THIS IS NOT AMERICA

THIS IS NOT AMERICA

ALAN FRIEDMAN

First published in Great Britain in 2017 by
Biteback Publishing Ltd
Westminster Tower
3 Albert Embankment
London SE1 7SP

ISBN 978-1-78590-235-2

10 9 8 7 6 5 4 3 2 1

A CIP catalogue record for this book is available from the British Library.

Set in Sabon

Printed and bound in Great Britain by
CPI Group (UK) Ltd, Croydon CR0 4YY

For Gabriella

post-truth *adjective*

Relating to or denoting circumstances in which objective facts are less influential in shaping public opinion than appeals to emotion and personal belief.

OXFORD DICTIONARY OF ENGLISH, OXFORD UNIVERSITY PRESS

ACKNOWLEDGEMENTS

When I first decided to write this book, at the end of 2015, almost nobody believed that Donald Trump would make it to the White House. I believed that he might well succeed and I was determined to investigate the root causes of the Trump phenomenon, first by travelling across the length and breadth of my country to listen to the stories of ordinary Americans out in the heartland, and then by sitting down with Trump himself. Many people helped me to organise this complicated voyage across the United States, and my heartfelt thanks go to these people, involved in research, planning and logistics.

My greatest thanks go to Luna De Bartolo, a talented young journalist who was at my side throughout the entire project, from start to finish, from early research to final fact-checking. Luna's professionalism was apparent throughout the project, whether in digging through piles of statistical data or in accompanying me across some of the poorest sections of Mississippi.

Flanking Luna was a small but capable team, including Andrea De Marco in New York and David Lachmann in Washington. Gabriele Franceschi, who has worked on documentaries with me in the past, once again proved himself an able filmmaker, both in our travels across America and in post-production back in Rome. In Florida, Vivian and Howard Packer provided hospitality and cultural context while people like Bill Luckett, the Mayor of Clarksdale, Mississippi, helped put me in touch with numerous people who could tell the story of their America.

In Britain, my special thanks go to the team at Biteback, led by Iain Dale and Olivia Beattie. This is my second book with Biteback, and I am pleased to work with this independent and iconoclastic British publishing house.

Final thanks go to a small group of special friends, who had the patience and kindness to read early drafts of various chapters and to endure endless discussions about the true nature of the Trump phenomenon and the real state of America. Among these are Eckart Sager, Justin Smith, Lionel Barber, Bruce Carpenter, Jamie Harpel, David Lachmann, Rory Sanders, Eric Reguly and Alex Amram.

Finally, to my agents Jonathan Ehrlich in New York and Niccolò Rositani Suckert in Florence, who encouraged me to give birth to this project, my sincerest gratitude.

And of course, last but not least, my biggest thanks go to the person this book is dedicated to, to my unflappable and patient Tuscan wife. *Grazie, Gabriella!*

CONTENTS

CHAPTER ONE

THE DAWN OF THE TRUMP ERA

> I never liked the idea of the euro from Day One. I don't like it much better right now. I think it actually complicates things. You have so much Brussels bureaucracy and so many different aspects, like taxation. When the idea of the euro first emerged I was not in love with it, and I don't think I have come any closer to falling in love with it.[1]

Donald Trump is talking down the euro. A moment later he will be talking down Angela Merkel, and then Barack Obama, and then Hillary Clinton. Then he will be talking up Brexit and Vladimir Putin. And then he will put in a plug for his newly refurbished golf course in Scotland. He's just that sort of guy.

Trump is seated at a highly lacquered mahogany table in the lounge section of *Trump Force One*, a garishly equipped Boeing 757 that is parked in the cargo zone of the George Bush Intercontinental Airport in Houston. It is 17 June 2016, three days after Trump's 70th birthday, five days after the Pulse shooting in Orlando, and a little over twelve months since the brash billionaire famously rode down the escalator at Trump Tower to announce his campaign for the presidency.

Outside, on the sweltering tarmac, in the 99-degree heat of a June afternoon, the big plane is surrounded by a dozen fierce-looking, armour-plated grey Chevy Suburbans that are full of Secret Service types and a few jet-black Cadillac Escalades owned by Trump's Texan donors.

The presumptive Republican nominee gestures for me to move his favourite red tie from the chair across from him, and for a moment I hold in my hands Donald Trump's famous red tie, the signature Brioni red power tie that he likes to wear, along with his hand-tailored Brioni suit, as he jets around America, campaigning for the White House. Trump has just flown in from a fundraiser in San Antonio, and he is preparing for another one here, in the wealthy suburbs of Houston. Only hours later he will fly to Phoenix and don his more incendiary public persona, leading thousands of supporters in an angry chant of 'Build that Wall! Build that Wall!' at a campaign rally. But right now he is in his lair, safe and secure, relaxed, affable, even low-key. It is 17 June 2016, and he has just about wrapped up the Republican nomination.

The shock waves of the shooting massacre at the Pulse Club in Orlando are still reverberating across America, and Trump seizes the occasion to condemn 'terrorism at a very disgusting level'. He swears that if he is elected President he will wipe ISIS and all 'radical Islamic terrorism' from the face of the earth. He does not say how he will do it. 'Believe me,' he repeats with a consummate salesman's sincerity, 'we will get the job done.'

Now Trump is hopping from subject to subject. Suddenly we are talking about his new golf course in Scotland. Later this week, Trump will fly to Scotland's scenic west coast to cut the ribbon at the official opening of the expensively revamped Trump Turnberry Resort and Golf Course in Ayrshire.

'I look forward to going to Scotland,' says a grinning Trump.

> We have spent a great deal of money on renovating Turnberry, about £200 million, and we have done a fantastic job. It is magnificent. We have gutted out the building and we have rebuilt the course to the highest specifications. The ninth hole is moved out toward the ocean. It's incredible.

Now we hop back to America and I ask him about Barack Obama.

Trump does not blanch; indeed, he instantly pivots to his idea of what constitutes a more presidential, even-handed, stance. 'Obama has been a very ineffective President. He refuses to use the term radical Islamic terrorism, which is a real problem because unless you are going to talk about it you are not going to solve the problem.'

Trump's gaze wanders, and he breaks up the interview for some small talk and barks a few orders to an aide before jumping back into the conversation. Now Trump is back in Scotland, at the golf course.

'I love Great Britain. My mother was born in Scotland, in Stornoway, and I am sure we will have a great relationship with Great Britain.'

The Trump who is now speaking is the property developer and brand-name franchiser who will land in Scotland on the morning after the Brexit vote, triumphant. Trump would later predict that his White House victory would be 'Brexit-plus'. He was right again, and again he would be triumphant.

On that Boeing 757, back in June 2016, Donald Trump would talk with glowing admiration of Vladimir Putin and, when told that the Russian dictator had praised him at a conference in St Petersburg just a day before, the Republican candidate for the White House would nearly blush. He would happily invite Putin to the White House, he declared, and the two would join forces to defeat ISIS and bad guys everywhere.

On the plane that day, Trump looked like what he really was, a deal-making property tycoon from New York with more chutzpah than sophistication, a man with accomplished flair for embellishing and promoting his own brand, his personal fairy tale, his own version of the truth. When we sat together that day in Texas, he was facing criticism for having stated his willingness to invite the mercurial North Korean leader Kim Jong-un to Washington for talks.[2] The thought of two such impulsive types getting together and talking nuclear weapons was causing mingled panic and derision among the chattering classes who derive their worldview from the pages of the *New York Times*. But Trump had no time for the intellectuals and the East Coast establishment who for decades had wrinkled their noses at his flamboyant antics.

'I'll talk to anybody,' says the author of *The Art of The Deal*.[3]

He is also clear about whom he likes and whom he doesn't like – until he changes his mind, of course, and that happens quite a lot. On this particular day he is happy to slam Germany's Angela Merkel, whom he accuses of making a 'massive mistake, a massive mistake' by allowing migrants and refugees from the war in Syria into Germany. He is happy to explain why the euro was a failed experiment that never should have been started, and he is more than happy to talk about how the Clinton Foundation had taken many millions of dollars from countries accused of financing Islamic terrorism. Later on, after the campaign was over, there would be plenty of time to unbundle various promises and revise his positions. For now, Trump is in full-scale campaign mode, which, as one of his top advisers put it, was an experience unlike any other political campaign he had ever worked on.

'He actually sits there at Trump Tower and asks us about his next *appearance* rather than his next campaign stop. He actually thinks about these as appearances, just like you would expect from a reality TV show star,' confided this campaign adviser, one of several who would be fired during the course of the 2016 campaign. Not surprisingly, when it came time to pick his Cabinet, the world would watch a string of celebrity politicians show up at Trump Tower on Fifth Avenue and 56th Street and suddenly the selection of the government of the United States began to resemble an episode of *The Apprentice*. Trump even tweeted at one point that he and he alone knew who were the real 'finalists' for his Cabinet.[4]

Throughout our conversation on board his private jet, the soon-to-be President appeared cool and crisp. The private Donald Trump looks very much like a wealthy New York businessman with nouveau riche tastes who is about to dine on a luxury cheeseburger at the 21 Club. But he is also a conversation hopper, a schmoozer who is in love with the sound of his own voice, and a man who seems to find it hard to focus for more than a few minutes on any single issue. He appears to suffer from Attention Deficit Disorder. I remember thinking that his relatively brief attention span, like his outsized personality and the way he tends to filter much of the world through the prism of his own ego, are traits not at all dissimilar to those of other self-made billionaires and oligarchs I had met in my travels.

In some ways Trump reminded me of the subject of my last biography, an intimate portrait of another brash and successful narcissist billionaire, an Italian named Silvio Berlusconi.[5] Like former Prime Minister Berlusconi, Trump has a certain repertoire of strongly held opinions and slogans which he is prepared to express almost anywhere and everywhere, on a reality show or on the campaign trail or at the White House. Like Berlusconi, he repeats his strongly held views as though the repetition of declarative statements were in some manner a form of argumentation. Donald Trump does not do analysis. He does declarations. Yet, like Berlusconi, if he feels he is in the company of somebody he can trust – or somebody he wants to sell himself to – his manner becomes solicitous, courteous, even disarming, and the tone of his voice is always calming, always charming, as though this is the way brash billionaires from the Queens area of New York are supposed to talk when they move to Fifth Avenue or get a four-year mandate to live at 1600 Pennsylvania Avenue.

I asked Trump right then and there on the plane if he saw any similarities between himself and Berlusconi. Trump did not seem flattered by the question; rather, he seemed somewhere between diffident and indifferent. 'I guess,' he replied after a bit of a pause, 'we are both two rich guys who went into politics.'

Trump and Berlusconi would also go down in the histories of their respective countries as the political leaders with the greatest unresolved conflicts of interest in their nations' histories.

In Berlusconi's case, he claimed he never needed a blind trust or a special separation of his business and political interests because he had given his children control of his media company, Mediaset. In Trump's case, he claimed he never needed a blind trust or a special separation of his business and political interests because he had given his children control of his company, the Trump Organization.[6]

In fact, until the election of President Donald Trump in November 2016, no other major advanced industrial democracy had ever seen such an unprecedented concentration of business and political power in the hands of one man, except for Berlusconi, and under his leadership things did not go very well for Italy. Sure, there were plenty of banana republics in South America or in Africa where plutocrats took over governments, or enriched themselves even as they governed. But this was America, and surely such things could never happen here, here in the USA!

Just an hour later after I left him, Trump was back in fighting form and on stage at a Houston rally, in front of about 5,000 supporters, slamming President Obama and Hillary Clinton and telling the crowd that he would be an aggressive advocate of gun rights if elected President.[7] Guns for everybody! Then, a few hours later, came the Arizona rallies and the chants of 'Build that Wall'.

Once off the plane and back in the sweltering Texas heat, I am shepherded into another SUV and driven away from the gathered motorcade by a friendly senior official of the Houston Fire Department's Aircraft Rescue division. In a thick Texas drawl he tells me about a recent visit to the UK and how much he loved going to British pubs. He asks me about my interview with Donald Trump, and I ask him whom he intends to vote for.

Although he declines to answer my query, he does offer one last insight. 'Ah have to say that the thing that's different with Mr Trump, or even with Bernie Sanders,' says the friendly Texan, 'is that whether you agree with them or not they talk straight, they speak their mind, and they talk in plain language, not like the normal politicians who give speeches and ya never know what they really mean. Ah kinda like that.'

I think about this as I leave the George Bush Intercontinental Airport and head back into Houston. Most political leaders give speeches. Donald Trump 'talks' to his supporters, he *converses* with the electorate. He is in many ways the exact opposite of Hillary Clinton, the policy wonk.

I think about this again when it is time for me to cast my vote in Broward County, Florida, at a few minutes before eight o'clock on the morning of 8 November 2016. On that particular Tuesday morning, in a gated community a few miles west of Fort Lauderdale, the designated polling station was the community clubhouse. By eight o'clock that morning the lines were already stretching out to the parking lot. It seemed that the voters of Florida were taking seriously their status as a battleground state, even though most voters didn't particularly like either of the candidates in this seemingly endless race for the White House.

At the clubhouse in this south Florida village, the polling booths are a makeshift space made of temporary plastic divider walls that come in portable briefcase units. You go in with a paper ballot, although they have resolved the problem of the 'hanging chads' that cost Al Gore the White House in the 2000 race; these were the old-fashioned ballots where you were supposed to punch through a hole and not leave any paper bits hanging. The malfunction of these ballots in 2000 cost Al Gore the White House and helped George W. Bush take the issue straight to the Supreme Court, which, being of a Republican majority, promptly handed him the election. But that was sixteen years ago; now the problem has been fixed. No, here at the clubhouse the ballot was large and long but very clear and clean, to be marked up with a special pencil. Aside from the presidential candidates there was an endless series of local and county officials and judges and prosecutors to vote for, as well as half a dozen referendums on legalising medical marijuana in Florida and on other regulatory issues that concerned small businesses in the Sunshine State.

The act of actually voting for President, by colouring in the space next to the candidate's name on the ballot, was almost a relief, for me and I suspect for millions of other Americans – the end of a bad dream, a period of fear and anger. Nobody could remember an election campaign so painful, so lengthy, so vulgar and squalid, so much like a nightmare rather than a shared civic experience. Most Americans just wanted to be done with it, forget about it and get on with their lives. So in 2016 the act of voting was for me, as perhaps it was for many millions of Americans, something of a catharsis, and it was actually a relief that it was over.

That night, as I sat in the broadcast tent of Italian state television's all-news channel, perched on the roof of the AFL-CIO Building on 16th Street in Washington, with the White House just behind us across Lafayette Park, I shared the national experience of watching Donald Trump power ahead in state after state and overtake Hillary Clinton to win the Electoral College and with it the presidency. On the video monitor to my right I could see Wolf Blitzer and John King puzzling over the result on CNN, as though something had not gone according to plan. The nation would never forget how Clinton operative John Podesta would come out at a little past 10 p.m. to tell the crowds at the Javits Center in New York to go home.[8] Nor would the nation ever forget the arrival of the Trump family in the ballroom of the New York Hilton on Sixth Avenue, and especially the various faces of young Barron Trump, the ten-year-old son who is Trump's fifth child.

But what kind of America had just given Trump his upset victory? After the dirtiest and the most vulgar presidential election in recent American history, Trump was now the winner, and he was destined to preside over a wounded nation, a country that had been riven by fear and anger, by unprecedented levels of racism, a society whose politics had been polarised as almost never before, or at least not in the past half century, or at least not in living memory, and mainly by him.

What kind of America had just elected Trump? And who was the real Donald Trump: the ideologue or the pragmatist? And what were the underlying causes of America's existential crisis, its polarised and deeply divided society?

To understand Trump, in some ways a quintessential New Yorker, one needs to understand the psychology of New Yorkers. In particular, one needs to understand the way New Yorkers from Manhattan tend to look down at New Yorkers who come from any of the city's other four boroughs, the Bronx, Staten Island, Brooklyn and Queens.

Donald Trump came from the outlying borough of Queens, from a suburban neighbourhood called Jamaica Estates. He grew up in a spacious house on a tree-lined hill in this little enclave of Queens, the son of wealthy real estate broker turned property developer named Fred Trump.

Trump, unsurprisingly for a kid from Queens, had a chip on his shoulder about the glamour and social acceptance of Manhattan's Upper East Side. It was not so much an inferiority complex as a drive to arrive, a desire for acceptance. Even though he was driven to a private school in nearby Forest Hills in one of his father's chauffeured limousines, he felt he had not arrived. He might have been from a wealthy enclave, but it was still Queens, an outlying borough, and his father might have been a rich property developer, but he was still an outsider. Jamaica Estates was a very white neighbourhood in Queens, and as Trump's father put up apartment buildings elsewhere in the borough, he found himself accused of racial discrimination. Donald started his career working for his father. Both father and son were accused in the 1970s by New York prosecutors of refusing to rent or sell to black people, a charge the Trump family has always denied. The court records from the 1970s show, however, that they paid settlements to avoid any admission of guilt.[9]

In the 1970s, Queens was the location for what was for a time America's most popular television show, a dark comedy called *All in the Family*. The programme featured a bigoted and racist white man without a college degree who was named Archie Bunker. He lived in a working-man's house in a working-man's neighbourhood. And where did he live? In the Queens section of New York. Today,

Donald Trump is President of the United States after having run an electoral campaign steeped in the language and mindset of Archie Bunker's Queens. So among the many influences that shaped and formed the young Donald Trump, he happened to grow up in an area of New York City steeped in racism and bigotry, an area where each new immigrant group becomes the lowest rung on the social ladder in the great American melting pot.

To put it in social terms, Manhattanite snobs tend to use a disparaging term for New Yorkers from outer boroughs like Queens and Brooklyn and Staten Island and for those who live across the Hudson River in New Jersey. The term is 'bridge and tunnel' crowd, meaning people who can only arrive in Manhattan by physically travelling over a bridge or through a tunnel under the Hudson River or the East River. It is not uncommon to hear a New Yorker say, 'Let's not go to that restaurant or bar on Saturday night because it is going to be full of bridge and tunnel types.'

In 1971, three years after graduating from college, at the age of twenty-five, Trump finally shed his 'bridge and tunnel' skin and moved into an apartment on Manhattan's Upper East Side for the first time. He was about to take over his father's company. He was aiming to make it in Manhattan. The suburban outsider from Queens had arrived.

'I was a kid from Queens who worked in Brooklyn, and suddenly I had an apartment on the Upper East Side ... I became a city guy instead of a kid from the boroughs,' Trump writes in *The Art of the Deal*.

To understand Donald Trump, one needs to understand the importance for him of penetrating what he perceived to be the inner sanctum of the very power elite that as a politician he has railed against. The word *arriviste* refers to someone who craves applause and social acceptance because they have arrived. In New York City, Donald Trump has always been considered an *arriviste* developer from Queens. He has been pretty much shunned by old money and by old families, as seems fitting for a man who has shamelessly sold the public on the glories of his money-making, a man who for decades has showcased his own gaudy lifestyle as a model of conspicuous consumption. In Donald Trump's world, opulence is a value and the more something shines, the better it is.

To understand the aggression in Trump's rhetoric, in his public persona, in his sometimes shrill and hysterical outbursts, it is helpful to understand that among his early mentors back in the 1970s was a hugely controversial lawyer named Roy Cohn.[10] Back in the 1970s, Trump was the rambunctious scion of a real estate empire, a young developer anxious to leave his mark on New York. Roy Cohn was a legendary fixer, a ruthless lawyer who had served as the chief counsel to Senator Joseph McCarthy's anti-Communist witch-hunts, a dark period for America if ever there was one. Cohn was now serving as a mob consigliere, with clients including 'Fat Tony' Salerno, boss of the Genovese crime family, the most powerful Mafia group in New York, and Paul Castellano, head of what was said to be the second largest family, the Gambinos. The two men met by chance one night at Le Club, a hangout for Manhattan's rich and famous. Trump introduced himself to Cohn, who was sitting at a nearby table. He asked his advice, specifically about how he and his father should handle allegations from the US Department of Justice that they had been discriminating against black people by denying them rental apartments.

'My view', Cohn told Trump at the time, 'is tell them to go to hell and fight the thing in court.' He also counselled Trump that when somebody comes at you with a threat, the best response is to hit them ten times harder and scare them away. Cohn helped Trump beat the US government accusations of racism in 1973, and went on to become one of his most important mentors, helping him in legal battles and marital affairs and introducing him to some of New York's leading power brokers and socialites. The Cohn method, which Trump adopted, was a very simple formula for beating your adversary: attack, counter-attack and never apologise.

So it was not surprising that Roy Cohn would join Trump and

New York Mayor Ed Koch at the glitzy October 1983 opening of Trump Tower on Fifth Avenue, complete with Donald's palatial triplex penthouse, his own personal Versailles.[11] The property was located right next to the legendary Fifth Avenue flagship Tiffany store. The 58-storey building featured a six-storey atrium lined with imported pink marble and an eighty-foot waterfall. It was pure opulence. The luxurious skyscraper attracted well-known retail stores and celebrity renters and brought Trump national attention for the first time.

It was at the same time that Trump was investing in the profitable casino gambling business, starting with the opening of the Trump Plaza in Atlantic City, New Jersey. Then came the Trump Castle, and finally he was able to acquire the largest hotel casino in the world, the Taj Mahal at Atlantic City, which opened in 1990.[12] In 2016, in the middle of his presidential campaign, the Trump Taj Mahal would close its doors after multiple bankruptcies and a lengthy strike.[13]

In 1989, he branched out to purchase the Eastern Air Lines Shuttle for $365 million, which he promptly renamed the Trump Shuttle. After failing to make it profitable, Trump defaulted on his loans, and the airline venture ended three years later, in 1992.[14]

All of his casino ventures ended up going bankrupt, and yet Trump was able to walk away from every project, often by declaring bankruptcy and then making a deal with his bank creditors or by selling off some collateral to pay them back.[15]

In all of his business ventures, Trump's greatest talent appeared to be his ability to market himself, to promote his own name. He became the brand. His national celebrity grew exponentially with the launch of his 1987 book, *The Art of the Deal*. The book was on the *New York Times* bestseller list for forty-eight weeks and made millions of dollars.[16] After that, Trump would put his name on every building, whether he built it himself or just franchised his name out to others. In Manhattan, where the name Trump still meant brash and tawdry to many, neighbourhood groups were formed on several occasions, mainly on the West Side of the island, to try, often unsuccessfully, to oppose Trump-proposed projects. But Donald Trump never seemed to have problems getting permission for his extravagant and often risky property developments; he made sure he maintained excellent relations with politicians from Ronald Reagan to Bill Clinton, and he made campaign contributions to all of them over the years, from left to right,[17] contributing half a dozen times to Hillary Clinton's campaigns and donating $100,000 to the Clinton Foundation.[18]

Trump's rocky personal life has received plenty of press attention over the years, as befits a man who seemed to enjoy being featured on the gossip pages of the *New York Post* as much as being written up in the financial pages of the *Wall Street Journal.*

His three marriages, two of them to Eastern European-born fashion models and one to a failed actress, are the stuff of tabloid trash. In 1977, Trump married Ivana Zelníčková Winklmayr, a fashion model from Czechoslovakia. The couple had three children, Donald Jr (1977), Ivanka (1981) and Eric (1984). A messy and highly publicised divorce was finalised in 1992 after Ivana discovered that her husband had been having an affair with Marla Maples. That same year would see the bankruptcy of Trump Plaza,[19] a year after the Trump Taj Mahal went bankrupt for the first time.[20] Trump, who had been cheating on his wife with Marla Maples for years, finally married her in December 1993, just a few weeks after the birth of their daughter Tiffany. Marla Maples would last for six years in holy matrimony with Donald Trump, until she was 'fired' when Trump filed for divorce in 1997. In January 2005, Trump married for a third time, this time to a Slovenian model named Melania Knauss, who was more than twenty years his junior.

Among the many celebrity guests at the extravagant wedding, held at Trump's Mar-a-Lago estate in Florida, were Hillary Clinton and former President Bill Clinton.[21] In 2006, Melania gave birth to a boy, whom they named Barron.

By then Trump was already reinventing himself again, this time as an entertainment figure, the host of the hit reality show *The Apprentice*. The first season in 2004 had earned the highest ratings on television that year after the Super Bowl, and earned Trump a star on the Hollywood Walk of Fame in 2007. Finally, the kid from Queens had found the kind of national celebrity he had craved. *The Apprentice* presented the Trump Organization as a wonderful place to work and Trump as a master businessman, a financial sage. It made Trump feel good about himself and helped his family to make more money with the Trump brand. It also made Trump feel supremely confident about his abilities with women. It was back in 2005 that he was secretly recorded offering his private opinion about women on a Hollywood backlot: 'I'm automatically attracted to beautiful women,' said the future President of the United States back in 2005. 'I just start kissing them. It's like a magnet. Just kiss. I don't even wait. And when you're a star they let you do it. You can do anything ... Grab them by the pussy. You can do anything.'[22]

This was the Donald Trump who rode down the escalator in Trump Tower on 16 June 2015 and announced to the world that he was going to launch his campaign for the White House, complete with plans to build a wall that would keep out Mexican 'rapists and criminals', to repeal Obamacare and to make America great again.[23] He was long on bravado and short on detail, as always. The reality star had morphed into a presidential candidate, and the most nativist and xenophobic populist presidential candidate since the anti-immigrant Native American Party of the 1850s, commonly known as the Know Nothings.

After the ugliest and most vicious presidential campaign in American history, Donald Trump actually pulled it off. In a campaign that saw racism and anger spreading across America, much of it incited by his own inflammatory declarations on the campaign trail, Trump managed to shout his way to the White House. He lost the popular vote; Hillary Clinton won nearly 3 million votes more than Trump across the United States, representing a 2 per cent margin of victory for her in the popular vote.[24] But Trump won the Electoral

College, and the stage was now set for a most unusual presidency. In cultural terms, America seemed happy to say goodbye to the well-intentioned but ineffectual Obama regime and hand its destiny to a man who by comparison made George W. Bush seem like an intellectual. The new President of the United States appeared to have more in common with Kim Kardashian than with Abraham Lincoln. But the will of the people is sovereign, and the people of America had made their choice.

As I watched the Trump administration take office, I wondered how his ultra-conservative and loyalist team could possibly help the nation to heal when so many of them were themselves so extreme. I wondered about what had happened to American society and to its political culture and economy to explain the extreme bitterness and popular distrust that had corroded America's soul even before the campaign of 2016. How and, above all, why had the nation been so ripped apart, so deeply divided, so lacerated? What were the underlying causes? And what could we do to make things better?

The recent resurgence of American populism, nativism, nationalism, xenophobia and Trump-style demagoguery, which has many echoes across a suffering European continent, meant that what used to be fringe politics – extremism – was now moving to the mainstream. But how did we get here? And is there a way out?

I had decided to write this book ten months before Election Day, and to use the opportunity to travel across America and attempt a fresh look at our troubled country, visiting the working poor of the 'Walmart society' and examining the most divisive issues on the ground, from racism, immigration, Obamacare and gun violence to severe income inequalities and the perennial boom-and-bust follies of Wall Street. I wanted to also look at America's abundant strengths: the dynamism of its people, the drive to succeed, the raw energy, the technological innovation of Silicon Valley, the avant-garde projects of the green economy and the fact that despite a powerful conservative movement, after eight years of the Obama administration America had become a much more progressive nation when it came to social issues, from gay marriage to abortion rights and the legalisation of marijuana. Now, most of Trump's supporters instead expected a return to more 'Christian' values and the shape of future American society would depend on key judicial appointments that would be made by President Trump, beginning with the Supreme Court.

I wanted to write a book not about the 2016 presidential election but about America itself, a portrait, a moving picture, if you will, of America and Americans toward the end of the second decade of a new century, seemingly troubled, suffering, somehow disorientated and yet still (by default) the strongest nation on earth. But the key question to which I wanted an answer was: what had really happened to my country? What were the underlying causes of America's current malaise? Did it have more to do with unprecedented levels of poverty, with 43 million Americans, or 13.5 per cent of the population, below the poverty line and a total of more than 100 million Americans, which is nearly 33 per cent of the population, falling into the ranks of the working poor?[25] Or did it have something to do with a growing sense among those of the working class endangered by the decline of manufacturing jobs in the age of globalisation and automation that the US government had become indifferent to their economic needs? Or was it just the politics of a dehumanised society with a chronic dose of attention-deficit disorder, a blind love of television stars and a tendency to applaud the snappiest sound bite on Twitter? Did Americans even care or understand that meanwhile, outside, there was an increasingly dangerous world? And what would the Trump presidency mean for Britain, for Europe, for the rest of the world? Could America recover from the national fatigue of two failed wars in Iraq and Afghanistan? Some would argue that the mistakes of both President Obama and his former Secretary of State Hillary Clinton in places like Iraq, Libya and Syria had been so colossal that they had contributed to the rise of ISIS and the chaos across much of the Middle East following the Arab Spring. But did Americans understand or care? Did they see how Vladimir Putin was busy redrawing the geopolitical map of half of Europe and the Middle East while they had been busy watching Trump and Clinton trading insults? Trump promised to change all of this, to make friends with Putin and bring radical change to American foreign policy.

This, in essence, is the heart of this book: a look at the underlying reasons for the current state of American society, and an assessment of the nation in the wake of the election of a new American President, at a time of great global economic and geopolitical uncertainty, in a world fraught with danger. How did we get here, and how do we get ourselves out of this situation? *Can* we get ourselves out of this situation?

The pages that follow are an attempt, therefore, to explore America through the lives of ordinary Americans on the ground in the deepest heartland of America, *l'Amerique profonde*. The goal was to capture and record this unhappy moment in American history in order to consider whether there are truly ways to heal the nation and recover our famous strength and unity through diversity, or whether the social and economic stresses of recent years have become too heavy to bear, the divisions too deep, the outlook too uncertain. While America has looked inward and been consumed by the epic battle between Hillary Clinton and Donald Trump, the world has moved on and become a far more dangerous place.

The problem is that America, including the America that put Donald Trump in the White House, has been living for a long time in what can only be called a form of collective denial, a negation of the daily injustices that are visited upon millions of Americans every day, those who have been left behind, those who never got to live the American dream.

Donald Trump has promised to make America great again. But at the outset it is worth posing a rather more basic question. What was America's greatness? Was America really once the shining City on the Hill, the light of the world? Did the America of our dreams, the

America of noble ideals and streets paved in gold, ever really exist, or was it a sort of figment of our collective imagination?

Once upon a time, long before Donald Trump had moved to the Upper East Side of Manhattan and somewhere between the legends of Camelot and John F. Kennedy, of Ronald Reagan and the Cold War, surely there was an America we could all be proud of. Or was there?

CHAPTER TWO

ONCE UPON A TIME IN AMERICA...

A chicken in every pot.

A two-car garage.

And the conviction that just so long as you worked hard and applied yourself, you could get ahead.

That was the American dream; at least, that is what we were taught in school back in the day.

The American dream was all about upward social mobility and the promise of a better tomorrow. Confidence. Optimism. Fair play. This was the American ideal, a vast and wealthy land of shared prosperity where anybody could get a piece of the pie. Equal rights and opportunities for everyone to get rich, to make it, irrespective of race, creed or colour.

This was the belief that was inculcated into our collective consciousness throughout much of the twentieth century. This was our vision of a utopian society, our social mythology. The nation of immigrants who came to seek their fortune in the New World would always be welcomed by Lady Liberty. 'Give me your tired, your poor, your huddled masses yearning to breathe free...'

This was America, the land of Horatio Alger, of rags-to-riches stories that stretched from Wall Street to Main Street, the America of the fabled prosperity of the Eisenhower years, the tweed-jacketed grandeur of the Kennedy era, the glamorous America of JFK and Jackie. The booming 1960s. Camelot, and all of that.

It was an America of noble ideals, of honour and dignity, a

melting pot of fairness and freedom, the proverbial America whose streets were paved with gold. This was the United States that set the moral standard for the rest of the world to follow, this was John Winthrop's 'model of Christian charity' or, in Ronald Reagan's idiom, the 'Shining City upon a Hill'.

Or was it?

Was it real or was it just a grand illusion? One great big spin? A mythology maintained by a self-perpetuating elite? A fairy tale written by cheerleading historians who had only remembered to put in the good stuff and had glossed over the bad? History, after all, is usually written by the winners. Is that why our nation's history has always seemed so ebullient and successful, so white and male? Was it because the storyline of our nation's history was written predominantly by well-fed white journalists and academics who, starting in the Kennedy era, were themselves steadily co-opted into the power elite? Was Harvard part of the problem?

It may seem odd, but the question needs to be asked: did the America of true values and Jeffersonian ideals ever really exist, in the Eisenhower, the Kennedy or the Reagan years? Or even in the Jeffersonian era? Michelle Obama aptly noted in the summer of 2016 that the White House was a house that had been built by African-American slaves. Did the American dream ever really exist for black people? Or for the working poor and working-class white factory workers? Was there ever really an America of social justice and endless opportunity? A level playing field for everyone? Or were the 'good old days' just a figment of our collective consciousness, the feel-good story that was repeated to us over and over again by our leaders, our educators and our corporate media, until we had collectively bought the story, hook, line and sinker?

There once was a time when we would not have had a doubt. There once was a time when everything seemed possible, when we had faith in the system. Once upon a time in America it seemed like everybody believed in the American dream.

In the 1950s, the 1960s and even into the 1970s most Americans grew up believing that change for the better was possible, that the good guys always triumphed over the bad guys. It was the America of John Wayne, of Clint Eastwood, of Woodward and Bernstein, and of Superman, who always fought for *truth, justice and the American way*. It was a far more innocent world back then. A world of comic books and baseball games, of big automobiles and sprawling suburban development. The American way of life was based on community and civic culture. We grew up thinking of our political leaders as statesmen, and we grew up believing in the fundamental goodness of the American people.

• • •

The first time I campaigned for a presidential candidate was in 1968. I was twelve years old at the time, a bit young perhaps to be campaigning but I happily distributed leaflets door-to-door in uptown Manhattan for Senator Bobby Kennedy. It was the time of flower power and the hippies. Bobby was my hero, and the hero of millions of young Americans. He was a better man than his brother, more pure of thought and determination, a man who wanted to end war and bring peace, who understood the folly of Vietnam, a man who believed in racial harmony, who sought to bring an end to racism and segregation and KKK lynching of blacks, and the persistent harassment by law enforcement officials of African-Americans, yes, even back then, especially back then.

Many young people believed in Bobby Kennedy in 1968 (the way many would believe in Bernie Sanders nearly a half-century later) because America in 1968 was a nation set atop a tinder box, perched upon an explosive mix of racial divisions and anti-war protest movements, a society that was more torn apart than at any time since the Civil War. In that moment of our history, Bobby Kennedy symbolised hope and the promise of strength and unity through our cultural diversity. He was the best of the Kennedys.

These thoughts raced across my brain on that blistering June day in

Houston, Texas when I boarded Donald Trump's Boeing 757. I thought of Kennedy when Trump welcomed me to his parlour on the plane and started making small talk. Quite a contrast. The noble statesman and the populist buffoon. And as I considered the man before me, who was now chatting amiably about Brexit and immigration, I wondered how and why America had fallen so low, how had it come to pass that my country, the land of opportunity and justice for all, was now fated to having to choose between two of the most distrusted candidates ever seen in a presidential election: a demagogic real estate mogul turned reality-show star and the Lady Macbeth of the famous Clinton dynasty, a cynical opportunist who believed she had a birthright to the presidency. Hillary Clinton had claimed her mantle after a raft of leaked emails revealed that her Democratic National Committee had discussed using smear tactics against Bernie Sanders, along with other political treachery that was worthy of the Borgias. She had withstood the allegations of pay-to-play access to the State Department via the back door of the Clinton Foundation. The GOP candidate, meanwhile, had withstood smearing a Gold Star family (the term for those who have lost loved ones to military service) and taken the Band-Aid off racism in America with his virulent incitements to hate. Now the choice was between Trump and Clinton. How had America fallen so low? How had we entered into such a deep and prolonged period of suffering, of fear and anguish, of protracted national agony? What was really behind our collective national howl?

On the plane that June afternoon in Houston, Donald Trump also talked about the death of the American dream, expounding on his theory that millions of Americans no longer had any realistic hopes of getting ahead. I thought about that when I left the plane and dived into the air-conditioned comfort of a Fire Marshal's Chevy Suburban for the drive across the runways of Houston Airport. And I thought about it again, long and hard, just a few days later, on 7 July, when American society suffered another trauma, and eerily enough in Dallas, a city that for generations had been trying to live down its reputation as the City of Hate.

With Dallas, everything changed. The shootings of five white police officers were part of an already bloody season of racism, violence and domestic terrorism that had seen dozens of unarmed blacks killed by trigger-happy white policemen. America seemed to be at a tipping point, if not a breaking point. Once again the city was scarred by national tragedy.

It had happened here before here, in November 1963, and just a few steps away, in nearby Dealey Plaza.

Indeed, there seemed something perversely symmetrical in the way hapless Dallas found itself bookending two of the greatest moments of national anguish of the past half-century. The first jolt had come in this city, the first seismic shock to the constitution of the American people.

The shots that rang out in Dealey Plaza did more than strike down a President: they presaged a half-century-long and collective loss of innocence, a period in our nation's history in which the promise of shared prosperity was shattered every few years by a new national trauma, by tragedy and defeat, a sort of slow-motion and collective sense of being violated, and over time, a syncopation of our recent history, one trauma after another, in a lengthy, periodic and protracted loss of our national innocence. Could this be our nation's real legacy of the last half-century?

After the death of JFK in 1963 came more societal upheaval, more trauma, and over an extended period of time. Five years later America witnessed the riots and assassinations of 1968, the resignation of a President in disgrace over the Watergate scandal in 1974, a staggering defeat in Vietnam in 1975, the rise of the Ayatollahs and the Iran hostage crisis from November 1979 until January 1981, and then still later the first Bush war against Saddam Hussein with Operation Desert Storm in 1991, the first attack on the World Trade Center in 1993 and the national trauma of 9/11 in 2001, followed by the prolonged battle with Osama bin Laden and the Bush wars in Afghanistan one month after 9/11, and then, on false pretences, the second Bush war against Saddam Hussein, the invasion of Iraq in March 2003, and then, years later, in an ever more dangerous world, the chaos of the Arab Spring in 2010/11 and the emergence of ISIS terrorism, the disasters in Iraq, Syria and Libya, and finally, in more recent times, an ever more frequent outbreak of gun violence in the United States, ISIS-inspired but not ISIS-perpetrated terrorism, racist hate crime massacres and school shootings across Middle America, perpetrated not by foreign enemies but by home-grown terrorists, by American sociopaths and racists, by the enemy within.

For more than half a century, America has experienced rising levels of violence, both at home and abroad. The nation has gone through trauma after trauma, until it felt as though we couldn't take any more.

In November 1963, the murder of a young President in Dallas shocked an idealistic nation. In July 2016, the murder of five policemen in Dallas struck a nation that was already shell-shocked, reeling, punch-drunk and disorientated by a decades-long case of nationwide post-traumatic stress syndrome. But something was missing. After running through the normal eleven-day news cycle, we stopped talking about Dallas again.

It was almost as though we were no longer capable of treating shock and trauma as more than a news moment on CNN or on social media, as though we were somehow inured to the pain. And so after Dallas, as on so many other occasions, we went through the 'normal' news cycle, the makeshift memorial, the wreaths of flowers and messages and candles, the meetings of families of the victims, the days of tributes and religious gatherings and the search for unity, and, as always, the sad and predictable words of outrage from the White House, from a despondent-sounding Barack Obama, the Consoler-in-Chief of an increasingly desolate nation.

Dallas I shattered our innocence and coincided with a period of social conflict across the racial and political divide. Dallas II should have called into question our social cohesion and forced us to ask ourselves what had happened to the American way of life. Instead, sadly, it seemed like just another piece of breaking news, consumed, digested, commented and then forgotten by a society that had become all too accustomed to such fare.

Dallas I had come at a different time, in a world that could be more easily shocked, and where information about our leaders was parsed by the elites with the cooperation of a relatively docile press corps. In a world without smart phones or all-news cable and satellite channels, without internet or social media, the romantic 1960s legend of JFK and his vision of America was far easier to burnish and protect.

It would take a long time after JFK's assassination before we began to understand that the great hero of Camelot actually had feet of clay, that this noble President was really one the coldest of the Cold Warriors, with dangerous instincts about the use of military force. In fact, seen from a distance, the Kennedy era looks far less romantic and much more a case of thirty-four months of living dangerously with an inexperienced ideologue at the helm. If the world was a dangerous place, that was also because we helped to make it that way, with a legacy of robust, even virulent anti-Communism that ran from Harry Truman straight through to Eisenhower, Kennedy, Johnson, Nixon and Reagan.

The Vietnam engagement that JFK started by sending military advisers in the early 1960s would escalate to a long and protracted war and it would create a nightly moment of shared national trauma as Walter Cronkite closed his news programme on CBS every evening by announcing the daily body count in Vietnam. The war would run for more than a decade and it would end in complete failure in 1975. But it would take at least two more wars after Vietnam, this time in Afghanistan and in Iraq, both of them botched, before Americans would realise the limits of their power. It would take a long time, well into the start of the twenty-first century, before America would begin to realise that it had not done so well in its role as the world's policeman. Perhaps America had mismanaged its empire, even the golden opportunity of a unipolar world that had come after the collapse of the Berlin Wall, because Americans do not do so well at managing empire. As a rule, America never sought empire; rather, we were sort of thrust into the role by chance. Unless there was oil involved. That was different.

America's ascendency to global superpower status actually began with the end of the Second World War, as America became an accidental empire virtually by default, at the end of a war that had decimated Europe and left the United States essentially the last man standing: the only wealthy, powerful, fully rearmed and economically dominant power left on earth. With that kind of strength, and American idealism, it seemed that we could do no wrong. But we did.

One could point to Hiroshima as a moment of loss of innocence and one could argue about whether it was a good or bad thing for America to become the first nation on earth to use nuclear weapons against a civilian population. But perhaps the biggest mistake made by America in the aftermath of the Second World War may have been the idea that some form of forceful containment, some form of aggressive and proactive cold war against the Soviet Union was needed in order to staunch the menace of global Communism. This obsession ushered in an era of robust and muscular American exceptionalism on a global scale.

It began in 1947 when a young State Department officer named George Kennan penned an anonymous article for the most respected journal of the foreign policy establishment, *Foreign Affairs*.[1] The article's author identified himself only as 'X' but the article proved to be the most influential op-ed in American history. It warned of the risks of Soviet Communism and preached the idea of containment, of making the premise of American foreign policy an all-out effort to counter the perceived threat from Moscow and to model all of Washington's decisions on this premise. The idea proved dangerous, and at times disastrous, and soon triggered a tit-for-tat atmosphere between Moscow and Washington, a climate of mutual recrimination, an unprecedented nuclear arms race, and a phase in which veiled nuclear threats began to characterise relations between the United States and the Soviet Union. This simplified good vs evil approach to world politics begat the Cold War in the late 1940s, helped trigger the building of the Berlin Wall in 1961 by the Russians, and fuelled the paranoia that led to the Bay of Pigs Invasion in 1961 and the Cuban Missile Crisis in 1962.

Back in the 1950s, while America was trying to contain the Soviets, American politics was plunged into a paranoid witch-hunt for Communists, everywhere and anywhere, in Wall Street, in Hollywood, in every sphere of American life. A crusading senator whose rage matched that of Donald Trump set about trying to rid America of Communist spies, fellow travellers, sympathisers and secret party members. His name was Joe McCarthy. His chief counsel was Roy Cohn, the man who would twenty years later become one of Donald Trump's early mentors. As a result of the McCarthy hearings and leaks and televised harangues, the lives of thousands of honest and talented Americans were ruined, destroyed by the fear-mongering ways of McCarthyism and the Un-American Activities Committee in the 1950s. It was a dark period in American history, a testament to how, even in the best of economic times, many Americans could be easily manipulated by fear-based policy-making and demagogy. But the American dream was still alive, and Americans were getting richer. The McCarthy witch-hunt did not really affect the lives of most ordinary Americans. Black-and-white television sets were increasingly visible in the living rooms of suburban homes, as were TV dinners, and the spirit of the nation was a form of patriotic contentment. The President, nicknamed Ike, was an admired former war hero and amiable golfer named Dwight Eisenhower, and his time in office, against the backdrop of the post-war boom, became known as the Eisenhower years. It was a decade that saw McCarthyism and the rise of dark figures such as FBI director J. Edgar Hoover, but it was also a time of innocent recreation, of 1950s fun, as evinced by the culture of drive-in movies and icons such as Doris Day, Elvis Presley, Buddy Holly and *The Mouseketeers*.

The contradictions of such a complex nation as America are many. Thanks to a booming defence industry and American manufacturing power, America was growing, building the famous middle class and new suburbs, complete with the proverbial two-car garage. The Eisenhower 1950s created a sense of entitlement to economic prosperity and growth. It seemed to be building from the ground up at the time; it seemed that anyone with enough drive could make it – and in many cases this was true. The wave of economic growth would float many ships and make many Americans prosperous, and it would take many years until we began to understand the way American growth and prosperity had warped away from the traditional middle class and ultimately settled in the coffers of the new power elites. These elites included not just billionaires but multinational corporations that would achieve a global reach, a number of them thanks to the continuing build-up of the arms industry which came with the deepening of the Cold War in those same years. Eisenhower was a military man, and so he understood the risks inherent in a constant and continuous arms race, but he was also an honest man and a quintessential Middle American, who was worried by the incestuous and symbiotic relationship between the Pentagon and the arms makers. Before leaving office he would warn his fellow Americans of the dangers of creating 'a military industrial complex'. His warning would not be heeded. The American dream was now becoming a two-headed proposition: to enjoy rising prosperity at home and the ability to wage war abroad in the name of American democracy. The Cold War fuelled the arms race and vice versa.

Interestingly, the 1950s was still a period of relative income equality; certainly, there was a great deal more equality than exists today. Thanks to the welfare state that had been created by FDR, thanks to make-work programmes and infrastructure investments and other job creation and social assistance programmes, the underclass had found a safety net and fewer Americans were suffering. Trade unions like the United Auto Workers and the Teamsters were also developing and they managed to obtain a number of benefits for the workers of America, including health and pension benefits that became established baselines. At the same time, there were more steeply progressive income tax brackets and the upper middle classes and the rich actually did pay their fair share in taxes. At one point in the 1950s, the top tax rate for a very wealthy person in America reached 92 per cent; the top rate averaged around 70 per cent for most of the next two decades,[2] part of the legacy of FDR, the wealthy Democrat who was considered a traitor by the wealthy classes.

In the 1950s, income disparities were nowhere near as severe as they are today, and the poor enjoyed the benefits of a generous social safety net, so one could reasonably say that the American dream was, relatively speaking, and at least for much of the white population of the United States, alive and well.

In retrospect, American society was far more cohesive and egalitarian back in the 1950s and Dwight D. Eisenhower was a far safer pair of hands than his successor would prove. When it came to domestic policy, JFK would be the man to tell Martin Luther King Jr, back in 1962, that unfortunately he would not be pressing forward with his support for civil rights legislation because of upcoming mid-term elections. JFK dropped the ball on civil rights. On international politics and his dealings with the Kremlin, JFK would turn out to be quite a jumpy fellow.

John F. Kennedy was an aggressive Cold Warrior, steeped in anti-Communism, and no less so than his rival in the 1960 presidential election, Richard Nixon. It was Kennedy who would legitimise the 'domino theory' of US military intervention in south-east Asia and other far-flung places, on the grounds that if just one country went Communist then there would be a domino effect around the region and the world. Kennedy's greatest failure would prove to be the legacy of his sowing the seeds of Vietnam, a war that, ironically, would haunt his rival Nixon throughout his own presidency a decade later. Kennedy made the decision to go into Vietnam, continuing the 1950s American tradition of fighting Communists wherever they could be found, in faraway countries or at home under the bed, or on a Hollywood backlot. JFK famously sparred on several occasions with the Kremlin in a dangerous nuclear game of chicken and he dragged the United States into an unwinnable war in faraway south-east Asia because he believed in the domino theory.

Kennedy's assassination left poor Vice-President Lyndon Johnson to clean up the mess in Vietnam, but President Johnson couldn't do it, in part because he was distracted by a different war, this one on the home front: American society was going through some of the worst convulsions it had known since the Civil War. And unlike his predecessor, LBJ wanted to wage a war on poverty and create the Great Society at home. He wanted to secure some minimum form of social justice and equity for African-Americans, who were still being lynched and discriminated against and in many places denied their right to vote. But the guns-and-butter dream of eliminating poverty while financing the Vietnam War proved untenable.

America was a powder keg back then, a nation divided, in that awful spring of 1968, just before Bobby Kennedy was assassinated that June, and not long after the murder of Martin Luther King Jr that April. The violence that swept the country would come to the city of Chicago that August, during the Democratic National Convention that chose Hubert Humphrey as its presidential candidate. The mayor of the city was an autocrat and on his watch the police brutality against anti-war protesters marching in the streets of Chicago was there for all to see: it was live on national television. It would leave a nation scarred, another unprecedented social eruption during a year in which more than 100 American cities had been swept by race riots and violent confrontations between protesters and the police. Then, as now, the Republican candidate, in this case Richard Nixon, had called himself the candidate of 'law and order'.

At the time, the war in Vietnam was still raging. Lyndon Johnson, who had inherited the presidency in 1963, was by now deeply unpopular because of the war and had announced that he would not seek re-election. The two most outspoken anti-war Democratic presidential primary candidates were Senator Robert F. Kennedy from New York and a senator from Minnesota named Eugene McCarthy.

On the radio that year you could listen to a song by a popular folk group called Peter, Paul and Mary; it was called 'If You Love Your Country' and the opening lyrics became an anthem for the peace movement: 'If you love your country, and the things for which it stands, vote for Gene McCarthy and bring peace to our land!'

Peace did not come to our land. Richard M. Nixon bested Hubert H. Humphrey in November 1968. The war continued.

On 15 November 1969, more than half a million young people pinned a blue badge that featured a white dove on their shirts and boarded buses for Washington to join what was then the largest anti-war protest in US history: the National Moratorium March on Washington. It was a mostly peaceful demonstration that day in Washington, although scuffles broke out in front of the White House, where Nixon was now ensconced as the new President.

The rally featured speeches by various anti-war politicians, including Senator McCarthy and another left-wing Democratic senator from South Dakota named George McGovern. The rally also included musical performances by Peter, Paul and Mary, Arlo Guthrie and Pete Seeger, who led the crowd in the singing of John Lennon's 'Give Peace a Chance'.

Nixon had promised in his 1968 campaign to begin a troop withdrawal but he had yet to take action. The new American President was unmoved by the peace protest, and he would later claim that he watched sports on television in the White House while it happened.

The anti-war movement continued to gain support in 1970, particularly after Kissinger's invasion of Cambodia and the shooting of unarmed student protesters at Kent State University.

The war would eventually cost America more than 58,000 lives and when it finally ended in 1975 – in a withdrawal that sent US troops scurrying out of Saigon – the Nixon administration tried to spin this, the first US defeat since the Second World War, as something they called 'Peace with Honor'. As the Viet Cong approached Saigon, both South Vietnamese citizens and American personnel fled and soon there were reports of American citizens clamouring up ladders and onto the roof of the US embassy, trying desperately to board Marine helicopters that flew them to the safety of waiting American warships off the coast of Vietnam, such as the aircraft carrier USS *Midway*. It was a dramatic and pathetic mass evacuation, the biggest humiliation of the United States in history, and the lasting images were the scenes of chaos as desperate people tried to escape and surplus helicopters were pushed over the side of ships and into the South China Sea in order to make room for more.

That was 30 April 1975, and the shock of the American defeat in Vietnam was yet another national trauma, after the murders of John F. Kennedy, Martin Luther King Jr and Bobby Kennedy. Like the assassinations, it would leave a lasting scar on our collective consciousness, just as had been the case a few months before, in August 1974, when another helicopter had carried out a more peaceful evacuation. In this case the helicopter was *Marine One*, which had lifted off from the White House lawn in the middle of August 1974 after Richard Nixon had resigned rather than face an impeachment trial in the Senate after he had been caught lying about the cover-up of the Watergate scandal.

By the mid-1970s, when Nixon resigned and the Vietnam War ended, America was still leading the world, but it was spending enormous parts of its energy and resources on fighting the Kremlin. The anti-Communist strand in American politics and foreign policy, in retrospect, was a substantial drain on resources and at times a substantial distraction. Yet nothing in the Cold War had prepared the Americans for what came next, or for their new President, a peanut farmer from Georgia named Jimmy Carter. Carter was a devout Christian who believed in human rights and he was the first and only President of the United States who actually used the power of the White House to put pressure on governments accused of human rights violations, from Chile to South Africa. But he was also magnificently unprepared for a dangerous and complicated world. It was in the mid-1970s that we learned about Arab oil producers, who began to enter American living rooms on the nightly news. We learned about something called OPEC, an organisation of petroleum-exporting countries that was willing to use the oil weapon against the United States. So we learned about lining up at the gas station and the speed limit was lowered to 55 miles per hour.

Jimmy Carter would eventually lose himself in the minutiae of the presidency, though he was a good man with a good heart, well-intentioned. Unfortunately for him, and for America, it was on his watch, in November 1979, that trauma struck again, this time as the US Embassy in Tehran was overrun by Iranian students who took fifty-two hostages and held them captive for a period of fourteen months. The hostages would be released only on the day Jimmy Carter left the White House on 20 January 1981, following his defeat the previous November at the hands of Ronald Reagan. Seeing fifty-two Americans treated like dirt for more than a year in Tehran as a helpless White House stood by was certainly another national trauma, a sickening experience. America was also sick of high inflation and a bad economy and oil prices and hostages and the peanut farmer from Georgia. By 1980, most Americans wanted some good news, some better times and perhaps a more happy-go-lucky leader.

With Ronald Reagan they got their wish. They got a feel-good President with a fondness for American exceptionalism. The term refers to the supposedly special and superior character of the United States as a uniquely free nation based on democratic ideals and personal liberties. But it also encompasses the idea that the US has a unique mission to transform the rest of the world.

Reagan embodied American exceptionalism and the roaring 1980s. He was all about jelly beans, big smiles and lots of optimism, and the promise that we would outspend the Soviets in order to defeat the 'Evil Empire'. At home it was a period of consumer hedonism, of big tax cuts, of Reaganomics and so-called trickle-down economics, which argued that policies that favoured the wealthy and privileged would eventually trickle down to the poor. The cup would runneth over, as it were, and everyone would gain. Unfortunately, for tens of millions of Americans, it did not work out that way.

In 1981, President Reagan became the first of three two-term Presidents who over the next thirty years would progressively slash America's spending on welfare benefits for the poor. Reagan led a powerful conservative Republican movement that promised to roll back the welfare state, privatise social security and increase defence spending. Call it more guns, less butter.

Trickle-down economics meant huge tax cuts, especially for the upper middle classes and the rich, greatly increased Pentagon spending, deregulation for big business, a policy of aggressively trying to roll back Communism (rather than just containing it), a stronger military, and appeals to family values. That was the Reagan era: the dismantling of many of the legacies of the New Deal and related progressive social and economic policies that had been in place in America since the 1930s, since their introduction by Franklin Delano Roosevelt.

Much of the Reagan era was a period of apparent national prosperity, but it marked the beginning of early globalisation and the first emergence of serious income disparities across American society. So not everyone enjoyed the booming 1980s or the follies of Gordon Gekko's Wall Street. This was, however, the era of the Yuppies, the young urban professionals, actually baby boomers born in the 1950s and 1960s, who were identified by the Madison Avenue advertising agencies as the demographic target that possessed the greatest consumer spending power. Throughout it all, Reagan had the national consensus, he was a much-loved President and he always smiled a great big smile for the cameras.

Smile or no smile, the Reagan years saw the start of an economic and social revolution in America, the rolling back of much of the Roosevelt-era legacy of the welfare state. It was a process of denuding the welfare state, of slashing tens of billions of dollars off the welfare budget, and it would continue for nearly thirty years, spanning the presidencies of Ronald Reagan in the 1980s, Bill Clinton in the 1990s and George W. Bush in the 2000s. In fits and starts, but consistently throughout the period from 1981 to 2001, the social safety net was dismantled, welfare cuts totalled tens of billions of dollars, and the percentage of our GDP spent on welfare shrank from 3.5 per cent to just 2.3 per cent.[3]

The welfare cuts were made by two Republicans and one Democrat who in the 1990s adopted a number of Republican policies, and together they managed to deactivate many of the federal policies and programmes that had underpinned our social cohesion at a national level, much of the super-structure of the social safety net and its associated machinery that Franklin Roosevelt had left behind.

If Reagan set about the task deliberately, with a free-market liberal's style and enthusiasm, Bill Clinton in the 1990s represented a more ambiguous approach; some would say more cynical. Clinton was part of the wave of progressive yet pro-business Democrats, those who were willing to reduce welfare spending, continue a number of Reagan tax cuts and look benignly upon the actions of the big banks on Wall Street. In Washington they called it 'triangulation' when Bill Clinton would get into an alliance with moderate Republicans and accept policies that were, objectively speaking, Republican.

By 1994, a Republican-dominated Congress was urging President Bill Clinton to make good on his campaign promise to 'end welfare as we know it'. He did.

By 2000, after a decade of Reagan welfare cuts and eight years of Bill Clinton's welfare reforms, the nation's welfare rolls had fallen sharply, to their lowest level in decades. But the figures masked a stark reality: many millions of people had simply been kicked off the welfare rolls.

It was also during the Clinton presidency in the 1990s that the seeds were sown for what would later become a global crisis of unprecedented dimensions in the financial world. Long before the collapse of Lehman Brothers in 2008, Bill Clinton's team was co-operating with Alan Greenspan's Federal Reserve to allow dangerous derivatives trading and securitisation of subprime mortgages. During the 1990s, banking deregulation proceeded as though a Republican were in the White House.

President Bill Clinton allowed huge helpings of deregulation that opened the door to the growth of the virtually unregulated securitised and bundled subprime mortgage market. It was with the Clinton administration's blessing that dangerous derivatives trading jumped by a quantum proportion, paving the way alongside the subprime mortgage market, for looming financial disaster.

It was under Clinton that the FDR-era Glass–Steagall Act was repealed, the law that had been set up after the Great Depression to protect savers and which forced banks to keep separate their commercial banking – i.e., taking deposits and making loans – from their investment banking businesses, like trading stocks and bonds. Wall Street was unleashed during the Clinton years, even more than under Reagan. Greed was back on Wall Street, and Washington looked away. The Treasury under Clinton was being run by Bob Rubin, the former boss of Goldman Sachs, and the Federal Reserve by Alan Greenspan, a former consultant to a notorious savings and loan fraudster from the 1980s named Charles Keating.

If the Reagan 1980s had seen the start of the rollback of the welfare state in America and an unleashing of the brashest speculative impulses on Wall Street, then the Clinton 1990s saw still further deregulation of the financial services sector and a series of free trade deals that would help America in the short-term but would ultimately cost jobs as the price of doing business in a globalised economy. Deals like the North American Free Trade Agreement (NAFTA) tend to bring more benefits than drawbacks but free trade does come with a price, and in free trade deals at least some domestic factory jobs tend to be lost to lower-cost foreign trading partners.

Slowly but surely, the more deleterious effects of globalisation were creeping forth.

The 1980s and 1990s weren't just about welfare reform and deregulation on Wall Street; they were also about the progressive declawing of American trade unions. Nothing symbolised the steady loss of power of the trade unions more than the way Ronald Reagan fired 11,000 air traffic controllers in one stroke, signing one executive order that would break the trade union for ever, much as Prime Minister Margaret Thatcher would do four years later in Britain, when she broke the will of the coal miners' union. Unions were being progressively weakened and disarmed, and worker benefits that had seemed normal for decades were suddenly being called into question. Across the United States, the manufacturing economy was giving way, over the decades, to a service economy. This, in turn, has given rise to the explosion of service sector 'McJobs' and a new working-poor segment of society, a new American underclass.

Over a period of three decades, American Presidents of both parties have progressively removed much of the social safety net, dismantled much of the welfare state and dramatically cut spending on the most vulnerable parts of our population. Guess what? It hurts. Someone is feeling the pain. Today, the rise in political populism is simply the most visible manifestation of widespread fear and anger emanating from that part of America which feels most exposed, at risk, unable to cope. In America today there are more than 43 million people living below the poverty line, or about 13.5 per cent of the American population.[4]

Once upon a time in America, there may have been a more equitable society, an American dream, a place with greater opportunity for nearly everyone and decidedly less gaping income disparities. Back in the 1950s, the unions were still strong and were demanding and obtaining more worker benefits, the state was still functioning under the full authority of FDR's welfare legacy, and the economic growth for much of the time was buoyant enough to float many people's boats, even those who may not have been so clever or intrepid.

Once upon a time, there was an America that felt it could leave the doors unlocked and go about its merry way, feeling somehow protected because we were Americans and we lived in America.

But that illusion ended on the morning of 11 September 2001. The destruction of the Twin Towers of the World Trade Center was another jolt to our national system, perhaps the biggest and most painful shock and our most profound loss-of-innocence moment since the Second World War. After all, back then we had been attacked by the Japanese at Pearl Harbor, in faraway Hawaii. This was downtown Manhattan.

As history would have it, the President on duty that September was the son of former President George Herbert Walker Bush, the man who had started the First Gulf War against Saddam Hussein in 1990. This President, George Walker Bush, was a real-life Texan with a studied swagger and a fondness for simplicity. Bush's response to 9/11 was to launch a poorly planned war in Afghanistan a few weeks later and then, on the back of what later turned out to be misleading and manipulated evidence of weapons of mass destruction, a second poorly planned war against Saddam Hussein, the US invasion of Iraq, in early 2003.

The effect of the war in Afghanistan, at least for a time, may have been to temporarily disrupt Osama bin Laden and the Al Qaeda infrastructure which cooperated with the Taliban in Afghanistan. But in the long run, no imperial power has ever won a war in Afghanistan: not the British, not the Russians, not America.

The effect of the mismanagement of the Second Gulf War in Iraq and its aftermath was to consign political and military influence over much of Iraqi territory first to the ayatollahs of Tehran and then later, during the Obama administration, to the warlords of ISIS, following a disastrously planned exit from Iraq which created a power vacuum that was quickly filled by the followers of the Caliphate.

Together, the wars in Afghanistan and Iraq have cost trillions of dollars,[5] not to mention the loss of hundreds of thousands of Iraqi and Afghani lives over the past fifteen years.[6]

But in the early twenty-first century America seemed oblivious to these wars, with many Americans approving of Bush's cowboy antics. The war on terrorism had replaced the Cold War as America's primary foreign policy; a common enemy had been identified. Washington had a bogeyman in Osama bin Laden. Meanwhile, behind the scenes, the Bush machinery functioned very well under the watchful guidance of Bush surrogates such as Karl Rove, Dick Cheney and Donald Rumsfeld. On the domestic front, the Bush years saw a radicalisation of the Republican agenda by the neo-cons and even by many who could today be called Tea Party or Trump supporters. The paradigm of American politics had been shifting to the right for decades, but now the shift became a lurch.

While he waged war on terrorism abroad, at home, in social and economic terms President George W. Bush continued to dismantle the social safety net that Ronald Reagan and Bill Clinton had already slashed severely between 1981 and 2001.

The results were hailed by the White House as a success, but they masked another statistic, and this one more serious: poverty rates were rising as welfare was being cut. From the time Bush took office in 2001 until his departure from the White House in January 2009, the poverty rate increased from 11.7 per cent to 13.2 per cent.[7]

It was just as Bush was preparing to leave office, in the autumn of 2008, that financial disaster struck. The derivatives trading and subprime mortgages had come home to roost. The collapse of Lehman Brothers in September 2008 was followed by a worsening of the crisis, from finance to the real economy, and Bush set in place the emergency partial nationalisations of car companies and banks, the massive bailouts of Detroit and Wall Street that his successor, Barack Obama, would continue.

Years of quantitative easing from the Federal Reserve seemed to find the American economy still in a lethargic state, and the financial crisis spread across the Atlantic to Europe. The Great Recession brought with it years of economic stagnation, persistently high unemployment, low consumer confidence, increasing mortgage foreclosures and personal bankruptcies, rising federal debt and a general sense of hopelessness among millions of Americans that began to become the norm. It really began to look as though mediocrity was the new normal. Americans were losing faith in America.

Obama had come to office on a tsunami of enthusiasm and hope, with his 'Yes We Can!' campaign chant creating a (temporary) confidence across America and the world. The new President seemed so eloquent, so different; the first African-American President of the United States, a highly articulate black man with a Harvard law degree and a noble demeanour, and he would surely bring America back to the greatness of the Kennedy era, wouldn't he?

The old men in Oslo who give out the Nobel Prize seemed to think so; within months of Obama moving into the White House they awarded him the Peace Prize – more a vote of confidence and an appreciation of his rhetorical abilities than an earned award, but then again the same prize had once been awarded to the likes of Henry Kissinger, who had supposedly achieved 'Peace with Honor' in Vietnam during the Nixon days.

Obama tried and failed to do many things that might have made America a more equitable society. To be fair, for much of his time in office he was faced with the legacy of two intractable wars, a financial crisis, a lingering recession that at times felt like a depression, and life-threatening risks for some of America's biggest banks and car makers. Obamacare, still highly controversial and divisive across the political spectrum, was perhaps the single most visible manifestation of Obama's vision for America. Much of the rest is less edifying stuff, the non-achievements of a well-meaning President who found himself caught in the gridlock of partisan politics.

While Obama continued the Bush rescue of Detroit and Wall Street, he also forged ahead with free trade negotiations, almost matching Bill Clinton's NAFTA agreement with his own

Trans-Pacific Partnership. But globalisation had a dark underside and by the time Obama left office, America was in no mood for more trade deals that had cost factory jobs.

Obama's greatest failure, by his own admission, was the bungling of Libya during the height of the Arab Spring. In early 2011, the protests in Cairo's Tahrir Square had swept away President Hosni Mubarak and ushered in the Arab Spring, the debut of the Facebook generation's rebellion across the Arab world. The deserts of the Middle East were suddenly ransacked by a violent wind, by a dust storm of global dimensions that came masquerading as the quest for democracy and then morphed into anarchy and fragmentation, into tribal and ethnic war, into failed states and semi-states and rival militia groups competing with terrorists to overthrow dictators.

In March 2011, when it looked like Libya's Colonel Muammar Gaddafi was about to fall, Secretary of State Hillary Clinton travelled to a special summit in Paris and, while President Obama was busy on a state visit to Brazil, she gave her backing to a move by President Nicolas Sarkozy of France to launch bombing raids and go for regime change in Libya. Sarkozy sent his fighter jets, backed by David Cameron, the hapless and neophyte Prime Minister of Britain at the time. And Hillary Clinton gave her blessing.

Obama's biggest mistake was trying constantly to ride the wave of the Arab Spring like a surfer, trying desperately to make sure he was on the right side of history. In the end, the destruction of Gaddafi without any plan for the future achieved exactly what the Pentagon and CIA had warned Secretary Clinton would happen when they had advised her against it. It helped open a power vacuum which the followers of ISIS would soon fill. The same could be said of Obama's hurried exit from Iraq, or his zig-zag uncertainty over what to do in Syria.

It can be reasonably argued, without taking political sides, that the result of US policy during the Arab Spring was to make it easier for ISIS to occupy new territories and capture US military equipment left behind, along with millions or billions of dollars of cash and enough oilfields to finance years of medieval-style horror across the Middle East and the world. The terrorism was at first limited to Europe, especially to Paris and Brussels.

The rise of ISIS only really began to strike home in America when ISIS-inspired murderers began their rampages in San Bernardino, California in December 2015 and in Orlando, Florida six months later, in June 2016. It was one thing for Islamic terrorists to attack Paris and Brussels, far away and across the Atlantic. But this was California, this was Florida, this was the homeland.

The spring and summer of 2016 was also a period of more frequent, and more visible, shootings of unarmed black youths by police, of rising racism and of general gun violence across America. The violence played out against the backdrop of the most vitriolic presidential contest in American history. Donald Trump sought to capitalise on the violence and presented himself as the candidate of 'law and order' while Hillary Clinton accused Trump supporters of being 'racist, sexist, homophobic, xenophobic and Islamophobic'.[8]

Sadly, Barack Obama seemed powerless throughout his last term in office to do anything about the higher levels of violence and racism, just as he was unable to stem the rise of poverty among poor white and black Americans. By the time Obama left office, poverty had reached the highest level in decades.

There is heavy irony in the surge in racism and the equal surge in poverty among African-Americans under America's first African-American president.

Until the arrival of Bernie Sanders and Donald Trump, both of whom were attracting large numbers of angry followers, political scholars and commentators had largely neglected to comment on one particular aspect of having an African-American in the White House: the racist backlash. After the election of Trump in November 2016, and the outbreak of hundreds of hate crimes, the talking heads began wondering aloud whether there had been a sinister and politically relevant 'whitelash' against the Obama era. Many working-class whites saw Obama as part of the problem, and given that for nearly half the population real wages had not risen for a decade or more, they were seething. Add together a real decline in net incomes and living standards caused by the Great Recession with a left-of-centre African-American in the White House and it is easier to understand the racism that took root across America, especially among the working poor, the underclass.

It did not seem to matter during the race for the White House in 2016 that on paper the US economy seemed to be growing, albeit at a relatively weak 2 per cent. Nor did it matter that unemployment numbers seemed to be at record lows, perhaps because an unprecedented number of Americans had simply dropped out of the labour market; they had given up hope, perhaps because there were so many service industry jobs that paid little more than the minimum wage of $7.25 per hour.

By November 2016, as Americans went about the unpleasant business of electing a new President, choosing between the two most disliked candidates in the nation's history, the reality was that many had simply lost faith in the chances of a better tomorrow, of better jobs and a better education for the next generation, of improving living standards. For many white working-class people, but also for tens of millions of other Americans, life had proven to be a raw deal. They had lost faith in the American dream.

By now there were 43 million Americans below the poverty line and a total of more than 100 million who were struggling to make ends meet on salaries that were less than twice the poverty level. The poverty line was just over $24,000 a year for a family of four, but nearly half of the poor actually subsist on less than $12,000 for a family with two children.[9] That is roughly eight dollars a day per person.

In a nation of 319 million people, in the richest country in the world, roughly a third of the population in 2015 was either living below the poverty level or was still so poor they risked social marginalisation. The American dream meant nothing for most of these people, who struggled to get by, formed part of the underclass or the working poor or the lower middle class, and who did much of their shopping at Walmart, the mammoth low-cost discount chain that with $482 billion of annual revenues is also the world's biggest corporation.[10]

The American dream? Once upon a time there was an America that believed in the dream. Maybe.

By now many Americans were living in a society lacerated by anger and fear and yet somehow strangely inured to it, a society that was getting used to resurgent political populism on TV and resurgent racism on the streets, a nation where gun violence and police shootings of unarmed blacks seemed at times a weekly or even occurrence, a challenge of epidemic proportions.

Had the America of equal opportunity and shared national prosperity ever really existed? Or had it all been a charade?

To understand what has happened to America, we need to understand the underlying causes of this unhappy period in our nation's history, a phase which in other countries might be called a national crisis.

The root causes are economic.

CHAPTER THREE

THE WALMART SOCIETY

> I was working for Walmart in the deli department, serving food, making salads, cooking food, slicing meat. I had started on $8.15 an hour back in the summer of 2014 and I really liked the job. Then I got pregnant, and at the end of 2015 there were a few times where I thought I was losing my baby and so I'd go to a hospital and get checked out, or I'd be very, very sick and I'd have to go see my doctor and get help, and it would get in the way of work. But I'd always bring written medical excuses, and then they'd go and tell me that Walmart doesn't take medical excuses. I begged them to move me to another department because the food smells and everything was making me nauseous. But they ended up firing me instead. They treated me like dirt and fired me when I got pregnant.

Nita Fischer[1] sits forward on the edge of her worn beige sofa, in a tiny and cluttered living room that is stuffed with junk, with the baby crib, the sofa and the TV set, with piles of dirty clothes and baby toys, prescription medicines and papers scattered across the floor. She is a pale and overweight young woman with a plain face, brown hair and a faint voice. When she speaks she seems to drift off, losing focus. She looks depressed, at times despondent. But she laces her utterances with an occasional giggle, a self-deprecating smile, and it is then that the true pathos of her life condition emerges. The fake pinewood panelling behind her is decorated with stick-on Disney princess decals and one small golden crucifix. The kitchen sink is stacked with filthy dishes. Detritus is everywhere.

We are in a tiny, grey clapboard hovel in a poor section of Lake Charles, Louisiana, a coastal town of just over 75,000 people where nearly a quarter of the population lives below the poverty line.[2] Each of the dozen or so grey prefab houses on the strip is the same, with a small air conditioner sticking out of one of its windows, chipped and peeling sidings and a small car out front. We are less than twenty feet from the railroad tracks on West Sallier Street.

This area of south-western Louisiana – a swathe of land that runs from Port Arthur in eastern Texas along the Gulf of Mexico and toward Lafayette – is surrounded by huge and monstrous refineries and petrochemical plants that have gouged away much of the natural beauty. Lake Charles, although also surrounded by the petrochemicals industry, has built a couple of modern skyscraper casino resorts to try to cash in on the gaming and tourism industries. The bigger one, the 26-storey L'Auberge Casino Resort, employs 2,400 workers. Nearby oil refineries and a liquefied natural gas terminal and shopping malls make up much of the rest of the economy. In fact, the city's economy is sustained by the oil and gas sector, by tourism and by large-scale shopping malls with huge warehouse-style supermarkets like Walmart.

Nita Fischer is twenty-four years old. She is a single mother who says her husband, who worked on repairing air conditioners, 'upped and ran off' when he discovered she was pregnant. 'He didn't want a baby,' says Nita. She never made it through college, although she did take some classes at nearby McNeese State University before dropping out. She didn't finish college, but she did accumulate $36,000 of student debt.

At first, Nita Fischer was like many of Walmart's 2 million employees, who are known as 'associates' inside the $482 billion company. She worked at Walmart, she shopped at Walmart and she lived near Walmart. Her wage increases were minimal, but over a period of eighteen months she did work her way up to a salary of $10.17 an hour. It was tough, but she managed to get by.

'Everything was going perfectly until I got pregnant,' says Nita. She remembers clearly the day she was fired.

> It was 15 January 2016. I went to work and I'm in the deli, doing my thing for an hour. I'm showing off a picture of the ultrasound of my baby because I had a medical appointment the day before. And then they call me to the office because I was off for two days because the night before that when I was closing I had a little accident at work. I slipped and the sink hit my tummy real good and so I told the management and they said I should go to the hospital and get checked out. And everything was fine, but then I was off for two days after the accident and then the next day I get fired! At first I thought they would call me into the office, talk to me about the accident that happened, but they pretty much told me I'm fired and that I can reapply in ninety days. The thing is they knew how far long I was. I was six or seven months pregnant by then.

At this point, based on Nita's recollection and confirmation from her pro bono lawyers, she asked the assistant manager at the Walmart store why she was being fired.

> They had pulled me into the office and they're like saying: 'You know why you're here, right?' And I'm like: 'No.' And they're like: 'Well, we have to let you go.' And I'm like: 'Why?' And they're like: 'Your absences.' I'm like: 'Really? These were medically excused absences. Really? So in other words you're firing me because I'm pregnant, because I have medical excuses for all of my absences.' And then they're like: 'Well, Walmart doesn't take medical excuses.' And I'm like: 'That's bull crap.'

The Walmart management told Nita that she would have been fine if she had had her leave of absence papers finished for her maternity leave. Through no fault of her own, the leave of absence paperwork was not returned to her by 15 January.

Nita found herself suddenly without any income, and in less than three months she was due to give birth. But she still waited the ninety days and filed an application for a new job at another Walmart branch, and she was hired, and put back on a $9 an hour salary as a fresh starter two months after her son was born. She is meanwhile bringing action before the Equal Employment Opportunity Commission against the mammoth Walmart for unfair dismissal. But her condition today, with a newborn baby, is significantly worse than it was before she was fired by Walmart.

Nita Fischer has fallen into the poverty trap, and she and her baby are living below the poverty threshold.[3] She is now an official member of the working poor and has been forced to get food stamps and Medicaid and declare personal bankruptcy. She has $36,000 of student debt and $21,000 of credit card bills that she could not pay back. Her utility bills have not been paid for many months. Her parents try to help her out with the rent, but her father is an out-of-work tugboat captain and her mother makes about $600 a month doing part-time work at a neighbourhood church.

Nita says she is currently struggling on about $1,100 of gross pay a month from Walmart. Her rent costs $395 a month, her monthly bankruptcy settlement payment costs a further $400 a month, and her car insurance costs another $402 a month. The water and electricity bills, around $90 a month, 'just sit there and don't get paid', says Nita. Some of the deficit is made up by contributions from her mother.

Nita Fischer, with one child, is now officially below the poverty line. She does not have enough money to buy food for her baby. She says her own daily lunch usually consists of a bowl of cereal or a pint of ice cream. To feed her baby she has had to seek welfare benefits under a federal programme called WIC, which stands for the Special Supplemental Nutrition Program for Women, Infants and Children. WIC helps low-income pregnant women, infants and children under the age of five.

Nita gets $279 worth of food stamps each month and uses all of them, of course, at Walmart. 'I get off work,' she says, 'and I need some food or milk, so I just go shopping with my food stamps back at Walmart.'

Walmart, when asked to comment on Nita's claims of unfair dismissal for pregnancy, claimed that its store 'worked with Ms Fischer during her pregnancy to provide appropriate accommodations, including providing her with light duty work. Unfortunately she didn't always work all of the hours she was scheduled, causing extra work for the other associates in her store.'[4]

Nita's lawyer begs to differ. 'This is entirely inaccurate,' says Elizabeth Gedmark, an attorney at A Better Balance, a non-profit legal advocacy group that is donating its services to Nita Fischer.[5]

> Walmart did not work with Ms Fischer during her pregnancy. They did not seek alternative accommodations. They did not provide her with light duty work. She was in the process of requesting a leave of absence for her pregnancy and they fired her the day after she fell and injured herself. They refused her medical excuses. She was fired for her pregnancy-related absences and for her pregnancy. At Walmart they are treating pregnant women as second-class citizens.

Dina Bakst, co-president of A Better Balance, says the case of Nita Fischer is just one of many, including many single women, often single mothers, who fall out of the labour force or onto its lowest rungs, and find themselves unable to cope.

'We have seen many fall out of the workforce and see their long-term prospects imperilled. This ripple effect of so many challenges makes it so difficult for so many low-wage women in America. They are one of the biggest segments of poverty in America,' says Bakst. 'It is shameful that in 2016 pregnant workers are still being treated like second-class citizens. In Walmart's case there is an extraordinary lack of human decency and respect for the worker, but this is not just about Walmart. We see this trend all across America.'

Walmart is for many the bogeyman of American exploitative capitalism in the early twenty-first century. The Walton family of Bentonville, Arkansas is the richest family in America, worth over $130 billion.[6] The family has built Walmart into a half a trillion dollar a year company that is notorious among the 1.3 million members of the United Food and Commercial Workers International (UFCW) for myriad cases of unfair practices.

'There is plenty of evidence of Walmart refusing to accept doctor's notes, there are plenty of cases,' says Randy Parraz, an official at the UFCW.[7] 'They do plenty of things that are illegal, but just try and go after them,' scoffs Parraz, citing the David-vs-Goliath nature of Nita Fischer's case against Walmart and those of so many other workers at Walmart and elsewhere across the landscape of giant shopping malls, big-box stores and fast food establishments that we call America.

More than 2.3 million Americans work for Walmart, nearly twice the total number of men and women employed in our armed services. Walmart's nearly 5,000 stores across America occupy almost 700 million square feet. That's enough space for 11,800 football fields. More than half of Americans live within five miles of a Walmart store, and 90 per cent of Americans live within fifteen miles.[8]

Charles Fishman, the journalist whose 2006 book *The Wal-Mart Effect* is the single best chronicle of how this Arkansas-based discount store became the world's largest retailer, noted the vast influence of the Walton family.

'Wal-Mart isn't just a store, or a huge company, or a phenomenon any more,' writes Fishman. 'Wal-Mart shapes where we shop, the products we buy and the prices we pay – even for those who never shop there.' The Walmart effect, as Fishman explains, touches the lives of literally every American, and every day.

Every week of the year more than 260 million customers go into a Walmart store, somewhere in the world. That is 37 million customers a day. 'Wal-Mart changes the world every day,' notes Fishman, 'Wal-Mart has changed business, work, the shape and well-being of communities and everyday life in the United States and around the world.'

Randy Parrazz is a bit blunter:

> Walmart has helped create the working poor in America. They drive out competitors, they pay low wages, so they force people to come back and buy from them. They deny many benefits. They have a way of doing business in which they will fire you and then rehire you at a lower wage. There is very little stability in the number of hours a worker is allowed to work and so they have forced a lot of their low-wage workers onto welfare. Walmart has helped to create this new American underclass.

The company's detractors are many. The accusations are numerous. Walmart uses foreign labour, including child workers in places like Bangladesh. Walmart underpays women and neglects pregnant workers. The company discriminates against workers with disabilities and against elderly employees. The company is accused of wage theft, of not paying the real number of hours worked, of providing poor health care for its workers, of cheating and mistreating its workers in every way that you could imagine. Among the loudest complaints by far is the alleged mistreatment of workers and unfair dismissal practices against pregnant women. At Walmart, it is OK to reject a written note from a doctor who is treating a work-related injury in the deli department. At Walmart, it is even OK to sue a brain-damaged former worker to recover health benefits needed to pay for her life as an invalid in a nursing home.

Deborah Shank was a Walmart shelf stocker who suffered severe brain damage when her car was hit by a truck.[9] She was a full-time employee and so Walmart health insurance paid for her medical costs. The woman's family received a settlement from the trucking company that left her with $417,000. That money was put into a trust for her long-term care in the nursing home.

Then, Walmart went after the money, suing Ms Shank to collect reimbursement for $470,000 in medical costs that had been covered by her health insurance at Walmart. Amazingly, the practice is not unusual. Walmart's health plans have a so-called 'subrogration' policy that allows the employer to recover costs if a worker ever receives damages in a settlement related to their injury.

A week after Ms Shank lost her case against Walmart, she received the news that her eighteen-year-old son, a soldier in the US Army, had been killed in Iraq. Walmart came under a heavy barrage of negative publicity, but wouldn't budge. Rules are rules.

Finally, a crusade by MSNBC personality Keith Olbermann in the spring of 2008 helped embarrass Walmart into backing down.

'A week after Walmart beat her in court, Mrs Shank lost her eighteen-year-old son in Iraq,' noted Olbermann.

> Because of her brain damage from the accident, her memory is intermittent. So every time she asks about him, they have to tell her he's dead. It's as if she's hearing it for the first time. Walmart is suing her for all the money she has in the world. Walmart, always low prices, always low humanity.[10]

Following this broadcast, Walmart dropped its claim on the money that was in Ms Shank's nursing home trust. For once, the Waltons had been embarrassed into backing down.

Today, in a nation of institutionalised social injustice and an expanding underclass, you could say that we are living in a Walmart Society.

Walmart is in some ways a manifestation of the contemporary American dream in 21st-century America. It is the meeting place for local society, the symbol of having arrived in life. For many of the new American underclass, the famous chicken in every pot and the two-car garage have now become just a roof over one's head, some form of accommodation, but always a car, always a car so that one can drive to shop at the big-box stores and the local Walmart super centre. Yet there are also legions of Walmart workers who do not have a car. A catch-22 of the Walmart Society is that in much of rural America the public transport is poor and barely transports many of the working poor to their jobs.

The armies of Walmart cashiers, many of them earning the minimum wage of $7.25 an hour, live in Walmart, shop in Walmart and otherwise tend to live an often downtrodden life. They are part of the new low-wage underclass. The same is true for the endless employees of fast food outlets across the nation, the infamous McJobs that have helped to expand the ranks of the working poor. The truly sad part of America's economic recovery story is that despite slowly rising median incomes, America in 2017 is still wheezing from the effects of the Great Recession that struck in 2008, with large pockets of the nation still hurting or worse. For many of those in employment, real net wages (adjusted for inflation) have barely increased over the past twenty years.[11] Many of the jobs that were lost offered relatively decent pay. The new jobs we are adding, in a nation that has seen its manufacturing sector shrink to less than a quarter of our national output, tend to be mostly low-level, service sector positions. Middle-class jobs have been replaced by McJobs.

In many ways, what happened during the Great Recession and its aftermath since 2008 was really the aggravation of an already developing trend, where technological change and globalisation have shaped an economy that creates new work at the top and bottom, but very little in the middle.

Perhaps the greatest irony is that as America has shifted to a service economy dominated by fast food, shopping malls and mass retailing, and as that service sector has created a new underclass of the working poor, we have all ended up subsidising Walmart and other low-wage retail giants as taxpayers.

'When companies pay too little for workers to provide for their families, workers rely on public assistance programs to meet their basic needs,' says Ken Jacobs, head of the University of California Berkeley Labor Center and co-author of an exhaustive report on how rising numbers of low-wage workers for Walmart and others are being subsidised by welfare.[12]

The 2015 study by the University of California noted that while the US economy was recovering from years of lethargy, persistent low wages are costing taxpayers more than $150 billion a year in public support for working families at the lower rungs of society.[13]

The underlying causes of this plunge into poverty for tens of millions of Americans began, according to the study, with the decline in the real hourly wages of the median American worker and the trend toward employer cuts in benefits. The result today is a concentration of low-paid, struggling workers who are increasingly relying on the government to put food on the table and pay for health coverage. Almost three-quarters of enrollees in the country's biggest public support programmes are members of working families, the study found.

The study concluded that US taxpayers bridge the gap, by providing more than $152.8 billion a year in funding for working families receiving four key anti-poverty programmes that are known generically as welfare: Medicaid, Temporary Assistance for Needy Families, food stamps and the earned-income tax credit.

On the receiving end, one figure pretty much says it all: about 52 per cent of all fast food workers across America today rely on public assistance, on food stamps or Medicaid or some form of welfare. All 52 per cent are below the poverty line.

Welcome to the Walmart Society.

It is therefore not surprising that Bernie Sanders has called Walmart 'the major beneficiary of welfare in America'[14] and has repeatedly attacked the family that owns it. 'The major welfare abuser in America is the wealthiest family in America, the Walton family,' says Sanders. 'This one family owns more wealth than the bottom 40 per cent of the American people.'[15]

Sanders is a politician, and his simplifications have elements of demagoguery and populism. But he has done more than any other politician to raise awareness of the state of America's new underclass and the perverse ironies of the Walmart Society.

'Isn't it weird', Sanders asked a cheering Iowa crowd at the start of his presidential campaign, 'that many of the people who work at Walmart are on Medicaid, which *you* pay for; they're on food stamps, which *you* pay for; they're in government-subsidised housing, which *you* pay for because the Walton family refuses to provide the wages and benefits their workers deserve.'[16]

Perhaps a more eloquent summation of the irony of the Walmart Society was given by Professor Robert Reich of the University of California, while giving testimony on Capitol Hill.[17]

> I do not think that taxpayers in this country ought to be subsidising the wealthiest family in this country or any company and any corporation that is paying its workers so little that those workers, in order to have a decent living, have got to rely on food stamps, Medicaid, subsidised housing and so on. That is corporate welfare of the worst kind. But more broadly, let me simply say that Walmart is the largest employer in the United States. It is paying its workers, if you include its part-time workers, on average $8.80 an hour. Now, compare that to 1955, when the largest employer in the United States was General Motors and it was paying its workers in today's dollars $37 an hour.

The problem of poverty in America, however, is much bigger than Walmart.

Even though US Census data showed that 2015 saw the first real recovery in median income since 2008, income remained below 2007 pre-recession levels. Poverty in America, although down in 2015, remained among the highest, as a percentage of society, among Western industrialised nations. Wages were still below 2007 levels in 2015, and most of the income rises were occurring in urban centres, in cities.[18] Those in many of the rural areas of the Midwest, the West, the South and the South-east felt no improvement whatsoever.

It is not surprising that many of these dejected Americans became supporters of Bernie Sanders, on the one hand, and of Donald Trump on the other. Both politicians, as different as they may have been, seemed to project solidarity with the working poor, the low-wage portions of America, the lower middle class and white working classes. Sanders spoke with compassion about the plight of the poor while Trump marched into the room and made lavish promises, announcing that he would fix everything. Many poor people believed Trump.

Back in Lake Charles, Louisiana, Nita Fischer was among those who were drawn to Trump. She fidgets slightly when asked the question. Was she going to vote for Donald Trump?

'Um-hm!' she replies in a singsong voice, nodding her head vigorously and breaking into her first smile of the day.

'We need to get rid of Ding-Dong in the White House and get somebody who will help us out and unite us and fix this economy,' says Nita Fischer.

'I think Donald Trump is going to put America back to work and stop all these freeloaders from living off the government,' says Nita, her voice now going slightly shrill.

Nita Fischer, discriminated against for being pregnant and now a single mother with a baby son, who is only getting by thanks to food stamps, offers the opinion of the working poor toward the even less fortunate of America's underclass.

Freeloaders? Living off the government? Who does she mean?

Nita nods her head in a righteous manner.

'Freeloaders!' says Nita, as though the answer should be self-evident.

> Like somebody who don't want to work and they just live off the government for money. They choose not to work and they're capable of working. I've seen so many people who just sit on their butt, not doing nothing, and I'm like, 'Really? Get a job, stop living off of my taxpaying dollars and just get a job! You don't want to work? Then if you're not even trying to find a job, I think you shouldn't get anything.'

Nita speaks with her own sense of dignity and pride as she looks one rung down the social ladder. She is a member of the working poor who is speaking about those well below the official poverty thresholds in America. In America, in 2015, you were poor if you earned less than $12,331 a year as an individual, or, for example, if you were a family with two children and earning a combined total of less than $24,036. Nita is now earning $13,000 a year, below the established poverty level for a single mother with one child, which would be just over $16,000 a year.[19]

Nita's son Austin is also growing up poor, below the poverty line, along with 14.5 million other American children. Nearly 20 per cent of all American children are currently living in poverty.[20] It is a staggering number in the richest nation on the planet. And nearly 2 million children are living in extreme poverty, in conditions not dissimilar to subsistence farmers in Zambia.[21]

In America today it is not too hard to find extreme poverty. If you drive north from Lake Charles, Louisiana and take US-165 for three or four hours, and then follow US-278 east and across the Mississippi River, you soon find yourself driving past huge cotton plantations near Greenville, Mississippi and into a region that has been called 'the most Southern place on earth'. It is also the poorest region of the poorest state in the entire United States of America.

Welcome to the Mississippi Delta.

The Delta is actually not a delta but rather a rich and fertile alluvial plain created by thousands of years of flooding. The bottomland is moist and lush. This is the authentic backwoods of Mississippi, a land of mosquito-infested swamps and abandoned cotton gins that runs for 200 miles from Vicksburg all the way up to the northernmost border with Tennessee, just minutes south of Memphis. As one gas station attendant in Vicksburg put it, 'We got a whole lotta nothin' here.'

At its widest point the Delta has a girth of seventy miles; its boundaries are the Mississippi River and the Yazoo River. The mighty Mississippi regularly overflows its banks, and the levees in the Delta have been known to break, on many occasions. When they built the levees to hold back the huge Mississippi River floods that happened every year, the floodplains and the marshes dried up, and the silt from the river left behind a wonderfully fertilised land that was perfect for growing cotton.

Although the Mississippi Delta would eventually come to be known as a quintessential example of the Old South, or the Deep South, with its wealthy white plantation owners and its impoverished black sharecroppers and tenant farmers, only 10 per cent of the land had been cleared at the end of the Civil War in 1865. Back then, most of the Delta's bottomland was still covered in forest. Initially slaves and then, after the Civil War, newly freed African-Americans were put to work clearing the land, building the plantations and working them, whether as slaves in antebellum Mississippi or later as sharecroppers or tenant farmers. But in the twentieth century the supremacy of 'King Cotton' faced two major challenges: first the mechanisation of the refining process that put many out of work in the 1960s and 1970s. Second, more recently, in the age of globalisation, international companies from China and Japan and around the world have been buying up many of the Mississippi plantations, cutting human capital still further. The fastest-growing industry in the Mississippi Delta used to be cotton. Today it is a toss-up between agriculture and the rapidly expanding business of incarceration, mainly of black men, in several penitentiaries that fill the otherwise empty landscape.

The Delta has one big cultural claim to fame, as the original home of the blues. Yet even this is an art form whose origins lie in the region's economic hardship.

It was on these cotton plantations in the Mississippi Delta that most of the most famous blues musicians in American history were born or raised, as sharecroppers who picked cotton or worked in the cotton gin during the day and shopped at the plantation's commissary, using their labour in return for food credits. By night, they played a new and mournful form of music, a melodic and at times haunting howl of anguish, expressed with rhythm and resignation. In the 1930s and 1940s, this music became known as the blues, and later it would become the foundation of all the rock and roll music that would follow.

Muddy Waters grew up in a tenant farmer's shack in Clarksdale, Mississippi, in the heart of the Delta. He shopped at the plantation commissary and expressed the giant sadness of the life of his fellow man in song, in blues that came out of his belly like a sometimes wretched prayer, a harmonic and wrenching melody.

Muddy Waters. B.B. King. Robert Johnson. Howlin' Wolf. Their names are many, and music buffs everywhere know that the Mississippi Delta was rich in soil, music and culture. But its economy began a century-long freefall with the first signs of mechanised cotton pickers in the 1920s. The mechanisation of cotton, which intensified over the decades, at first sparked what the locals called the Great Migration, of many black sharecroppers and tenant farmers from the Delta to St Louis and Chicago. Then it led to some of the highest unemployment in America. Today, unemployment in the Delta is close to double the national average of 5 per cent, and among African-Americans it is even higher.[22] In much of the Delta, the poverty rate still hovers between 35 and 40 per cent, against a national average of 13.5 per cent.[23]

Today, the Delta feels somehow cut off from the rest of America, even more than Appalachia in West Virginia. The Delta is like a piece of abandoned territory whose people have been tossed onto the junk heap. Driving along the dirt roads, one sees nothing but trailer parks and prefabs, an endless landscape of boarded-up gas stations and abandoned shops, of broken-down communities and barefoot children. It is a bleak and desolate reality, all the more shocking to see in the middle of America; a 200-mile-long garbage dump where more than a third of the people have largely been cast off by the rest of society, by globalisation and by the juggernaut of the American economy. Human detritus. Not needed. No thanks. Sorry.

The Mississippi Delta is noteworthy for the number of records it holds, perhaps first and foremost as the poorest part of America pretty much uninterruptedly for the past 150 years, since the end of the Civil War. It wins a lot of prizes, but for all the wrong reasons. This is the birthplace of the most extreme forms of racism in America, the lynching capital of America. In the state of Mississippi, there are three times as many black men in prison as whites.[24] Year after year, Mississippi scores the lowest education scores in America, the highest illiteracy rate, the highest teenage birth rate, the lowest life expectancy and, unsurprisingly, the highest child poverty in America.[25]

In the 2015 Census, child poverty declined by 1 per cent at a national level. In Mississippi, it rose by 7 per cent, the only increase in the United States. The child poverty rate for Mississippi now stands at more than 30 per cent.[26]

Up in Clarksdale, Mississippi, in the heart of the Delta, in the little former plantation town where blues singer Muddy Waters grew up, Mayor Bill Luckett says that child poverty is the saddest part of the whole sad story.[27]

'Our overall poverty rate is up there between 37 and 38 per cent,' says Mayor Luckett, a big, larger-than-life man with a white beard and a gentle disposition. Indeed, in Clarksdale, overall poverty is close to three times the national average.[28]

The gregarious Luckett, who speaks with a soothing Southern drawl that has won him acting gigs in a number of movies, comes from old money but has distinguished himself as a civil rights and anti-poverty activist. Part-time lawyer, part-time real estate mogul, part-time blues club owner (with actor and local celebrity Morgan Freeman), he is in many ways the progressive face of left-of-centre Democratic politics in a state that is solidly red. At sixty-eight, he is still a hyperactive sort of fellow with a passion for the blues and the militancy of a social activist. All this and a country lawyer's faux-humble demeanour. The Mississippi Delta is a place of exotic and complex contradictions, a place of extremes such as the millionaire's row of newly built mansions along the golf course on the edge of Clarksdale and the dilapidated and crumbling wooden huts of the poorest of African-Americans living along Florida Avenue, literally on the wrong side of the tracks in this Delta town. Luckett seems to embody all of these contradictions, as he drives his pick-up truck into the parking lot of his (and Morgan Freeman's) nightclub, Ground Blues Zero.

When he sweeps into the place, a former cotton gin converted into a graffiti-covered juke joint, it is with the force of a friendly hurricane. 'Hey. How y'all doin'?' he asks a couple of tourists from Amsterdam who are eating fried baloney sandwiches and staring in rapture at the stage, where a morbidly obese child prodigy, the sixteen-year-old blues performer known as Christone 'Kingfish' Ingram, is plucking at the guitar. 'Kingfish even played at the White House, for Michelle and Barack Obama,' notes Luckett as he proceeds across the club. 'Buongiorno,' says Luckett, with a Southern twang, to a table of photographers from Rome. 'Oh yeah,' says a proud Bill Luckett, 'we get visitors from around the world.' Now he greets some locals, both blacks and whites from Clarksdale, and he notes how here there are citizens of both colours, sitting together and united as a community, united by the music. Although he complains that he and Morgan Freeman have not seen a penny back from Ground Blues Zero since they opened the place back in 2001, Luckett has used the club and the promotion of an annual blues festival to help create jobs in the otherwise battered community. Tourism is now driving Clarksdale's efforts to create some jobs, but the city's high crime rate has been holding back progress.

Over some delicious but clearly unhealthy fried green tomatoes, bacon cheeseburgers and fried potatoes, Luckett notes that another of the records held by the Mississippi Delta is as the most obese place in America.

'We have the highest diabetes rate in America,' says Luckett. 'This is a food desert with the highest level of obesity, the highest level of heart disease, the highest in child malnutrition, the highest in you name it,' says Luckett, with a look of frustration spreading across his face. 'Here we are in the middle of the most fertile farming land in America and we are living in a food desert,' he adds with a deep sigh.

The rich soil, however, does not stop the people of Clarksdale and the surrounding Coahoma County from living in what is pretty much the poorest county in the poorest state in America.

What is a food desert? In poorer parts of America, and not just here in Clarksdale, it is very hard to find any fresh produce. Most of the local staple diet consists of processed and packaged goods bought from local convenience stores and discounts like the Save-A-Lot chain. Prodigious quantities of fried chicken are sold by gas stations up and down the highway and a large part of the local diet is made up of carbohydrate-rich and cholesterol-laden snack foods and beer and Coca-Cola.

On the subjects of malnutrition, obesity and child poverty, Luckett recommends a conversation with a Harvard law graduate named Desta Reff,[29] a strong and independent woman who has come to live in Clarksdale, working as part of Harvard's Delta Fellows outreach programme, in this case helping to educate poor mothers about pre-natal care and early childhood. Ms Reff, who speaks openly of her mixed heritage as the offspring of a black father and a white mother and of her own wife and two children, agrees with Luckett about the serious illness and malnutrition that plague the Delta.

'We do indeed live in the middle of a food desert,' she says.

> All of the Delta is basically a food desert, which means there is no access to fresh food. So, in Clarksdale we do have a Walmart and we have a Kroger, but you go fifteen minutes away to Jonestown or thirty minutes to Sumner, and there is nothing. They have to come here to get food. I remember being in a meeting with the Mayor of Jonestown, which is a small Delta town, it's got about 1,200 people. They were talking about how they were working on plans to get a Dollar General or some sort of dollar store to

> open up there, and how that would be great because then people could buy food.

The lack of fresh food has the greatest impact on poor children, who, according to Ms Reff, still get most of their food from convenience stores that stock the usual fare of sandwiches, snacks and chips.

'Fresh food access is really difficult. It's really hard to find fresh fruits and vegetables, even if you have the money to buy them, which a lot of our families don't,' says Reff.

'There is a concept I was not familiar with before moving here, it's like malnutrition and obesity coming together,' she says.

> A lot of these kids maybe have only one meal a day, but that meal is chips and juice and like hotdogs. But it's not nutrition dense. They're not getting the nutrients they need, and they're actually hungry because they're only fed once. The problem is that what they are fed is this overly processed and fattening food, and that is literally all they have access to, whether or not they can get access to a store. It is also because this is all they have access to economically, because it's what they can afford.

The irony of this food desert is not lost on the Harvard-trained social worker. Desta Reff acknowledges the contrast between the rich alluvial soil that feeds mega-cotton plantations and endless fields of soybean, corn, wheat, rice and sorghum, and the near impossibility of getting easy access to fresh food. Even more moving is her explanation of why, given all this fertile soil, the poor in Clarksdale don't cultivate a tiny vegetable garden on their land.

> Aside from the fact that we lost most of those skill sets several generations ago, we should remember that there is a strong correlation between poverty and being African-American. There is a strong resistance to farming, to manual labour on farms because of what that means. I don't even think it's conscious, it's very

> subconscious. People are very resistant to it. In fact, people will almost brag about their lack of exercise. They'll take the car across the street and it's like a point of pride. I think it's subconscious.

Back in the Mayor's office, on Sunflower Avenue, Bill Luckett is talking about poverty in the Delta. He is remembering the time he ran for governor, in the Democratic primary of 2011. He lost, as any progressive Democrat would in such a staunchly Republican state, but he made the hallmark of his campaign the link between poverty and education. For Luckett, as for many poverty experts across America, the key to eliminating poverty lies in education.

> I wrote a paper at the University of Virginia back in the late '60s and I wrote then about the fact that Mississippi ranked first in poverty and fiftieth in education. Well, we still hold those positions, except we have dropped to fifty-first in education because the District of Columbia is now included in the mix. So we are a dead last place in so many categories.

His solution is to devote more resources to early childhood education in a state where attendance at kindergarten is voluntary and there are no publicly mandated schools for three- or four-year-olds.

> Unless and until we educate better, we are going to just stay in the same cycle, and it's a cycle of poverty. You look at the third-grade reading levels of students in Mississippi and it is an uncannily accurate predictor of how many prison beds we will need fifteen years later. Uncannily accurate. When kids can't read in the third grade, they tend to drop out. They don't finish high school, a lot of them go to crime, and then they don't have a high school diploma and then they eventually can't pass a drug test. Those are the two biggest impediments to employing people here in Clarksdale. Most businesses, including city government, require a high school diploma or a GED equivalent and passing a drug test, and that

keeps a lot of people from being employed, except for day jobs like yard work and that sort of thing.

In 1965, President Lyndon B. Johnson's War on Poverty provided a panoply of job training, adult education and loans. Early childhood education, alongside health and nutrition, was a top priority in the Head Start Program that Johnson launched for low-income families. But that was before the welfare cutbacks of the 1980s and 1990s, and long before the cold winds of globalisation began to blow away low-skilled jobs.

Forty years later, Marian Wright Edelman, a Hillary Clinton mentor who is founder of the Children's Defense Fund, is still aghast at the state of affairs. 'Over 80 per cent of the black children in Mississippi cannot read or compute at grade level in fourth or eighth grade,' she told PBS in 2016. 'What is a child to do if they can't read and compute at the most basic levels?'[30]

In many parts of America, the answer to that question is often determined by which side of the tracks you grew up on.

In April 1967, Senator Robert F. Kennedy visited the Delta to see for himself how bad the poverty was. At the time, Kennedy remarked to his aide, Peter Edelman, Marian's husband, that it was worse than anything he had seen in a third world country.

Edelman rightly puts the Mississippi into a national and global context. 'What has happened over the last forty years', he argues, 'is that we have had a major change in our economy. Good jobs have gone to technology and globalisation and the consequence is that half of our population is not earning enough to support their families.'[31]

All true, but what is striking is how accurate Bobby Kennedy's comparison to third world conditions remains today. Even though the overall poverty rate declined in 2015, the number of Americans living in extreme poverty was and is still increasing.

'I've spent time in Africa,' says Desta Reff.

I lived in Zimbabwe for a while. My father is from Ethiopia, I've

> seen third-world poverty, and there are circumstances here where it is not that dissimilar. There are people here who don't have electricity or running water, who live in conditions that you wouldn't believe for someone living in America.

Richard Grant, a well-travelled British author and journalist who has also made a home for himself in the Mississippi Delta, has no doubt about the similarities.

> If you come to America from Europe, I think one of the things that shocks you initially is how poor people are, and how many poor people there are, but also the fact that they almost all have cars somehow. You can usually see a car parked outside the tumbledown trailer by the dirt road. There is poverty in Mississippi that really reminds me of being in Haiti or Tanzania. Life expectancy in some Mississippi counties is equivalent to Zambia and Bangladesh. It is incredible to have this poverty in the middle of a nation this wealthy.[32]

The World Bank sets the international poverty line at about two dollars a day, a level that actually exists in the United States today.

According to Professor Luke Shaefer, a poverty expert at the University of Michigan, there are more than 1.5 million families in the United States today that live on two dollars a day.[33] Many of these families are single-parent households, with an average of two children. In other words, in the United States, in 2017, nearly 4 million Americans, more than half of them children, live at the same level as the poorest subsistence farmers in Africa.

Shaefer and sociologist Kathryn Edin have done a great deal of ground-breaking research to identify and chronicle the lives of these millions of Americans who subsist on two dollars a day. Their 2015 book was aptly titled *$2.00 A Day: Living on Almost Nothing in America*.

Not surprisingly, Shaefer, who also travelled to inner-city Chicago and the Appalachian region of West Virginia during his research, found one of the biggest concentrations of $2 a day poverty in the Mississippi Delta. What he saw left him stunned.

> In a lot of the small towns that we visited, it wasn't just that there weren't enough jobs to go around. There were simply *no jobs*, and it had been that way for a long time, since the mechanisation of agriculture. It never recovered, and the situation was compounded by its own particular racial challenges that go back generations and generations.

'In many of the small towns we were in, it felt like you could probably throw a stone and hit the house of someone who was living below the two-dollar-a-day threshold,' he adds.

Shaefer says that if he had his choice between living on two dollars a day in America and in sub-Saharan Africa, he might prefer to be 'transported' to Africa. 'At least there I would have some access to fresh produce and I might have a greater degree of autonomy.'

In fact, based on several indicators that Shaefer and his colleagues have examined, people living in extreme poverty in America can actually fare worse than poor people in third world countries. 'We have looked at things like life expectancy, infant mortality, risk of homicide and risk of incarceration,' says Shaefer. 'On all of these indicators, things look worse for Americans than they do for a whole host of people in much poorer countries.'

The Delta may represent the worst case of national poverty in statistical terms, but it is part of a pattern of poverty that stretches across the nation, with extreme poverty clustered mostly in inner-city areas of major cities and in rural stretches of America.

Some 43 million Americans live in poverty, and a total of more than 100 million Americans live on less than twice the poverty level, which puts a full one third of the American population either below the poverty threshold or struggling to get by and at constant risk of facing social marginalisation. And yes, there is a strong correlation between poverty and race. In 2015, one in every eight white men, 11.6 per cent, were below the poverty line in America, but for African-Americans the ratio was more than double: one out of every four men, or 24.1 per cent.[34]

If the fate of the Mississippi Delta was sealed when cotton picking was mechanised in the 1920s, the town of Allendale, South Carolina suffered an even more dire fate. This town of 4,000 souls, 65 per cent of them African-Americans, is located on Highway 301, which until the 1960s was the well-travelled main artery for north–south traffic, up and down America's east coast. It was the essential thoroughfare for snowbirds and vacationers from as far away as Canada and New York who were on their way to Florida. Allendale's fate was sealed back in the late 1960s when US I-95 made its debut, a new interstate highway that ran just forty miles over to the east, bypassing Allendale and virtually taking away its reason to exist.

Today, Allendale is a no man's land of boarded and vacant storefronts, crumbling wooden shacks, dusty trailer parks, a Hardee's, a Subway and a couple of gas stations. Along the once glorious Highway 301 lie the ruins of abandoned motels and seafood restaurants, reminiscent of better days. Rusted signs hang from the hinges of these skeleton-like motels; otherwise, there are only empty lots and weatherworn shacks and hovels as far as the eye can see. Allendale is a forlorn sort of ghost town, a forgotten place that today knows only decay and decrepitude. In Allendale, the unemployment rate is more than double the national average at 11.4 per cent,[35] and the poverty level is nearly triple, at 32.5 per cent.[36]

In the middle of town, across the parking lot from the Allendale County Department of Social Services, is a corner patch of worn grass whose most prominent feature is the twin set of portacabin toilets out front. A few yards behind and to the left of the toilets is a small white painted sign stuck into the ground in front of a white prefabricated mobile office unit that looks temporarily propped up on cement blocks. The sign reads: 'Allendale County Alive, Empowering Our Community One Life at a Time'.

Up some makeshift stairs and at the end of a narrow corridor of green carpet tiles and fluorescent glare is the spartan office of Wilbur Cave, who runs the non-profit affordable housing development organisation.[37]

A warm and cheerful man with a strong spiritual side, Wilbur Cave has devoted the past fourteen years to fighting poverty in Allendale County, one house at a time.

'I was born and raised about eight miles from here in the adjoining county of Barnwell in a small community called Kline, South Carolina,' says Cave as he begins to explain how he came to work with the deeply poor in Allendale. The only people eligible for Allendale County Alive's services are those who live on less than half the poverty threshold, on less than $6,000 of cash income a year.

> My father was a minister and my mother was a school teacher. And there were three of us in my family, a brother and a sister. We attended schools here in Allendale County. After high school I attended the University of South Carolina and eventually graduated from there and worked in the public school system in Barnwell for a number of years. Then I worked for a US congressman for about five and a half years. That was Congressman Butler Derrick, who is now deceased, but he represented the 3rd Congressional District of South Carolina for a long time. From there I ran for a state representative seat and was elected and served from 1994 to 1998. I resigned my seat to take a position with the Democratic governor who was elected in 1998, Jim Hodges. I was involved in constituent services. Then I got hired here in 2003 and I have been here since.

It was in 2003 that Wilbur Cave was named the director of the non-profit Allendale County Alive, which still had $250,000 worth of federal grants left over in its kitty. The non-profit organisation has always operated on a shoestring and has always had more work than it could handle. Originally set up as a non-profit community development corporation, Allendale County Alive received $250,000 of federal funding a year until 2009. But after that, as Cave notes, it started decreasing, and now the non-profit is receiving about $100,000 a year.

For Wilbur Cave, in a community where 40 per cent of the population was below the poverty line, the number one priority was housing. The goal was literally to ensure that the deeply poor would at least have a roof over their heads. As a long-time anti-poverty activist, Wilbur Cave knew that 'you can't sustain efforts in health care and literacy, which are deeply needed here, if you can't pay the light bill, if you can't keep the house running. You can't do those things because you have no revenues and no assets and no earnings.'

So, in 2003, Wilbur Cave started with the basics, doing housing rehabs on shacks that were falling apart, trying to help the poorest families attain stable and affordable housing.

'We would get money to help owner-occupied families with very low household income to fix and repair essentials like roofs, heating, cooling, the electric function. These were families who did not have the ability get the house rewired,' Cave recalls.

> Today, we focus on the challenge of developing affordable housing: Aside from the housing rehab part, we also now buy houses, rehab them and make them available for rent. We also buy houses, repair them and sell them. We also buy those houses and then do what is called a 'lease option' for families who are in our counselling when we have a housing counselling component. And we also have a small business loan programme, a kind of micro-credits lending facility for small businesses, with loans of up to $25,000.

As if that were not enough, Wilbur Cave and his five-person team in the mobile prefab also help the elderly and disabled to cash their social security checks and manage their family finances.

> We are also what is called a social security representative payee.

> We manage the income of social security recipients who for some reason can't handle things, so we pay their bills and then we give them a stipend. In business parlance you would call it a loss leader but it is something that is needed in our community. Most of the folks we're dealing with don't have vehicles and whatever and they'd have to maybe try to go forty, fifty miles away for somebody to handle that for them. So, we do it for them.

Wilbur Cave is the noble face of a nation that has largely turned its back on these people. He is just one of millions of Americans who volunteer their time and dedicate their lives to helping the poor and the deeply poor to survive in a nation that for the most part doesn't care.

'I feel I am here because I am spiritually called to be here. This is where I am supposed to be,' says Cave in a determined and deeply natural voice, his eyes sparkling, his smile firm. 'I have witnessed acts of heroic strength and fortitude from ordinary folk in these parts. We have been able to provide to families in this community, but I have also witnessed amazing courage and fortitude here,' says Cave, a much-loved local figure.

Wilbur Cave is at one with these people, and his solidarity oozes out of every pore in his skin. At the local Subway, nearly every diner stops by to say hello to Wilbur, or signals a howdy from across the room. In the trailer parks, they all salute Wilbur, waving from their doors, signalling their appreciation.

Cave says that he finds the work rewarding. His most inspiring experience came just a couple of years ago.

> I remember one day my uncle came back here, and he was just kind of upset. He told the lady upfront that he really needed to talk to me. 'Hey, look,' he told me, 'You've got to come with me. I got to show you something right now. You got to stop whatever you're doing. You got to come.' And so he took me over to a gentleman's house, and he had me to go in a house and frankly I was scared to walk much in the house because it was in such bad

shape, I mean. And this was a guy who was in a wheelchair. His name was Lawrence McGraw. And I'm sitting there wondering how the heck he hadn't fallen through the floors because this house is in really bad shape. My uncle said, 'You know I brought you here because I want you to figure out how do something for this guy.' Well, the first thing that was very obvious was there wasn't anything we could do to that house, OK, because it was too far gone. So I was challenged by this.

So, I figured out that we were going to tear down this house, this existing house, and build him a brand new house that would allow him to move around comfortably in his wheelchair. But we were dealing with a tight budget here. I mean, you know, it happened during the time when things were kind of slowing down in the housing market. So I found a contractor who did it cheaply and said, 'I'm going to do this because I want to keep my team working. I want to keep my guys working.' And the town and county helped us with the permits and stuff and we got the place built in something like six months, from tearing the place down and getting the lot cleared and moving Mr McGraw back inside.

Wilbur Cave is passionate about helping poor folk to have a roof over their heads, but he does not speak easily about racism and the plight of African-Americans in Allendale County. He is a gentle soul who likes to live in optimism rather than in fear. But he acknowledges the strong correlation between poverty and being born black in America. Around these parts, that is plain for the eye to see.

In nearby Orangeburg, just forty-five miles along the faded glory of Highway 301, Calvin Wright[38] knows all about the correlation between poverty and race. He has been an anti-poverty campaigner since the 1960s, since the launch of President Lyndon Johnson's War on Poverty in 1964 and the establishment of 1,000 community action centres across America. These would later serve as incubators and bundlers for a bewildering array of anti-poverty programmes administered through federal, state and local agencies. Remarkably, despite thirty years of cuts in welfare spending, a number of Johnson's anti-poverty programmes have continued to receive funding.

Today, at sixty-nine, Calvin Wright runs the OCAB Community Action Agency in Orangeburg. OCAB is the acronym which stands for the four counties in South Carolina it serves: Orangeburg, Calhoun, Allendale and Bamberg counties. Wright has been in charge since way back in 1983. In 2016, which marked the 50th anniversary year of the community centre, Calvin Wright was administering an annual budget of more than $8 million, with a staff of 154 full-time and another sixty part-time workers. He has built a sprawling centre on the side of a highway that offers Head Start education for pre-schoolers, medical and dental treatment for disadvantaged children, job training and a range of local programmes and micro-grants that are managed by local branch offices across four counties in this depressed part of South Carolina, all of them with poverty rates close to 40 per cent.

Calvin Wright is also a former civil rights activist.

Back in 1964, as a teenager, he led the fight for African-Americans to use the whites-only swimming area in the nearby Edisto River here in Orangeburg, South Carolina. The town's response was to close down the entire swimming area so that nobody could use it. He recalls the infamous Orangeburg Massacre back in February 1968, when three students were shot to death and twenty-eight wounded by South Carolina state police. The troopers came onto the campus of the all-black South Carolina State College in Orangeburg and opened fire on the unarmed gathering of students one night. The incident came after three days of violent protests by the students, who had been protesting the fact that they were not allowed to enter the All-Star Bowling Alley in downtown Orangeburg. The National Guard and South Carolina state police had been sent in by the governor, and a number of students, including female students, were beaten by the police.

'The young people just wanted to desegregate the bowling alley,' recalls Wright. 'It is terrible how it was handled and has never been fully explained. No one in any official capacity was ever brought to justice. Nobody in an official capacity was ever arrested or prosecuted.'

Instead, after the police shooting of unarmed black students that became known as the Orangeburg Massacre, one of the protesters, who had himself been wounded by the gunfire, was arrested, charged and convicted of inciting a riot.

Calvin Wright may not have been in Orangeburg when the massacre occurred (he was away in the army at the time), but he has felt the humiliating sting of racism on his own skin. That is why he became a student activist.

'I joined the civil rights movement as a juvenile. I was fifteen or sixteen years old. It was when I was a high school student. I got arrested some twelve times during the civil rights movement, sometimes twice in the same day.'

Wright remembers growing up in segregated America, long after the Civil Rights Act of 1965.

> The day after that law passed, I got together with a group of friends and we travelled from county to county all around here. We wanted to see if we could eat our way through desegregated South Carolina; it was kind of a test. Not a single place would serve us. If you were black and went into a shoe store back then, why, they wouldn't let you try on the shoes. In clothing stores, blacks were not allowed to try the clothes on. So the protests started in Orangeburg. And I joined many of them. I affiliated with a youth chapter of the NAACP and for one solid year I walked the streets of Orangeburg with a picket sign saying 'Don't shop downtown!' We weren't even allowed to eat at the local Kress counter. I was arrested there several times for protesting. Why should you spend your money in Kress if you were not allowed to sit down and eat? You could order and wait for them to give your food, and then you had to take it out. But you could not sit at the counter and eat it. So many days, at 12 noon, I would be at the Kress counter sitting on a seat and as the white folks getting off for lunch came

> in they wouldn't sit next to us. So we would move, or they would either rope us off or call the cops to have us arrested, and we'd be hauled off to jail. At one point they removed the seats at Kress from the counter so then nobody could sit.

In January 1969, Calvin Wright returned from a two-year tour of duty in Vietnam with an honourable discharge. He had been serving as a military policeman. Wright went to the local employment bureau and asked for help in finding a job. When the head of the office heard that he had been a military policeman, he told Wright that the Orangeburg Police was looking to hire.

> He called over to the chief of police while I was sitting there in front of him, and he told the chief, 'I got a vet here who was a military policemen and he would be good for you.' But after a while I could tell by the expression on his face what the chief of police was saying. After he got off the phone, the head of the employment office said he was sorry, but they couldn't use me because I was too big to fit into their police cars.

Calvin Wright stands up to show that he is more than six feet tall, but he smiles as he reflects on the subtle ways of racism, even for Vietnam veterans. Over the years, the ironies kept on coming.

In the 1970s, Wright was conducting a state-wide study of veterans.

> I had the opportunity to travel this entire state talking to veterans, seeing where they were and what kind of services they were receiving. I drove a government vehicle and actually I remember driving to Greenville, South Carolina one time and I had to stay overnight. I went to this hotel and they denied me service. True story.

'Things have improved over the years,' says Wright, especially when it comes to what he calls 'public accommodations' or the rights of blacks to be allowed entry into hotels and restaurants. 'But when it comes to job opportunities,' says Wright, 'we're still lagging, woefully lagging.'

As a community and civil rights activist, Wright also believes that the mere fact of having in Barack Obama the first African-American President in American history has unleashed a backlash of newly inspired resentment and racism against blacks everywhere.

'I studied sociology in college, and we were taught that the more minorities advanced, the more difficult it would become for them. There's an old saying: "People don't mind you getting ahead as long as you don't get ahead of them."'

There may have been an African-American in the White House for eight years but the ethnic group was still suffering as Obama left office. The poverty rate for black Americans was 24.1 per cent, compared to 9.1 per cent of whites.[39] The median income of blacks was less than 65 per cent the national average,[40] and unemployment among young black men aged sixteen to twenty-four was running at nearly 21 per cent, almost twice the national average.[41]

For Calvin Wright, anti-poverty practitioner, the correlation between poverty, unemployment and discrimination against African-Americans could not be clearer.

> The anti-poverty programs are working, but it is going to take time. The poverty rates are higher for African-Americans because of lack of education, discrimination, not being prepared, not having the skill sets for some of the jobs that are being offered. Discrimination plays a big part in it. Discrimination is still here and it is part of the reason why so many blacks are unemployed or underemployed. The same is true when it comes to poverty. The reasons are education and discrimination.

At the University of Michigan, Luke Shaefer confirms Calvin Wright's assessment:

> African-Americans are less likely to get called for a job interview, and even with the same credentials, they are less likely to get hired than whites. We have a long history of segregation policies that have effectively limited where African-Americans can live. On some fronts we made some progress. But there are generations of discrimination in actions and policies and laws.

For Shaefer as a social scientist, this means that it is not surprising that the proportion of African-Americans living in deep and extreme poverty in America, defined as earning less than $6,000 of cash income a year, is 10.9 per cent, or more than twice the level of whites.[42] Yet the problem of resurgent racism across America goes well beyond the realm of statistics. It spills over into the real world with the persistent social and economic punishment it inflicts on African-Americans, just because of the colour of their skin. Even more alarming are the racial violence, police shootings and hate crimes which have peppered the landscape of everyday America in recent years.

For Calvin Wright in Orangeburg, South Carolina, it feels as though the bad old days are coming back, and with a vengeance. He is angry and troubled by the victory of Trump, and he worries about the potential for higher poverty again and rising racial tension. What worries him most is the rise in racism, and the harsh reaction to organisations like Black Lives Matter.

'It's worrying me even more now than it used to. It's almost as though we are trying to legitimise racism again, to make it mainstream. It concerns me greatly,' says Wright.

He is not alone. As America went about the business of choosing a new President in 2016, the country was not merely suffering from severe income inequality and the creation of a new underclass, a new McJobs-based service sector of the working poor, an American-style lumpenproletariat that could also be called the Walmart Society. It was not just that America was barely coping with the problem of the deeply poor and the extremely poor, many of whom lived in conditions which compared unfavourably with third world poverty. That was bad enough. The poverty and unemployment were bad enough at the bottom rung of society. The problem was that poverty and unemployment mingled with mounting racism and violence against blacks. What was even more troubling was that it had all become almost routine in American society; it did not seem to trigger a collective reaction of outrage. On the contrary, Americans took violence against blacks in their stride, as they had black poverty and black unemployment.

The Disney version of American society that we saw on television, on our Olympic team and on talk shows, looked fairly balanced when it came to ethnic diversity. But on the ground, things were very different, and black America pretty much had the worst of the deal.

On CNN and Fox News, the talking heads would dissect the latest shooting for twenty-four hours and then they would move on to the next subject. Sure, there was plenty of coverage every time Donald Trump got into trouble for saying something about the condition of blacks or about the Ku Klux Klan, and sure, there were endless predictions by talking heads of how Hillary Clinton was going to sweep the African-American vote. There was, however, precious little in the way of policy prescription from the candidates, or any exploration of the root causes of resurgent racism from the talking heads. Sure, the latest police shooting of an unarmed black man made the national news, and sometimes two or even three times a week. We all knew what was going on, but there was a part of America that looked away. In 2016, some sixteen years into the twentieth century and some fifty years after Martin Luther King Jr had first expressed his dream, much of white America seemed to be in denial about what was happening before their eyes. For a significant number of white Americans, it seemed that black lives didn't really matter.

CHAPTER FOUR

BLACK LIVES MATTER

'You can still see the bullet holes over there, in the wall,' whispers Eric Manning.[1]

The newly installed pastor at the Mother Emanuel African Methodist Episcopal Church of Charleston, South Carolina gestures furtively to a wall panel in the church basement. He is not comfortable with such a morbid display, such a stark and vivid reminder of the tragedy that struck here at the AME Church, as the locals refer to the venerable old institution on Calhoun Street.

The ceiling tiles, where bullets sprayed when a white racist named Dylann Roof opened fire, have been replaced. Yet there are at least three bullet holes still visible in the plywood panelling on the wall, near the entrance to this large room in the basement area of the AME Church, just below the main sanctuary. This is the only remaining trace of the murder of nine worshippers who were attending a Bible study class on that Wednesday evening, 17 June 2015.

The pastor sighs deeply as he speaks of the horror that visited this place, in what was supposed to be the most sacred sanctuary for black Americans in Charleston, in fact in all of the south-eastern United States.

'This is a church that is still hurting,' says Rev. Manning. 'This is a church that's still trying to heal.'

Manning, who was born in the year that Martin Luther King Jr was assassinated, says he is 'deeply humbled' at having been chosen to lead a congregation so steeped in history. As the oldest African Methodist Episcopal church south of Baltimore, the AME Church on Calhoun Street has been a part of some of the most significant events in US history, for the past 200 years. A better target for a white racist there could not be.

The AME denomination was born out of the struggle for black liberation. The church's origins go back to the Free African Society of the late eighteenth century, but Mother Emanuel was formed in 1818 by a black pastor and freed slave from Charleston named Morris Brown. In 1822, Rev. Brown, and another freed slave and church co-founder, Denmark Vesey, were suspected of being the ringleaders of a vast planned slave uprising. Brown fled Charleston. Vesey and his alleged co-conspirators were rounded up by the Charleston authorities and quickly hanged. The church was burned to the ground.

Parishioners rebuilt the church but it was closed down in 1834 because of laws across much of the country that made it illegal for slaves to come together to worship in a church. Until the end of the Civil War in 1865, AME Church members were forced to hold meetings in secret; underground worship in the days of the underground railway. In those decades, the secret places of worship for slaves were known as 'hush harbors'.

In 1909, Booker T. Washington, the greatest leader of black Americans at the start of the twentieth century, came to visit the AME Church. In the 1950s and 1960s, the church became a safe haven for the foot soldiers of the civil rights movement, a centre for African-American non-violent activism. Dr Martin Luther King Jr preached from its pulpit in 1962. Seven years later his widow, Coretta Scott King, led a Charleston hospital workers protest of 1,500 people right to its steps, and faced down bayonet-touting National Guardsmen who made 900 arrests, right there, in front of the church on Calhoun Street, on a street named for the most pro-slavery senator in the history of the United States.

A few days after the massacre in June 2015, President Barack Obama came to Charleston to deliver his eulogy to Rev. Clementa Pinckney, the much admired South Carolina state senator and leader of the AME Church who had been gunned down along with the others. By now the victims had become nationally known as the 'Mother Emanuel Nine'.

Obama spoke from the heart, not just as the President but clearly also as an African-American President. He recalled how 'the Church is, and always has been, the center of African-American life, a place to call our own in a too often hostile world, a sanctuary from so many hardships'.[2]

'There is no better example of this tradition than Mother Emanuel,' said Obama,

> a church built by blacks seeking liberty, burned to the ground because its founders sought to end slavery, only to rise again, a phoenix from these ashes. When there were laws banning all black church gatherings, services happened here anyway, in defiance of unjust laws. Dr Martin Luther King Jr preached from its pulpit and marches began from its steps.

Obama called Mother Emanuel 'a sacred place'.

But the sacred place had been soiled, and very badly. Obama said the holy sanctuary was meant to be 'inviolate'. Yet the sanctuary had been violated.

This was by no means the first time a black church, or even the AME Church in Charleston specifically, has been attacked by angry white racists. America's history over the past century is filled with church bombings and Ku Klux Klan attacks of every size and description. But the massacre of the Mother Emmanuel 9 seemed to resonate with America in a way that other mass shootings did not. It was that blatant, and that horrible.

Rev. Eric Manning compares the Charleston church shooting with another brutal and notorious attack on a black church: the 1963 bombing of the 16th Street Baptist Church in Birmingham, Alabama. That was another pivotal moment in African-American history, in another church where Dr Martin Luther King Jr had led prayer. The difference was that the Alabama church bombing occurred at a time when the civil rights movement was still in its early days and there had already been dozens of such bombings by Ku Klux Klan members. It was a period of numerous lynchings that brought no punishment, of Jim Crow laws in full force that restricted the most basic rights of black Americans. It was a time when segregation was a way of life.

The 16th Street Church bombing involved KKK members who planted sticks of dynamite directly under the church's front steps. The ensuing explosion shredded the bodies of four little girls, aged eleven to fourteen, who were, as it happened, attending Bible Study class. The bombing marked a turning point during the civil rights movement and contributed to support for the passage of the Civil Rights Act less than a year later, in 1964. It would, however, take another fourteen years before any of the perpetrators were finally convicted of the crime in Birmingham. After the Charleston Church massacre of June 2015, some black commentators described it as the '9/11 of the Black Church' and said it should have been another pivotal point in black history, an alarm bell. That was certainly Obama's message, but across the national landscape it seems to have fallen largely on deaf ears.

Sadly enough, the Charleston massacre, an act of terror by any measure, seemed to be just another blip of information, a huge and grotesque factoid, another digital data point, another set of pixels along the fast-flowing media screen of information overload that we navigate each day on our smart phones and tablets. Oddly, in America, the overexposure has not prevented a case of collective denial.

For civil rights leader Jesse Jackson, there is also a direct comparison to be made between the AME Church massacre in Charleston and the 16th Street Baptist Church bombing in Birmingham.

'Not unlike the four little girls killed in a church bombing in Birmingham, Alabama, in 1963,' he declared in June 2015, 'the nation and the world are saddened and outraged at the hatred and senseless killing of nine African-Americans in the historic Emanuel AME Church in Charleston, South Carolina.'[3]

But Jackson went further, making a grave accusation against the Washington political establishment, which by now included Barack Obama. 'The nation and its leadership are still failing to see, understand and come to grips with the underlying economic and political circumstances that led to such a tragedy,' Jackson noted.

The shooting in Charleston, he added,

> is the result of institutionalised racism, centuries of dehumanisation and the current denial of economic and political equality of opportunity. Today, everyone is outraged at the killings, but there is not the same outrage that African-Americans have the highest rates of infant mortality, unemployment, of being denied access to capital and bank loans, of imprisonment, segregated housing and home foreclosures, segregated and underfunded public schools, poverty, heart disease, liver disease, diabetes, mental health issues, HIV/Aids and more.

Jackson concluded that America could no longer afford to ignore the gaping examples of institutionalised racism in a society that still, more than a half-century after the passage of the Civil Rights Act, continues to deny many African-Americans the same basic job and educational opportunities as whites.

Down in the basement of the AME Church, Eric Manning has turned away from the bullet-scarred wall and is standing near a framed colour photograph of the Mother Emanuel Nine. He is explaining how a large number of the congregation members, especially some older members, cannot bear to see the bullet holes any more. It is simply too painful. So there is a delicate debate underway among church members to ascertain whether there is more honour for the dead in remembering, by seeing, or is it better to replace the wall panels and move on?

Manning admits this is a bone of contention among the members of the congregation. Some are in favour of leaving the wall as it is, as a reminder for future generations. The majority want to move on.

A few blocks away, over at the Charleston branch of the National Association for the Advancement of Colored People, the Reverend Joe Darby says it is time to move on. Darby is an imposing figure, battle-weary, supremely articulate and still defiant after all these years, after so many battles.[4] He is the Presiding Elder of the Beaufort District of the AME Church and the First Vice-President of the Charleston Branch of the NAACP. The branch's long-serving president, a cheerful woman named Dot Scott, also believes it is time to move on. She and Rev. Darby sit together in the little two-storeyed grey wooden house that serves as their headquarters. Both have deep ties to the AME Church and both were personal friends with most of the members who were attending Bible Study on that Wednesday evening in June 2015.

'I think that they need to keep a picture or a piece of the wall for historic purposes,' says Mrs Scott, more than a year after the shooting occurred.

> One of my best friends is a member of that church, and she says it's painful for people to be reminded in that way, to continuously see it. So I think that something needs to be done to enshrine it, even if that means they take the wall out and preserve the wall. But they need to do something so they can move on. Folks need to heal.

Rev. Darby, a veteran civil rights activist and pillar of the black community in Charleston, nods his agreement. 'There needs to be a way to memorialise the panels, to create a relic room or something. But the congregation needs to move on.'

The reverend notes that part of the reason why the congregation has found it so hard to move on goes well beyond the problem of bullet holes in the basement. The AME Church has become something of a Ground Zero in the iconography of 21st-century social media's collective awareness of racism in America. The church has been given the CNN treatment. It has been tweeted and facebooked and trended into this iconic condition by American society. The church, with its proud history, has finally become a symbol again – once again, ironically, a symbol of racism and racial violence in America.

'Part of the problem', says Darby, 'is that the church is no longer just a church. It's part shrine, part memorial, part tourist attraction. You've got tour buses that pull up out front all the time so that people can take pictures of the church.'

Dot Scott frowns in agreement. 'People are not coming to the church, and they're angry that they can't even get a parking space. It's not being treated as their church, but as this famous edifice.'

Sure enough, the floral tribute on the curb out front is refreshed on a daily basis, another street-side memorial in a nation where the proliferation of street-side memorials makes this appear to be the leading growth industry. The church's response is a simple black panel out front, with white lettering in a glass frame with words that read: 'We thank you for your many acts of kindness.'

The concept of tragedy as spectacle and victims or survivors as instant celebrities is a relatively recent phenomenon in America, an outgrowth of the all-news TV channel environment and the online data flow society in which we live. Family members, wives, children, brothers-in-law, parishioners, Facebook friends and Instagram contacts have suddenly become the new go-to celebrities.

Joe Darby says that members of the AME Church congregation have not been spared the treatment, even though they are real people trying to go about their real lives and not members of the cast of a reality show.

> We were getting white tourists all of the time, who would come in and sit down, particularly during the height of tourist season. They'd look around, they'd sit for maybe ten minutes of the service and then they get this look on their faces like 'This is not what I expected! These black people are not entertaining at all! They're not jumping enough or dancing enough!' And then they would leave, because they weren't there to worship. They were there as part of the tourist experience. We even had a tour group

> from the Netherlands and they asked me if they could come in. I said 'You're welcome to worship with us,' and he said, 'Will there be jumping? We want to see jumping.' And I said, 'You need to go 125 miles to Riverbanks zoological garden. You can see all of the monkeys there you want to see.'

Joe Darby is a passionate man. He talks about how racism has been 'baked into the system' by culture and habit, and over a prolonged period of time. He says that America's economic success, for the two centuries that preceded the end of the Civil War, was based in large part on acts of genocide perpetrated against Native Americans, which resulted in their land being confiscated, and then based on an economy whose business model relied upon the enslavement of black people brought over from Africa.

'Racism is baked into the American condition,' says Darby.

> You've got a nation that was founded on a strange form of agrarian capitalism that depended on people owning people, all across the nation at one point. You've got a ruling class that owned people, but they also called themselves people of faith. So they had to rationalise slavery and say, 'These people are not people like us. They are an inferior species, and owning them is really doing them a favor. We're taking them out of the jungles, giving them a different life.' You also had a much larger white class that was dirt poor and that should have had an affinity with the slaves. How do you control that class? You say to that class that these people are not only different; they're dangerous, and if you're not careful they will rape your women. They will kill you. They will take what you got. So you have to help us to control them because you may be poor, but at least you're white. That's baked into America. It's always been there.

For Darby, and for so many other black leaders across America, the great civil rights legislation of the 1960s did not produce a fair and equitable society. It simply did away with what Darby calls 'legalised apartheid'.

'Laws', notes the reverend, 'don't change hearts.' Instead, he says that the civil rights laws

> simply drove racism underground for a while. It was unacceptable for somebody to be a wacky racist. People would be criticised, people would be vilified because that was not the norm. So most folks kind of kept it to themselves. Now, it's become OK to say you who you really are again.

Darby goes into something of a rant about the way, in his opinion, Donald Trump's string of inflammatory remarks incited racism throughout the 2016 presidential campaign. 'Suddenly there's this wealthy, successful, crazy guy who is saying that it's all right to be a racist,' he declares with deprecating irony.

Dot Scott stirs in her chair. She is not so sure. 'It would be far too easy to say that Trump is causing it all,' she says with a sigh. 'No, Trump is just ripping the Band-Aid off racism in America, and he's not being very careful about it.'

Beneath the Band-Aid lay a festering national wound, an infection that had never fully gone away after the Civil War, after the years of reconstruction, after the dawn of the twentieth century, throughout the decades after the Second World War. The wound is still festering today, fifty years after the landmark legislation of the 1960s. Not even the election of the first African-American President in 2008 brought national healing. On the contrary, the election of Barack Obama seems to have stirred still more racism in America.

In fact, the greatest irony is the way racism has been rekindled by the very fact of there being an African-American in the White House. In the summer of 2016, a Gallup opinion poll showed that six in ten Americans believed that racism against blacks was widespread in the United States. Some 61 per cent held this opinion, up from 51 per cent in 2009, when Obama first took office.[5]

The spate of white-on-black police killings of unarmed black men seemed to be a stain that was spreading across the map of America. The murders of unarmed blacks continued; they seemed, in fact, to accelerate, at least in the collective consciousness of online America. The nation appeared to be at war with itself. Something terrible had happened to the nation's amygdala, some fight-or-flight response in white policemen seemed to be malfunctioning. By 2015 and 2016, policemen were killing unarmed blacks at more than twice the rate of unarmed whites.[6] This, too, was sadly part of the cruel legacy of the Obama years.

The fact is that during the presidency of Barack Obama, racism in America became more socially acceptable in some places, more mainstream than fringe, more common than it used to be. Or at least that is the way it seemed to nearly two thirds of all Americans.

Joe Darby believes that the Obama presidency has brought scores of previously invisible racists 'out of the woodwork, out of the woods'. He says they were always there; it has just become more acceptable to come out of the closet. 'They were there and they are here today,' says Darby. 'There are many people in America who still cannot accept the idea of a successful black person, period, much less a black person as President of the United States.'

Darby gives Obama a pass on his inability to stop racism from worsening during his eight years in office. 'He had to tiptoe on egg shells,' says Darby. 'He had no choice. No other President's nationality has been questioned. Particularly in his first term he had to be very careful about what he said. In his second term he has become bolder, and has said some important things about gun violence and how it relates to race.'

By the spring and summer of 2016, when the United States was hit by what seemed like a rash of hate crimes and police shootings of unarmed blacks, Obama was speaking plaintively, repeatedly and ever more forcefully about the link between racism and violence in America.

In early July 2016, just hours before the tragedy in Dallas,

Obama was having to act again as Consoler-in-Chief to the nation, this time after stepping off a plane in Warsaw, Poland to attend a NATO summit. He was speaking about two separate incidents that had resulted in the death, at the hands of white police, of two black Americans in two different American cities: Alton Sterling, who was shot by police in Baton Rouge, Louisiana on 5 July and Philando Castile, who was killed by police in St Antony, Minnesota on 6 July. The first victim was filmed being shot by police while they held him to the ground in front of his car,[7] and the second victim was captured in a graphic video filmed by his girlfriend inside their car.[8] Both videos were highly disturbing but typical of the genre, which by now had become part of what the public had almost come to expect, the release of a police dashboard camcorder or body camera or a closed circuit video, or, as occurred in these cases, of a smartphone video filmed in real time by a passer-by or by the wife or girlfriend or friend of the victim.

Each time Obama spoke about a police shooting that summer, his face was a mixture of anger and pain; at times he would seem to scowl in frustration. As the shootings continued, and as the YouTube videos continued to show police violence against unarmed blacks across the nation, Obama would sometimes use his remarks to argue for gun control and at other times he would call for racial harmony. On occasion, he tried to lay out the facts to a weary nation. Unfortunately, the nation did not seem to be listening.

After the events in Baton Rouge, Obama went through a laundry list of examples of bias and racism against African-Americans, although he limited himself to listing only cases of injustice and discrimination in law enforcement and in the courts. It was a succinct and precise summary, but it was all the sadder as it came from the first African-American President who in the final months of his second term was unable to change the national mood of fear and anger, a man who for eight years had borne witness to the worsening of race relations in America.

'All of us as Americans should be troubled by the news. These are not isolated incidents. They are symptomatic of a broader set of racial disparities that exist in our criminal justice system,' Obama said.[9]

He then offered a few statistics 'to try to put into context why emotions are so raw around these issues'.

'African-Americans', Obama declared,

> are 30 per cent more likely than whites to be pulled over. After being pulled over, African-Americans and Hispanics are three times more likely to be searched. Last year, African-Americans were shot by police at more than twice the rate of whites. African-Americans are arrested at twice the rate of whites. African-American defendants are 75 per cent more likely to be charged with offenses carrying mandatory minimums. They receive sentences that are almost 10 per cent longer than comparable whites arrested for the same crime.

'So if you add it all up,' said Obama, 'the African-American and Hispanic population who make up only 30 per cent of the general population make up more than half of the incarcerated population. Now, these are facts.'

At the Southern Poverty Law Center, they already have all of these facts. They make their life's work the dissemination of these facts in a desperate effort to create national awareness and eradicate hatred and racism, especially when it comes to the cruel overlap between racism, poverty and social exclusion. In all of the United States there is probably no greater database, no better tracking of racism and hate than at the Southern Poverty Law Center.

Jody Owens runs the SPLC's office in Jackson, Mississippi. He is a graduate of Howard University's School of Law who grew up in a family of civil rights activists, 'campaigning, protesting and being involved in different movements'.[10]

Owens believes that racism in America has worsened as a result of having an African-American President. He also seems to agree with Rev. Joe Darby that America's first black President has been 'tiptoeing on eggshells'.

'I think President Obama is trying to be a President of all Americans, and not just a black President,' says Owens,

> and I think he has done a great job. But to be a President for all America the President has had to recognise the ugly reality of where we are as a country, due to failed policies and systems that were put in place by previous Presidents who came decades before him.

Owens says that Obama got it right when he spoke about the disproportionately high level of incarceration among black Americans. Black youths, for example, between the ages of eighteen and nineteen (1,072 prisoners per 100,000 black male residents aged eighteen to nineteen) are more than ten times more likely to be in state or federal prison than whites (102 per 100,000). Blacks represent about 13 per cent of the national population, but they make up 37 per cent of the entire national prison population.[11]

'You have a criminal justice system that is not fair,' says Jody Owens.

> We know that, percentage-wise, people of color are not committing more crimes than whites, but they are being prosecuted at higher rates. We incarcerate more people than any other industrialised nation in the world in the United States and unfortunately the people who have been most affected are the minority population. We see it from a lack of representation in the criminal justice system. We see it in the ways blacks are targeted. It was always easier to arrest or prosecute and throw the key away for people of color.

Owens has no trouble in citing examples of the gaping disparities between whites and blacks when it comes to charging and sentencing.

'You might see a white child take someone's car and they are charged with joyriding, which might be a misdemeanor. You might see a black person take the car and they get charged with stolen vehicle or high-speed chase.'

'Unfortunately in this country right now,' says Owens,

> we still have a society where black men who look like me are viewed differently than white men. Black boys are suspended and expelled from school at higher percentages than their white counterparts. So if you make a society where 'these people' are considered more dangerous or somehow different, a society where you don't have to know 'these people' or understand them, then you can justify treating them differently. Once you dehumanise them, it's easy to treat them differently and that's what we have seen all too often, whether it's Baton Rouge or whether it's Florida. We see it throughout this country, that black folks are treated differently when it comes to law enforcement.

Obama made the same point when he spoke of the shootings in Minnesota and Baton Rouge in that torrid summer of 2016. After providing a laundry list of examples of institutionalised discrimination against blacks in law enforcement and in the courts, Obama paused ever so briefly, his lips pursed with anguish.

'When incidents like this occur,' he said, 'there's a big chunk of our fellow citizenry that feels as if they are not being treated the same because of the color of their skin. And that hurts. And that should trouble all of us.'[12]

Baton Rouge or St Anthony, Sanford or Ferguson, Tulsa or Charlotte. The list seems endless. Hundreds of white-on-black police shootings each year, at times as many as two or three in a single week. Always the controversy over graphic video shot on camcorders and iPhones. So many unarmed blacks apparently cut down by police incompetence or by racist instinct. How could this be? What had happened to America?

In 2016, America remained a divided country, along race lines, along economic lines and along societal and class lines. The black underclass and the black working poor, and even middle-class black families faced greater dangers in their everyday lives than their white equivalents. Even though the overwhelming majority of law enforcement officials were evidently not racist, the frequency of these incidents gave a starkly different impression. The police appeared to be biased. Elsewhere in society, race relations only seemed to be under control. The reality was that de facto segregation of school systems continued to be a reality, with more whites opting for private schools in the cities and so-called academies in the suburbs and rural areas, and inner-city and rural blacks relegated largely to failing public and largely black and Hispanic schools. More black children were poor than their white equivalents, three times as many in 2015.[13] More black children were living in extreme poverty, too. Educational and job opportunities for blacks lagged significantly behind those extended to whites. America was integrated in name, but a more insidious form of racism, fuelled by fear and anger, ensured that the cards were still stacked against black Americans.

By almost every measure, in 2016, as America went to the polls to elect a new President, the African-American community continued to be victimised by white-on-black racism, some of it in the streets and some of it involving law enforcement. It was in this setting that the most visible manifestation of racism in America soon became the string of shootings of unarmed blacks by white policemen. What began as sporadic tragedy had turned into a national epidemic.

Or had it always been this way? Were more blacks actually being shot by police, harassed by police, discriminated against because of their colour in 2016? Or were we simply more aware of it all because of television and social media?

Jody Owens says that to measure the level of racism in America today, you need to understand the historic backdrop.

> We're at a very interesting place in our history. We are seeing political parties and candidates like Donald Trump tapping into a certain hatred that people have, a certain belief that they cannot

> achieve what they want in life because of those other people. We are seeing a level of anger against blacks that we have not seen since the early 1950s, since the days of Jim Crow and segregation. We're seeing that cycle come back around again now.

Owens sighs. He is sitting in the conference room of the Jackson, Mississippi office of the Southern Poverty Law Center, underneath the glare of the fluorescent lighting. He is speaking now about hate crimes and racism, but it is as though he is speaking with an interior voice, as he recounts a very personal and intimate memory.

> As a black man who grew up in Mississippi, I can tell you that my father tells me stories of people who would just disappear, because someone white got mad at them. And they would be found in a ditch, they would be harmed. We have lost lives in our family, relatives of ours have died solely because of the color of their skin. Sixty years ago it wasn't uncommon for a white person to be able to take the life of a person of color and not even be fined. So now we come sixty years forward and we are seeing more and more hate crimes being reported, more white policemen shooting unarmed persons of color.

The bottom line, for Jody Owens and for the great majority of black leaders in America, is that despite significant improvements in race relations in America over the decades, the behaviour of white law enforcement officials has not really changed that much. No, there are not more cases of black unarmed men being shot by the police today than in the past, says Jody Owens. It *has* always been this way. We just didn't see it so often, on handheld devices, so graphically, in such high resolution, so unignorable.

'The only thing that is new today is the use of iPhones and video,' says Owens. It is thanks to all-news TV channels and the round-the-clock news cycle, and the use of iPhones and YouTube and Facebook and Twitter that America's awareness has been heightened about a facet of life in America that has been prevalent since the days of the cotton gin.

Back in Charleston, Reverend Joe Darby has come to pretty much the same conclusion as Jody Owens.

'The wave of police shootings is nothing new,' he says.

> It's just that there's video now. If it weren't for video you would not have had the devastating report on the Baltimore PD that just came out. Video is just documentation of what black folks have been saying for years. That's why one of my favorite T-shirts that the Black Lives Matter folks wear says 'Do You Believe Us Now?'

There can be no doubt. The evolution of the instant-replay video of police shootings and racial violence has been a game changer, as radical a *you-are-there* moment for Americans as was the introduction of CNN's first live broadcasts of the bombing of Baghdad back in the summer of 1990. In the cultural anthropology of 21st-century America, the instant-replay version of events has shocked and inflamed public opinion, but has it really changed hearts and minds?

The self-evident truths that come across in the instant-replay iPhone records of police shootings are often deeply disturbing. Like flashing memes, the victims skate across the digital landscape on our tablets and across our TV screens. The images become burned into our digital memory, another YouTube moment, another video that has gone viral. Who can forget the image of the unarmed black man in Tulsa, Oklahoma, Terence Crutcher, standing near his vehicle in the middle of a street, his hands held high seconds before being shot?[14] Who can forget the image of Alton Sterling, the unarmed black man who was shot several times and at close range, while being held down on the ground by two white policemen in Baton Rouge? Who can forget the image of the fatal police shooting of Keith Lamont Scott in Charlotte, North Carolina, complete with the audio of his wife begging the police not to shoot her husband just seconds before they did just that?[15]

The shooting of Trayvon Martin came long before the current vogue for instant-replay video versions of white-on-black police shootings, way back in February 2012. There were no passers-by or family members on hand with an iPhone to record what happened for posterity and the courts. But the shot that killed the teenager was captured in a 911 call from a concerned neighbour.[16] The shooter was a trigger-happy neighbourhood vigilante named George Zimmerman. It was the night of 26 February 2012, just after 7 p.m. in the gated community of Sanford, Florida. The victim was a seventeen-year-old boy named Trayvon Martin, a high-school student wearing a hoodie and jeans who had gone to buy some candy and soda and was talking on his cell phone to his girlfriend when the vigilante saw him. Zimmerman was heard on 911 complaining about how 'these punks always get away'.

Eighteen months later, Zimmerman, who became the symbol of racial violence for much of black America, would be tried for, and quickly acquitted of, the murder of Trayvon Martin.[17] Not second-degree murder as charged, not even manslaughter. Not guilty. It was a decision that enraged all of black America, including Barack Obama. 'If I had a son, he would look like Trayvon,' said Obama.[18] A black member of the local AME Church in Sanford put it this way: 'I can assure you that if I had been a black man, and if I had killed a seventeen-year-old white boy under the conditions that boy was murdered, I'd be doing time in jail right now.'

Trayvon Martin's mother, a strong and determined woman named Sybrina Fulton,[19] has since become something of a celebrity on the macabre circuit of solidarity meetings, families-of-victims events and other social groupings that have sprouted as a result of the many cases of white-on-black racial violence and police shootings in recent years. Ms Fulton's high point came during her appearance on stage at the Democratic National Convention in July 2016 in Philadelphia.[20] She called herself a 'reluctant member' of the Mothers of the Movement, the group of mothers of unarmed black youths who had lost their lives in cases of racial violence. She endorsed Hillary Clinton for President, but she told the crowd in Philadelphia: 'I am here for Trayvon, who is in heaven.'

Fulton has since convened a group named the Circle of Mothers and created the Trayvon Martin Foundation in order to seek some form of justice, even if it is only through the retelling of her story as an example of how bad things have always been for black America. At the end of one of her Circle of Mothers meetings, held in a small hotel in Miami Lakes, Florida, just a mile from Miami Gardens, where her son grew up, Sybrina Fulton sits down to remember her emotions back in July 2013 when she heard that her son's killer had been acquitted.

'There was a little bit of everything,' says Ms Fulton.

> It was definitely anger, it was definitely sadness. I was disappointed, I was outraged. I just felt like the system just did not work. And that's what empowered me to go ahead and move forward with the foundation, so had there been a guilty verdict, I don't know if I would have continued to fight.

The murder of Trayvon Martin may not have been captured on an iPhone, but it did lead to riots and protests and national anger. For a brief moment, perhaps the length of a few news cycles, it roused the nation's consciousness about racial profiling. The killing of Trayvon Martin also led to the creation of a hashtag, #BlackLivesMatter, which turned into a rallying cry, a cause and then a movement.

The day after George Zimmerman was acquitted of murdering Trayvon Martin, a California activist named Alicia Garza took to Facebook to comment on the events, reminding her fellow black men and women that 'black lives matter'. Her friend Patrisse Cullors spotted the post and put it on Twitter, and from there the movement was born.

The acquittal of Zimmerman also led to many comparisons with the 1950s acquittal of the killers of Emmett Till, a fourteen-year-old black teenager from Chicago who was horribly tortured and murdered by white racists while visiting family in Mississippi in 1955.

Till had allegedly flirted with a white woman at a grocery store, and for this he was murdered and his body dumped in the river. Martin was simply loitering in a gated community while talking on his cell phone, the victim of racial profiling.

A white jury in Mississippi took a little over an hour to acquit Emmett Till's killers back in 1955. A mostly white jury in Florida took sixteen hours to acquit Trayvon Martin's killer in 2013.

The acquittal of George Zimmerman enflamed and divided public opinion across America. To many African-Americans it seemed beyond belief.

Oprah Winfrey told a startled nation that she saw a direct and clear parallel between the murders of seventeen-year-old Trayvon Martin and fourteen-year-old Emmett Till. 'In my mind, same thing,' she famously declared.[21]

Three relatives of Emmett Till came forward and weighed in on Oprah's controversial comparison. They agreed. A cousin of Till's, Erica Gordon-Taylor, said the country was still 'confronted with many hate crimes that are very similar to what Emmett Till suffered'.[22] The not guilty verdict in the killing of Trayvon Martin, she added, showed that racial profiling remained a national problem.

'Across the country, when you're still confronted with the same type of injustices and the same type of tragedies, it's hard to say that we have moved on from fifty years ago,' Ms Gordon-Taylor said.

In 1955, Emmett Till's death became a symbol of racial hatred and violence in America. It inspired civil rights leaders to act.

Martin Luther King Jr described it as 'one of the most brutal and inhuman crimes of the twentieth century'[23] and it was no coincidence that his famous march on Washington – the moment when he said 'I have a dream!' – was held on 28 August 1963, on the anniversary of Emmett Till's murder.

In 2013, Trayvon Martin's death also became a symbol of racial hatred and violence in America, but it inspired only anger and fear, and even a white backlash, following the creation of the Black Lives Matter movement.

Black Lives Matter became a symbol of militancy for many whites. Trump supporters sneered at the movement. Older whites confused it with the militant Black Panthers movement from the 1960s, while others simply believed that it was somehow dangerous and violent. The moment that triggered the white backlash came on 7 July 2016, on that fateful day in Dallas when a black sniper took down five white policemen during a peaceful march that had been sponsored by Black Lives Matter.

Dallas should have caused a period of national reflection. But it came amid a fast-moving series of events, just days after the white-on-black police shootings in Baton Rouge and St Anthony that had so moved Barack Obama. It was followed by a steady stream of more racial violence, more police shootings of unarmed black youths elsewhere. The Dallas shootings may have momentarily shocked the nation, but they did not lead to any soul searching. On the contrary, it seemed as if Dallas had once again ripped the Band-Aid off racism in America, and the principal beneficiary was Donald Trump, by now just two weeks away from wrapping up the GOP nomination.

A new hashtag had emerged online in the dark days after Dallas. This time, the message was again insidiously misleading. The hashtag, in an evident response to Black Lives Matter movement, was #AllLivesMatter.

By the time the Republican National Convention opened its doors at the Quicken Loans Arena in Cleveland, Ohio on 18 July, with Donald Trump positioning himself as the 'law and order' candidate, the hashtag #AllLivesMatter had become a highly provocative symbol of the white backlash in American society.

The roar of the crowd inside the Quicken Loans Arena would reach its greatest intensity on the final night of the Republican Convention, when Trump's most prominent black supporter, a pastor named Mark Burns, would rouse the Republican delegates, whipping them into a frenzy of derision for the Black Lives Matter movement.

The firebrand black pastor from South Carolina drew thunderous applause and cheering from the crowd as he screamed at the top of his lungs and led them in a chant of 'All Lives Matter!'

Pastor Burns brought the house down when he attacked the 'divisive rhetoric of the Black Lives Matter movement'. He rabble-roused the crowd even more when he declared to the packed arena that 'in a Donald Trump administration, *all* lives matter'.[24]

For her part, Alicia Garza offered a simple but direct response to the backlash against Black Lives Matter: 'To say that all lives matter in response to black people saying that black lives matter is actually saying that black lives don't matter.'

Garza tried to explain the reality of the Black Lives Matter movement.

> We are not just a movement that is focused on police violence and police brutality. The reality is that black people in this country have been plagued by a pervasive and dominant system. When we look at issues of housing, employment, education, health care and health care access, black people are at the bottom of those disparities.[25]

But Alicia Garza had herself squabbled with the movement, and in a nation so shell-shocked and punch-drunk with almost daily TV reports of violence, most Americans had never even heard her name. The war of the hashtags became a symbol of a divided nation, along racial lines.

Perhaps the most eloquent defence of the Black Lives Matter movement came in the autumn of 2016, and from a most unlikely source, the white CEO of a famous American corporation, AT&T. Randall Stephenson, in a little-reported speech to AT&T employees at a conference in Dallas, stood up and denounced the wave of racism sweeping the United States, urging people to try to better understand each other through an open and honest dialogue on race.[26]

'We've got a problem,' he said in front of more than 2,000 AT&T

employees. 'Our communities are being destroyed by racial tension, and we're too polite to talk about it.'

Stephenson told his employees it was wrong to disparage Black Lives Matter, and it had to stop.

> When a parent says, 'I love my son', you don't say, 'What about your daughter?' When the President says, 'God Bless America', we don't say, 'Shouldn't God bless other countries?' So when a person struggling with what is being broadcast on our airways says, 'Black Lives Matter', we should not say, 'All Lives Matter' to justify ignoring the real need for change.

But few Americans knew the name of the CEO of AT&T, a Fortune 500 company with $150 billion of annual revenues.[27] Stephenson's cry of anguish, his proclamation that 'racial tension is ripping apart the very fabric of our communities' was not big news. In fact, it was invisible. In the greater scheme of the constant 24-hour-a-day news flow, Stephenson's valiant defence of Black Lives Matter went virtually unreported.

The root causes of racism may be partly cultural and partly economic, but against the backdrop of a tawdry presidential election season, the anger quotient had never seemed higher. Was this what it felt like to see racial violence erupt onto the streets, wondered those who had never lived through the 1960s. The problem is that it was not supposed to be this way in 2016. This was not the America we had been promised, not the America we had told ourselves about.

'Race', said a sullen Reverend Joe Darby, 'is the serious defect that America has not dealt with, and that we still have to deal with.'

After the Charleston shootings, Jesse Jackson had spoken of 'institutionalised racism', and 'centuries of dehumanisation'.[28]

Yet America, after the election of Donald Trump as President in November 2016, was still living a form of collective denial. For many the election of Trump was a confirmation that racism was alive and well across large swathes of America. Even worse, the rise in hate crimes and the newfound confidence of white supremacists implied that the rise of Donald Trump had fanned the flames of racism across the country, and his tepid attempts to disassociate himself from his racist supporters would appear half-hearted at best.

If African-Americans were looking for a signal from President Trump, they got one just days after the election when Trump appointed Senator Jeff Sessions from Alabama as his new Attorney General.[29] The ultra-conservative seventy-year-old senator was an anti-immigrant firebrand,[30] an enemy of free trade and a long-time opponent of voting rights laws for blacks. Back in February 2016, Sessions had also been also the first sitting member of the US Senate to endorse Trump during the primary season.[31]

To the heirs of Rev. Dr Martin Luther King Jr, Senator Sessions was anathema, the racist's racist, a career segregationist from the Deep South.

Back in 1986, when Ronald Reagan nominated Sessions to a federal judgeship, it all came out. First it was revealed during his confirmation hearing in the Senate that Sessions had called a white civil rights attorney 'a disgrace to his race' and then that he had called a black prosecutor he worked with 'boy'.[32]

Sessions claimed he had only been joking when he said the Ku Klux Klan was 'OK', but he could not erase the words he had used to describe the NAACP and the Southern Christian Leadership Conference (which was founded by Rev. Dr Martin Luther King Jr). He called them 'un-American' and 'Communist-inspired' organisations.[33]

At the time, Senator Edward Kennedy, a member of the judiciary committee that was about to vote down his nomination as a federal judge, called Sessions 'a throwback to a disgraceful era'.[34] Others just called him a racist. Today, Sessions is part of the Trump mainstream, a master of doublespeak and quite capable of denying all charges of racism. After all, this is the man who stood by Trump throughout the 2016 campaign, a loyal stalwart with an agenda. This is Jeff Sessions, who, after the leaking of the Hollywood video with Trump's 'grab them by the pussy' remark in October 2016, was instantly forgiving. 'I don't characterise that as sexual assault,' he deadpanned.[35]

If black Americans began to feel more anxious after the November 2016 election, that was understandable. After all, as head of the Justice Department, Jeff Sessions has the power to radically change how the federal government oversees civil rights laws, how it handles voting rights issues, and how it deals with the nation's immigration laws.

Jeff Sessions is a politician, like Trump, who has profited from the 'whitelash' of racist resentment against the Obama administration in recent years. Like Trump, he has always known how best to exploit people's emotions and fears, stoking the flames of hatred with demagogic rhetoric and then issuing bold-faced denials of his behaviour.

But America is not focused on the identity and ideological baggage of Jeff Sessions. Not many people are really interested. America is only able to deal with simplicities, and can barely distinguish between real and fake news these days. America, after the election of Donald Trump to the White House, is shell-shocked by the digital overload. Incidents of racial violence, even cops and vigilantes shooting unarmed black youths? That is just another violent intrusion into our day, a glance at the iPhone, a moment of cable TV. The plight of African-Americans in the United States of America is a minor matter in our daily lives. There is plenty of other news that is battling for our shrinking attention span. What else is new? Another one. Oh, that's too bad. How horrible. Do black lives really matter in the United States of America in the Trump era? Based on his behaviour as President, apparently not. For the average American in 2017, racial violence is a relatively minor concern, and Donald Trump has hardly made it a priority. Racial violence in the Trump era is merely a series of media blips on our collective conscience, just part of the information overload. We shrug each incident away, we avert our eyes, and we move on to the next item, the next story.

• • •

For Sybrina Fulton, back in Florida with nothing but the memories of her son, there cannot be enough consciousness-raising about racism in America. For Sybrina Fulton, black lives do matter and it matters that other Americans know what is going on in their country. She agrees, however, that the shooting of unarmed black youths has always happened, and long before the shooting of Trayvon Martin. She welcomes the new use of video and social media to disseminate America's racial atrocities. She hopes and prays it will make a difference.

> I think that it's always been around, but what's happening now is that there is just more awareness. People are opening their eyes. In the past, people really didn't realise it was happening because it wasn't occurring in their lives. Now there's more videos out there, there's more people sniffing out the social media. You know, they are posting these things. Now they can actually see that these people are unarmed, and they are being shot and killed, and nobody is being held accountable. So I think America is waking up. They are starting to wake up and notice that there is a problem in this country with gun violence.

Gun violence. Sybrina Fulton does not deny that gun violence and racism often go together.

'There is an issue with senseless gun violence, and there is an issue with racism, and so we have to be aware of those things,' she says. But on her to-do list, the biggest priority is gun control.

'I think we need to have gun control in this country,' says Trayvon Martin's mom.

> It shouldn't be so easy for somebody to get their hands on guns. I think certain guns are for war, and not just to simply protect yourself. Why would you need an assault rifle unless you are

> going hunting or unless you are at war? I think if you are going to protect yourself you don't need a semi-automatic weapon.

By the summer of 2016, the semi-automatic weapon, the assault rifle, had become the weapon of choice in many killings across America, from San Bernardino to Orlando. They used to be banned by law. But the ban expired in 2004 and Congress opted not to renew it. So it was pretty easy to buy assault rifles across America, even if you were a suspected terrorist on the FBI watch list.

For Barack Obama, as for Sybrina Fulton, the challenge of gun control had seemed even greater than the challenge of resurgent racism, although a careful examination of his repeated melancholy remarks during his last year in office might conclude that it had been something of a toss-up.

If at the start of 2012 Trayvon Martin had become the poster-child for racial violence in America, another, even more horrifying event would come towards the end of that same year, and it would come to symbolise, for Barack Obama and for many Americans, the sickened state of American society, a society in which semi-automatic weapons are regularly used to gun down Americans of all colours, shapes and sizes, including frighteningly high numbers of American schoolchildren, dozens and dozens of innocent schoolchildren.

CHAPTER FIVE

GUNS KILL

The President of the United States was crying.

Barack Obama stood at the podium of the White House Briefing Room, tears streaming down his cheeks. From time to time he tried to brush the tears aside, dabbing at them with an index finger. He choked up, and paused, and then, for what seemed like an eternity but was actually only a few seconds, he appeared to struggle to retain his composure. It was 3.30 on the afternoon of 14 December 2012 when Obama appeared on live national television, just hours after the massacre of twenty schoolchildren and six adults in the classrooms and corridors of the Sandy Hook Elementary School in Newtown, Connecticut.

'As a country we have been through this too many times,' said a grim and weary Obama. 'Whether it is an elementary school in Newtown, or a shopping mall in Oregon, or a temple in Wisconsin, or a movie theater in Aurora, or a street corner in Chicago...'

The first tears came when Obama noted that 'the majority of those who died today were children, beautiful little kids between the ages of five and ten years old'. He then declared mournfully a nation's grief: 'Our hearts are broken,' said Obama, adding that he was speaking not just as the President but as a parent.[1]

The parents of Newtown, Connecticut on that day would live through every parent's worst nightmare.

The first call to 911 had come at around 9.35 a.m. that morning, from a teacher at the school. An 'active shooter' had opened fire inside the school. But it took more than an hour before the full extent of the horror became clear. By 10.30 that morning, ambulances began arriving and stretchers were being set up at a nearby fire station. By 11 a.m., police gave the first indications of multiple fatalities inside the school. By noon, it became clear that most of the fatalities were children. Teachers were seen escorting survivors out of the school and over to the fire station.

Only later would it emerge that the shooter was a mentally disturbed twenty-year-old named Adam Lanza, and that the children he had mown down with his mother's assault rifle were six- and seven-year-olds, a total of twenty schoolchildren. Twenty innocent schoolchildren. First graders. Lanza had first shot his own mother in the face, at home, and then driven a mile to the Sandy Hook Elementary School, located amid the rolling hills of this bucolic Connecticut community.

At the Sandy Hook Elementary School that Friday morning, some of the first graders were getting ready to make gingerbread houses in preparation for the Christmastime festivities. After all, Christmas was just eleven days away. Adam Lanza shot his way right into the school then went from room to room, emptying rounds of ammunition into children and teachers until he had killed twenty children and six adults, including teachers and the school principal. Then, as occurs so often in these atrocities, the shooter took his own life.

The parents of the twenty slain children could never be consoled, and the entire community, like the nation, was shattered. The images of the surviving children being led out of the school by teachers, marching single-file, each one with their arms placed on the shoulders of the student ahead of them, were replayed across American media until we had memorised the whole tragedy, the school, the shooting, the children fleeing, the police cars and ambulances, the fire station that became a makeshift staging post. The tragedy at Sandy Hook captured the imagination of a nation, created a moment of shared national horror and revulsion.

Dave Stowe[2] had two children at school in Newtown that day, one daughter at a nearby pre-school and the other daughter, herself seven years old, at another school less than a mile away from Sandy Hook Elementary School. Stowe was a normal Newtown parent, who worked in graphic communications, in an office in Stamford, Connecticut, about an hour away. He remembers the day with chilling clarity.

'I was sitting at my desk,' recalls Stowe,

> and I got a reverse 911 call on my cell phone. What that is, is that you can sign up with a district and any time there is any important information you'll get an automated call. The initial call came right when I got to work, and it said there was an active shooter situation in a Newtown school, and they didn't identify the school. Well, I had one child in school and another was actually with my wife that day at pre-school. So I called my wife immediately. She was with my younger daughter, and they didn't know what was going on either. And then ten minutes later we got a second 911 call that said the active shooter situation was at Sandy Hook Elementary School. So initially and immediately, I'm relieved, because my child is safe. And then literally, within seconds, I have these tremendous feelings of guilt and horror because my kids play with the kids at Sandy Hook. I have a lot of friends here, I have many, many friends that we hang out with all the time, our kids played together.

Dave Stowe, an ordinary-looking suburban father in a short-sleeved shirt and chinos, stands in front of the perimeter of the newly reconstructed Sandy Hook Elementary School, which opened in September 2016, nearly four years after the tragedy. The old school was demolished, but not the memories. He is gesturing to the nearby fire station, which became the staging area for first responders.

Stowe says that when the shooting took place, his seven-year-old daughter was hidden in her classroom at a nearby school, about a mile away.

> They are the closest school to Sandy Hook, and in her class the

> teacher took them and they were locked in a closet in the dark in silence for about an hour. All the schools in Newtown were locked down that day, including the pre-school where my younger daughter was with my wife.

Stowe remembers racing home to Newtown after the second 911 call.

> I jumped in my car and rushed home, which was like the longest ride in my life because I just wanted to be home. On that ride home that day I kind of made a promise to myself that I was going to do whatever I could for my children, for my girls, to make a difference and make the world a safer place. At the time I had no idea what that meant or what that would become.

Dave Stowe became an activist. Today he serves as vice-chair of the Newtown Action Alliance, a gun violence prevention group that was formed by the parents of Sandy Hook victims and survivors, along with other parents from the community. Another community, another group of grieving activists, survivors and families of the victims.

'That day I will never forget,' says Stowe.

> I got home with my wife and we waited at the bus stop for my older daughter, and we talked to her and told her what had happened in a very age-appropriate manner. But no parent should ever have to hear that their child has been murdered or have to tell their siblings that. I don't wish on anyone to have to sit down with their eight-year-old and tell them what happened.

Just two days after the Sandy Hook massacre, Barack Obama came to Newtown to join the parents and families of the Connecticut village in their mourning. His eyes would well up with tears again, this time during the prayer vigil on 16 December, when it came time to read the list of the twenty children and six adults who had been slain by Adam Lanza.

As would be the case on many other occasions, Obama used the event to argue for tighter gun control. 'We can't tolerate this any more. These tragedies must end,' said the President, in a desultory tone of voice.[3]

'Surely we can do better than this,' he argued plaintively.

> If there is even *one* step we can take to save another child, or another parent, or another town, from the grief that has visited Tucson, and Aurora, and Oak Creek, and Newtown, and communities from Columbine to Blacksburg before that, then surely we have an obligation to try.

Obama's list of recent gun shooting tragedies was relatively short back in December 2012. Tragically, it was destined to grow much longer and even more horrific during Obama's second term in office.

The nation had grappled with gun violence and mass shootings before, long before the tragedy at Sandy Hook. Gun rampages were an American way of life. The massacres at McDonald's and in offices across America in the early 1990s had led to Congress approving a ban on the sale of assault weapons,[4] the infamous semi-automatic rifles that were modelled on the MR-16 machine guns used by US soldiers in Vietnam. The weapon was designed with just one purpose: to create the most lethal weapon for combat troops, starting in Vietnam. The AR-15, made by the Bushmaster division of Remington Arms, was a civilian version but nearly as lethal. It could fire more than thirty bullets without reloading. So how did a weapon like that end up on the floor of a first-grade classroom in a sleepy town in Connecticut?

The AR-15 assault rifle was the weapon that Adam Lanza had used to take down twenty schoolchildren and six adults in a matter of seconds, firing multiple rounds from his magazine before pausing to reload.

As previously noted, the assault rifle had been banned back in 1994, but when the ten-year ban expired in 2004, Congress opted not to renew it. The gun lobby had spent many millions of dollars making certain that almost nobody in Congress would dare to renew it again. Gun control, by the early years of the twenty-first century, was becoming the great lost cause of American politics.

By the time a newly re-elected Barack Obama faced the prayer vigil in Sandy Hook in December 2012, the assault rifle had become the weapon of choice across America for mass murderers everywhere. A lawyer for the families of Sandy Hook victims who were suing Remington Arms, makers of the AR-15, called it 'the gold standard for mass shooters'.[5]

Another semi-automatic weapon, in this case a Glock 9-millimetre semi-automatic pistol, had been used by another mass shooter nearly two years before Sandy Hook. The rampage occurred back on 8 January 2011, in the parking lot of a Safeway supermarket in Tucson, Arizona. That was where a shooter had opened fire on Congresswoman Gabrielle Giffords while she was greeting her constituents, leaving Giffords with a disabling brain injury, a dozen wounded, and six people dead, including a federal judge.[6]

Over the years, after almost every mass shooting in America, Democrats on Capitol Hill would try to revive the gun control issue. It was a familiar pattern. Each time new legislation was tabled, the National Rifle Association managed to intimidate, cajole and threaten into submission the requisite number of members of Congress needed to block the legislation. So far every major attempt has failed, including the many pieces of legislation that were introduced following the shooting of Gabrielle Giffords.

After the shooting of a sitting member of the House of Representatives, Democrats were once again becoming bolder in challenging the gun lobby. Surely something had to be done about the assault rifles, the semi-automatic weapons? The ban on their sale had expired back in 2004, and nobody, not the White House of Barack Obama nor the US Congress, seriously believed that the ban could be easily reinstated. Yet even more limited and common-sense legislation was destined to fail.

Just two weeks after the Tucson shooting in January 2011, new gun control legislation was introduced by Senator Frank Lautenberg, a New Jersey Democrat, and Rep. Carolyn McCarthy, a House Democrat from Long Island and a long-time gun control activist member of Congress whose own husband had been murdered in a mass shooting. There were three separate bills, none of them particularly radical or extreme.[7]

One would have closed the so-called gun show loophole by requiring sellers at gun shows to perform the same background checks that licensed gun dealers must conduct. Another would have banned the manufacture and sale of magazines with a capacity of more than ten rounds of ammunition. The third proposal would have stopped a person on the terrorist watch list from obtaining explosives or guns.

None of them gained traction in Congress.

In July 2012, more than a year after the Tucson shooting, America was again facing the tragedy of gun violence, this time a shooting massacre in a movie theatre in the little town of Aurora, Colorado. The shooter's weapon was the Bushmaster AR-15 assault rifle.

Since the semi-automatic weapon had been designed for US Army combat troops in order to help them to kill as many enemy soldiers as possible in the shortest possible amount of time, it was not surprising that the Aurora shooter was able to kill a dozen people and wound another fifty-eight so quickly and efficiently. This was largely thanks to the rifle's large magazine clip. The moviegoers inside the crowded theatre in Aurora didn't stand a chance.

After Aurora, Rep. Carolyn McCarthy, by now the leading gun control advocate in Congress, kept pressing her case.

She proposed laws to limit the magazine in an assault rifle to just ten rounds, a small and common-sense step by any measure. But she seemed pessimistic that such a proposal stood any chance in Congress, especially in the middle of an election year.

'We know the atmosphere in Congress now,' she said in an interview that summer.

> Several Republicans said they would vote for it if it came to the floor, but the current leadership will not allow it to get a vote. The NRA and the gun manufacturers put a lot of money in to scare legislators – not just federal, but at the state level too – and they are saying 'Support this and we'll take you out. You won't get re-elected.'[8]

The NRA would make good on its threats. The gun lobby scared the bejesus out of most lawmakers.

At the time, McCarthy did not dare push for a renewed ban on assault rifles. But she thought a ban on large clips would at least reduce the number of people killed by semi-automatic weapons.

The Aurora massacre came right in the middle of the presidential election campaign, at a time when Barack Obama was fighting it out with Republican candidate Mitt Romney.

Romney, unsurprisingly as the Republican nominee, was in lockstep with the National Rifle Association, the most powerful lobby in Washington and the sworn enemy of even the most reasonable and *de minimus* gun control proposals.

Barack Obama was between a rock and a hard place. He was running for re-election as President, and so he was extremely cautious when it came to gun control, a flashpoint issue that smart presidential candidates tended to avoid rather than confront head on. In fact, even though he had been a lifelong gun control advocate, Barack Obama had remained nearly silent about the issue through most of his first term in office.

On his visit to Aurora that July, Obama expressed his condolences but little more. He seemed genuinely gun-shy on the issue at hand and would limit his pronouncements for the rest of the campaign to careful generalities.

To many gun control advocates, even after the horror of Aurora, it seemed that hopes for gun control were dead that year.

After Sandy Hook, Robert Shrum, a savvy Democratic political consultant and veteran of the presidential campaigns of Al Gore and John Kerry, called for Obama to stop being so timid and to finally take action on gun control. He decried the murder of innocent schoolchildren in Newtown and called America a 'killing field' of gun violence, from its inner cities to its suburban shopping malls and beyond.[9]

Barack Obama's work on gun control was so modest that it could not be considered in any way meaningful during his first term in office. He essentially avoided the topic in the White House, and even signed into law two bills that included provisions expanding gun access, one in national parks and one on Amtrak trains. In 2010, the respected Brady Campaign to Prevent Gun Violence report had given Obama an 'F' for leadership on gun control.[10]

The truth was that Obama only summoned up the passion and the political courage to tackle gun control following his re-election in November 2012, and after Sandy Hook. Presumably he felt more secure now, knowing he would never again have to face an election campaign. What Obama could not change was the fact that Republicans held the majority in the House of Representatives, while many Democrats were too frightened of the NRA to do very much.

Thus, when tragedy struck at Sandy Hook, on that Friday morning in December 2012, a day that Obama would call the worst of his presidency, some mechanism was triggered in Obama's brain. With some synaptic response or perhaps with long-repressed anger, he shifted from flight to fight response on the issue of gun control. Barack Obama finally found his voice. Sandy Hook changed something in Obama, who now became passionate and outspoken about gun control. He appeared variously anguished, outraged and energised. Most of all, he was searching for something to do, some action to take, even though all of his efforts would eventually come to nought. In the months and years that followed Sandy Hook, the public Obama would alternate between phases of deep frustration, grim and tense anger and further moments of genuine heartbreak.

He would describe himself as a parent, as a father; he would regularly be seen trying to console the families of victims of mass shootings and other forms of gun violence. He would denounce the constant carnage that slid across America's television screen awareness, but in the end he was up against interests more powerful than his presidency, in Congress, in the gun lobby and across a seemingly unapologetic America.

Four months after Sandy Hook, on 17 April 2013, Barack Obama, Rep. Carolyn McCarthy and the parents of the children who had died in Newtown, gathered at the White House in what proved to be a moment of painful defeat. Their hopes for new gun control legislation were dashed once more. The law that came up for a vote four months after Sandy Hook was itself quite modest; it was mainly about enhancing a few background checks. Yet it was voted down in the Senate. What was especially striking was how small most of the changes being proposed actually were in the greater scheme of things, in a nation where the Second Amendment of the Constitution was venerated by millions of Americans in a militant, fundamentalist, and at times almost religious manner.

The expansion of background checks contained in the legislation was not a huge step. The compromise had actually been put together by two lifelong NRA members, Republican Pat Toomey from Pennsylvania and Democratic Senator Joe Manchin from West Virginia. The legislation[11] did not challenge the Second Amendment. It was careful, even cautious. The aim of the bill was simply to make it harder for criminals and those with severe mental illness to buy guns over the internet and at gun shows. The same rules already applied in gun shops, which covered 60 per cent of all sales. So this was a relatively small move. But the bill failed.[12] Not one of the key elements got the sixty votes needed to become law. In rapid succession they were voted down: a bipartisan compromise to expand background checks for gun buyers, a ban on assault weapons and a ban on high-capacity gun magazines. All gone. Obama had been outmanoeuvred, frustrated and blocked. Again.

The author, together with Donald Trump aboard his Boeing 757, parked in the Cargo Zone of the George Bush Intercontinental Airport in Houston, Texas, 17 June 2016.

Juanita 'Nita' Fischer, a single mother who was fired by Walmart during her pregnancy. Today, although rehired by Walmart, she is unable to feed her infant son without food stamps and welfare.

Mayor Bill Luckett of Clarksdale, Mississippi. 'Clarksdale is culturally rich, the home of the Blues, but the Mississippi Delta is the poorest part of the poorest state in the United States.'

Desta Reff, a Harvard Delta Fellow, has chosen to live and work amid the poverty of Clarksdale, Mississippi. 'This place is a food desert. Most people do not have access to any fresh fruits or vegetables.'

The author with Wilbur Cave, who runs the Allendale County Alive community centre in Allendale, South Carolina.

The author with Calvin Wright, a veteran of the battle for civil rights and today the head of the OCAB community centre in Orangeburg, South Carolina. 'Today, the problem is that racism has become institutionalized.'

The author with Reverend Eric Manning, Pastor of the Mother Emanuel African Methodist Episcopal Church in Charleston, South Carolina. The two are standing in front of a commemoration of the nine victims of the massacre of 7 June 2015. In January 2017 the killer, Dylann Roof, was convicted and sentenced to death.

The author and his collaborator Luna De Bartolo, with Ms Dot Scott and Reverend Joseph Darby, respectively the president and vice-president of the Charleston, South Carolina branch of the NAACP. 'Trump is ripping the Band-Aid off racism in America,' says Scott.

The author with Jody Owens, director of the Southern Poverty Law Center in Jackson, Mississippi. 'It has always been easier to arrest or convict black people, and then throw away the key.'

The author with Sybrina Fulton, the activist mother of Trayvon Martin, who was killed by a white vigilante on 26 February 2012. The shooting of Trayvon Martin shook America and inspired the founders of the Black Lives Matter movement.

The author with David Stowe, vice-president of the Newtown Action Alliance, which brings together parents of the victims of the massacre at Sandy Hook Elementary School in Newton, Connecticut on 14 December 2012.

The author with Mario Reyes, a deputy in the Sheriff's Office of Laredo, Texas, with a colleague. Reyes is a veteran of the border wars along the Rio Grande.

Hector Garza, president of the local Laredo branch of the National Border Patrol Council, is the man who first invited Donald Trump to visit back in the summer of 2015. 'We understood that Trump really cared about the border issue.'

Urbino 'Benny' Martinez, Sheriff of Brooks County, Texas. From his office in Falfurrias, Texas, Martinez has been on the front line against Mexican drug cartels and people smuggling. 'A great deal of our work involves recovering corpses of Mexican migrants out in the brush.'

Rosalind Hines, who works on health care in Allendale, South Carolina. She was shocked to discover that free national health care is available in most of Europe.

Gary Brock of Ormond Beach, Florida works as a waiter in a steakhouse and earns $5 an hour plus tips. 'For me, Obamacare saved my life. I had always wanted to have health insurance.'

The author with President Vladimir Putin during an interview in the Chimney Room at the Kremlin, 27 July 2015.

The President, by now looking both scornful and mournful, stood in the Rose Garden, flanked by Newtown families, a scowling Vice-President Joe Biden and former Congresswoman Gabrielle Giffords, who had limped over from the Oval Office to join the others. Obama, looking indignant, quoted opinion polls showing that the enhanced background checks were supported by 90 per cent of the American public. Then, in the most explicit terms ever used by a sitting President, he blamed the NRA for essentially threatening both Republicans and Democrats with harsh retribution if they voted in favour.

'I've talked to several of these senators,' said Obama, 'and they worry that the gun lobby will come after them and spend a lot of money and paint them as anti-Second Amendment.'

'All in all,' Obama concluded, 'this was a pretty shameful day for Washington.'[13]

Over at the Fairfax, Virginia offices of the NRA, they were uncorking the champagne.

The NRA, and gun lovers across America, had good reason to celebrate. They had once again protected their strict interpretation of the Second Amendment, of the right to bear arms. They had virtually made gun control a taboo subject, a politically radioactive issue. They had spent more than $32 million on campaign contributions, ads and on attacks during the 2012 campaign that were funded by political action committees, or, as they are known in US politics, PACs.[14]

With the defeat of gun control legislation in April 2013, they became even stronger, and more allied with the obscure forces of Tea Party radicals as well as their more traditional Republican and gun-owning base. For the rest of his term, the NRA would continue to obfuscate Obama's legislative attempts at tightening gun laws, stopping him dead in his tracks each and every time.

By the start of 2016, despite the lingering shock of the San Bernardino attack in which fourteen people were killed, gun control really did look like it had become the great lost cause of American politics. In the five years since the shooting of Rep. Gabrielle

Giffords and eighteen other people in Tucson, Arizona in January 2011, lawmakers had introduced more than 100 gun control proposals in Congress. Not one of them made it into law. Not one. In fact, very few of the proposals even made it to the floor of the House or Senate for a vote.

Resistance to gun control in America is about far more than just a powerful Washington lobby. It is about tampering with the American way of life, the freedom to bear arms, the deeply entrenched and widespread desire to own guns and rifles for hunting and shooting and self-defence.

Today there are about 350 million guns in circulation in America, more than one weapon for every man, woman and child, in a nation of 319 million people.[15] The actual number of gun owners in America is more than 100 million people, around 31 per cent of the population.[16]

In 2015, there was more than one shooting a day in the United States that left four or more people wounded or dead.[17] More than one mass shooting a day, every single day, each day of the year, the whole year through.

Americans are ten times more likely to die from gun violence than citizens of other advanced high-income democracies. Compared to twenty-two other OECD nations, the US gun-related murder rate is twenty-five times higher.[18] Roughly 30,000 Americans die each year because of gun violence, although about two thirds of these deaths are suicides.[19] Yet even legislative attempts to ensure the safe storage of weapons at home so as to make it more difficult for children to play with guns have consistently failed.

The gun lobbyists argue that better background checks and controls on assault weapons would not make a difference in reducing crime rates. The gun control advocates, and the families of victims, have been asking for comparatively little in terms of substance, so little that their own critics maintain that merely enhancing background checks is almost useless in a nation so prone to violence and with so many guns already in circulation.

America is a country where even after the shooting of President Ronald Reagan in 1981 it took more than a dozen years before Congress would approve the most basic background checks. This came in the form of the so-called Brady Bill,[20] signed into law by President Bill Clinton in 1993 and named for Ronald Reagan's chief of staff, who was wounded severely in the 1981 assassination attempt on the President by John Hinckley. The time limit on the assault rifle ban that became law in 1994 was just one of the many flaws in the legislation. But the gun lobby was furious and afterwards Bill Clinton and many Democrats blamed gun control as the main reason they had lost the House of Representatives to a Republican majority in the mid-term elections of 1994.

Back in 1994, Tom Diaz[21] was a staffer working for Congressman Charles Schumer, a New York Democrat who is today the Senate Minority Leader but who back then was a leading gun control proponent and part of the push to approve the ban on assault rifles in the House of Representatives. Diaz, once a gun enthusiast, became an ardent advocate of gun control. His first book, *Making a Killing: The Business of Guns in America*,[22] was widely considered to be among the most influential anti-gun books ever written. Having been there at the creation, he agrees that the assault rifle ban was deeply flawed, and not only because it expired after ten years.

'There were a couple of problems with the assault weapons ban,' recalls Diaz.

> It was part of a crime bill that Bill Clinton really needed, but the people in Congress didn't truly understand what they were doing. It was a case of cutting and pasting labels and so they named some guns and not others, and they named some of the characteristics which were really not relevant to the designed purpose and functioning of these military weapons. So it was really an ineffective law. It had a sunset provision that meant it expired in ten years and it did not apply to all the guns already in existence.

> So in effect it was a pass. But many people blamed this law for the Democrats losing control of Congress.

After the loss of the mid-term elections in 1994, and for decades to come, gun control would be considered too hot to handle by the majority of American politicians.

'The conventional wisdom was that gun control was the third rail of politics,' recalls Diaz.

> You couldn't touch it. Any Democrat who chose to do so would be done. When Rahm Emanuel was Barack Obama's first chief of staff, he made it quite clear that no one in the administration – not the Attorney General, not ATF [the Bureau of Alcohol, Tobacco, Firearms and Explosives], not anybody – was to advance any idea about gun control. So basically gun control withered on the vine. Until Sandy Hook. After Sandy Hook, Aurora, San Bernardino and Orlando, I think something changed in the dynamic of gun politics. At least I would like to think so.

At the start of 2016, the nation was still grieving at the shock of San Bernardino. Social media was still buzzing, and there was once again talk of tightening gun control laws, or at least imposing better background checks. Once again the Republican-controlled Congress displayed little appetite for gun control, especially at the start of a presidential election year. The outgoing President was having none of it. Obama was moved again by the violence in San Bernardino, and he had been working closely with Vice-President Joe Biden, trying to come up with new initiatives, new measures that he could implement without having to go to Congress.

In early January of 2016, Obama announced what he called a series of 'executive actions'.[23] It was mostly a group therapy session for Obama, his allies in Congress and in gun control advocacy, and the families of shooting massacres. It was noble-sounding and worthy stuff, but hardly radical gun control. Obama pledged to hire

200 more ATF agents and investigators to help process applications faster, and to require firearms dealers to report more lost or stolen guns on a more timely basis. These were hardly measures that would make a dent in America's soaring gun market. The critics would say it was at best a stir-fried repackaging of existing gun control initiatives and other repackaged programmes. Yet when Obama stood before the cameras on 5 January 2016, he was a determined man, defiant and eloquent.

'I'm not on the ballot again. I'm not looking to score some points,' he said. 'But we need to feel a sense of urgency about it. Because people are dying, and the constant excuses for inaction no longer suffice.'

Obama recalled the death toll of gun violence in what seemed like a litany. 'Every single year more than 30,000 Americans have their lives cut short by guns,' said Obama. 'Suicides. Domestic violence. Gang shootouts. Accidents. Hundreds of thousands of Americans have lost brothers and sisters, or buried their own children.'

'The United States', Obama proclaimed,

> is not the only country on Earth with violent or dangerous people. We are not inherently more prone to violence. But we are the only advanced country on Earth that sees this kind of mass violence erupt with this kind of frequency. It doesn't happen in other advanced countries. *It's not even close.* Somehow we've become numb to it and we start thinking that this is normal.

It was only towards the end of more than forty minutes of remarks in the East Room of the White House that Obama would become emotional, and once again over Sandy Hook. 'Every time I think about those kids it gets me mad,'[24] said the President, pausing to brush away a tear.

Thus Obama may have opened his final year in office with passionate hopes of pressing the cause of better background checks and other limited gun control measures. But it was not meant to be.

The Obama administration's last hope of achieving any useful gun control legislation died in June 2016. Once again, what was on the table were just a handful of relatively small improvements in background checks, like extending the three-day background period to sales over the internet and at gun shows.[25]

The vote came on 20 June, just over a week after the mass shooting at the Pulse nightclub in Orlando. But that didn't bother the Republicans or the NRA, who were out in full force. That didn't stop the Senate from voting down even the idea of extending 72-hour background checks to terror suspects who were on the FBI watch list. You could be on the FBI's no-fly list but you could still buy a gun, easily. With Republicans holding the majority in both houses of Congress, the background check measures didn't stand a chance, and even the modest Republican-sponsored measures went down to defeat. It made no difference that a Democratic senator, Chris Murphy from Connecticut, had pulled the stunt of staging a fifteen-hour-long filibuster just to get the Senate to vote.[26] It made no difference that House Democrats staged a noisy sit-in two days later, protesting the way their Republican counterparts had even dodged the issue of expanding background checks to include terror suspects on the FBI watch list, and just a week after the terrible events of Orlando.[27] For the hardline Republicans, any attempt at expanding background checks was an assault on their constitutional rights to bear arms.

Today, as a result of this inaction, it is still with the greatest of ease that suspected terrorists and mentally ill people are legally able to purchase lethal weapons, often without getting either a licence or a background check.

It was with ease in 2012 that Adam Lanza's mother in Newtown, Connecticut could legally purchase the AR-15 assault rifle and Glock semi-automatic and other weapons that her son would find at home and turn upon the children of Sandy Hook. It was with equal ease that Omar Mateen could buy the AR-15 that he would use at the Pulse club in Orlando in 2016. Ease of purchase for a gun-crazed nation. The number of Americans who want to possess and display the assault rifle as a form of home decoration is staggering. Up on the wall. Roughly 8 million assault rifles are in circulation across America.[28] Eight million civilian versions of the M-16 combat rifle. This is a not legal issue. This is cultural. Americans love assault rifles and Americans love guns. It is deep in our culture, an integral part of our national heritage, deeply ingrained in our frontier mentality, in the desire to be free of any restriction or regulation of our lives. The problem with gun control is that it goes against the grain of our national identity.

Guns are as American as covered wagons and the OK Corral. Handguns. Semi-automatic weapons. Machine guns. Assault rifles. If the US military can build bunker-busting bombs to drop on Al Qaeda and drones that rain terror from the sky, then why shouldn't American gun owners have the satisfaction of holding extreme power in their hands too? Guns don't kill people, says the NRA. But guns do kill more efficiently when their technology is enhanced. Tightening background checks or restrictions on the purchase of guns won't make any difference, says the NRA. But something like half of the mass shooters in recent American history wouldn't have been able to purchase a gun if such background checks had already been in place.

Curiously, history shows that mass shootings do not improve the ability of Democrats in Congress to push through tighter gun controls; they often have the opposite effect, as the gun lobby marshals its forces to defeat a perceived threat. Mass shootings tend to trigger renewed efforts for gun control legislation. It happens every time. But the prospect of new gun control laws tends to lead to a spike in assault rifle sales, as people rush out to buy them, fearing that new laws could place greater restrictions on their ability to purchase them. The same thing happened across America in the autumn of 2016 when it looked like Hillary Clinton might win the White House: gun sales jumped as people rushed out to avoid future controls. Once Donald Trump was proclaimed winner in November

2016, the NRA and the gun enthusiasts rejoiced and sighed with relief and gun sales slumped again.[29]

After the Orlando shooting, where once again the weapon of choice turned out to be an assault rifle, Hillary Clinton called for the reinstatement of a ban on assault rifles.

'I believe weapons of war have no place on our streets,' she said just a day after the Orlando shooting in June 2016.

> We may have our disagreements on gun safety regulations, but we should all be able to agree on a few things. If the FBI is watching you for suspected terrorist links, you shouldn't be able to just go buy a gun with no questions asked. You shouldn't be able to exploit loopholes and evade criminal background checks by buying online or at a gun show. And yes, if you're too dangerous to get on a plane, you are too dangerous to buy a gun in America.[30]

In the course of the Democratic primary season, Hillary Clinton had been speaking far more openly about gun control than was usual in a presidential campaign. But with Bernie Sanders wrapping up the more progressive vote in the primaries, Clinton had to appeal to the base. To burnish her gun control credentials, she even used an endorsement in a specially made television ad which featured the daughter of Dawn Hochsprung, the principal of Sandy Hook Elementary who was among those gunned down by Adam Lanza in December 2012.[31]

As the primary season drew to a close, Hillary Clinton had continued to talk tough about the gun lobby. She openly accused the NRA of using their money and power to coerce members of Congress to do their bidding.[32] None of this was new, but it was unusual for Clinton to be so vocal.

Cynics like Tom Diaz suggested this was made easier for her because opinion polls showed that when it came to background checks on suspected terrorists, the vast majority of America was in favour. It was in any case smart politics for Clinton to try to co-opt the more liberal part of the Democratic Party; that was the key challenge going into the Democratic National Convention of July 2016, trying to achieve unity and to reach out to the Sanders left. There was even more urgency in the task in the wake of the resignation of Democratic National Committee chairperson Debbie Wasserman Schultz, who had been accused by the Sanders camp of working behind the scenes with Team Clinton to rig the vote. This charge included a controversy about several hundred so-called Super Delegates who were in the Clinton camp but who were not elected as transparently as other delegates during the state primaries.[33]

At the Democratic Convention, Hillary Clinton continued to reach out to progressives on gun control. The platform called for strengthening background checks, especially when it came to terrorists, criminals and those with severe mental health issues. It promised to 'keep weapons of war – such as assault weapons and large-capacity ammunition magazines – off our streets'.[34]

But after the convention was over and once the general election campaign got underway after Labor Day, the issue of gun control seemed to fade away once again. It came up briefly during the third televised presidential debate, on 19 October 2016, but Hillary Clinton fluffed her moment by complaining about how unfair it was that she was being targeted by millions of dollars' worth of negative advertising that was being financed by the NRA.

'I am honored to have the endorsement of the NRA,' Trump shot back at her, before he proceeded to declare his undying fealty to the Second Amendment and pledged to appoint justices of the Supreme Court who would do everything in their power to defend the Second Amendment.[35]

Between Clinton's own campaign difficulties in the autumn of 2016 and the turbulent gyrations in Donald Trump's campaign, gun control sort of slipped off to the side as Election Day neared. It was always a rouser for Trump at rallies of the base, but Clinton did not really pursue the issue; by then she had too many other problems.

In the campaign of 2016, the NRA spent an unprecedented

amount to help elect Donald Trump as President, spending more than $50 million on ads promoting Trump and attacking Hillary Clinton.[36] With the victory of Trump, the NRA could feel satisfied that it had spent its money wisely, and the gun lobby began working almost immediately to monetise its investment. It let it be known which judges it would like to see nominated to the Supreme Court by President Trump, judges with a known track record of advocating an individual's right to own weapons.

The NRA also began working with the Republican Congress to push for legislation that would make concealed-carry permits issued in one state valid in all fifty states, similar to a driver's licence. Actually, if the truth be known, the NRA favours doing away with permits entirely, believing that the right to carry concealed weapons is a constitutional right. They call this alleged constitutional right to carry a concealed weapon by the awkward-sounding name of 'constitutional carry'.

Tom Diaz says that neither is out of the question, now that the Republicans control all branches of government. In fact, he is pretty sure the concealed-carry legislation will be enacted by the Republican Congress and signed into law by President Donald Trump.

'Trump is a godsend for the gun lobby, and for the guns industry,' says Diaz.

> Now, with the Trump administration, no matter what happens we can be sure of one thing: that the industry will figure out how to manipulate the situation to sell more guns. That is the one certainty.
>
> That is why I think you will see approval of concealed-carry legislation, and a loosening of restrictions on assault rifles and on background checks. Because they need to sell those guns. For nearly twenty years the whole concealed-carry thing has been a marketing device to get people to buy more handguns. Whatever happens you can be certain that the gun industry will be figuring out ways to use the situation to sell more guns.

What does this mean for American society? America's premier expert on gun control and the gun industry sees a dark future. Diaz says that with Trump in the White House and the Republicans in charge of Congress, and with a new gun rights ideologue appointed to the Supreme Court, the game is over for gun control advocates. And that, Diaz worries, will in time lead to more guns and more violence and more of a risk to the social fabric, to social cohesion. In his vision of an unshackled gun lobby, a darker American society will evolve. We will become more used to and even more inured to shooting massacres, to racial violence, to inner-city crime, to suicides and to children killed by guns in their own homes.

'I am worried about the potential for a serious rise in violence across society. In the future we will have to take a look at things like what do you do in shopping centers to protect yourself,' says Diaz. 'We'll be living in a sort of dystopian society where everybody has to worry about the guy who's going to come at you with a gun,' he added.

'With Trump in the White House I think it is now quite likely that we will move in this direction,' says Diaz, who proceeds to insult the 45th President of the United States with a variety of colourful epithets.

To avoid such a dark and dystopian future, what is needed is meaningful gun control. But that is not going to happen any time soon. Instead, the number of mass shootings will probably remain among the highest in Western society, a fact of life in America.

There are simply too many guns out there and too many Americans who are not interested in having the conversation. The election of Donald Trump proved as much.

The desire of so many Americans to answer violence by arming themselves with lethal weaponry that was designed for combat troops is a vision of a society desensitised by gun violence and in a collective state of denial. Trump is the perfect avatar for that segment of society.

In 2016, Donald Trump made himself the 'law and order'

candidate and the Defender of the Second Amendment. He basked in his NRA endorsement and promised to do them proud. He empathised with their anger and he embraced their cause. Yet the frenzy he was able to whip up over the Second Amendment was nothing compared to the toxic cocktail that Trump prepared when he made the issue of immigration one of his signature themes. In a matter of months, little more than a year, Trump had transformed an entire American ethnic minority into punching bags, into outcasts, lesser beings. Trump, playing upon the most primordial fears of his base, turned *Mexican* into a curse word. He would break up families and deport millions of Mexican-Americans who had been living in America for decades. He would build a wall and force Mexico to pay for it. His virulent rhetoric would soon unleash a tidal wave of uninformed sentiment, most of it steeped in fear and anger.

If gun control had seemed the most partisan issue in American politics, it was about to be eclipsed by an even more divisive one. Donald Trump was going to build a wall.

CHAPTER SIX

A NATION OF IMMIGRANTS

> This is where the people smugglers come across. Sometimes they'll come in multiple groups. We have a surveillance tower up there by the thicket, but they'll try to cross at different points in the river, in multiple groups of ten or fifteen each, all at the same time. So they spread our assets real thin and they hope that one of the groups will make it through. They come either by raft or by swimming and sometimes, when the river is low and the water is shallow, like knee-deep, they even just wade right across the Rio Grande and come up the banks. Then they change into clean clothes that they bring across in a plastic bag and they are good to go. They just walk out into the streets of Laredo at rush-hour and blend in with the local population.

Mario Reyes[1] is pushing past the brush as he makes his way along a dirt path just a few yards from the river, a path that is lined by scrub vegetation and cane and mesquite trees. He points out discarded pieces of clothing and the ruins of plastic bags and beer cans that adorn the wild grass and scrub. Reyes is a chunky, barrel-chested man of solid muscle, a veteran of the never-ending border wars. He is carrying thirty pounds of Kevlar vest under his regulation khaki shirt and a semi-automatic Beretta on his holster. He is a big, friendly man with a badge and a matter-of-fact demeanour, the thinking man's grunt, a border town warrior.

Mario Reyes is a deputy in the Sheriff's Office in Laredo, Texas.

Laredo is America's most Hispanic city, a border town where 96 per cent of the population is of Mexican origin.[2] With the heavily guarded World Trade Bridge spanning the Rio Grande, Laredo is the entry and transit point for a whopping 40 per cent of all trade between Mexico and the United States, the largest port of entry along the US–Mexico border. More than 8,000 trucks cross the border at Laredo every day.[3] It is also, as Deputy Reyes notes, a Ground Zero for illegal immigration into the United States, one of the concentration points for people smuggling along America's 2,000-mile-long border with Mexico.

On the dirt path there are several footprints still fresh in the mud. The temperature is 97 degrees in the shade, the humidity oppressive and the air is deathly still except for the steady beating of the cicadas. Deputy Reyes gestures to the mighty Rio Grande, which from here doesn't look so mighty. It is little more than fifty feet across to Mexico from here, on a bluff overlooking the bank, just a few miles from downtown Laredo.

'Sometimes in Laredo you can hear the gunfire from across the river, on the Mexican side in the town of Nuevo Laredo, Mexico,' says Reyes matter-of-factly. 'Right over there, you can hear them shooting at each other in broad daylight. That's the cartel factions fighting with each other. They control all of the migrant smuggling, absolutely all of it.'

People smuggling, drug smuggling and money laundering are the three biggest growth industries in this badly tarnished border zone. The violence occasionally spills over the border from Nuevo Laredo, where the ruling cartel is a violent gang of militaristic killers known as Los Zetas.

Considered by the US government to be 'the most technologically advanced, sophisticated, vicious, ruthlessly violent and dangerous cartel operating in Mexico',[4] Los Zetas has expanded its activities beyond drug trafficking and also runs profitable sex-trafficking and gun-running rackets. The origins of Los Zetas date back to the 1990s, when commandos of the Mexican Army deserted their ranks and became the enforcement arm of the equally notorious Gulf Cartel.

The Gulf Cartel controlled a strip of Mexico that runs due south of Brownsville, Texas and along the Gulf of Mexico, but in 2010 Los Zetas broke away from the Gulf Cartel and took over the Laredo area, with its control stretching as far to the south as Monterrey.[5] Los Zetas is now the largest drug cartel in Mexico, even bigger than the Sinaloa Cartel, made famous by the repeated arrests and prison escapes and re-arrests of its leader, Joaquin Guzmán, known in the tabloids as 'El Chapo'.[6]

While drug trafficking may be the most profitable activity of the cartels, people smuggling is also big business, and the cartels continue to operate across large tracts of Mexico largely unhampered by the government of Mexico or the army. Much of the cocaine trade that was once controlled by Pablo Escobar's Medellín Cartel in Colombia now flows through Mexico, and much of it is right here in the Laredo area, along with the constant bread-and-butter business of people smuggling.

After years of cartel violence, the town of Laredo, Texas today looks tawdry and weatherworn. Once a tourist town with a cheerful Mexican-American flavour, a place where Americans would come to buy trinkets or watch the annual Jalapeño-Eating Contest on Washington's birthday, Laredo is now a ghost town reeling from the border wars. Violent crime is up, the economy is down, and the boarded storefronts tell a familiar story.

Out here on the bluff just a few yards from the Rio Grande, Reyes is pointing again to the Mexican side, this time to a clump of trees.

> That is where the cartel's scouts will hang out, trying to conduct counter-surveillance of us, to see who is here from the Sheriff's Office, who is here from Border Patrol, who is here from Immigration and Customs Enforcement and so on. They keep watch 24/7 and they watch when our cars go by, they have night-vision goggles just like us, and they use their cell phones to direct traffic, telling the *coyotes* when to make a run for it.

The word *coyote*, explains Reyes, is the name they use around here for people smugglers.

'The *coyotes* used to be local freelance smugglers,' says Reyes, 'but not any more. Now they all work for the cartel.'

For US law enforcement officials along the border with Mexico, it is a constant game of cat and mouse. Reyes gestures up to the pole-mounted camera in the distance, the radar, the vibration sensors and motion sensors. 'There is no physical wall here, but there is a virtual wall with the border patrols and the sensors along the river banks that will trigger and let us know when somebody is crossing,' says Reyes.

> But there is always somebody watching on the other side and they know our shifts, our timetables and they know when to make their move. That's all they do. They have plenty of time on their hands so they'll just be sitting there, watching, waiting, calculating.

Mario Reyes fires up his black Webb County Sheriff's Office Chevy Tahoe and steers it away from the river embankment and back towards downtown Laredo. He drives along these border roads almost every day of his life. He grew up in Laredo. He is on the front line of America's war on illegal immigration, and he knows the Rio Grande better than most. But ask him what he thinks of Donald Trump's idea of building a wall with Mexico and the deputy flinches. He seems uncomfortable. Mario Reyes, the grunt's grunt, wonders aloud where on earth such a wall would be built. 'Down the middle of the Rio Grande? I don't think they could build that wall in the middle of the Rio Grande,' he says earnestly.

'What is really needed here,' says Reyes finally,

> is not a wall, which would be ineffective and a waste of money. We need funds for better surveillance technology and more boots on the ground, more officers being hired for the Sheriff's Office,

> more agents for the Border Patrol and not just here but all the way along the border, all the way from California to Brownsville, Texas. A wall would be obsolete. There are hundreds of miles of wall in certain parts of Arizona, in the desert, and it is obsolete there too. Wherever there is a fence or a wall, people will find ways around it. They dig tunnels, they go over it, they find ways to go around it. I guess it's because of the drive to try and have a better life and stuff like that.

Stuff like that. People, families, children, the search for a better life. Immigrants being reunited with their families or striving for a better life. That might be the single most important cultural, political and economic cornerstone of our shared American history, the most unifying national characteristic: we are, and we always have been, a nation of immigrants. An immigrant nation. But Donald Trump was having none of that. He made immigration and securing the border with Mexico his biggest issue, and he unveiled his notorious plan to build a wall with Mexico on the very day that he declared his candidacy for the presidency of the United States.

It was on 16 June 2015, amid the kitsch glitter of a ballroom in Trump Tower, that Donald Trump declared his presidential bid. He did so with his trademark incendiary style, stoking fear and racism from the very start by accusing Mexico of sending 'criminals and rapists' and by promising to put an end to Barack Obama's attempts at immigration reform and start mass deportations. His solution? He would build a really big wall on the nation's southern border.

'I would build a great wall, and nobody builds walls better than me. Believe me. And I'll build it very inexpensively. I'll build a great, great wall on our southern border and I will have Mexico pay for that wall. Mark my words,' said Trump as he announced his campaign for the White House.[7]

Later on in his campaign Trump would refine his policy to a mantra, a chorus, and he would often stir up the crowd at a rally and gleefully lead his fans in a roaring chant that would become emblazoned upon America's collective consciousness like the refrain from a popular song on the radio: 'Build That Wall! Build That Wall!' they chanted in unison at the Republican National Convention in Cleveland. 'Build That Wall!' they chanted at Trump rallies in Texas and Arizona.

Trump had seized the mantle of immigration hardliner, with his frequent talk of setting up a Deportation Force and his regular ethnic slurs against Mexicans. The scorched earth policy worked; he would say anything, it seemed, no matter how outrageous or disconcerting. He would attack a Mexican-American judge.[8] He would speak of Mexican rapists and criminals.[9] He would make the building of the wall his signature theme, his trademark. It became more than a campaign slogan; it became a brand awareness tool for the brash billionaire from New York. Each utterance became more incendiary. In Trump's hands, the challenge of immigration became a matter of fighting 'illegal criminal aliens' who were pouring across the border. He pledged zero tolerance and made wild and unsubstantiated claims that there were 2 million undocumented immigrants with criminal records living in the United States.[10] In his dystopian view of things, it was easy: 'They don't come in here,' he said, 'because on Day One, my first hour in office, those people are gone!'[11]

Trump basked in the glory as hardline crowds repeated the chant, and then, on a late summer day at the end of August 2016, Trump refined his pledge in the purest of Trumpspeak. His ultimate proclamation came on 31 August 2016 during an emotional rally in Phoenix, Arizona, and just hours after flying down to Mexico City for a meeting with the hapless President of Mexico, Enrique Peña Nieto. The flying visit was meant to project statesmanship but it ended up looking more like an episode of *Celebrity Survivor*. That night, however, Trump went hardline again. He promised again to make Mexico pay '100 per cent' for the wall, and he declared at the top of his lungs that he would build an 'impenetrable, physical, tall, powerful, beautiful Southern border wall'.[12]

Impenetrable. Physical. Tall. Powerful. Beautiful.

A surprising number of Americans actually bought the pitch. In a nation of significant socio-economic unease at the lower rungs of society, in a nation still struggling with low growth nearly a decade after the onset of the Great Recession, in a nation where health care was not yet as affordable as the Obama administration might have desired, in a nation of resurgent and overt racism, in a nation where jobs for the unskilled were becoming scarcer and low-cost labour competition from newly arrived Mexicans could be seen as a threat, a surprisingly large number of people thought that maybe Trump had the right idea, perhaps he had the best solution. A huge number of Americans bought into Trump's populist rhetoric and believed that he was absolutely right about building a wall. The wall became Trump's biggest and best-known idea, his trademark piece, his *schtick*.

In July 2015, just one month after launching his presidential campaign, Trump came to Laredo, Texas.[13] He stepped off his Boeing 757 and donned his by now iconic white 'Make America Great Again' baseball cap for the first time that day. He spent more than four hours touring the border region in a lavish motorcade that was followed by two busloads full of reporters. The man who invited him to Laredo was an enthusiastic fan of Trump's who worked in law enforcement on the Rio Grande. His name was Hector Garza,[14] a Border Patrol agent but also a union official. Garza is president of Local 2455 in Laredo, part of the National Border Patrol Council, the union which brought together 16,500 Border Patrol agents at the national level.

'The Border Patrol – they're the ones that invited me here,'[15] said Trump after posing for eighteen assembled photographers and camera crews. He then left Laredo Airport and headed into town. He had come, Trump wanted everyone present to know, 'despite the great danger' to himself.[16]

Hector Garza is toying with a quesadilla and sipping a Diet Coke at the Palenque Grill, a well-regarded local eatery that specialises in

North Pacific Mexican cuisine. Mexican love songs are playing on the restaurant's creaky sound system and the place is full of Latino families and businessmen out for a treat. Garza is talking about cartels and border wars and why he loves Donald Trump. He mentions that Deputy Mario Reyes over at the Sheriff's Office is an old friend of his. 'We were in high school together here in Laredo, although he was a couple of grades ahead of me. He is a very good old friend of mine from high school,' says Garza.

Hector Garza beams with pride as he recalls how he first helped to engineer the Trump visit to Laredo. He smiles again when he recounts how he supported the endorsement of Trump by the National Border Patrol Council. Trump, says Garza, is the first politician to really understand the challenges faced by Border Patrol agents.

'You know, we are out there risking our lives every day and we are not getting the support we need,' complains Garza. He repeats the story told by his friend Mario Reyes of the multiple crossings by people smugglers and says it happens every day.

> We don't have enough manpower, and all of this is happening in an area that is 300 miles long and where there are as many as 500 attempts a day to cross the Rio Grande. Try to multiply what is happening here across the entire 2,000 miles of the US–Mexico border and you can see what we are up against.

Garza rolls his eyes up to the ceiling to make his point and complains that in his opinion the Obama administration has actually damaged efforts to secure the border with Mexico. 'Every time they talked about immigration reform and the path to citizenship it caused a surge in illegal crossings because everyone wanted to get in and take advantage of what they thought was going to be an amnesty,' says Garza.

But when he speaks of Donald Trump there is a twinkle in Hector Garza's eye. He is really proud of his union's decision to endorse Donald Trump for the White House, an announcement that was made at the height of the Republican primary season in March 2016.

'We need a person in the White House,' the National Border Patrol Council declared,

> who doesn't fear the media, who doesn't embrace political correctness, who doesn't need the money, who is familiar with success, who won't bow to foreign dictators, who is pro-military and values law enforcement, and who is angry for America and not subservient to the interests of other nations. Donald Trump is such a man.

Hector Garza smiles as he recalls the endorsement. He can't wait to tell the story of the small part he played it in Donald Trump's campaign against illegal immigration.

'When Mr Trump announced that he was running for President, he was talking strongly about border security, and as Border Patrol agents, we care about border security, we see it every day,' says Garza. 'So a lot of the statements that Mr Trump was making about the border resonated with the agents that our union represents. We invited Mr Trump to the border and Mr Trump did accept our invitation and he made a quick tour to the border.'

Garza recalls that he had to meet with Trump in private because the union had not yet endorsed him at the national level.

'I could tell that Mr Trump was concerned about the border and that his intentions were real. He was very interested in learning more about the border and trying to see how we can provide better border security,' recounts Garza.

'Our organisation was the first to talk to Mr Trump right here in Laredo. So we were happy when the rest of the locals came on board and they decided at a national level that we would endorse Mr Trump.'

When it comes to Donald Trump's signature promise to build a big and spectacular wall along the entire southern border and make

Mexico pay for it, even the ebullient Hector Garza nearly chokes on his tortilla.

'I, uh, I really don't have an opinion on Mexico paying for it,' says the slightly flushed local union official. 'I really don't have an opinion on that. What I can tell you is that we do need a physical barrier along the border in *some parts* of the border and in *some other areas* we just need better infrastructure and technology.'

'One of the biggest challenges that we have', says Agent Garza,

> is the lack of resources, lack of manpower, lack of technology along the border. For example, we have Border Patrol agents that go on in the field and they're not able to communicate with one another because of the lack of radio towers, and because sometimes the ones we have don't function. Another big issue that we have is the lack of infrastructure, the lack of roads, the lack of access to the border and the lack of lateral movement along the border.

Garza says it is this lack of easy access along the Rio Grande that accounts for the success of the people smugglers who launch the simultaneous group crossings at different places along the river. 'That is why we need better roads, quicker access to the river, better lateral movement,' he concludes.

Garza's friend Mario Reyes would agree. In the brotherhood of south Texas law enforcement, these men agree on about just about everything, except for Donald Trump's idea of building a great big impenetrable wall along the entire 2,000 miles of the US–Mexico border, somewhere next to or in the middle of the Rio Grande, through the scrub and up in the mountains, and across the scorching desert that divides the two countries between Brownsville, Texas on the Gulf of Mexico and San Diego on the Pacific Ocean.

Over in neighbouring Brooks County, in the town of Falfurrias, Texas, some ninety miles east of Laredo on the intersection of Texas State Highway 285 and US Highway 281, Sheriff Benny Martinez[17] has a slightly different point of view. But then Sheriff Martinez, who has to cover more than 900 square miles of rough terrain with a staff of just seven people, faces a different sort of challenge.

Sheriff Martinez has too many migrant corpses on his hands.

Falfurrias is a hardscrabble Texas town of 5,000 hardy souls 'that comprises mainly ranchland and scrub and abandoned oil and gas sites. It is home to the biggest inland highway checkpoint operated by the Border Patrol, the notorious Falfurrias Station on Highway 281, about seventy miles north of the Rio Grande and about an hour south of Corpus Christi. The challenge that Sheriff Martinez faces is not the catching and deporting of migrants who come through the checkpoint, hidden in the air ducts or engine blocks or in other hiding places in trailer trucks. That is the Border Patrol's job, and they do it pretty well out on Highway 281.

The problem that Sheriff Urbino 'Benny' Martinez of Brooks County faces is of a different order of magnitude because his role more often than not tends to involve recovering bodies. In some ways he is as much an undertaker as a policeman. Sheriff Martinez faces the truly horrible collateral damage of illegal immigration, almost every working day.

A lanky man of sixty in a military khaki shirt, blue jeans and cowboy boots, Sheriff Martinez is a gentle and hospitable fellow with a craggy face, with a wave of long and scraggly grey hair. He was a Texas State Trooper for twenty-nine years before he retired and got himself elected as Sheriff of Brooks County in November 2016, running unopposed on the Democratic ticket. He had previously served for years in Falfurrias as Chief Deputy Sheriff. Benny Martinez has been around the county for a very long time and he has pretty much seen it all, including the mass graves of migrants discovered a few years back out in the desert scrub. As the administrator of a budget of less than $1 million a year for both law enforcement and the running of the Brooks County Jail, Martinez complains that he doesn't have enough funds to meet the challenge and is still awaiting federal reimbursements for his off-budget emergency spending on what he euphemistically calls 'the recovery and the disposal of the deceased'.

'We have a checkpoint that probably runs at 10,000–11,000 vehicles per day, it is probably one of the busiest in the Southwest Corridor, and that means immigration, narcotics and in the nearby brush lots of dead bodies,' he confides with a sigh.

At the Falfurrias checkpoint over on Highway 281, lines of green-uniformed agents armed with automatic licence-plate readers talk to drivers and passengers about their citizenship while drug-sniffing dogs move up and down the lines of cars. High above the checkpoint, a massive blimp, which is called an aerostat, watches over the surrounding brush and ranchland, searching for migrants or smugglers who are dropped off just south of the checkpoint so they can try to make the long walk around it.

'We call them drop-offs,' says Sheriff Martinez, describing the groups of migrants that smugglers will leave in the area just south of the Falfurrias checkpoint. They will be dropped off, Martinez explains, so that they can then travel on foot across the remote and rugged terrain and across the county, to be picked up at a highway north of the checkpoint so that can then continue their journey into the interior of the United States. The problem, says the sheriff, is not that there are too many drop-offs who make the trek and manage to evade the checkpoint. The problem is that too many of the drop-offs don't make it through the trek.

'Often there will be a vehicle that is carrying ten to fifteen passengers who are undocumented crossers. They get dropped off and they go off into the brush,' recounts Martinez. 'During their journey across this rough and treacherous terrain they often get lost or they get injured. When they get sick or they can't keep up, they get left behind. So we have to go into the brush for the recovery of the deceased, the bodies,' says Martinez, his voice trailing off in sadness as he recalls cases of older Mexican migrants he has found dead and the corpses of mothers and infants trying to make it across the hostile terrain.

'That's just one issue,' he continues.

> The other issue is that the young females that are coming across usually get violated. They get sexually assaulted as they come across. So, that's another issue that we have to deal with. Then you have the issues of those who are wanted for crimes like murder in different states. So, we hold those until they are transported to respective states. So that's what happens here in Brooks County.

Martinez goes on to explain that while the journey itself is long and hard, the smugglers tend to minimise the risk when they drop off their human cargo. 'They're just told to start walking, for two or three days. But it takes a little bit longer than that and they are crossing a very sandy terrain. It's really very sandy. You know, we have huge sand dunes out there. This is the coastal south,' notes the sheriff.

> The vegetation is thick. The motte out there is a very thick shrub, a thick bush, and it's very hard to get through. So the migrants will try and go underneath it. They'll find a way to get in there. But often they don't bring enough food or enough water, enough things to survive the elements out there, and they're probably walking for five or six days, a thirty-mile trek over treacherous terrain.

It is in this extreme terrain, and in these extreme conditions, that Sheriff Martinez has handled the deaths of hundreds of migrants, and he has had to call for extra resources to deal with this, the raw side of America's immigration problem. Although immigration is a federal issue and the Border Patrol is part of the Department of Homeland Security, the local Sheriff's Office is tasked with recovering the dead and handling arrested drug smugglers and other criminals before they are put on trial. Perhaps that is why Sheriff Martinez seems so overwhelmed.

As an elected sheriff and as a Democrat, Benny Martinez bristles with indignation at the mention of Donald Trump and his idea of building a wall.

'I don't agree with the wall,' says Martinez pensively.

> I truly believe that what we need is more resources on the ground, more boots on the ground and more technology. A wall would just give more funding to the private sector versus actually trying to solve the issue. We have to distinguish between the criminal element that comes across and the mother and child. I've yet to see a mother and child who are crossing over the border as a threat to the United States. I would rather go after the criminal element who leave these people out there to die on the brush, knowing that they are going to die.

As for the other big idea in Donald Trump's anti-immigration platform, that of mass deportations, that doesn't look so attractive either to this first-generation American sheriff whose parents both came from Mexico. Benny Martinez grimaces at the idea of separating families and trying to deport America's 11 million undocumented immigrants.

'They should stay in the United States,' says Martinez.

> Some of them have been around for twenty years. They should be allowed to become citizens if they have made a life here and [if] they pay taxes then they are contributing to the economy. Even though they are undocumented, they have to rent some place. They have to eat. They have to have transportation to get to and from work. So they are creating economic growth.

In fact, despite all the scaremongering about Mexican immigrants during the 2016 presidential campaign, there is abundant evidence that Trump's claims about the supposed hordes of Mexican criminals pouring over the border were without any foundation in truth, as were his claims that the immigrants were taking away American jobs.

In September 2016, just weeks ahead of Election Day, an authoritative 500-page study of the economic impact of immigration would offer the last word on what had by now become a white-hot campaign issue in the race for the White House.[18] The report from the National Academies of Sciences, Engineering and Medicine concluded that immigration does more good than harm to the economy and even called immigration 'integral to the nation's economic growth'.

'The prospects for long-run economic growth in the United States would be considerably dimmed without the contributions of high-skilled immigrants,' the report said.

Immigrants, as the report noted, bring new ideas and add labour to an American workforce that would otherwise be shrinking. In historic terms, it was clear that waves of immigrants coming into the US had over time helped grow the economy. The report also said that contrary to Trump's claims that jobs were being lost and wages were being driven down, there had been little noticeable impact on the wages or employment levels of native-born Americans as a result of immigration.

The study, featuring more than twenty of the nation's leading academics, was the first such broad look at immigration in nearly two decades. It was published in the autumn of 2016, at the most heated moment of debate over the topic during the presidential race. But it was largely ignored.

'Immigration enlarges the economy while leaving the native population slightly better off on average, but the greatest beneficiaries of immigration are the immigrants themselves as they avail themselves of opportunities not available to them in their home countries,' the report concluded. Immigration, it said, had also led to more innovation, more entrepreneurship and greater technological change across the economy.

The federal economy, meanwhile, benefits from first-generation immigrants because they pay taxes and utilise few federal benefits, such as social security and Medicare.

The number of immigrants now living in the United States is approximately 43 million people, just a little over 13 per cent of the population.[19] Immigrants are defined as foreign-born residents of the United States, be they naturalised citizens, lawful permanent residents, visa holders or the unauthorised. If you add the American-born children of immigrants to the mix, it turns out that one in every four Americans is either an immigrant or the child of one. Immigrants in the United States and their US-born children now number approximately 81 million people, or 26 per cent of the overall population.[20]

In a recent analysis of immigration trends by the Pew Research Center, Mexican immigrants accounted for approximately 28 per cent of the foreign born in the United States, making them by far the largest immigrant group in the country.[21] But India and China were trailing closely behind, and by 2013 Mexicans had fallen to third place in terms of the flow of new immigrants, behind both India and China.[22] In Donald Trump's numerous anti-immigrant harangues, he never seemed keen to speak of the Indians or the Chinese who had filled the halls of Harvard and Yale and Silicon Valley, bringing with them technology innovation, a huge strength in software, engineering and the sciences, and a disproportionately large contribution to the management of high-tech industries and the success of many innovative businesses in the American economy.

Trump was focused instead on the criminal aliens, on the bad *hombres*[23] who would come surging over the border and take everything away from us. In his dystopian vision, there was an uncontrollable flow of bad guys coming from Mexico, a rising tide that could not be stopped. The hard data reveals a starkly different reality.

More Mexican immigrants have actually returned to Mexico from the US than have migrated here since the end of the Great Recession, according to the Pew study.[24] Census data for the period from 2009 to 2014 shows that 1 million Mexicans and their families, including US-born children, left the US for Mexico while a smaller number, an estimated 870,000 Mexican nationals, actually left Mexico to come to the United States.

The Pew analysis ascribed the net drop in the flow of Mexican immigrants to several reasons, including the fact that the lethargic recovery of the US economy after the Great Recession had made the US less attractive to potential Mexican migrants. Contrary to Trump's more paranoid assertions, the Pew data showed that stricter enforcement of US immigration laws at the US–Mexico border had also contributed to the reduction of Mexican immigrants coming to the US in recent years. Even without The Wall.

As for the 11 million undocumented immigrants living in the United States, the families who had become the target of Trump's set speech on immigration, it turned out that a large majority, two thirds of them, had lived in the US for at least a decade. The median period was more than thirteen years. Sure, just over half the 11 million unauthorised immigrants were from Mexico, but only 7 per cent of the Mexican unauthorised immigrants had lived in the US for less than five years, the Pew study found.[25] Like other immigrants who had come to seek their fortune in America, they had settled down, raised families and for the most part contributed to their communities.

The problem today for Mexican immigrants, and for all other Americans who are concerned with the immigration debate, is not the facts and figures. These are clear enough. It is the fact that for several years now, and long before the arrival of Donald Trump, there has been a swelling in the ranks of anti-immigrant and xenophobic politicians in America. The Tea Party has played its part in influencing many Republicans. Radical anti-immigrant leaders have made wild-eyed assertions for many years in places like Arizona, where for a time, and until the intervention of the Supreme Court, overtly racist state laws allowed law enforcement officials to conduct random racial profiling on any Arizona street corner.[26] For years, the fear-mongering has grown, throughout America and not just throughout America's south-west. By the time Donald Trump came on the scene in June 2015, the gap between reality and populist rhetoric on immigration had already widened, and not just in the United States.

Across the entire Western world, in more than a dozen advanced democracies, a wave of anti-immigrant sentiment and populist rhetoric had turned into a tsunami of hate-driven politics that ended up threatening some of the most basic tenets of how responsible politicians and political leaders conduct public discourse in a democracy. Extreme populist groups, often making immigration their primary campaign issue, had doubled and tripled their share of the national vote across Europe, jumping from 5 per cent to 10 or 15 per cent and even higher in many countries.

In Europe, as in the United States, nativism, xenophobia and anti-immigrant politics used to live out on the political fringe. Mainstream politicians of the centre-left or centre-right did not make gratuitous attacks on illegal immigrants, nor did they stoke the fears of working-class voters who might feel threatened by immigrants. It was not considered acceptable in public discourse in either the United States or Europe to make ethnic slurs or to speak of racial profiling or to propose banning entire religions or ethnic groups from entering a country. In the United States, between June 2015 and November 2016, Donald Trump had broken all the taboos. He had introduced an inflammatory rhetoric and rabble-rousing technique that seemed to incite anger, fear and hate. For his harshest critics, but also for any student of history, his style and his pronouncements seemed to resemble the virulent rhetoric that had been employed in the 1930s by Adolf Hitler and members of the Nazi Party in Germany.

In Britain, meanwhile, at the height of the US presidential campaign in June 2016, more than half of British voters decided in a national referendum to leave the European Union.[27] After more than forty years of membership, a Trump-like nationalist named

Nigel Farage and an erratic former Mayor of London named Boris Johnson, led the Leave campaign to victory, to their much-cherished goal of Brexit. Front and centre in the Brexit campaign there had been a drive to stop immigrants, a proposal to secure the borders, a pitch to the fears of the working class, a clever preying on fears of economic insecurity. It was only months after the Brexit vote that disillusioned voters in places like Sunderland in the north of England realised that their local car factories had only been kept alive thanks to European Union subsidies, which would now be promptly cancelled as the UK was planning to give up its EU membership. Half of the support for Brexit was driven by a fear of immigrants. The other half was sheer ignorance. The financial and economic costs to Britain will likely be heavy, and it is unlikely that Prime Minister Theresa May will succeed in retaining free trade with the European Union without budging on other issues, such as the free movement of people, and the entry of immigrants into Britain.

In France, on the eve of another presidential election, the party that has consistently polled the biggest number of supporters is the National Front, a one-time fringe party whose leader, Jean-Marie Le Pen, was best known for his anti-Semitic and anti-immigrant tirades. His daughter, Marine Le Pen, now leads a toned-down version of the old National Front, but she still whips up the crowds with her anti-immigrant populism and even though she was defeated in the presidential election in France in May 2017, Marine Le Pen still got more than one third of the national vote.[28] She is still a factor in French politics.

In Germany, the anti-immigrant fringe party Alternative für Deutschland (AfD) seems to be a lesser threat, and Chancellor Angela Merkel is well positioned to fend off the wave of populism and secure another term. Yet Merkel, who used to be a much-loved and respected figure, has risked her political career over the thorny subject of immigration. Her open-door policy for refugees from the Middle East carried a heavy political cost, but she was eventually able to regain her footing. As the leader of a country that had forced millions to flee when it committed genocide back in the 1940s, her actions seemed reasonable. But it turned out that Merkel had made the mistake of her political life in 2015 when she said that Germany would open its doors to a million refugees from the bloody war in Syria. Merkel's open-border policy created political confusion and sent her poll numbers down, but when she tried to walk back her commitment, that had an even more disruptive impact on German politics. The new American President meanwhile poured gas on the flames by attacking Merkel's immigration policy and calling it 'a catastrophic mistake'. But Trump is not well loved in Germany, which tends to prefer the current President's predecessor, Barack Obama. And Angela Merkel, strangely enough, may be emerging as the Western world's premier statesperson, the wisest and most moderate leader on either side of the Atlantic.

In Hungary, Prime Minister Viktor Orbán, a 'mini-Trump' populist if ever there was one, has clamped down on the media and built barbed-wire fences and walls to keep refugees and migrants from entering his country. He preaches against Muslims; he scorns the idea of taking any refugees into Hungary.

In Italy, the anti-immigrant Northern League has seen its appeal expand and now commands 13 to 14 per cent in the national polls. Matteo Salvini, the party's demagogic leader, has made a point of forging a strong friendship with Marine Le Pen in France. His adoration of Donald Trump is evident in all his public statements and he even travelled to a Trump rally in Philadelphia and got himself a selfie, if not the candidate's full attention. But it is the populist anti-establishment party led by right-wing comedian Beppe Grillo that most closely resembles a Trumpist movement in Italy. The Five Star Movement is probably Italy's single most popular party, and to avoid a populist takeover of the government in upcoming elections, former Prime Minister Matteo Renzi may well find himself needing the support of Silvio Berlusconi, the controversial 81-year-old media mogul and former Prime Minister. Berlusconi, although still ineligible to hold public office because of a 2013 criminal conviction on tax fraud, nonetheless leads the rump of his old party, Forza Italia, and could help Renzi block Grillo's populists.

In the Netherlands, anti-Muslim and nationalist firebrand Geert Wilders surged to the top of Dutch opinion polls but then lost the election.[29] He wants to stop Muslim immigration, ban the Koran and generally stop any immigration whatsoever. For years, Wilders has been building his political base on the fears of the less educated and less well off in his country. His Party for Freedom may not be governing, but it has a prominent position in Parliament.

In all of these countries, but also in Sweden, Finland and Denmark, and in Austria, Switzerland and Slovakia, xenophobic and often racist politicians have seen their fortunes rise. Anti-immigrant politics and extremist populism have flourished against the landscape of fear and anger, with the threat of jihadist terrorism thrown into the mix.

What Trump had in common with his European counterparts was an ability to preach his demagogy to the poorest classes of society, the least educated, the most unskilled workers, and to whip up an anti-immigrant sentiment with incendiary rhetoric. In the rise of populism across the West in recent years, the target of populist politicians has more often than not been the economic have-nots, those who live with the greatest degree of economic insecurity. This was certainly the case in Britain, where the Leave vote prevailed mostly among the less educated at the lower rungs of society.[30]

What made things worse in Britain, and in France and Germany and in the United States, was that the economic insecurity argument was frequently blended together with a more primordial fear that often played on latent racism and which was mainly about immigrants as a threat to cultural identity. This was part of the subtext in Trump's harangues against Mexicans. But the same could be said of the anti-Muslim rhetoric of Trump and so many other populists in the United States and in Europe. At a time of rising terrorism, with voters everywhere numbed by the scenes of carnage on the television news, it was grotesque but quite natural for Donald Trump and his European counterparts to make the fear of 'radical Islamic terrorism' a companion piece to their anti-immigrant harangue. Anti-Muslim politics has paid off for many extremist and populist parties, who suddenly discovered that they were no longer fringe. They had become mainstream.

In the entire debate over immigration that has divided America in recent years, perhaps the nastiest, the most outrageous, the most insidious and openly racist idea, was the proposal to ban all Muslims from entering the United States, an idea that was Trump's mantra for many months.[31] He would later try to refine the ban on Muslims to an ill-defined programme of 'extreme vetting', but when he came to office he would make one of his first acts of business the signing of an executive order placing a temporary ban on refugees and immigrants coming from Syria, Iraq, Iran, Libya, Somalia, Yemen and Sudan, on the grounds that terrorists might try to sneak into the United States from these countries disguised as refugees.[32] Yet Donald Trump, like many populist politicians in Europe, made the Muslims his principal target and blended anti-Muslim rhetoric into his anti-immigrant speeches. The racial anger in Trump's populist rhetoric went right off the deep end and for a time it began to sound very much like the resurgent nationalism of the 1930s. Donald Trump was, after all, the man who fully five years before the 2016 presidential election campaign had suggested that Barack Obama, the first African-American President of the United States, had not been born in the United States.[33]

Obama's efforts to find a solution to America's immigration crisis were to prove noble and constant. But he would ultimately fail. For years he could not persuade a Republican-controlled Congress to take an enlightened or common-sense approach to immigration reform, and his own attempts to impose immigration reform by way of executive order would eventually come unstuck, along with his much of his legacy on immigration policy, by a June 2016 ruling from a divided Supreme Court.[34]

Obama was not the only President to see his dreams of

immigration reform thwarted by the Republican right on Capitol Hill. His predecessor in the White House, George W. Bush, also failed during his entire eight years in office to achieve immigration reform, mainly because of opposition from right-wingers and radicals inside his own party.[35]

When Bush became President in 2001, he owed a piece of his victory to his ability to charm and persuade America's Latino community. Although today, in the wake of the Trump phenomenon, it might seem unusual for a Republican candidate to take such a position, George W. Bush actually cared about immigration reform and made it one of his national priorities while still a presidential candidate, back in 1999.[36] He went courting Latino votes in California, New Mexico, Arizona, Texas, Florida and New York. As a candidate, he emphasised his deep cultural connections to Mexico, reminding Latino voters that he spoke Spanish and that his brother Jeb Bush, then Florida's governor, was married to a Mexican-American woman.

Just weeks after taking office, Bush travelled to visit President Vicente Fox at his ranch in the central Mexican state of Guanajuato. The two leaders, both fond of cowboy boots and big talk, developed an immediate rapport. During that visit to Fox's ranch, they also mapped out plans for a coordinated approach to trade, drug enforcement and border security. On the thorny subject of Mexican immigrants,[37] Bush foresaw letting in more Mexicans as temporary workers and speeding up the transition to US citizenship, a position that would have been unthinkable for a Republican in the poisonous and partisan atmosphere of the 2016 election campaign.

The hardening of Republican views and the internecine battles inside the Republican Party between hardliners and moderates would paralyse the immigration issue for many years. Today it would be inconceivable for a Republican to be as 'liberal' on immigration as George W. Bush appears across the prism of time. Even more surprising, for those who have only known the incendiary rhetoric of Trump's anti-immigrant populism, is the fact that it was none other than President Ronald Reagan who signed into law the single biggest amnesty for undocumented Mexican immigrants in post-war history,[38] which back in 1986 provided around 3 million people with a path to citizenship.[39]

In the past, the most important immigration laws have traditionally been negotiated and agreed in a bipartisan manner in Congress. After all, they concern the highly sensitive issues of securing the nation's borders and deciding the rules under which immigrants can come to and remain in America. But the last successful and sweeping bipartisan immigration bill was passed more than a quarter of a century ago, in 1990.[40] It was Reagan's successor – President George Herbert Walker Bush – who signed a comprehensive overhaul of immigration that helped shape the pathway to legalisation for many unauthorised immigrants. Bush Sr signed the bill into law with a smiling Senator Teddy Kennedy, the bill's chief sponsor and patron, standing behind him in the Oval Office. Democratic Senator Ted Kennedy and Republican President George Bush, united on immigration reform. How times change. Ronald Reagan and George Herbert Walker Bush were actually the Presidents who did the most on immigration reform, and even the second Bush presidency began life on a hopeful note.

George W. Bush's plan to push through a deal on what he called 'guest workers' was sincere enough, in the summer of 2001. But immigration reform soon fell by the wayside, and for all the wrong reasons. President Fox actually came to Washington, on 5 September 2001, and he and Bush held their immigration summit, as planned.[41] Yet even before the ideas could be drafted into formal legislation, Bush began facing strong opposition from members of his own party. They were bitterly opposed to anything that could be considered a legalisation of immigrants and they labelled the idea an amnesty. Bush was already on the defensive.

What might have happened thereafter is anyone's guess, because the hand of fate intervened. The attacks on 11 September 2001 on the World Trade Center and the Pentagon immediately shifted the debate, making border security the paramount issue for the Bush administration and for the American public. Suddenly the border with Mexico was just another potential site of terrorist infiltration and President Bush was forced to set aside all attempts at immigration reform as he prepared to fight Al Qaeda and eventually Saddam Hussein. In all of his eight years in office, Bush never achieved anything on immigration reform. His early good intentions died on September 11 and for the rest of his time in office he faced too much opposition from inside his own party and too many distractions from the two wars he had started. Meanwhile, during the Bush years, many Congressional and Senate Republicans were undergoing a process of self-radicalisation' on immigration policy, just as they would on gun control and the Second Amendment, and on so many other issues that affected the shape and nature of American society.

When Barack Obama took office in 2009, he pledged to fix the broken immigration system with an ambitious set of legislative initiatives that would improve border enforcement and create a path to legal status for illegal immigrants. The aim was to allow the more than 11 million undocumented immigrants living across America to emerge from the shadows.

From 2009 to 2013, Tom Jawetz[42] served as chief counsel on the Immigration Subcommittee of the House Judiciary Committee, where he advised members of Congress and congressional staff on all areas of immigration law and policy. He watched Obama's dealings with Congress up close over the years and he was part of the process. Today Jawetz is vice-president of immigration policy at the Center for American Progress, a progressive Washington think tank.

Jawetz admits it has been painful to watch the way Congress has failed to deal with the immigration crisis and throughout both the eight years of the Bush administration and the succeeding eight years of the Obama administration.

'Our immigration system has not been reformed by Congress in any meaningful way in over twenty-five years. Yet we have a strong demand for immigrant labor in our workforce and millions of working families that risk being ripped apart,' says Jawetz. 'What we have really in America is an immigration system that has not kept up with the modern-day demands of our society, and one of the effects of that is we have ended up with a large unauthorised population.'

Jawetz reels off a long list of failed immigration reform efforts in Congress. He says there have been plenty of attempts to help design an immigration system that better reflects contemporary society. He recognises the goodwill of President George W. Bush back in 2001 before his efforts were shelved by the September 11 attacks. He says that Obama certainly signalled his intention to tackle immigration back in 2009 but then other, more urgent priorities prevailed, like dealing with the aftermath of the Great Recession, the collapse of Lehman Brothers and a full-scale financial crisis. Jawetz recalls:

> Clearly, in the midst of a financial collapse, the priority was going to be first and foremost stimulating the economy and dealing with our economic difficulties, and then another urgent policy priority for Obama was health care reforms. So immigration reform didn't happen. In 2010, the House passed a law which would have provided a path to citizenship for 'Dreamers', a defined set of young people who came to this country as children and who are American in everything but name. But that bill did not pass the Senate.

The last time the Obama administration would see any daylight from Congress on immigration reform was just after the 2012 presidential election that saw Republican nominee Mitt Romney go down in defeat. Republicans were still nursing their wounds and many were shocked at Obama's winning 71 per cent of the Hispanic vote. Romney's ill-judged remarks about deportation only worsened his losses among Latino voters, or so the pollsters proclaimed.

'After the 2012 election,' recalls Jawetz,

> there was a general consensus view among many Republicans that they had to put their opposition to immigration reform behind them, they had to become champions of immigration reform, that the Latino community wouldn't listen to them if they continue to be opposed to immigration reform. That momentum helped us for about six months.

In those six months, America's best chance at a major bipartisan reform was suddenly back on the table. Republicans, reeling from the Romney defeat and the collapse of the Latino vote, immediately coalesced behind immigration reform. Senator Charles Schumer of New York launched a bipartisan effort to write a comprehensive immigration reform bill, and early in 2013 he brought together four Democrats and four Republican senators in a group that became known as the 'Gang of Eight'. Among the Republican senators were Marco Rubio of Florida and John McCain of Arizona.

On Tuesday 16 April 2013, the Gang of Eight introduced on to the floor of the Senate the Border Security, Economic Opportunity, and Immigration Modernization Act of 2013, a genuinely bipartisan immigration law that had been produced during months of private negotiations by the Gang of Eight.[43]

Just one day later, on 17 April 2013, the Senate would vote down another bipartisan attempt, the famous background check improvements that gun control advocates had been pleading for ever since the recent tragedy at the Sandy Hook Elementary School.[44] Senator Rubio may have been part of the Gang of Eight on immigration, but a day after that law was presented, Rubio, still a darling of the Tea Party, helped defeat the gun control law.

The Gang of Eight's immigration reform law would essentially revamp much of the US immigration system. It would establish a thirteen-year path to citizenship for millions of undocumented immigrants, with several security benchmarks that had to be met in order to obtain a green card. The law would have added huge new resources to strengthen border security and it even required a mandatory workplace verification system for employers, in an attempt to ensure that jobs would only be given to immigrants who were authorised to work in the United States. It was a compromise law, but on balance it was an important step forward.

In the spring of 2013 there was still enough momentum for the Gang of Eight to push their legislation through the Senate. At the end of June, the Senate passed the immigration reforms by a vote of sixty-eight to thirty-two.[45] No fewer than fourteen Republican voters had crossed the aisle to vote with Democrats.

'The strong bipartisan vote we took today', proclaimed an ebullient Senator Schumer, 'is going to send a message across the country, and it's going to send a message to the other end of the Capitol as well. The bill has generated a level of support that we believe will be impossible for the House to ignore.'[46]

Senator Schumer was wrong. The House of Representatives, under the leadership of Speaker John Boehner, was perfectly willing and able to ignore the Senate legislation, and it did precisely that. Soon after the Senate approved the bill, it became clear that the Gang of Eight's valiant effort was not going anywhere.

Tom Jawetz, who followed the drama from a front-row seat in Congress, said that while many Republicans had been sensitive to Mitt Romney's devastatingly poor performance among Latinos, there was also a growing 'counter-narrative' about the lessons that Republicans should glean from the 2012 election:

> The counter-narrative that developed was that the 2012 election wasn't lost by Romney because he failed to turn out enough Latino voters. It was that he failed to turn out enough white voters, and they failed to support him in large enough margins. So the idea was that you could be a successful Republican candidate if you could track down those missing white voters. I don't think it's possible to truly understand Trump's candidacy without understanding how he was essentially pursuing this 'missing white voter' story that had been put out by all the pundits as a political strategy.

The result of the 2016 presidential election campaign suggests that the original Republican post-mortem on 2012 was actually wrong, and this counter-narrative was correct. At the end of the day, Trump certainly did not go after lost Latino voters. He pursued even more disgruntled white voters. And he won.

In any case, after the 2014 mid-term elections, Barack Obama was stuck. He was pretty much stalemated on Capitol Hill, in many areas but especially on immigration. Early that year, desperate to probe the limits of his presidential powers and try to do something to at least alleviate the condition of the millions of undocumented workers and their children who feared deportation, Obama had commissioned a study. He had directed the Secretary of Homeland Security to begin studying the immigration system to explore what administrative changes could be made to improve things without requiring Congressional approval.

'There was a lot of back and forth on this,' recalls Jawetz. 'Some people said that Obama should hold off because otherwise he was going to pre-empt the Congress, and in the end the administration held off significantly to give Congress breathing room. But it was becoming clear that the legislative effort was dead.'

It was amid this Congressional gridlock in November 2014, just days after the mid-term elections in which the Republicans had won control of Congress, that Obama made his move. He issued a flurry of executive actions on immigration, the most controversial of which was the one which would grant up to 5 million unauthorised immigrants and their children protection from deportation.[47]

In a nationally televised address, Obama declared:

> If you've been in America for more than five years, if you have children who are American citizens or legal residents, if you register for a criminal background check and you are willing to pay your fair share of taxes, you'll be able to apply to stay in this country temporarily without fear of deportation.

'You can come out of the shadows and get right with the law,' he added.[48]

The Republicans immediately accused Obama of abuse of power, of taking illegal and unconstitutional actions. The White House did its best to defend itself. Obama promised to 'take steps to deal responsibly with the millions of undocumented immigrants who live and work in our country'.

Unfortunately for Obama, the Supreme Court would eventually deal a deadly blow to his controversial executive orders on immigration. The actions had already been blocked by lower courts, who stopped their implementation after Texas and twenty-five other states sued, claiming the President had no power to order the changes.[49] In June 2016, the Supreme Court, by now without its Associate Justice the late Antonin Scalia, found itself deadlocked in a 4–4 vote on an appeal against the lower court.[50] In other words, the block on Obama's executive orders had been upheld by the highest court in the land. Obama's immigration legacy was suddenly imperilled.

As far as the Republicans were concerned, it was a great victory. Donald Trump was ecstatic. By the time the Supreme Court announced its deadlock in June 2016, Trump had already been on the scene for a full year, touting his plans for building a wall along with mass deportations. He reacted to the Supreme Court deadlock with a trademark tweet and a pledge that as President he would nominate only really tough Supreme Court judges who liked the idea of deportations and building really big walls to keep criminals and rapists out of the country. Trump tweeted that the court has 'kept us safe from exec amnesty -- for now'.[51]

As soon as Trump became President, he moved to sign his own executive orders on immigration, making good on his campaign promise to build a wall and telling agents of ICE and the Border Patrol that they should vigorously enforce the law against 'all the criminals and drug dealers' coming in from Mexico. The message was clear.

With Donald Trump at the White House, with Jeff Sessions, an anti-immigrant hardliner as Attorney General,[52] and with a Republican majority in the Congress, the entire paradigm of the immigration debate shifted, and quite radically. Trump rode a wave of anti-immigrant rhetoric to the White House, and as President he began to push through some of his most extreme ideas. By now there can be no doubt that US immigration policy has shifted dramatically away from Obama's attempts to create pathways to citizenship for the 11 million undocumented immigrants. Donald Trump has opted instead for the most intransigent and hardline position imaginable.

The simple reality is that the candidate with the harshest anti-immigrant platform in living memory is now the President of the United States.

CHAPTER SEVEN

OBAMA CARED

Gary Brock[1] considers himself a lucky man. The 59-year-old Maryland native lives a happy life together with his partner in a small house in the north Florida community of Ormond Beach, just an hour north of Orlando. Gary is a lean and boyish fellow in a Hawaiian shirt and flip-flops, seated in his favourite armchair in the tiny living room of a modest property in the Tomoka Meadows housing development. He sports a baseball cap and a set of tattoos up and down his arms and legs. The odour of dogs fills the house, but for now Gary has put the German Shepherds out in the garden, along with the family pig. Gary is saying that he has just celebrated his first anniversary of working as a server at the local steakhouse, where he takes home $5.07 an hour plus tips, below the minimum wage, and if he doesn't make enough tips they raise his hourly pay to the $7.25 minimum wage. He usually works a forty-hour week.

Ormond Beach is a township of nearly 40,000 people, where nearly half of the population lives on less than $25,000 a year, so Ormond Beach ranks as something of a low-income north Florida community. Its pristine white sandy beaches are filled with endless rows of big and boxy SUVs that drive right onto the beach and open their tailgates, the American way, a drive-by sort of visit to the beach, a hike from the tailgate twenty feet to the water's edge and back. Ormond Beach is filled with cheap fast food establishments, in all sorts of ethnic varieties. Gary has found a job at one of the more upscale restaurants. He has worked in the fast food industry for most of his life, although for a while he used to cut hair. He says that throughout his working life, in his many jobs, he could never afford health insurance. Until now.

'In the past I didn't have any health insurance. Most of the places where I worked didn't offer any health benefits, or it simply wasn't affordable, it wasn't even something I could think about getting,' he says matter-of-factly.

So how did Gary Brock get by for all these years?

'Basically I was just lucky,' he replies.

> I've always taken good care of myself and I have been healthy. But the first accident that happened to me was when I broke my wrist, and I didn't have health insurance. So I went to the emergency room, and there was a big bill for the emergency room. Then I had to be transported to a hospital to have emergency surgery. It was thousands of dollars! I wanted to do my part to pay, but I couldn't afford the thousands of dollars.

He says he first heard about Obama's controversial plan to offer nearly universal health care to all Americans back in 2008, during the presidential campaign.

> When the President was campaigning, I mean he talked about health insurance, and I was like thinking: 'Yes! That's something I'm definitely for.' I've always wanted to have health insurance. And when it became a reality after President Obama was elected and the Affordable Care Act was passed in 2010, I was very happy.
>
> Back then I was working at the fast food chain Denny's, with a woman who was a Democratic Party activist named Sharon, and she asked me to help make calls and tell people they could now get Obamacare. I said, 'Sure.' I'm excited about Obamacare for myself and I will do everything I can to get other people signed up ... So when the online health exchanges opened up in 2013, I couldn't wait. I got enrolled and went through the whole process.

> And I remember getting my first doctor. I was driving back from work and I saw a sign for Florida Blue Cross and Blue Shield for Florida. So I stopped by. There was a little doctor's office and I walked right in and said: 'Do you take Obamacare?' And the receptionist said: 'Yeah, we do.' So she took my name and number, and that's how I started with the doctor that I'm with now, Dr Tamaris. And the next thing I know I'm with the same doctor and I just felt very grateful that this receptionist went out of her way to help me with the Obamacare.

The insurance policy that Gary Brock enrolled for had a market cost of nearly $500 a month, nearly half of his monthly take-home pay. But the Obamacare plan gave Gary Brock a $470 tax credit, effectively a federal subsidy. The Florida waiter smiles with sincere gratitude.

'So I used the whole entire tax credit, and that brought my bill down to just $26 a month. And I thought this is great, for $26 a month I have an unlimited number of doctor visits and full coverage if there is an emergency.'

Soon after signing up for Obamacare, he accidentally got some poison in his eye.

> I had to go to the emergency room and have them clean up my eye. Thank God I had Obamacare. All it cost me to go to the emergency room was $50, where normally it would have been hundreds of dollars. And now my prescriptions cost me just $10 each. I do have an ongoing prescription that I have to take for shingles. That prescription would have normally cost me $248, but now I pay just $10. That makes a big difference for somebody like me.

Brock remembers another experience soon after he signed up for Obamacare:

> When I first got this health insurance, the doctor looked at me and

> he asked if I had ever gotten my colon checked. I said: 'Never, I've never had full lab work,' and I got that done, my first colonoscopy. That bill was $1,734. There is no way I could have ever paid that. But it was covered.

Then, smiling, he adds: 'I love my Obamacare.'

When Obamacare was signed into law in March 2010,[2] nearly 50 million Americans, more than 16 per cent of the US population, were like Gary Brock: completely uninsured, unprotected, without any health insurance whatsoever.[3] By 2016, thanks to Obamacare, that number had dropped to less than 30 million people, just above 9 per cent of the population.[4] That means that between 2010 and 2016 roughly 20 million Americans, including those with pre-existing conditions, were able to get health insurance for themselves and their families, most of them for the first time in their lives.

It is this number which most significantly describes the legacy of Barack Obama and of the much-maligned Obamacare. It is the number of Americans who today, for the first time in their lives, actually have some form of protection against otherwise prohibitive and unregulated medical costs. The big pharmaceuticals lobby has made sure that most prescription drug prices are unregulated, and medical costs have soared so much that many Americans still go bankrupt because of healthcare expenses. Yet thanks to the tax credit subsidies offered by Obamacare to low-income families, most of these 20 million Americans now pay less than $100 a month in cash for their health insurance.[5]

Unfortunately, the rollout of Obamacare's website did not go very well in 2013. There were plenty of glitches. The site didn't work at first. There was much confusion, as would be expected at a time of major change in the rules.[6] At the same time, the programme came under constant political attack from Republicans from the moment the legislation was first discussed in 2009, while the many imperfections of the Affordable Care Act have left millions of people still unable to get health coverage or Medicaid, falling into what is called 'the donut hole'.[7] To make matters worse, the cost of Obamacare premiums began jumping wildly just weeks ahead of the November 2016 election, with millions of lower-middle-class Americans now facing a rise in costs that was unsustainable again.[8]

Bill Clinton inadvertently admitted as much, with a campaign gaffe of significant proportions. While on the road in Flint, Michigan in early October 2016, the Democratic candidate's husband did the Trump campaign's dirty work for them, unintentionally. He called President Obama's signature policy reform 'the craziest thing in the world' and criticised the Affordable Care Act (ACA) for causing premiums to rise for many middle-class Americans who do not qualify for subsidies.

'So you've got this crazy system', declared Clinton, 'where all of a sudden 25 million more people have health care and then the people who are out there busting it, sometimes sixty hours a week, wind up with their premiums doubled and their coverage cut in half. It's the craziest thing in the world.'[9]

Oops.

Trump and the Republicans were gleeful. 'Just delicious. Bill Clinton slams ObamaCare as "craziest thing in the world"', tweeted Kellyanne Conway,[10] Trump's campaign manager.

A day later, at a rally in Ohio, Clinton tried to walk back his remarks, but he only made things worse. 'For the first time in our history, we are providing insurance to at least 90 per cent of our people,' he began, 'but there is a group of people, mostly small-business owners and employees who make just a little too much money to qualify for Medicaid expansion or for the tax incentives, who can't get affordable health insurance premiums in a lot of places.'[11]

Back at the White House, Obama's press secretary Josh Earnest looked unhappy. He said the only reason that people were not getting access to Medicaid, the emergency health cover that is provided to poor people in America, was that Republican-controlled states were refusing to cooperate with the Obamacare programme by taking federal funds and helping to provide more health care to the lowest rungs of society. By October 2016, that was more than half of America's fifty states.

As for Bill Clinton's criticism of the rise in premiums as 'the craziest thing in the world', the White House was not very pleased.

'It's not exactly clear to me what argument he was making, and so I'll let him and his team explain that,' an embarrassed Earnest told the White House press corps. 'The President', he insisted, 'is quite proud of the accomplishment of the Affordable Care Act.' He ticked off the achievements of Obamacare, noting that coverage had been expanded, that people who got sick no longer risked being kicked off their insurance policy or being called into bankruptcy court, that families could now keep children on their health insurance plans until the age of twenty-six, that people could for the first time get access to free check-ups and birth control, and so forth. As for Bill Clinton's unexpected outburst, Earnest remained phlegmatic: 'You would have to talk to President Clinton to find out what kind of message he was trying to send,' he deadpanned.[12]

In the Trump camp and among conservative Republicans who had been trying for six years to upend Obamacare, there was outright joy.

'With premiums continuing to skyrocket, state insurance markets collapsing and businesses struggling to comply with its job-killing mandates, even Democrats like Bill Clinton are coming to realise just what bad public policy Obamacare really is,' proclaimed Trump spokesman Jason Miller.[13]

For his part, Donald Trump made merry on the campaign trail, joking about Bill Clinton's gaffe with a crowd at an Arizona rally. 'I'll bet he went through hell last night,' he told his supporters. 'Can you imagine what he went through after making that statement? He went through hell. But you know honestly, there have been many nights when he's gone through hell with Hillary.'[14]

Yet while Donald Trump and legions of Republicans marched across America's television screens announcing their intention to 'repeal and replace' Obamacare, the system was actually helping millions of Americans, including those who had been denied health insurance in the past because they had a pre-existing condition. Obamacare decreed that insurers could not deny coverage because of a person's medical condition or history, thus stopping insurers from backing out of policies when people got sick. Obamacare meant that insurance companies could no longer charge women more than men for the same policies. Obamacare also stopped insurers from putting a cap on the amount of time or money they would spend on reimbursing a patient's health care costs. No wonder the insurance industry hated Obamacare.

Republicans especially hated the provision of Obamacare known as the 'individual mandate'. This part of the law obligates all Americans to have some form of health insurance or face penalties and fines if they do not sign up. This clause was challenged in the Supreme Court, which in 2012 upheld it, but it enraged Republicans, who saw it as encroaching on the individual freedoms and liberties of the Constitution.[15]

Out on the campaign trail, on television, in debates and at rallies, Trump's promise to repeal Obamacare became a key slogan, like the chanting of 'Build That Wall' or 'Lock Her Up'. Very rarely did either Trump or Hillary Clinton try to explain to the American people what they actually had in mind. The 2016 presidential campaign was not exactly an exercise in detailed policy debate. But at ground level, out in the heart of Middle America, Obamacare was actually making a difference.

Seated in the makeshift prefabricated mobile office headquarters of Allendale County Alive in Allendale, South Carolina, Rosalind Hines[16] is talking about the hundreds of Obamacare referrals she has made over the past three years, in her work assisting anti-poverty campaigner Wilbur Cave at the non-profit community development centre in this derelict town. Rosalind Hines used to work on pregnancy prevention educational campaigns in the area, in the schools of Allendale. But since 2013 she has been helping Wilbur Cave with the Affordable Care Act. Most of her cases are people earning an annual income of between $11,000 and $15,000, the working poor.

Hines is particularly passionate when she recounts an experience she had with a poor black woman in the community who had never been able to afford health insurance and could never get it because she had a pre-existing heart condition and the insurance companies would not take her on.

'I remember the case of this young lady, she was about thirty-six years old,' says the timid and soft-spoken Hines.

> She was battling a serious medical condition that was genetic, and she could never get any affordable health insurance. So before Obamacare her mother paid for all of her medicines, out of pocket. She couldn't afford it really but her mother sacrificed everything they had, and those bills were costing $1,000 a year.

Hines remembers sitting down with the young lady and explaining that with Obamacare the insurance companies could no longer deny her a policy because of her pre-existing condition, and with the subsidies and tax credits she could get a plan that would cost maybe as little as $25 or $30 a month. She says with a sigh:

> We sat down and talked and I explained, and we tried, and we were able to enrol her in Obamacare. And they gave her a four hundred and something dollar credit towards her monthly payments a month, so it was affordable then. She paid about $25 a month and could get her medicines and her medical care, finally.

Both the statistical and the anecdotal evidence clearly suggests that Obamacare, despite of all its many problems, has been making a genuine difference, in the heart of poor America, among the working poor of America.

Rosalind Hines says she doesn't understand why anyone would want to repeal Obamacare. As far as she is concerned, it has saved the lives of members of her community. To those who criticise Obamacare, she has a simple reply:

> Until you have someone or yourself who is in that predicament where you actually need the help because you have a pre-existing condition, well, then you are always going to be skeptical. I mean you can't change people's mindsets. All we can do is try to help those who actually need the help or who want the help.

Rosalind Hines is not a particularly worldly person. Her life is simple and her horizon extends from Allendale to a few other counties across the state of South Carolina. But the young woman becomes emotional when she learns about the existence of universal health care in Europe. Her jaw drops when she hears that health care is considered a universal right of citizens in Britain or France or Germany or Italy. The concept seems shocking to her, like a dream come true.

'Wow!' says Rosalind Hines, her eyes wide with astonishment. 'Everybody gets access to health care in Europe? Wow!'

Unlike Europeans, Americans do not consider universal health care to be a citizen's birthright, and so it was the most natural thing in the world for the Trump campaign to have made the repeal of Obamacare one of its central tenets. It was a classic Republican Party theme, and had been for years. But the problem of health care in America goes well beyond the inefficiencies of Obamacare. The fact is that the United States spends more per capita on health care than any other major industrial democracy in the world, and gets less for its money. While the United States spends on average about 17 per cent of the gross domestic product for a system that still excludes millions of Americans, the Europeans spend far less and guarantee universal health care to all of their citizens. The comparable levels of healthcare spending in Europe are 9 per cent in Italy and 11 per cent in Germany and France.[17]

Much of the problem has little to do with Obamacare and a lot more to do with America's savagely unregulated pharmaceuticals and healthcare industries. The US delivers roughly three times as many mammograms, two and a half times as many MRI scans, and a third more C-sections per capita than the average Western country, according to the OECD. The prices of branded prescription drugs in the US are, on average, about double those in other countries. The fees of specialist physicians are typically two to three times as high as in other countries. One of the biggest reasons for the expensive US costs are that the system produces more profits for drug manufacturers, for specialist physicians and for others who have considerable influence on policy.[18] It was against this dysfunctional backdrop that Barack Obama had tried to achieve a modicum of social equity.

And then came Trump.

Donald Trump took office on 20 January 2017 and began trying to dismantle Obamacare on Day One, in his very first executive order.[19] He pledged to work with Congressional Republicans to replace it with a better system. While he had carefully ring-fenced the most popular elements of Obamacare – the clause that guaranteed coverage for people with pre-existing conditions and the clause that allowed families to keep children on their policies up until the age of twenty-six – the rest of the Affordable Care Act seemed very much up for grabs. And soon even the pre-existing coverage promise would be thrown out the window as Trump and the Republicans began a long and difficult effort to make good on the campaign pledge to repeal and replace Obamacare.

The Republicans found themselves facing a determined new President who was making the repeal and replacement of Obamacare a top priority. Trump signalled his determination not merely with his executive order but also with the naming of a staunch enemy of Obamacare as his new Secretary of Health and Human Services.

Rep. Tom Price was a one-man death panel for Obamacare, a right-wing congressman from Georgia and a Tea Party darling who for years has been the most prominent critic of Obamacare on

Capitol Hill.[20] Price is an ultra-conservative, a right-winger with a 100 per cent approval rating from the National Rifle Association,[21] a sworn enemy of abortion and gay marriage,[22] and a key ally of House Speaker Paul Ryan. In fact, in 2015 Price replaced Ryan as chairman of the influential House Budget Committee, and he had been working for years on various pieces of draft legislation that aimed to repeal and replace the Affordable Care Act.[23]

If Donald Trump wanted an ideological and militant Cabinet Secretary who could help him dismantle and replace Obamacare, he could not have found anyone better than Tom Price. Price was the man for the job at hand, ready, able and willing. A specialist.

Senator Charles Schumer, the Democratic minority leader, said that nominating Price to the Trump administration 'is akin to asking the fox to guard the henhouse'.[24]

Over the years, Price has voted against federal funding for abortion and family planning groups like Planned Parenthood, and has opposed a bill that would have provided four weeks of parental leave for federal employees, as well as a law that now requires the Food and Drug Administration (FDA) to regulate tobacco as a drug.[25] What is more, Price is in favour of privatising Medicare: under his plan, those who qualify would be provided a voucher to be used as a subsidy for private insurance.[26]

An orthopaedic surgeon who served six terms in the House of Representatives, Price is much loved by right-wing think tanks like the American Enterprise Institute and by right-wingers in Congress. With his Southern drawl, his thinning but bouffant grey hair and his dark bushy eyebrows standing out from a pale and bespectacled face, he cuts a rather sinister figure. Price is an old hand at repealing Obamacare. He has made it his speciality in Congress. He has been proposing legislative alternatives to the Affordable Care Act since it was signed into law in 2010, and now, in the Trump administration, he would finally get to play a central role in the new administration's efforts to repeal it. But the influence of Tom Price goes far beyond his work in trying to repeal and replace Obamacare. He is also now America's most powerful man on health care. He controls the biggest budgets, the government's largest social programmes that have been pillars of American society since the 1960s, Medicare and Medicaid. He also has authority over agencies like the Food and Drug Administration, which is supposed to regulate America's pharmaceuticals industry. To run the FDA, Donald Trump named Scott Gottlieb,[27] a conservative financier with long-standing ties to the drug industry, an industry shill for Big Pharma who had worked for several drug companies, including GlaxoSmithKline and Vertex Pharmaceutical. Gottlieb, like Trump, was committed to slashing health regulations and even abolishing some clinical trials in order to speed up the process by which drugs are approved and come to market.

In order to assist Price in dismantling Obamacare, Trump chose as his new administrator of the Centers for Medicare and Medicaid Services a controversial behind-the-scenes Republican operative who had spent years trying to come up with a private sector alternative to Medicaid. Seema Verma, a darling of the conservatives with close ties to Vice-President Mike Pence, was a perfect partner to Tom Price for the task of dismantling Obamacare and rolling back the social safety nets of Medicare, guaranteed health care for the elderly, and Medicaid, guaranteed health care for the poor.[28]

Verma, a former adviser to Pence when he had been Governor of Indiana, had red-state policy chops. She had worked on creating an alternative to Medicaid called the Healthy Indiana Plan. The plan took advantage of a 2012 Supreme Court decision which allowed individual states more freedom in deciding whether or not to expand Medicaid as required by Obamacare. It gave the states enormous discretionary powers and most of the Republican states then proceeded to opt out of expanding Medicaid to more of the poor and disabled whom the programme was intended for. Seema Verma was fine with that. She embraced the state freedom and went about constructing her own free-market version of Medicaid for Pence. Her argument was that in order to qualify for medical care from Medicaid funds, even if you were poor, you had to make some payment: you had to have, as she put it, 'skin in the game'.

Medicaid, in Verma's opinion was 'dysfunctional' and there was too much oversight by the federal government. Medicaid had to be remodelled and improved.

Critics called her alternative a punitive plan that introduced work requirements and minimum premium payments for the poor. The plan required people to make a small monthly payment in order to access health insurance. Just a single missed payment could result in a six-month lockout period, where they would have no insurance coverage. Those provisions aren't allowed under traditional Medicaid, but Governor Mike Pence of Indiana, as conservative a Republican as it's possible to be, managed to get special permission to implement Verma's plan.

Many of the poor, the critics warned, would end up being disenfranchised by the Indiana model. When faced with the choice, the poor would not choose to have any 'skin in the game'.

But Seema Verma prospered. Her little-known private consulting firm, SVC Inc., has received a total of $3.5 million in Indiana state contracts.[29]

At the same time, while she was designing and implementing Indiana's conservative-friendly alternative to Medicaid, Verma was also working for one of the state's largest Medicaid vendors, a division of Silicon Valley giant Hewlett-Packard. That company, according to the *Indianapolis Star*, agreed to pay Verma more than $1 million in consulting fees and has landed more than $500 million in state contracts during her tenure as Indiana's go-to healthcare consultant.

'Verma's dual roles raise an important question,' the Indiana newspaper noted with irony. 'Who is she working for when she advises the state on how to spend billions of dollars in Medicaid funds – the taxpayers or one of the state's largest contractors?'

In a written statement, Verma did not deny her dual roles but she claimed that she played no role in Hewlett-Packard's contracts with the state. 'SVC has disclosed to both HP and the state the relationship with the other to be transparent,' Verma said. 'If any issue between HP and the state presented a conflict between the two, I recused myself from the process.'

But the recently ousted head of the state agency administering Verma's contract told the *Indianapolis Star* that Verma once attempted to negotiate with state officials on behalf of Hewlett-Packard, while also being paid by the state. Verma decided not to comment on this detail and, for its part, Hewlett-Packard said it could find no one in the company with any recollection of such a meeting.

Indeed. In the age of fake news and post-truth Breitbartian truisms, what is a little report in the *Indianapolis Star*? Certainly nothing to discourage the likes of Donald Trump.

Trump was positively delighted with his choices. With typical flourish, he proclaimed that Price and Verma would be 'the dream team that will transform our healthcare system for the benefit of all Americans'.[30] That was as much detail as he would be getting into for now. He would leave the rest to his dream team.

Given that Tom Price had repeatedly called for cutting Medicaid funding, and the new head of Medicaid, Seema Verma, had developed an alternative to Medicaid in Indiana that appealed to conservatives, the two really did seem to be a perfect fit. Indeed, the idea of throwing Medicaid funding back to the states, where it would be cut, and of requiring that under the Trumpcare plan even the very poor face work requirements or make payments was soon official administration policy.

Between the two of them, Price and Verma would control an annual budget of more than $1 trillion, and the fates of long-standing public health programmes for the very poor, disabled and elderly. Medicaid alone covers more than 74 million Americans, nearly one-quarter of the American population.[31] But with Donald Trump in the White House, all bets were now off the table.

Price and Verma were in full agreement with proposals by Trump and by Paul Ryan to transform Medicaid from a fully federally funded programme into a system where the federal government would give block grants to individual states. Many Republicans liked the idea of block grants because they gave more freedom to individual state governors, and at the start of 2017 the Republicans controlled thirty-one governorships. This would mean, as it already had in earlier block grant approaches to welfare funding, that states would either lose money or have the latitude to use these block grants for other purposes, and not necessarily for expanding Medicaid.

Allowing states to redirect the grants to other purposes could result in severe cuts in benefits for millions of patients across America, but the Republicans on Capitol Hill had already been on record for years arguing that Medicaid funding should be slashed by $1 trillion over the next decade.[32] This is the equivalent of cutting about a quarter of all Medicaid funding to America's poor. With the Republicans now in control of the full Congress, it looks as though Tom Price and Seema Verma may be able to remake Medicaid, and thereby dismantle a fundamental pillar of American social programmes since the 1960s.

Judith Solomon, vice-president for health policy at the Center on Budget and Policy Priorities, has said that Verma's alternative forms of Medicaid 'are not in line with decades of research that has shown that when you impose premiums on very low-income people, you depress participation'. Solomon added that for those at the lower rungs of American society, many often choose not to pay for a health care premium due to having other urgent needs. 'This logic', she concluded, 'goes directly against the traditional spirit of Medicaid, which has long provided healthcare safety nets for the poor.'[33]

Unfortunately, Judith Solomon's think tank is a left-leaning institution, and therefore no longer relevant in Donald Trump's Washington. The same might be said about Professor Luke Shaefer,[34] the University of Michigan social scientist and co-author of *$2.00 A Day: Living on Almost Nothing in America*.[35] He is still busy at the Gerald R. Ford School of Public Policy, trying to calculate the exact number of Americans living in extreme poverty, but the election of Donald Trump has cast a dark shadow over his professional life, and he says he is frightened, most of all about the fact that with Republicans fully in control of the White House, the Congress and soon, the Supreme Court, there will be nothing to stop them from cutting away the remaining strands of America's already rather frayed social safety net.

Luke Shaefer thinks that with Price and Verma at the helm of America's healthcare system, it is quite likely that they will eventually follow her Indiana model and even beyond. He thinks the Trump administration could well transform Medicaid into a system of block grants for individual states. The White House has already indicated it favours the block grant approach.

'I think my biggest worry', says Shaefer,

> is that they will change the structure of the entitlement programs to be more like the block grants that were used in the 1996 Clinton welfare reforms. That was a disaster which ended up getting less welfare cash to the very poor. And my worry is that they will do the same with Medicaid. They could shift everything to block grants and let the states decide.

The 1996 welfare reform legislation[36] that Shaefer was quoting was a dark day for America's poor, though it was cause for celebration for President Bill Clinton, who had pledged to 'end welfare as we know it'. The Clinton administration pushed through a law that replaced the traditional welfare system, known as Aid to Families with Dependent Children (AFDC), with a new set of block grants that was called Temporary Assistance for Needy Families (TANF). Now the states could do what they wanted with the welfare cash.

> Under the block grant system, the federal government gives you a certain amount of money, and if you use it for cash assistance, for cash welfare, then you have to abide by all these requirements.

> Or, you can use it for a variety of other things which they're not going to regulate. And so a lot of states have shifted away from doing what we think the welfare program should be doing, like providing cash aid or work help to people, and more towards doing things that were never the intention of the program.

Medicaid, says Shaefer, looks like it will go the way of block grants, and that could move more poor Americans off the state's ledgers and leave them without any visible means of support, even at the lowest rungs of society – especially at the lowest rungs. No health care, no welfare. The irony has already been noted by dozens of pundits and editorial writers: some of the poorest of America's working poor, many of whom saw in Trump their final hope for social justice, now stand to lose the most.

Trump's first attempts at repealing Obamacare did not go well,[37] and the legislation which was approved in the House of Representatives[38] became an instant controversy when the Congressional Budget Office predicted that Trump's slashing of Obamacare funds would result in the loss of health coverage by more than 20 million Americans.[39] Trump's trusted Secretary of Health Tom Price would prove of little use as the President soon found himself caught in the middle of a civil war inside the Republican Party, with hardliners wanting to abolish Obamacare entirely and moderate Republicans concerned that throwing too many Americans off the books could prove an electoral boomerang during the mid-term Congressional elections of 2018.

Trump's attempt to replace Obamacare with the American Healthcare Act in March 2017 was to prove his first legislative debacle, and a punishing political defeat. Trump embraced Speaker Paul Ryan's desire to ram through his own version of healthcare reform, and the New York billionaire didn't concern himself too much with the details. Trump and Ryan found their proposal derided by ultra-conservatives as 'Obamacare Lite'.[40] Nor did Trump seem to understand the dynamics inside the Republican Party, where the hardline conservatives, members of the Freedom Caucus, did not want to leave any federal healthcare entitlements standing. They wanted termination of everything, including essential healthcare basics for insurance such as maternity care or even ambulance and emergency services and prescription drugs. But some moderate Republicans were frightened by the forecasts of the Congressional Budget Office that at least 14 million Americans could lose health coverage within a year of Obamacare's repeal.[41] Trump was caught between a rock and a hard place, and his experience in building casinos or appearing on a Hollywood backlot did not prepare him for the intricacies of being President of the United States. He barked out an ultimatum, telling his party that they had one chance to repeal Obamacare and if they didn't take it he would just move on and let Obamacare 'implode'.[42] More than thirty Republicans didn't care what their new President thought; they just refused to budge. Trump and Ryan were forced to call off the vote on a Friday afternoon, 24 March 2017.[43] Ryan went before the cameras and admitted defeat while Trump, the President, sent out a tweet predicting that Obamacare would soon explode and telling Americans not to worry, and then he hopped on Air Force One and headed to Florida for a weekend at Mar-a-Lago and a round of golf.

The early defeat of Trump's efforts at healthcare reform showed America a President who did not seem very focused on the details of issues. Several members of Congress noted that at private meetings in the White House, Trump had appeared to be unfamiliar with the details of his own healthcare reform proposal. Yet the Republicans and Trump remain committed to undoing what was probably America's best shot at near universal health care and the second effort by the House would prove successful.[44] As noted, though, this version would deprive more than 20 million Americans of health insurance coverage, and that was causing a number of senators up for re-election in 2018 to hesitate.

Barack Obama had done his best and, in retrospect, he actually did help 20 million Americans to get affordable health care for the first time, as intended. Now, in some way and form in future, perhaps by the use of block grants or discretionary powers of the Health Secretary, major elements of the programme will be dismantled, and it remains likely that at the end of the process at least some of America's social safety net entitlement programmes will see their budgets cut; some of the sacred cows of American social policy for the past half-century will be sacrificed. Tom Price and Seema Verma will have no compunction about touching formally sacrosanct programmes such as Medicaid, and nor will Speaker Ryan. The Trump administration's early stumbling over repealing Obamacare will not stop the administration from trying to roll back the last remnants of Franklin Delano Roosevelt's and Lyndon B. Johnson's legacies. In the new era of post-truth populism, Trump is able to promise (via tweet) to spend more money on health care while slashing its funding. Not a problem.

Over time, if Trump and the ultra-conservatives get their way, the net effect of their form of healthcare reform could prove devastating for at least 20 million Americans and probably for many more – and not only for those who risk losing Obamacare. Senior citizens, the disabled, the mentally ill and the poor are all likely to suffer at the hands of the Trump administration's budget cuts. The most likely scenario over the years is that there will be deep cuts in net spending, real reductions in overall healthcare budgets and subsidies, and cuts to the bottom line, and as a result there will be real and substantially increased suffering at the lowest levels of American society – a great deal more suffering.

CHAPTER EIGHT

THE FRACKING OF A NATION

Five hundred billion dollars. Half a trillion dollars.

That was the value placed by Vladimir Putin on the deal that had just been signed with his old friend Rex Tillerson.[1] The diminutive but steely eyed Putin stood smiling for the cameras, in a well-appointed room at his vacation residence on the Black Sea. Tillerson, a tall, strapping Texan who headed ExxonMobil, America's biggest oil company, returned Putin's affection with a toothy grin.

The two raised their glasses of champagne in a toast. They had just finalised a deal between ExxonMobil and the Russian state oil company Rosneft that would give Exxon permission to develop the vast offshore reserves in Russia's Arctic and Black Seas. In return, Rosneft would get 30 per cent minority stakes in a number of Exxon's North America-based oil projects. The hydrocarbon deposits of the Russian Arctic were estimated to be about 22 per cent of world reserves, or equivalent to all the oil in the North Sea, hence the Putin prediction that the deal would be worth $500 billion.

By any standards, it was a deal between two major players: on the one hand, the Russian dictator, and on the other the head of ExxonMobil, which by 2011 had become a corporate sovereign power in its own right, a state-within-a-state, a US corporation so big that if it had been a country it would have the 41st largest economy in the world.[2]

ExxonMobil did not have a good reputation as a great defender of either the environment or human rights. But Rex Tillerson had proved himself very adept at making profitable oil deals with African dictators and warlords in places like Chad and Kurdistan, as well as with his old friend Putin, whom he first met back in 1999.[3] In fact, Rex Tillerson was no ordinary ExxonMobil chairman and chief executive officer. He was a Big Oil power broker who ran a secretive corporation that had its own foreign policy, its own security services and its own intelligence arm. ExxonMobil often hired former CIA officials and as a rule it did not take kindly to nosy reporters or environmental activists.

'Reporting on Exxon was not only harder than reporting on the bin Ladens; it was harder than reporting on the CIA by an order of magnitude,'[4] said Steve Coll, the journalist who wrote about the company in a book called *Private Empire: ExxonMobil and American Power*.[5]

Rex Tillerson's ExxonMobil, according to Coll, 'has a culture of intimidation that they bring to bear in their external relations, and it is plenty understood inside the corporation too. They make people nervous, they make people afraid.'

None of this would bother the likes of Vladimir Putin, who in 2013 awarded Tillerson the highest honour that can be bestowed on a foreigner in Russia, the Order of Friendship.[6]

Tillerson is also good friends with the notorious head of Rosneft, Igor Sechin, a former interpreter who worked as chief of staff for Putin when he was deputy mayor in St Petersburg in the mid-1990s. Sechin, who is sometimes described as the second most powerful man in Russia, is a hawkish hardliner who is feared even by many Russian government officials. Sechin was believed to have been behind the carving up of the private oil company Yukos (at Putin's behest) and the jailing of its owner, Mikhail Khodorkovsky, then Russia's richest man, in 2003.[7] Sechin, who spoke fondly of racing his Harley-Davidson alongside his friend Rex Tillerson,[8] was a crafty and seasoned operative, a power broker extraordinaire in Putin's Russia.

Tillerson was by all accounts the most powerful and effective CEO in ExxonMobil's history, which is no small thing given the company's history from the days when it was John D. Rockefeller's Standard Oil of New Jersey through its infamous 1989 oil spillage in Alaska, the notorious Exxon Valdez.[9] The ExxonMobil boss was used to jetting across the planet with ease, making deals with African autocrats or Kurdish separatists in Iraq, turning a blind eye to collateral damage that his deals might cause in human rights or the environment. Tillerson was a realist, a pragmatist, a one-time Eagle Scout who would get the job done and take no prisoners. 'He is one tough cookie,' said a former colleague.[10]

ExxonMobil itself is a $340 billion[11] monolith that while operating on the world stage has at times found itself at odds with official US foreign policy. Rex Tillerson rose to the top of ExxonMobil in large part thanks to his close relationship with Putin and his ability to get big oil deals done in Russia. Tillerson's involvement in Russia dates back to 1998, when he was appointed head of the Exxon subsidiary in Russia in charge of an oil and gas project on Sakhalin Island, off the coast of Siberia. This huge project put Tillerson in line to become the corporation's vice-president, president and eventually its chairman and chief executive officer.

More recently, in 2011, during the Obama administration, Tillerson enraged the Obama administration's State Department when he struck a deal with Iraq's autonomous Kurdish government, undermining Iraq's central government at a time when the US was trying to bolster it.[12] He informed the State Department only after the deal was done.

As ExxonMobil chief, Tillerson has been a vigorous opponent of US sanctions against Russia, which he has called ineffective.[13] For Rex Tillerson, Putin's smash-and-grab annexation of Crimea was not a business concern, just a local political development. Why impose sanctions on Russia, and on individual oligarchs and apparatchiks like Igor Sechin of Rosneft, the Putin crony who was personally named in Obama's sanctions? For Tillerson, crony capitalism and an expansionist Russia were just part of the game – not a worry, just a part of the local landscape.

Tillerson, says Coll, despite his huge power and lack of a moral compass, is 'a personable guy'.[14] A big bruiser of a man with a big smile and a Texan swagger. Like many of the Big Oil corporate titans who stride confidently around the world stage, and like many of the oligarchs and warlords they deal with on a daily basis, Tillerson is a tough guy. And Donald Trump likes tough guys. He likes strong leaders. That much is clear. So it was not that surprising that when Trump and Tillerson met for the first time at Trump Tower in early December 2016, they hit it off immediately.[15] Good chemistry.

Donald Trump didn't actually meet Tillerson until a week before he would announce his nomination as Secretary of State. But he had been receiving recommendations and pitches on behalf of Tillerson from two of the national security veterans of the Bush administration: Condoleezza Rice, the former National Security Adviser, and Robert Gates, the former Secretary of Defense and former director of Central Intelligence.[16] What they had in common was not just that they were both Bush family stalwarts who had loyally toed the line under George W. Bush. They were also financially tied to Rex Tillerson's ExxonMobil. Their private strategic consulting firm, RiceHadleyGates, was a paid vendor to ExxonMobil.[17] In other words, both Rice and Gates worked for ExxonMobil when they recommended Tillerson to Trump. They were on the ExxonMobil payroll. But in the increasingly foggy and surreal world of ethics in Trump's presidency, where a conflict of interest is not a conflict of interest, where the President's sons and daughters move in the shadows between the US government and the Trump family holdings, the fact that Gates and Rice were endorsing a fee-paying client wouldn't really matter. With Donald Trump, this sort of detail would not matter at all. Nor did it matter that Gates had written a scathing attack on Trump in the *Wall Street Journal*, saying that 'a thin-skinned, temperamental, shoot-from-the-hip and lip, uninformed commander-in-chief is too great a risk for America'.[18] Apparently it didn't matter when the thin-skinned, temperamental fellow in question was the President of the United States who was appointing one of your biggest clients as the new Secretary of State. Nor did it matter that only a month before Election Day Condi Rice had called for Trump to drop out of the race.[19] No. Nothing really mattered.

Nor would it matter that another big endorsement for Tillerson had come from the Bush family's oldest consigliere, former Secretary of State James Baker, whose law firm in Houston just happened to be a paid consultant, like his friends Condoleezza Rice and Robert Gates, to Rex Tillerson's ExxonMobil.[20]

In the political calculus, Trump was co-opting some former critics and the Bush family, and bringing the Republican establishment into line. He would coax and cajole, and if it suited him he would be forgiving. In the Trump worldview, there were bygones to be forgotten and bygones to be stored away for later use. What counted now was the man himself, the man who had beaten all the other contestants in Trump's reality TV selection of a Secretary of State. What counted was the winner, the Celebrity Apprentice, the man who had beaten Mitt Romney and Rudy Giuliani to grasp the mantle at State. Sure, Tillerson's Russian ties would come back to haunt him, over and over again, but for now he was Trump's latest discovery, the man whom Donald Trump would call 'one of the truly great business leaders of the world' in the early morning tweet which doubled as his formal announcement of Tillerson's nomination as Secretary of State.[21]

In fact, on the day he announced Tillerson, Trump also had his team bleed out the news of his choice of another Texan with a Big Oil pedigree, another friend of fossil fuels and a climate change denier. Rick Perry was known by many Americans as the former Governor of Texas who had become a failed presidential candidate during a Republican primary season debate. Many had ridiculed the hapless Perry for his 'Oops' moment in November 2011. While participating in a televised debate, he was sounding off about his conservative credentials and announced that as President he would be abolishing three entire government departments.

'There's three agencies of government that are gone when I get there,' said Perry, extending his left hand to count them one by one. 'And that's Commerce, Education, and... uh, oh, what's the third one there... uh... let me see...' He stumbled, he paused, he could not remember. The audience at the debate broke out in laughter. And it all played out in living colour on live national television. Rick Perry, never a man known for his keen intellect, seemed more obtuse than Forrest Gump. He tried to remember again, amid titters from the public: 'Commerce, Education, and...' Nope. Perry was stumped a second time. The CNBC anchor asked Perry if he could actually remember the name of the third agency that he wanted to abolish. The Texas governor, looking a bit forlorn, tried again. 'The third agency of government... I would do away with Education...' He stumbled again and this time the journalist prompted him with the word: 'Commerce.' A grateful Perry went on: 'Yes, Commerce,' he repeated. 'And let's see...' He stumbled again. 'I can't. Third. Sorry. Oops.'[22] And that was it. The self-immolation of a cowboy Republican candidate from Texas. Rick Perry.

So which government department did Donald Trump give Rick Perry to manage? The Department of Energy.[23] The agency that he wanted to abolish. The agency whose regulations on the energy industry he had been fighting to repeal for years. Call it a coincidence, although it seemed to fit a broader pattern. To run the Energy Department, Donald Trump had named a man who was the darling of the Texas oil and gas community, a true friend to fossil fuels. As the nation's top energy regulator he had named a man who wanted to dismantle most of the nation's principal energy regulations.

Like Tillerson, Rick Perry had a cowboy swagger; he rarely left home without his signature cowboy boots. The two men knew each other, as could be expected in such a small community of oil men and politicians. Perry had deep ties with the Texas oil industry. In fact, just weeks after he left the governor's office, Perry began serving on the corporate boards of two energy firms linked to Texas billionaire and Republican donor Kelcy Warren. Perry was on the board of Warren's Energy Transfer Partners and his Sunoco Logistics

Partners LP.[24] These two companies, both owned by Warren, had developed the controversial Dakota Access Pipeline project, the $3.8 billion project carrying oil from North Dakota to Illinois that had sparked national protests and which was perhaps, by the end of 2016, the brightest flashpoint in the war between environmentalists and Big Oil.[25] Perry's benefactors had plenty of cash, and plenty of it had been invested in his past political campaigns for governor.[26] The oil industry, starting with Kelcy Warren, gave him $1.6 million for his presidential primary campaign in 2011/12. In 2016, Sunoco, which was a Trump donor, announced plans to buy Energy Transfer Partners for more than $21 billion.[27] Perry, when he was named by Trump to be Secretary of Energy, owned hundreds of thousands of dollars' worth of shares in both Energy Transfer Partners and Sunoco Logistics, as did his wife.[28] On paper, he had a slight problem, a little conflict of interest.

Towards the end of the Obama administration, in December 2016, a last-ditch effort was made by Democrats to block the Dakota Access Pipeline, which would have gone across the sacred lands and burial grounds of a Sioux reservation in North Dakota and would have been installed below the Missouri River, the only source of drinking water for the local Indian tribe. Kelcy Warren's company swore there was no danger of oil leakages from the pipeline contaminating the Sioux tribe's drinking water, but Warren's companies had a pretty poor track record, having been found guilty of nearly 200 pipeline leaks since 2010.[29] For months, the Indians, together with environmental activists, had set up camp on the disputed land. Thousands of protesters, many of them sleeping in makeshift tepees, were treated savagely by the local police, suffering water cannons in the freezing North Dakota cold and being forced back by vicious dogs and anti-riot police. But the Obama administration managed to squeak through a temporary halt to the pipeline's construction. The US Army Corp of Engineers, in November 2016, had decided to delay the pipeline in order to allow more time for talks with the Native Americans of the Standing Rock Sioux tribe and with other pipeline opponents. The idea was to find an alternative route for the pipeline, even though Donald Trump and Rick Perry had promised to get the pipeline completed.[30] The army decision counted, but so would the departments of Energy, Interior, Justice and the Environmental Protection Agency, all of which play a role in sensitive matters such as this one.

Fortunately for the oil companies, Donald Trump has named either oil industry executives or oil industry cheerleaders to all of these sensitive government jobs, and in his first days in office Trump signed executive orders to allow the Dakota Access Pipeline to go ahead. Trump didn't mind that his new Secretary of Energy had been sitting on the board of the company that had developed the pipeline.

Like Donald Trump, his one-time rival and now his boss, Rick Perry has for years been a climate change denier. Both men are sworn enemies of the kind of environmental regulations developed during the Obama administration. Both men have regularly complained about the bureaucracy of the Environmental Protection Agency (EPA), which has been until now the one bastion of scientific authority in the federal government that has worked hard to protect America's clean water and clean air. Until now.

While ExxonMobil and the rest of the Texas oil industry were rejoicing in the appointments of Rex Tillerson and Rick Perry, an even more militant right-wing ideologue and oil-friendly Republican was then named by Trump to run the Environmental Protection Agency itself.

Scott Pruitt, the Oklahoma Attorney General, has a lifelong record of promoting hydrocarbons and opposing alternative and renewable energy.[31] He is a genuine climate change denier. He has sued the EPA to stop carbon emission regulations. Pruitt rejects mainstream climate science with as much ideological, nearly religious fervour as a right-wing Republican from Alabama might reject Darwin's theory of evolution. His entire career has been about trying to undermine mainstream science on behalf of Big Oil.

An ardent opponent of President Barack Obama's measures to stem climate change, Pruitt has enraged environmental activists for many years. The co-chairman of his 2013 election campaign in Oklahoma was Harold Hamm, another billionaire friend of Trump's who is CEO of Continental Resources, the oil and gas fracking group. A sworn enemy of the environmentalists and a big donor to Trump's election campaign, Hamm had recommended Pruitt to Trump, and he was thrilled with the choice of a man who in the past, as Oklahoma Attorney General, had brought lawsuits against the EPA. Here was a man who believed in opening up public lands for oil and gas exploration, a man who had devoted himself to defending the fracking industry and oil and gas companies by attacking the EPA in multiple lawsuits and public tirades.

In an editorial in the conservative magazine *National Review* in May 2016, Pruitt railed against Obama's efforts to reduce carbon emissions from US power plants, the clean power protections for Americans that were bitterly opposed by the oil and gas industry. He used the occasion of the article to pour scorn on the idea of climate change.

'That debate is far from settled,' wrote Pruitt. 'Scientists continue to disagree about the degree and extent of global warming and its connection to the actions of mankind.'[32]

The new head of the EPA was another climate change denier, just like the new President and the new Secretary of Energy. But Scott Pruitt was far more than this. He was a genuine hero to conservative Republican activists and he had been one of the main architects over the years of the legal battles against Obama's climate change policies.[33] He has sued the EPA over the Clean Power Plan, the principal Obama-era policy that was aimed at reducing US greenhouse gas emissions. He has also sued the EPA over its regulations seeking to curtail the emissions of methane, a powerful greenhouse gas, from the oil and gas sector.

Pruitt has described the EPA's attempts to control greenhouse emissions and reduce America's carbon footprint as 'unlawful and overreaching'[34] and he has sworn to dismantle many of the EPA's regulations. In short, he has sworn to reverse nearly all of the environmental regulations that were created by the Obama administration in its attempt to take urgent action on the challenges posed by climate change.

Environmental groups were apoplectic at the nomination of Pruitt to the EPA, perhaps even more than they had been about Rick Perry taking over the Department of Energy. Pruitt, they complained, was a long-standing puppet of the fossil fuel industry who would push back against air pollution standards and favour the oil and gas industry as he always had. Pruitt was a champion of the Dakota Access Pipeline and all pipelines across America.

Rick Perry, meanwhile, had also sat on the board of the company that was behind the controversial Dakota Access Pipeline, Energy Transfer Partners. Kelcy Warren, the billionaire Texan owner of Energy Transfer Partners, had given $6 million to Rick Perry's 2016 campaign[35] and had also contributed heavily to Donald Trump's presidential campaign in 2016.[36] And whose fracked oil would be part of the oil that was to be transported from North Dakota once the pipeline was unblocked by the Trump administration? The fracked oil came from billionaire oilman Harold Hamm's Continental Resources, the oil company that had nurtured the career of Scott Pruitt.[37]

In other words, while the new Secretary of Energy's campaigns had been financed by Kelcy Warren, the owner of Energy Transfer Partners, which had then hired him on their board, the 500,000 barrels of fracked oil that would be travelling through the Dakota Access Pipeline would come from the company owned by Harold Hamm, the principal financial backer and election campaign chairman of former Oklahoma Attorney General Scott Pruitt, who would, in turn, now be running the Trump administration's EPA. Trump himself had now promised to reverse Obama's environmental regulations and to get the Dakota Access Pipeline moving again. Trump never bothered to mention that until the summer of 2016 he had been a major shareholder of Kelcy Warren's Energy Transfer Partners, the company behind the Dakota Access Pipeline.

Financial disclosure documents filed by Trump show in fact that he had financial ties to at least two of the pipeline developers. The disclosure forms show that Trump had significant investment holdings in the fossil fuel sector, with shares in ExxonMobil, Chevron, Halliburton, Occidental Petroleum, ConocoPhillips, Shell, Schlumberger and BHP Billiton. They also show that Trump was a major shareholder in Kelcy Warren's Energy Transfer Partners. In May 2016, he disclosed owning between $15,000 and $50,000 in Energy Transfer Partners. This figure was down from the previous level of $500,000–$1 million in 2015. Trump also disclosed that he had between $100,000 and $250,000 worth of shareholdings in Phillips 66, which would own about a quarter of the Dakota Access Pipeline upon completion.[38]

After the election was over, it was revealed that Trump had sold off his shares of Energy Transfer Partners during the summer of 2016. Hope Hicks, the Trump spokeswoman, confirmed this to the *Washington Post* in a little-noticed story, but she did not say whether he had sold his Phillips 66 or any other oil stocks.[39] The news should have been a major talking point for the talking heads, a matter of national attention, but in the dawning of the Age of Trump it was a minor matter, a mere blip across the news screen, a matter that was dwarfed by the greater affairs of state, by President-elect Trump's undiplomatic conversations with the President of Taiwan,[40] or his latest tweet against *Saturday Night Live*[41] or *Vanity Fair*.[42] America was interested in Trump's attempts to deny the CIA's evidence of Russian hacking into the Democratic National Committee. He positively hated the fact that even President Obama had said it was pretty clear that Putin had been behind the interference and it was pretty clear that Trump was the intended beneficiary of Putin's interference in the US election. Against larger and more scandalous matters, against the loudening din of debate over the nomination of Putin's friend Rex Tillerson as US Secretary of State, the tiny matter of Trump's shareholdings in obscure US oil pipeline companies pretty much got lost in the sauce. So what if Donald Trump had been a big investor in Kelcy Warren's Dakota Access Pipeline and had now appointed a trifecta of oil industry executives and cheerleaders to the State Department, the Energy Department and the EPA? Such minor conflicts would be little more than a nuisance.

The environmental community was aghast. They had come face to face with their worst nightmare, a kind of green Armageddon. Environmental advocacy groups like the Sierra Club and Greenpeace and Friends of the Earth all bemoaned the appointments, along with the Democrats on Capitol Hill. They decried the way Big Oil had suddenly come marching back into Washington, amassing huge influence and decision-making power. Just like that. All in the space of one week in December 2016, just days before Christmas. The environmentalists denounced the fact that Trump had just given some of the wealthiest oil executives in the country an unprecedented power over the air that Americans breathe and the water they drink. They feared, sensibly enough, that a solidly fossil fuels agenda of drilling on public lands, allowing pipelines anywhere and rolling back clean air regulations would seriously endanger America's public health. They feared, reasonably enough, that filling the Cabinet with climate change deniers would ultimately endanger the planet.

'Having Scott Pruitt in charge of EPA is like putting an arsonist in charge of fighting fires,' said Michael Brune, the distraught-sounding executive director of the Sierra Club.[43]

'In a Donald Trump administration,' said Ed Markey, a Democratic senator from Massachusetts, 'America's foreign policy, energy policy and environmental policy are all linked by one thing: oil.' Markey said that Trump was creating 'a Cabinet of Big Oil all-stars with the plan to drag us back to nineteenth-century dirty energy sources and derail our 21st-century clean energy future.'[44]

Like nearly all of Trump's primary appointments, Scott Pruitt has been a harsh critic of Obama's immigration policies. He has sued the Obama administration not just to stop environmental regulations but also to block Obamacare. He has protested against excessive regulation of banks and bankers. He has been an outspoken opponent of abortion who would like to see the Supreme Court deny a woman's right to choose.[45] He has called for public schools to issue a bible to every student.[46] And he has consistently received the highest rating and the warm endorsement of the National Rifle Association.[47] Scott Pruitt, like Rick Perry, and Donald Trump, was much loved by gun owners and the gun lobby.

Ça va sans dire.

On climate change, Scott Pruitt, unsurprisingly, had come to the defence of ExxonMobil well before he was named to run the EPA. In November 2015, the Attorney General of New York, Eric Schneiderman, subpoenaed ExxonMobil as part of an investigation to determine whether the company lied to the public and to investors about the risks of climate change. The investigation, which would soon be joined by the Attorneys General of nearly twenty other US states, seemed to show the oil giant had known about the damaging effects of climate change for decades but had covered it up and spent millions on a misinformation campaign; Pruitt was among ExxonMobil's first defenders.[48] The investigation in fact focused on a period of at least a decade during which ExxonMobil funded outside groups that sought to undermine climate science, cast doubt on global warming, and through a clever mix of supposed expert opinion and op-ed packaging made ExxonMobil look like a caring company rather than the willing partner of Vladimir Putin's dangerous push into the Russian Arctic. In the lexicon of the current post-truth political environment, one could say that the investigation was really focused on ExxonMobil's funding of the 1980s and 1990s equivalent of fake news.

In order to roll back environmental regulations and give the oil industry a green light to frack and drill its way around America, the Trump administration had to fill its ranks with a Secretary of the Interior who would not mind letting Big Oil have a bit more access to public land. Like the new Secretary of Energy and the new EPA chief, the new Secretary of the Interior was another climate change sceptic.

Rep. Ryan Zinke, a former Navy Seal and freshman Republican congressman from Montana, was Trump's choice as Secretary of the Interior, a position that would give him wide authority over one fifth of the nation's land, offshore drilling, parks and wildlife, and even relations with American Indian tribes. In its closing days, the Obama administration had tried to make use of an old law to impose a ban on offshore drilling in the Arctic, but the Trump administration was pledged to undo this. Zinke was in many ways the perfect adjunct in Big Oil's takeover of Washington. He was a staunch supporter of fossil fuels and one of the most anti-environment lawmakers on Capitol Hill. He scored a dismal 3 per cent lifetime environmental voting record from the League of Conservation Voters.[49] His political campaign had been backed by Oasis Petroleum, a Texas-based oil and gas company.[50] He was also a staunch ally of the coal industry and of pipeline companies everywhere.

Zinke had personally opposed the Obama administration's proposals to regulate drilling and fracking operations on federal and American Indian lands.[51] He voted in favour of lifting the forty-year-old crude oil export ban.[52] He co-sponsored legislation to hasten pipeline approval for oil companies, and he showed a blatant disregard for the treaty rights of indigenous Native American tribes when they interfere with the construction of coal terminals.

As his transition aides merrily admitted, Donald Trump had outsourced the selection of Secretary of the Interior to his son Donald Jr,[53] who was allowed to be an influential member of the Trump transition team but who would after 20 January 2017 have no role in government, according to his father's public pronouncements. Donald Jr was an avid hunter, and he liked Zinke on the spot. Zinke would not disappoint, especially when it came to climate change.

'It's not a hoax, but it's not proven science either,' Zinke said. 'But you don't dismantle America's power and energy on a maybe. We need to be energy independent first. We need to do it better, which we can, but it is not a settled science.'[54]

Donald Jr may have also liked the way Zinke expressed himself. He once called Hillary Clinton the 'anti-Christ'.[55]

Thanks to Donald Jr's decision to appoint Ryan Zinke to his father's Cabinet, America would not only have yet another fossil fuels promoter and climate change denier; it would also have a hunter's hunter, an avid hunter, a gun-loving and gun-owning hunter, a Montana version of *The Deer Hunter* as Secretary of the Interior. According to the Center for Biological Diversity, Ryan Zinke wanted to kill a lot of animals. 'His brief political career', the Center declared upon hearing of his nomination,

> has been substantially devoted to attacking endangered species and the Endangered Species Act. He led efforts to strip federal protections for endangered wolves, lynx and sage grouse, voted to exempt massive agribusiness and water developers from Endangered Species Act limitations, and opposed efforts to crack down on the international black market ivory trade.[56]

Not wanting to crack down on the international black market in ivory pretty much tells us what we need to know. Zinke filled out the troika in charge of US energy policy pretty nicely. Perry, Pruitt and Zinke. Three sworn enemies of the environment. Of course, in order to manage the rolling back of energy and environmental regulations, the White House would need an effective conservative hardliner to be installed as head of the Office of Management and Budget, as the President's budget director. For that rather sensitive post, Donald Trump chose a South Carolina Republican congressman who just happened to be... a climate change denier as well.

Rep. Mick Mulvaney was part of the Tea Party Wave of 2010, which brought to Congress a flock of rather militant Republican hardliners.[57] He called the established facts of climate change a 'questionable science'.[58] He voted in favour of more offshore drilling and he voted against the idea of the EPA regulating greenhouse gas emissions at all. He voted in favour of lifting restrictions on the fossil fuels industry and against the idea of further federal funding of the development of alternative and renewable forms of energy.[59] Mulvaney was also a founding member in 2015 of the House Freedom Caucus, a congressional grouping of Tea Party right-wingers who were very sympathetic to the idea of deregulation.[60]

In December 2016, the House Freedom Caucus gave President Trump a list of hundreds of regulations he could repeal early in his administration.[61] They suggested that he open up more federal land to oil exploration, pull out of the Paris climate accords, kill the State Department's office on climate change and abolish the position of Special Envoy on Climate Change, and basically cancel any offices inside the federal government that the Obama administration had opened to keep track of climate change. At the same time, the Trump transition team had demanded that the Energy Department turn over a list of all federal employees who had worked on climate change policies.[62] Fearing they would be the subject of a Trump administration purge, the Obama White House refused to comply with the request, saying that it looked like 'an attempt to target civil servants, career federal government employees'.[63] This, too, was part of the dawn of the Age of Trump, in which it is far more than political correctness which is being thrown out the window.

With the Trump administration now in office and the Republicans in charge of the House and Senate, there are no more obstacles to the Trump administration's drive to put fossil fuels at the centre of US policy and to turn the clock back on climate change policy and environmental regulation by decades. The oil and gas industry can look forward to the Trump administration leasing more federal lands for drilling, lifting the moratorium on coal leases on federal lands, and progressively reversing the Obama administration's Clean Power Plan for reducing carbon dioxide emissions.

On the campaign trail, Trump promised to undo all of President Obama's climate regulations and to review numerous environmental rules for possible repeal. Trump, Perry, Pruitt and Mulvaney were all fans of fracking and of any number of dirty oil and gas exploration technologies that frightened many communities across America.

Donald Trump himself would briefly reach out to the other side, holding his reality TV-style quickie meetings with the hapless Al Gore[64] or the grinning Leonardo DiCaprio,[65] as a way of showing that he was listening, that he was open to hearing more about climate change. His daughter Ivanka, more than anyone else, would often seem to be the acceptable face of the Trump family, especially on issue likes climate change. Climate change is one of her pet subjects,[66] along with her plan for paid maternity leave and child-care tax credits.[67] But a careful look at the actual composition of the people who today manage and implement America's energy and environmental policy in the Trump administration suggests the true nature of things, as do the anti-environmental policies that have been introduced, including massive cutbacks at the Environmental Protection Agency and the continued denial of climate science, not to mention the rejection of the Paris accords on climate change that until the Trump era had bound the entire world.[68]

Ivanka, and not her father Donald, was the person who invited former Vice-President Al Gore to Trump Tower. Dad just dropped in for part of the chat. But it mattered little in the end when it came to Trump's decisions on climate change. Ivanka, who was supposed to represent the voice of moderation in the Trump White House, was everywhere, as was her controversial husband Jared Kushner, a top consigliere in the new reality TV extravaganza which moved into the White House on 20 January 2017. Kushner would find himself at the centre of scandal and controversy, in the tradition of his own family; his own father had gone to jail on multiple charges and had even hired a prostitute to lure his brother-in-law, who was cooperating with federal investigators, and arranged to have a secretly recorded tape of an encounter between the two sent to his sister.[69]

In the Kardashian era of American politics, when Donald Trump found time between tweets to meet with Kim Kardashian's husband

Kanye West, members of the extended First Family are supposed to be divided into those who tend to business and those who tend to politics. Ivanka Trump seems to do both. Jared Kushner has not sold his real estate holdings.[70] Yet they are everywhere. One of Jared's pet subjects, in a portfolio that ranges from sorting out peace in the Middle East to advising on US technology innovation, is Silicon Valley. So when Donald Trump and his Silicon Valley friend and backer Peter Thiel held a 'tech summit' at Trump Tower in December 2016, Ivanka and Jared Kushner were both in the room. So were Donald Jr and Eric Trump.[71] The White House would say that was because back in December 2016 they were still working things out, and now they know exactly how to handle the conflict of interest thing. But for the startled Silicon Valley billionaires, the tech summit turned out to be another episode of a reality TV show, another Trumpian photo opportunity that in some ways was on the same order as the humiliation of Mitt Romney. The former presidential candidate and enemy of Trump during the 2016 campaign had been brought to heel by Trump, who had him come to 'audition' for the role of Secretary of State on two embarrassing occasions. Now it seemed that the crème de la crème of Silicon Valley were also willing to prostrate themselves before Trump.

Tim Cook of Apple and Larry Page and Eric Schmidt of Google and Jeff Bezos of Amazon and Elon Musk of Tesla and Sheryl Sandberg of Facebook all accepted Peter Thiel's invitation to the meeting at Trump Tower. All of the Silicon Valley moguls had been loudly and raucously anti-Trump, and now they were being summoned by the President-elect. It was an offer they could not afford to refuse. Bill Gates, being the grand old man of Silicon Valley, had qualified for a private one-on-one with Trump a couple of days before. He had come out raving inexplicably about how Donald Trump could be the energiser of a new 'Kennedy era' set of innovations.[72]

Gates, who was a close and devoted friend of the Clintons, did not appear to have great faith in Trump's commitment to either the environment or technology innovation. While the billionaire brains of Silicon Valley were taking tea at Trump Tower, Gates was getting together with Warren Buffett and other billionaires to launch a billion-dollar fund that would aim to create technology innovation for renewable and alternative energy.[73] What Gates and Buffett and some ninety-seven of the world scientific community knew was that climate change was real, and not a hoax. Barack Obama, notwithstanding all his defects, had gotten it right on climate change and had proven himself the greatest defender of clean air and clean water and the rights of Native Americans in American history. The Obama administration's backing of a green economy, a clean energy economy, had undoubtedly shown leadership at the world level, and it was thanks to this leadership that China, the world's worst polluter, had signed on to the Paris accords.[74] As far as the US economy was concerned, the number of clean energy jobs had overtaken oil drilling jobs by 2015.[75] For the first time ever, the number of US jobs created in the solar energy sector overtook those in oil and natural gas extraction, helping drive a global surge in employment in the clean energy business as fossil-fuel companies faltered. But Donald Trump and his team intended to reverse this trend. Trump promised to bring back jobs to the coal mining communities of West Virginia. He promised to unleash the full power of Big Oil. He promised to undo the auto emission controls of the Obama era, and the Clean Power Act which protected American citizens from pollution.

Each and every one of Trump's Cabinet picks, without exception, was committed to cutting federal funding of renewable and alternative energies and promoting the rebirth of good old-fashioned fossil fuels. Green tech was not very high on the Trump administration's list of priorities.

As for technology innovation in general, the Trump administration had been fighting a war against the leaders of Silicon Valley for much of the past eighteen months. The leaders of Apple and Amazon had been firmly in the Hillary camp. But now the tech giants found themselves on the defensive. Events had taken an unexpected turn.

The arrival of Donald Trump at the White House was about to give a whole new meaning to the Silicon Valley concept of *disruption*.

CHAPTER NINE

THE DISRUPTOR-IN-CHIEF

It was a cold day in December, but there were scores of tourists and well-wishers on the street. There were Trump supporters and protesters and plenty of ordinary New Yorkers milling about on the corner of 56th Street and Fifth Avenue. The Manhattan White House, otherwise known as Trump Tower, was bustling with transition planning and score settling. The cameras were lined up in a row in the ornate lobby, ready to capture the moment when Trump's official 'Greeter Girl' – a 26-year-old native of Irvine, California named Madeleine Westerhout – officially started meeting and greeting the celebrity contestants as they entered the building and were accompanied to the elevator. For the press pool gathered in the lobby, Westerhout appearing at the elevator bay was a sign that somebody important was about to arrive, sending cameras into ready position. Some of the more important VIP visitors got to use a side entrance on 56th Street, but most of the visitors, especially the Cabinet nominees, entered the gold lobby and, on their way to the bank of elevators, passed by the Trump Grill and the famed escalator from whence the President-elect had so famously descended. Outside on the sidewalk, New York's finest were massed alongside a gaggle of Secret Service and Trump private security men, as the unruly crowd of bystanders spilled over into the traffic-congested Fifth Avenue.

It had been like this for weeks. Like contestants in a real-life reality show, winners and losers had been summoned to Trump Tower to pay homage, to be judged, to kiss the ring, to be chosen for government service, to be told if they were hired or fired, to be given their fifteen minutes of glory and fame in the sunlight of the cameras, and then to be swept up the tower to be received in the ornate and golden glamour of America's newly elected Sun King, the glorious Donald J. Trump.

It was on 14 December that Donald Trump summoned the moguls of Silicon Valley to Trump Tower for what his transition team called a 'tech summit'. As in most Trump family matters, he decided to give an active role to a family member, in this case his son-in-law Jared Kushner, the billionaire husband of Ivanka. Kushner would serve as point man and work closely with Trump's Silicon Valley backer and close buddy, the billionaire co-founder of PayPal, Peter Thiel.

The role of Thiel, as the lone Trump supporter in Silicon Valley, had been an enigma for much of the campaign. A libertarian who enjoyed shocking people, Thiel had been a Silicon Valley outsider who became a Trump insider. He had enjoyed a prominent speaking role on stage at the Republican National Convention in Cleveland, where he spent most of his allotted time singing Trump's praises. Toward the end of his speech, almost as an afterthought, he had mentioned his homosexuality.[1] His support for Trump would earn him the enduring wrath of gay activists across America. To PayPal co-founder Elon Musk and the rest of Silicon Valley's otherwise pro-Clinton community, Thiel was the on the wrong side. But, like it or not, he was now the tech supremo on Trump's transition team and the gateway to the Trump administration for Silicon Valley. For today's meeting he had worked closely with Jared Kushner to help Trump put together the guest list.

This was not Trump's first sector summit. He had already called together the media elite of America, many of whom he had personally attacked during the election campaign of 2016. That meeting had not gone too well. In a gathering of some of the most influential figures in America's TV news industry, the Sun King had proclaimed his disdain. 'We are in a room of liars, the deceitful, dishonest media who got it all wrong,' Trump told the gathered news executives.[2]

Trump would be more conciliatory the following day at a separate meeting with the *New York Times*,[3] but nothing of the sort was planned for the *Washington Post*. Trump had a personal beef with the newspaper's owner, Jeff Bezos, who was also the owner of Amazon. He had attacked the *Washington Post* on numerous occasions and banned its journalists from the Trump campaign.[4] He had accused Bezos of using the newspaper as a weapon against him and threatened Amazon repeatedly, saying: 'If I become President, oh, do they have problems. They're going to have such problems.'[5]

Trump's tirades against Bezos went on for many months. He started with a Twitter outburst during the campaign, when the *Washington Post* began investigating his business dealings. One day, upon waking, Trump launched a series of vitriolic tweets against Bezos. 'The Washington Post, which loses a fortune, is owned by Jeff Bezos for purposes of keeping taxes down at his no profit company, Amazon,' Trump wrote. 'If Amazon ever had to pay fair taxes, its stock would crash and it would crumble like a paper bag. The Washington Post scam is saving it!'

Bezos at first responded to Trump's tweets in a light-hearted manner, offering to send him into outer space with his Blue Origin rocket business. 'Finally trashed by Donald Trump,' tweeted Bezos. 'Will still reserve him a seat on the Blue Origin rocket #sendDonaldtospace'.[6]

But the war of words between Bezos and Trump soon escalated, and the Amazon chief became one of the most outspoken critics of Trump in Silicon Valley, eventually accusing Trump of behaviour which 'erodes our democracy around the edges'.[7]

Bezos changed his tone abruptly when the result of the presidential election was confirmed on 8 November. 'Congratulations to Donald Trump,' he now tweeted. 'I for one give him my most open mind and wish him great success in his service to the country.'[8]

Trump's son-in-law Jared Kushner and Peter Thiel, his friend from Silicon Valley, also wanted closure, following a fierce campaign in which Trump had also launched multiple attacks against Apple and its CEO, Tim Cook. Trump had even called for a boycott of Apple products.[9] Cook, an openly gay activist, was among Trump's biggest enemies in Silicon Valley, along with Tesla's enigmatic Elon Musk, the Clinton supporter who also had irreconcilable differences with Trump.

So, on 14 December, it was the turn of Silicon Valley to be summoned to Trump Tower. Donald Trump was convening his tech summit. It was not an invitation one could easily decline. Although most of the Silicon Valley leaders thought Trump was a buffoon or worse, nearly all would respond dutifully to the summons. With the exception of Hollywood, there was probably no other business elite in America as anti-Trump as the thought leaders of American technology innovation. They had been, almost to a man, Hillary supporters.

The meeting at Trump Tower was held in true Trump style, hurriedly arranged and looking more like a photo opportunity than a serious conclave. It was sandwiched into a busy transition week. Just a day before, with word leaking out about the nomination of Rex Tillerson as Secretary of State, Trump had found the time to welcome Kanye West to Trump Tower for what looked like the most awkward photo opportunity in the history of reality television.[10] A fellow member of the dynasty class of America's reality TV industry, Kim Kardashian's husband seemed somehow ill at ease. Trump was all smiles with Kanye, but just a few hours after he had finished the tech summit, the impulsive real estate tycoon would unleash another Twitter outburst. This time he let loose an angry burst of insults against Graydon Carter, the editor of *Vanity Fair*, a long-time nemesis in Trump's Twittersphere. *Vanity Fair*, it appeared, was guilty of having trashed the food and service at the Trump Grill in Trump Tower, in a poisonous online review, thus triggering the attack.[11]

Against this backdrop of celebrity nominations and meetings and insults, the tech summit began to take on surreal proportions. It appeared to be another celebrity episode in the expanding reality show that was soon to become the Trump presidency. And quite a show it was. The Silicon Valley moguls were led one by one through the gold lobby of Trump Tower, they were taken up the gold elevators, and then, after an hour or so, they were taken downstairs again and marched back out in front of the cameras. The moment was heavy with symbolism. Trump symbolism.

Kara Swisher, America's leading technology journalist, described it as 'a media-saturated geek reality show episode, in which real billionaires walk the gauntlet of prostration at Trump Tower and get exactly nothing for handing over their dignity so easily'.[12]

In true Trump style, never one to miss a branding opportunity, the President-elect had made sure that there was a bottle of his own Trump Ice Natural Spring Water placed in front of every tech leader. In the television industry, they would call this product placement. At the centre of the table, with Mike Pence to his right, sat President-elect Trump, a dazzling floor-to-ceiling window view of the Plaza and a corner of Central Park behind his shoulders. To his left sat Peter Thiel, the billionaire black sheep who was now Trump's Silicon Valley guru. Billionaire corporate vulture turned Secretary of Commerce Wilbur Ross sat at one end of the table, whispering to Gary Cohn, the Goldman Sachs president who had just been named chairman of the National Economic Council. Most of the leaders of America's tech giants looked distinctly uncomfortable. Some appeared hesitant; others looked carefully around the table. Most put on their best Silicon Valley smiley faces. Trump's children, Ivanka, Don Jr and Eric, sat at the Fifth Avenue end of the table, sandwiched between the president of Microsoft and the CEO of Intel. Eric even extended a welcome to the tech leaders, as though he were a co-host of the event.

The awkwardness of the whole thing was apparent from the moment they began, going around the room one by one, with the tech leaders introducing themselves to Trump as though they were participants in a speed-dating competition. Some used the occasion to make little speeches or to toss slogans or greetings into the air. The tech leaders were for the most part subdued, even subservient, always very respectful, while Trump was grinning broadly. He was doing his best impression of paternalistic and friendly, a condescending smile plastered across his face. He was clearly enjoying himself, even revelling in the attention of so many celebrity tech stars, the vanquished legion of Hillary supporters from Silicon Valley.

Tim Cook, seated appropriately to the left of Peter Thiel, kicked it off.

'Tim Cook, very good to be here. And I look very forward to talking to the President-elect about the things that we can do to help you achieve some things you want.'

Trump smiled graciously at the solicitous CEO of Apple.

'Great, Tim,' he muttered.

Next came Safra Catz, CEO of the powerful Oracle software group, which had been originally built by billionaire Larry Ellison on the back of CIA and Pentagon contracts. Catz had already decided to sign on to the Trump transition team, and was now in the Peter Thiel camp, the only other tech leader in the room who had joined Team Trump. 'I'm actually privileged and honored to even be here,' said a humble Catz, adding that she was looking forward to helping the Trump administration.

The Sun King nodded and awarded the Oracle chief two thank-yous in a row.

Elon Musk, with a wan smile, presented himself as modestly as he could as the builder of 'rockets and cars and solar stuff' and then informed Trump that he was 'really excited about expanding our manufacturing footprint in the US'.

The CEO of Microsoft, Satya Nadella, was perfunctory, offering just his name and rank, while the CEO of IBM, Ginni Rometty, mumbled something about it being 'great to be here'. Chuck Robbins, the CEO of Cisco Systems, another company with an appetite for hefty government contracts, said he was 'happy to be here, happy to help, and happy to work with you'. He was happy.

Jared Kushner, Reince Priebus and Steve Bannon introduced themselves, and Ivanka's husband was an active participant in the meeting, according to those present. Then came Google's Eric Schmidt, who squeaked out a meagre and somewhat soprano greeting: 'Eric Schmidt, Alphabet/Google, and completely agree with what's been said.'

Trump was smiling broadly, a look of satisfaction and achievement as the tech leaders presented their credentials. Louis XIV would not have behaved differently at court in Versailles as the senior nobles of France presented themselves, one by one. Trump had a positively golden smile on his face, worthy of Versailles.

After a few more executives and the Trump kids had introduced themselves, it was finally the turn of Jeff Bezos. The man who just a few weeks before had warned that Trump was eroding democracy now sounded more like the Prodigal Son returned home to do penance. He had already shown his pragmatism the day after Trump was elected President; now he was effusive.

'Jeff Bezos, Amazon.com,' he said breathlessly. 'I'm super excited about the possibility that this could be the *innovation administration*.'

Trump smiled again. How sweet it was to be the King, the new Sun King of America.

But the *innovation administration*? Seriously?

Trump listened in silence as they finished going around the table, smiling benevolently and nodding. Finally, when everyone had settled down, Trump gave the leaders of Silicon Valley a warm welcome, Trump-style. It was a welcome that could have come right off the floorshow of a Las Vegas casino.

'Well, I just want to thank everybody. This is a truly amazing group of people,' said Trump. 'I won't tell you the hundreds of calls we've had asking to come to this meeting.'

Polite laughter.

Trump had somehow managed to make it sound like the tech leaders who were gathered around the table had made it through a tough competition or a talent search to be here. He even joked with Peter Thiel about how hard it had been to decide which company leaders to invite. He thanked Thiel for everything he had done, giving him a thumbs-up, *Apprentice*-style, and then he bragged to the tech leaders that Thiel 'got the most applause' when he spoke in Cleveland at the Republican National Convention. Then he gave Thiel a funny backwards handshake, wherein Trump extended his left hand to the back of Thiel's right hand and Trump then extended his own right hand to pat the knuckles of Thiel's right hand, which was left hanging in mid-air against the back of Trump's left hand.

'I'm here to help you folks do well,' Trump told the tech leaders, and then he blathered on for a moment about himself, about his standing in the polls and about the bounce on Wall Street since Election Day. 'You're all doing well right now and I'm honored by the bounce,' he said, as if the tech companies should be thanking him for helping their stock prices to rise. 'They're all talking about the bounce, so right now everybody in this room has to like me at least a little bit,' Trump continued in his trademark *braggadocio* style, betraying both his Queens-bred insecurity and the need for constant ego reinforcement.

Then came the pep talk: 'We're going to try and have that bounce continue and perhaps even more importantly we want you to keep going with the incredible innovation. There's nobody like you in the world. *In the world*, there's nobody like the people in this room.'

Finally, Trump stared at the leaders of Google and Apple and Amazon and, perhaps trying to sound accessible and gracious, he told them that they could 'call my people'. It was the moment that betrayed the real outer-borough kid from Queens. The original Trump psyche came crashing through the velvety surface. Magnanimous Trump was trying to be friendly and conciliatory to the crowd of Silicon Valley leaders he had just trashed during the election campaign. He was evidently delighted to see them all here in Trump Tower. But the way his words came out sounded rather particular.

'Anything we can do to help this go along,' he said, 'we're going to be there for you, and you'll call my people, you'll call me, it doesn't make any difference, we have no formal chain of command around here.'[13]

To a true New Yorker's ear, telling somebody to 'call my people' is subtly different from telling them to 'call me'. So the ultimate message from the outer-borough kid to the billionaires of Silicon Valley was clear enough, for those who cared to decode it. *You'll call my people.*

By now America's tech aristocracy had been humbled, subjected to the Trump treatment. They were done. They were cooked. They were frozen like rabbits caught in front of the flashing headlights of the bulldozer known as Trump. Nearly all of them scurried away from Trump Tower on that cool December day without a statement, without a Facebook post, without an Instagram, without a message to their employees. No comment. The exception was, of all people, the billionaire owner of Amazon and the *Washington Post*. Jeff Bezos had gushed in front of Donald Trump upstairs and now he would gush in front of the cameras in the lobby, looking a bit like Mitt Romney praising Trump after stepping out of a dinner in Trump Tower when he was auditioning for the role of Secretary of State.

In fact, Silicon Valley's crème de la crème, most of them Hillary supporters, had just been given the Romney treatment. Summoned to a meeting they could not refuse, warmly welcomed, and then paraded in front of the cameras for posterity and for the personal pleasure of the Sun King, who could rub his hands in glee, many floors above, high in his lair, in the tower triplex of the Manhattan White House, high atop Trump Tower.

The tech leaders had met with a magnanimous Trump, which again was more in keeping with the role he had perfected during his two convocations of the hapless Romney, when the man who had called Trump 'a phoney and a con man'[14] had been reduced to the role of a supplicant, singing for his supper at Trump Tower.[15]

Donald Trump liked supplicants.

Jeff Bezos, whom Trump had insulted throughout the 2016

campaign, had come to Jesus. So had Apple's Tim Cook, whom Trump had threatened with a boycott.

When he emerged from Trump Tower after the tech summit, Jeff Bezos was a lamb. He made nice.

'I found today's meeting with the President-elect, his transition team, and tech leaders to be very productive,' announced the effusive Amazon boss. 'I shared the view that the administration should make innovation one of its key pillars, which would create a huge number of jobs across the whole country, in all sectors, not just tech – agriculture, infrastructure, manufacturing – everywhere.'[16]

The man who had accused Trump of eroding democracy was now on bended knee, spinning a yarn about an *innovation administration*, behaving like a billionaire corporate chieftain as carefully amoral as Rex Tillerson.

For Kara Swisher, Bezos's behaviour was not very hard to understand.[17]

'I suspect his personal opinions are different from the way he talked,' she says.

> But he's got a lot of issues. He's got a big company and a big newspaper. He wants to minimise the damage. He wants to make a deal. He realises that he probably went too far when he didn't think Trump would really win and so now that he has won he feels that he has to dial it back. He is concerned at what Trump could do against Amazon on taxes. He is protecting his interests.

As for Tim Cook, he sent a message to Apple employees in which he tried to justify his pilgrimage to Trump Tower, claiming that in order to protect Apple interests he had to be a participant. 'The way that you influence these issues is to be in the arena,'[18] wrote the cautious CEO of Apple.

The fact that Cook had opposed Trump and the Republican Party over LGBT rights and had been a solid Hillary Clinton supporter had to be somehow forgotten now. Business was business.

'Cook', as Kara Swisher put it,

> was not there as the CEO of Gay America, but as the CEO of Apple. And he is going to be pressured by Trump on manufacturing issues, on not having manufacturing in this country. He faces accusations from Trump that he makes everything in China, and that could impact the brand. After all, nothing in Apple products is made in the United States. It is all made in China.

Yet Trump's newfound power over the leaders of Silicon Valley was not just about threats or about what he could do to punish them. Trump also had a few important carrots to offer. Back in late August 2016, he had offered special tax breaks for Silicon Valley and other US corporations that agreed to repatriate their vast holdings of offshore cash. The idea was to bring back the war chest of overseas cash. But on the day Trump made the offer, Tim Cook was co-hosting a fundraiser for Hillary Clinton.[19]

Apple holds more than $200 billion in offshore funds,[20] so Cook stands to gain mightily for Apple shareholders if he plays his cards right. The combined total of offshore funds held by US corporations is said to be more than $2 trillion[21], a large chunk of which is held by tech companies.[22] If Trump arranges special repatriation terms and cuts the US corporate tax rate to 15 or 20 per cent, it is highly likely that these funds will indeed be brought back to America.

Swisher warns, however, that this does not necessarily mean the money will be used to create new tech jobs in America.

> It will probably fuel a new round of mergers and acquisitions, expansions, and it will be great for the stock and for shareholders, but I don't know that it will lead to a fundamental shift of jobs back into America. They might open up a token facility here or there, a factory with maybe 800 jobs here or there symbolically, and Trump will be able to tour these facilities for a photo opportunity. But the bottom line for shareholders is keeping costs down.

The bottom line seems in fact to explain the timid and cautious behaviour of America's tech chieftains. Swisher says Trump did not need to cow the tech leaders because they were already docile and humble.

'They did it to themselves. They humbled themselves by going to Trump Tower and saying nothing, by not standing up for what they supposedly believe in,' said Swisher.

'I have talked to a lot of people who were there,' continues Swisher, 'and they all had reasons for doing this, and most of them are economic. These people like to pass themselves off as different, as holier than thou, as more lofty and sanctimonious. They have a grand vision of themselves.'

'The reality', says Swisher,

> is that the tech sector is now a mature industry and in many ways these Silicon Valley leaders are comparable to ExxonMobil's Rex Tillerson, except that he seems to be more savvy and these people act like they were twelve years old. They are irresponsible. They claim they have no power to do anything about fake news, which is a lie. They are abrogating their responsibility and just protecting the bottom line.

For much of Silicon Valley, and especially for men like Tim Cook and Jeff Bezos, Trump was a business risk of colossal proportions. They were genuinely frightened about what Trump could do to Apple or Amazon, but then again they were also genuinely interested in what Trump could offer them.

So much for Silicon Valley's noble ideals and dreams of a better world.

Things had not gone very differently a day before the tech summit, when the Grand Old Man of Silicon Valley and Microsoft founder Bill Gates had been given his private audience. Gates had run the gauntlet of the marble-decked lobby of Trump Tower just a few minutes after Trump had finished his meeting with rapper

Kanye West. Gates was a close friend and supporter of the Clintons, a donor to the Clinton Foundation, but he seemed only too pleased to be here today, even if he had to play second fiddle in the celebrity line-up to the most important celebrity of the day, the rapper also known as Mr Kim Kardashian.

Gates didn't care if he had to follow Kanye. He had by now refashioned himself from monopolistic geek genius into billionaire philanthropist, and he naturally had his own private wish list to pitch to the Trump administration, starting with support for his new billion-dollar alternative energy technology innovation fund. Gates was, after all, a man of the world, a member of the permanent establishment as much as Goldman Sachs, the richest man on the planet, in fact, and the simple truth was that he, like others, would have to do business with the Trump White House. Yet when Gates emerged from Trump Tower he looked even more starry-eyed and sounded even more effusive than Jeff Bezos. Bill Gates went on national television and compared Donald Trump to John F. Kennedy.

> In the same way President Kennedy talked about the space mission and got the country behind that, I think whether it's education or stopping epidemics, other health breakthroughs, finishing polio and in this energy space, there can be a very upbeat message that [the Trump] administration is going to organise things, get rid of regulatory barriers, and have American leadership through innovation.[23]

For Bezos, it was the *innovation administration*. For Bill Gates, it was about a Kennedy era of *leadership through innovation*.

Team Trump, unsurprisingly, was delighted with the 'fantastic things' that Bill Gates had said about Donald Trump.[24] Another tech titan had taken a bittersweet bite of humble pie at Trump Tower. Bill Gates, the founder of Microsoft, had suddenly become the perfect avatar of the post-truth era, the age of Trump.

Had the rulers of Silicon Valley finally met their match? They had earned billions of dollars being disruptors, challenging the status quo of American life, challenging entire industries. But now they had found themselves face to face with a most unpredictable new President, a man who would give a whole new meaning to the Silicon Valley concept of 'disruption' and 'disruptors' in technology innovation. The politically correct and mollycoddled Hillary supporters from Silicon Valley, America's tech aristocracy, had indeed met their match. They had met the new Disruptor-In-Chief – the ultimate outsider, the outer-borough kid from Queens with a chip on his shoulder, the unprincipled property developer, the dealmaker, the political novice who would break all the rules in the book, and now the man who could send the share prices of publicly quoted companies into free-fall at the drop of a tweet.

Justin Smith,[25] the chief executive of Bloomberg Media, is something of a disruptor himself. At the age of twenty-five he built the first media bridges to China's leadership for the *International Herald Tribune*. He reinvented *The Economist* magazine and its online revenue model. He invented digital content platforms like *Quartz*. He turned around dying magazine brands like *The Atlantic* by going digital. And he is a respected digital thinker in Silicon Valley.

Smith sees a wide gulf between the mindset of Silicon Valley and the thinking at the Trump White House, and he doesn't doubt Trump's willingness to use the power of the presidency in a manner that he calls 'transactional'. He says he can imagine Trump getting deeply involved with the repatriation of offshore profits from Silicon Valley giants.

'I think there is a big and really immediate policy impact of the deal with tech firms on repatriation of foreign profits,' says Smith.

> I think we will see Trump cutting deals with tech companies and it will be a transactional tech policy. He will literally sit down, company by company, and say, 'Listen Apple, if you bring back this much cash we will you give you a tax amnesty or rebate.' This, in turn, could provide some short-term benefit to the economy

> and to the tech economy. It could be a significant trigger for tech M&A [mergers and acquisitions] activity if suddenly hundreds of billions of dollars of cash are brought back to the United States.

As for who will ultimately benefit from such large capital inflows into America, the answer seems to be the usual suspects: billionaire tech leaders and tech company shareholders. 'The lion's share of this cash, like the lion's share of the wealth creation that has characterised the growth of Silicon Valley, will go to specific privileged communities and especially to shareholders,' says Smith.

The Bloomberg Media chief thinks that even though Silicon Valley was caught off guard by the election of Trump, its position as the engine of global innovation in technology is not at risk.

'It was only in 2007 when the iPhone and Facebook were both invented,' says Smith. 'It's been a decade of incredible, transformative innovation and it looks like technology innovation is compounding with the dawning of the artificial intelligence era. The scale of disruption across industries and across geography is mind-boggling.'

America's technology innovation is indeed mind-boggling and it has undoubtedly created more tech billionaires and wealthy shareholders on Wall Street than any other industry for the past century. Unfortunately, the disruptive changes that are about to spread across America and the Western world may not be particularly helpful in job creation. In fact, the opposite may be true.

'My personal view', says Smith,

> is that ultimately the net impact of all this artificial intelligence and technology innovation on employment, on job levels, will be catastrophic. I'm of the view that the scale and the intensity of what we are seeing now, and the ubiquity of disruption across industries with AI and machine learning, is ultimately going to have a huge impact on employment.

Smith cites the example of Uber to prove his point.

'Look what's around the corner,' he says.

> Look at driverless cars and the impact on jobs. The single highest employment sector in all fifty states is drivers, whether cab drivers, taxi drivers, commercial drivers or truck drivers. We are just three or five years away from technologies that will completely disrupt what is arguably the largest employment segment in our economy. And that's just one example of what's coming.

Kara Swisher agrees.

'What's really coming is quantum leaps and innovations in AI, meaning drones and robotics. That's really going to replace jobs,' says Swisher. 'It's astonishing what's happening in automation. A lot of jobs will be eliminated. Ultimately, no matter what they tell you in Silicon Valley, technology will destroy jobs, and destroy a lot of them.'

In fact, an Oxford University study in 2013 forecast that up to 47 per cent of US jobs could be replaced by robots and automated technology in the next ten to twenty years.[26] Most experts agree that it will be technology, not trade, that eliminates the biggest number of jobs in America and across the Western world over time.

Trump talks a big game about bringing jobs back to America, but his claims are wildly exaggerated. Not even Donald Trump can hold back the forces of globalisation. He can tweet a victory from time to time, and he can stage a cameo appearance at a factory in the American heartland. He can tour the shop floor, smile for the cameras and then exaggerate the number of jobs that he has supposedly saved. But these will be symbolic moments. Trump has already shown how he will use the pulpit of the presidency on industrial policy. He can be a corporate bully, frightening the wits out of Boeing or Lockheed shareholders with a tweet, and he can shamefacedly take credit for the creation of new jobs that he had nothing to do with, jobs which had been planned long before his election in November 2016. Trump's corporate colleagues in his new Cabinet include fans of technology automation and robotics, and other job-reducing technologies. In the Trumpian view of the universe, technology innovation means cost reduction through robotics or automation, and if that means job reduction as well there is nothing personal intended. After all, business is business.

The truth is that the level of manufacturing in the United States has been in decline for many decades. Hard as it may be to believe, in a nation of 320 million Americans, today less than 20 per cent of jobs are in the manufacturing industry. The other 80 per cent are in the service sector.[27] But the economic dislocation that will be caused by robotics and automation in the United States will hit both the service and the manufacturing segments of the economy. Developments in artificial intelligence, robotics and biotechnology will disrupt the business world like a new industrial revolution, with administrative and office jobs as much at risk as factory workers and fast food industry employees. Technology may create a relative number of high-skilled jobs, even new types of jobs, but its net effect on the US economy will be to kill millions of jobs over the next decade or two.

Is Donald Trump aware of the subtle and nuanced paradoxes of technology policy in a nation where technology innovation has led the productivity revolution but could soon usher in a period of social displacement, even social upheaval as a result of job losses? Is the 45th President of the United States capable of understanding the difference between jobs that are lost as a result of globalisation and trade and outsourcing on the one hand, and on the other, jobs that are lost at home because of home-grown robotics and automation technology that is made right here in the USA? Kara Swisher has her doubts.

'He doesn't even understand it. He's still focused on West Virginia, telling them he is going to get them back their coal jobs. He doesn't really understand what's the next thing,' says Kara Swisher.

Trump may have a crude approach to jobs and technology, but Silicon Valley is even more concerned about the big issues of trade and immigration. Most of the tech giants have been unable to penetrate the China market, but they have been quite happy to produce products in China. A punitive Trump trade policy or, even worse, a trade war with China, would be in nobody's interest. But a Trump presidency that somehow pressured China into allowing Facebook and Google and Amazon more leeway in the Chinese market would be of interest to the scions of Silicon Valley.

During the tech summit at Trump Tower, Satya Nadella, Microsoft's CEO, raised the thorny issue of immigration with Trump, asking for help with the H-1B visas that Silicon Valley needed in order to attract highly skilled tech talent.[28] Trump appeared to respond favourably, asking how he could help. After all, these were not Mexican wetbacks; these were the kind of immigrants who are value enhancers for Silicon Valley, and in turn for Wall Street, and for the US economy, and Trump could see that much. But on a range of other issues that face America's technology innovation leaders and President Trump, it is likely to be a 'transactional' relationship, a set of agreements and deals, an exchange of favours between billionaires. If Trump, the dealmaker turned President, wants to do a deal with Silicon Valley, he can do so. He has all the levers of power that are needed.

As for the Silicon Valley aristocracy, they left their lofty and progressive values down in the cloakroom at Trump Tower. With Donald Trump, it was all about business. They had important interests to protect. He wanted to look good and be at the centre of attention. They could live with that. His trade and immigration policies could affect them. They had to be careful. But they stood to benefit mightily if they played their cards right. Favourable tax policies from the Trump administration could make them even more money, a great deal more. Repatriation of offshore cash could make their shareholders very happy. Deregulation on Wall Street could help them with their finances. There was every reason to smile and kiss the ring. So what if America's technology innovators were put off by the experience of dealing with Trump? That was the price of doing business these days. With the arrival of the Trump administration, the hordes of Hillary Clinton supporters in Silicon Valley would fall silent. They would come racing to be at the side of the victor, sucking up to Trump the way supplicants line up in front of Eastern European oligarchs when they are seeking favours.

For Silicon Valley, the arrival of Trump may even come to represent a coming of age, a moment when those fun-loving billionaire adolescent geeks and whizz kids began to look more like ageing corporate chieftains, like normal corporate executives and industry lobbyists, looking out for their shareholders, for their personal wealth and standing, and ready to eat some humble pie along the way if it serves the bottom line.

The leaders of American technology innovation used to be cleaner than clean, or, as Kara Swisher put it, holier than thou. They used to resemble one big Apple ad, with clean lines and bold vision. Until now. Now the iPhone had been stained. The coin had been devalued. The leaders of Silicon Valley had gathered meekly at the court of King Donald. They had paid homage to the Sun King, as they would throughout the Trump administration if it would help them to avoid damage or protect them from a derisive tweet – or far worse.

At the end of the day, the billionaire tech leaders from Silicon Valley stood to benefit mightily from cooperating with President Donald Trump. They could preserve and enhance their wealth and power. They could make more money. So what if they had to eat a bit of crow?

CHAPTER TEN

GOLDMAN SACHS FOR EVER

Steven Mnuchin, the new Secretary of the Treasury, is a controversial banker who spent seventeen years at Goldman Sachs, eventually rising to the position of managing partner. Mnuchin is second-generation Goldman Sachs; his father spent thirty-five years at the powerful Wall Street bank.[1]

Steve Bannon, the new chief strategist at the White House, made his bones as a merger and acquisitions banker with Goldman Sachs in the roaring 1980s, learning that greed was good first hand at the peak of Wall Street's hostile takeover and junk bond boom.[2]

Gary Cohn, the new chairman of the White House National Economic Council, was the president and chief operating officer of Goldman Sachs.[3]

Jay Clayton, the new head of the Securities and Exchange Commission, the man now in charge of regulating Goldman Sachs and the rest of Wall Street, is a lawyer who faithfully served Goldman Sachs on a number of multi-billion-dollar deals as a partner at Sullivan & Cromwell, which has been Goldman's go-to law firm for more than a century.[4]

Dina Powell, President Trump's Senior Counselor for Economic Initiatives and Deputy National Security Adviser for Strategy, as well as a top adviser to Trump's daughter Ivanka and her husband Jared Kushner, was a Goldman Sachs partner and head of the Goldman Sachs Foundation.[5]

There is no conspiracy here. Welcome to the government of

Goldman Sachs insiders, also known as the Trump administration. Nestled among the plutocrats and corporate raiders and Tea Party conservatives whom Trump has chosen to fill out his Cabinet, these Four Musketeers from the world of Goldman Sachs stand out, each of them to a man convinced of the need to slash corporate taxes and to roll back regulations on Wall Street, each of them a believer in unleashing the 'animal spirits' of the marketplace.

During the 2016 campaign, Trump attacked Wall Street repeatedly, singling out Goldman Sachs for criticism as the symbol of greed and evil, of some international financial conspiracy. He criticised Republican rival Ted Cruz for having financed his primary season campaign with a loan from Goldman Sachs,[6] and insulted his wife for having worked at Goldman Sachs.[7] He savaged Hillary Clinton for her close ties to Wall Street and Goldman Sachs and for having pocketed $675,000 for three private speeches at the powerful investment bank.[8]

'I know the guys at Goldman Sachs,' Trump had famously declared. 'They have total, total control over Cruz, just like they have total control over Hillary Clinton.'[9]

Toward the end of the 2016 campaign, one of Trump's last campaign ads featured an evil-looking Lloyd Blankfein, the CEO of Goldman Sachs, who also happened to be a Hillary Clinton supporter.[10] It was a spooky television ad, with a conspiratorial tone and overblown rhetoric. The voiceover didn't name Blankfein, but as his image flashed across the screen, looking like some international bogeyman, the narrator described 'a global power structure that is responsible for the economic decisions that have robbed our working class, stripped our country of its wealth and put that money into the pockets of a handful of large corporations and political entities'. The message was clear: Trump alone would stand up to Wall Street.

For months, Trump had blended together his attacks on Hillary Clinton and Goldman Sachs with tough talk on Wall Street. 'I am not going to let Wall Street get away with murder,' he bellowed. 'Wall Street has caused tremendous problems for us. We are going to tax Wall Street.'[11]

But *that* was the campaign. Now Trump was the President. If he wanted to stack his team with Goldman Sachs insiders, well, that was his prerogative. Already his spin doctors and surrogates were at pains to explain that if he wanted to hire Goldman Sachs people for his Cabinet that was OK because Trump supporters had faith in their leader and assumed that he knew what he was doing.

Trumpworld believed in their man and, as would be the case in so many other areas of policy, they did not take him literally. Nor did Goldman's CEO. After the election results were in, Lloyd Blankfein himself did not appear to be at all concerned about the prospect of a Trump presidency. Two days after the election, he sent a voicemail to company employees in which he seemed to praise Trump.

'The President-elect's commitment to infrastructure spending, government reform and tax reform', said Blankfein, 'will be good for growth and, therefore, will be good for our clients and for our firm.'[12]

Ultimately, Blankfein could only be pleased by the appointments that Trump had made, starting with the naming of his own right-hand man, Gary Cohn, the resident and COO who had served as Blankfein's principal deputy at Goldman Sachs, to the influential post of chairman of the White House's National Economic Council. That was a good start. But there were plenty of other reasons why the CEO of Goldman Sachs would feel that the Trump administration would be 'good for growth and therefore good for our clients and for our firm'.

In fact, what was underway at the dawn of the Trump administration was a restoration of Wall Street power that was perhaps unparalleled in American history. It was all the more apparent after eight years of government intervention and increased regulation under the presidency of Barack Obama, who had inherited a financial crisis in 2009 and had sought ways to help protect the nation from the risk of more speculative bubbles and more irresponsible behaviour by Wall Street.

Cohn, as president of Goldman, had complained about the

Obama administration coming down too hard on Goldman Sachs, but no one seemed to symbolise the greed and excesses on Wall Street more than Cohn's former colleague Steven Mnuchin, who after leaving Goldman Sachs had become a hedge fund manager and speculator. Mnuchin made a fortune buying a failed bank and then foreclosing on tens of thousands of mortgages after the collapse of the US housing market. The man whose signature would soon appear on the dollar bill had made his money off the depressed real estate market in a highly controversial manner. In California banking circles they had called him the 'King of Foreclosure'.

In 2009, Mnuchin led an investor group that put up $1.5 billion to buy a failed regional bank in California called IndyMac. The bank's collapse had been one of the largest bank failures in US history, but now the Federal Reserve was virtually throwing money at would-be bank saviours like Mnuchin's investor group. The fact that the government, through the Federal Deposit Insurance Corporation, agreed to cover 95 per cent of IndyMac's bad loan losses made the deal highly profitable for Mnuchin. He rebranded IndyMac as OneWest, a bank which proceeded to foreclose on mortgages in low-income and minority neighbourhoods across California.

IndyMac had been an aggressive seller of subprime mortgages, which had been at the heart of the financial crisis of 2008, and it had built its business on subprime mortgages. Now OneWest made its money by seizing properties from the holders of subprime mortgages. The bank was essentially a foreclosure machine. That was its business model. In 2015, Mnuchin sold the bank for more than $3 billion, double his investment, and then hopped on to the board of CIT Group, which had bought the bank after itself receiving billions of dollars of government handouts and guarantees.[13]

While Clinton may have made a few hundred thousand dollars giving speeches to Goldman Sachs, Mnuchin did far worse. He literally ran a bank that kicked tens of thousands of Americans out of their homes at the height of the housing crisis.[14] What is worse is that there is ample evidence that plenty of those foreclosures were illegal and fraudulent. According to a leaked memo from the office of the California Attorney General,[15] an investigation revealed thousands of violations including the backdating of foreclosure documents and the targeting of African-American families, who accounted for two thirds of all of the foreclosures.

The man named by Donald Trump to become Secretary of the Treasury had been the target of an investigation that had uncovered 'widespread misconduct' at his bank. The investigation showed how OneWest had pushed delinquent homeowners out of their homes by violating laws on notice and waiting periods and by illegally backdating key documents. In the memo, the state attorney general's consumer law division recommended filing charges against Mnuchin's bank, but that never happened.[16]

Mnuchin's response to the leaked investigation documents and the allegations of 'widespread misconduct' was to call the reports 'garbage', while Trump spokesman Sean Spicer painted Mnuchin as a hero.[17]

Senator Elizabeth Warren is a left-wing Democrat who has become America's most outspoken critic of Wall Street. She hovers slightly to the left of Bernie Sanders, and has never made a secret of her hostility to big banks. She summed up Steven Mnuchin with her usual invective.

'After years peddling the kind of dangerous mortgage-backed securities that eventually blew up the economy,' she said,

> Mnuchin swooped in after the crash to take a second bite out of families by aggressively – and sometimes illegally – foreclosing on their homes. This man has engaged in the worst kinds of practices on Wall Street and directly hurt thousands of working families – and now, Donald Trump wants to literally hand him the keys to the Treasury, where he can make big banks even richer at the expense of America's families.[18]

The senator's depiction of Steven Mnuchin is pretty close to the mark.

During his time at Goldman Sachs, Mnuchin had indeed been an ardent advocate of the risky securitised instruments that basically bundled subprime mortgages and sold them to investors. In other words, he had been part of the problem, an active participant in some of the most irresponsible Wall Street practices that would create the financial crisis from which he would later profit. The new Treasury Secretary could have been a poster boy for *Wall Street: Money Never Sleeps* or for *The Big Short*. He was an expert at buying up distressed assets, a speculator who made his money when companies and banks failed, just like his friend Wilbur Ross, the corporate vulture whom Trump named as Secretary of Commerce.

Mnuchin was brought into the Trump campaign in April 2016 as his chief fundraiser and as an economic adviser. During the campaign, he worked closely with Ross, a Trump crony and business partner who had become a key Trump adviser on trade and the economy. Ross was a billionaire in his own right, and a specialist at swooping in, vulture-like, and stripping assets away from a failed or failing company. Mnuchin might have done it with mortgage foreclosures, but Ross got rich by investing in faltering businesses like steel mills and coal mines that nobody else would touch.[19]

Among the failing businesses that Ross had invested in was Donald Trump's Taj Mahal casino in Atlantic City, New Jersey. In fact, it was Ross who saved Trump's empire back in 1990. At the time, Ross represented the bondholders of Trump's casino, along with Carl Icahn, the billionaire corporate raider and asset stripper who would also end up as a top White House adviser in the Trump administration. Ross was going to foreclose on Trump and send him into bankruptcy, but as he dealt with the brash New Yorker he began to like him, and to perceive value in the Trump brand itself. So Ross persuaded Icahn to support Trump and they embarked on a strategy that helped Trump to restructure and avoid personal bankruptcy. Ross and Icahn, in turn, became the primary shareholders in the Taj Mahal, while Trump retained a 25 per cent stake.[20]

Today, Ross is Secretary of Commerce and Icahn is special adviser to President Trump on financial regulation.[21] Both men have been accused by their critics of unethical behaviour, of callous disregard for the effect of their financial engineering on employment levels and for genuinely wolf-like predatory practices. If Mnuchin is poster boy for *The Big Short* then Ross and Icahn could be poster boys for *The Wolf of Wall Street*. Both Ross and Icahn, naturally, had worked closely on various large deals over the years with their friends at Goldman Sachs.

With Steven Mnuchin at the Treasury, and Gary Cohn and Steve Bannon at the White House, the team from Goldman Sachs was nearly complete. Carl Icahn, a scurrilous vulture investor who despised Securities and Exchange Commission (SEC) regulation, was advising the President on financial regulation. All that was needed now to round out the team was to put the SEC into the hands of the top lawyer to Goldman Sachs. Vulture-investor Carl Icahn helped Trump to find the right man: Jay Clayton.

Walter 'Jay' Clayton, the new head of the SEC, worked closely with Goldman Sachs throughout his career, having teamed up with the investment bank on a huge number of deals over the past decade. He has defended Goldman Sachs and other Wall Street banks from SEC regulators for years, especially in cases related to its role in the 2008–09 financial crisis. Clayton's wife is a Goldman wealth manager, another potential conflict of interest, though not in the eyes of the Trump administration.[22]

Clayton is the quintessential Wall Street insider, a senior cog in the machine that is committed to preserving the status quo, serving the establishment and, if possible, finding loopholes and leeway to avoid prosecution and fines for outrageous behaviour that has wrought havoc in the lives of millions of Americans, especially homeowners, since the Great Recession of 2008. He has been described as possibly the single most conflicted appointee in the Trump administration, and as the chief watchdog of the US securities industry he will have to recuse himself from numerous cases if he is to behave in an ethical manner.

Clayton represented Goldman Sachs when the firm received a $5 billion capital injection from Warren Buffett during the September 2008 financial meltdown on Wall Street.[23] He also represented Barclays bank during its controversial acquisition of the assets of Lehman Brothers.[24] He is a long-time defender of big banks and the excesses of Wall Street.

Even the *Wall Street Journal* noted that 'his past legal work raises potential conflicts of interest'.[25]

Clayton's nomination to head the SEC sent critics on the left into fits of apoplexy. Rep. Adam Schiff, a California Democrat, tweeted the good and bad news about Clayton with bitter irony. 'Good news: Trump's SEC pick Jay Clayton isn't another Wall Street billionaire. Bad news: He's their lawyer.'[26]

'It's hard to see how an attorney who's spent his career helping Wall Street beat the rap will keep President-elect Trump's promise to stop big banks and hedge funds from getting away with murder,' noted Senator Sherrod Brown, a Democrat from Ohio.[27]

In Trump's view, Clayton would do just fine. After all, he was well qualified for the job, and knew the industry. So what if he had been the principal defender of the wolves of Wall Street for decades? Trump said he had hired Clayton 'to undo many regulations which have stifled investment in American businesses'.[28] Indeed, Trump's new adviser on financial regulation, Carl Icahn, had recommended Clayton precisely for this task.[29] The fact that Icahn himself had an official designation as a special adviser to President Trump while maintaining day-to-day management of his multi-billion-dollar empire was just par for the course. It was unlikely that he would have any headaches with the SEC.

Aside from the mantra of deregulation, by now a clarion call that was echoed by the Republican Congress, Clayton shared another deep conviction with the 45th President of the United States. Both he and Trump want to undo the law that prohibits US corporations from paying foreign bribes, the Foreign Corrupt Practices Act.

In 2011, Clayton criticised the anti-bribery law, claiming that overzealous enforcement was 'causing lasting harm to the competitiveness of US-regulated companies and the US capital markets'. He called for the United States to 're-evaluate its approach to the problem of foreign corruption'.[30] In other words, Clayton was arguing that US corporations *should* be allowed to engage in bribery and pay-offs in order to become more competitive on world markets. Donald Trump heartily agreed. After all, greed is good. It could have been Gordon Gekko speaking. In 2012, Trump called the anti-bribery law 'horrible' and said it should be changed, but now he was the President, with a Republican majority in Congress and a cast of talented Wall Street deregulators in his Cabinet.

No wonder Wall Street began to party as soon as Trump's government began to take shape. Goldman Sachs saw its own share price soar by more than 30 per cent in the thirty days after Trump was elected.[31] Financial markets and investors were thrilled with the shape of Trump's Cabinet and his top economic appointments. But they were even more thrilled by what they were hearing. The prospects of huge corporate tax cuts and some form of fiscal stimulus by way of infrastructure investments were like manna from heaven, especially for a global economy that had been getting used to low growth and low interest rates and low inflation as a new way of life, as the new normal. The idea that began to take shape was that Trump's economic policies would ultimately be reflationary, and would contribute to faster US economic growth. Wall Street loved it. They especially liked the idea of big corporate tax cuts and a special tax amnesty to induce Apple and Microsoft and dozens of big corporations to bring back to America big piles of offshore corporate cash.

'Our number one priority is going to be tax reform,' proclaimed Steven Mnuchin on the day he was named Secretary of the Treasury. 'Cutting corporate taxes will create growth,' he declared, promising to serve up 'the biggest tax reform since Reagan'.

The Trump administration and the Republican majority in Congress are indeed moving ahead on tax reform, and US corporations and Wall Street banks, rather than the lower rungs of American society, stand to reap the greatest benefits.

'The reason why American companies don't bring cash back is because of the differential in tax rates,' Mnuchin explained. 'So the combination of lowering the corporate tax and a one-time 10 per cent repatriation tax will bring the cash back. We think there will be hundreds of billions if not trillions of dollars that are going to come back and create infrastructure and jobs.'[32]

The estimates of how much money will come back to America are staggering, but the likelihood of this money creating many new jobs is relatively low. Most of the repatriated cash is more likely to fuel another round of corporate mergers and takeovers, share buybacks and financial speculation.

Aside from tax cuts, the Trump administration's new senior economic and financial policymakers were also sworn, along with the Republican Congress, to roll back the regulation of banks and banking. They wanted to undo the Dodd–Frank law of 2010, a law that was introduced by the Obama administration in the wake of the financial crisis to provide safeguards against the banks using the money of depositors for the kind of speculative behaviour that had caused the financial crisis in the first place.

Mnuchin called the law 'way too complicated' and promised to 'strip back parts of Dodd–Frank that prevent banks from lending'. The new Treasury Secretary took special aim at a provision in the law called the 'Volcker rule', a consumer safeguard named after Paul Volcker, the former chairman of the Federal Reserve. The Volcker rule is designed to stop banks from betting with depositor-insured funds. Goldman Sachs had been complaining about that clause for years, claiming it was too complex and restrictive.

'The number one problem with the Volcker rule is it's way too complicated and people don't know how to interpret it,' said Mnuchin, mimicking the Goldman line. 'So we're going to look at what do with it, as we are with all of Dodd–Frank.'[33]

Carl Icahn, Steven Mnuchin, Wilbur Ross, Jay Clayton and all the merry band of Trump administration deregulators could now join forces with a Republican Congress to dismantle the few safeguards that had been erected in the wake of the Great Recession. Ross would throw figures around with wild abandon, complaining that excess regulation was costing America $1 trillion a year. But there was no way around the brutal reality of what was about to happen: the Trump administration would seek to undo the very regulations which were aimed at preventing another collapse of a major financial institution. They would work to undo a law that requires the regulation of risky derivatives trading by the SEC or by the Commodity Futures Trading Commission (CFTC). They would undo bank regulations and place Wall Street under the direction of Wall Street itself. By gutting the Dodd–Frank law and reining in watchdogs like the Consumer Financial Protection Bureau, Team Trump would allow the banks to engage in speculative practices once again, and this time without any real accountability.

Sadly, this was not the first time that a Treasury Secretary or a President had tried to unshackle Wall Street from regulation. For decades, there had been a push to roll back financial regulations and it was first embraced by President Ronald Reagan in the 1980s, then by his successor George H. W. Bush, and then by President Bill Clinton.

It was in the late 1990s, towards the end of the Clinton years, that Wall Street finally got what it wanted, namely a hands-off policy from Washington and a plethora of legislation that under the guise of modernising the financial system would actually reduce regulation and oversight, essentially leaving Wall Street to police itself. Nearly two decades before Trump, the Clinton administration rolled back the most important laws that had protected American savers and Main Street from the excesses of Wall Street since the Great Depression.

In 1998, the Secretary of the Treasury under Clinton was Robert Rubin, a financier who had previously spent twenty-six years at Goldman Sachs and was the star of the Wall Street establishment.[34]

Rubin believed in as little regulation as possible and he was served by free-market acolytes such as Larry Summers, his deputy and later his successor. Summers preached the gospel of deregulation just as much as his boss, and he was often the blunt instrument used by Rubin to cut deals on Capitol Hill. But Rubin's greatest ally in the war against regulation was Alan Greenspan, the powerful chairman of the Federal Reserve who had been a follower of libertarian goddess Ayn Rand, and who was himself bitterly opposed to the idea of any regulation of the markets.

Greenspan, Rubin and Summers were all riding high in the late 1990s. The economy was booming, housing starts were booming, Wall Street was bullish and the first wave of the tech stock boom was underway and creating the internet bubble. The Fed chairman and Rubin and Summers were masters of the universe when it came to the global economy. They had faced down financial crises in Mexico and Russia in the 1990s and now they were taking credit for solving the faraway Asian financial crisis of 1997–98. For this achievement, *Time* magazine would put their smiling faces on its cover and nickname the three men 'The Committee to Save the World'[35] and 'The Three Marketeers'.[36] They were lionised as heroes of the world economy. The fact that the Asian financial crisis had been solved by imposing draconian conditions on the struggling economies of south-east Asia, creating years of human suffering, was a detail that could be ignored. It was irrelevant. The point was that the Clinton administration had managed to use the International Monetary Fund to solve the problem and The Three Marketeers were credited with having avoided a global financial meltdown.

Meanwhile, back at home, Greenspan, Rubin and Summers were busy creating the conditions for an even bigger financial crisis, this time by allowing the geometric spread of dangerous derivatives trading that would later be a principal cause of the global financial crisis a decade later.

Ted Truman[37] has seen his share of global financial crises. He spent twenty-two years at the Federal Reserve, rising to lead the international finance division. In early 1998, Ted Truman was working for Alan Greenspan. He remembers Greenspan as a wily political animal, solidly pro-business and anti-regulation, but always shrewd in the way he got things done.

'He believed in letting the market regulate itself,' recalls Truman. 'He was a skeptic about what regulation could do, and he tended not to be proactive.'

Rubin and Greenspan, he adds, were in total ideological lock-step. Both men believed that the market could police itself.

In March 1998, one lone official of the Clinton administration, a derivatives expert who ran the little-known Commodity Futures Trading Commission, emerged from the bowels of the bureaucracy and tried to sound the alarm over risky derivatives trading. Brooksley Born was a smart corporate lawyer who probably knew more about derivatives trading than anyone else in Washington, including Alan Greenspan.

Born's warning was simple enough, but it did not play well with the zeitgeist of the times, with a roaring economy and a drunken stock market. But this brave woman persisted in telling the White House, the SEC, the Federal Reserve and the Treasury that in her opinion an unregulated derivatives market could pose grave dangers to the US economy.[38]

Ted Truman remembers her as being rather blunt and undiplomatic, even pushy. He also remembers what happened when she spoke up about the need for regulation of the dangerous derivatives market.

'She was not well liked by the Treasury or at the Federal Reserve and she wanted to get involved in the regulation of derivatives because she was seriously worried,' Truman recalls. 'But Rubin and Greenspan basically told her, "Well we are not so worried about derivatives and by the way, it's really none of your business. You don't know what you are talking about." They came down pretty heavily on her.'

The episode is important because it symbolised the only public challenge to the Greenspan–Rubin orthodoxy of leaving Wall Street as unregulated as possible. It was the Born Prophecy of 1998, and Greenspan and Rubin shot it down.

Born had good reason to be worried, because she had stumbled upon a problem that would prove to be at the heart of the 2008 financial crisis. Back in 1998, she worried that unregulated trading in derivatives could provoke a serious financial crisis. But nobody wanted to listen. When she came forward in the spring of 1998 with proposals to regulate the over-the-counter derivatives market,[39] she was met by fierce and hostile opposition from Wall Street lobbyists, and the combined wrath of Greenspan, Rubin and Summers.

At this point Greenspan himself entered the fray, saying publicly that there was no need for any new regulation of the derivatives market and that the Born proposal would threaten the very existence of financial markets. He stood logic upside down in his attempt to argue that markets get it right and do not require any regulation.

'Regulation of derivatives transactions that are privately negotiated by professionals is unnecessary,' Greenspan said with contempt as he attacked the Born proposal. 'Regulation that serves no useful purpose hinders the efficiency of markets to enlarge standards of living,' he declared in a Senate hearing.[40]

Ted Truman remembers the Brooksley Born incident as a turf battle, but former *Wall Street Journal* Fed-watcher David Wessel[41] points out that she was actually ahead of her time and that it was deeply unfortunate that the Federal Reserve and Treasury rushed forward so quickly to crush her.

'She may have over-reached herself a bit in her desire to regulate derivatives,' recalls Wessel.

> But she was prescient in her warning of the problems that derivatives could cause. Unfortunately she did it in a way that was politically ham-fisted, and she got totally zapped by Rubin, Summers and Greenspan. They came down on her like a ton of bricks. They told her not to try and regulate derivatives. She floated her proposal anyway and they publicly trashed her.

Much of the dirty work would be done by Larry Summers, who was by then serving as Rubin's deputy. He was effectively Rubin's enforcer, an arrogant intellectual with the blunt demeanour of a bad-humoured butcher. Many considered Summers to be Rubin's hatchet man when it came to shutting down Ms Born and her attempts at regulation. Summers was put in charge of yelling at Brooksley Born, of cajoling and threatening and pushing her to give up. Born was indeed finally stopped dead in her tracks, by Summers and Rubin and Greenspan. Wall Street would win the day and Born would eventually resign from her post in frustration.[42] But The Three Marketeers were not content to just shut her down. Greenspan went back in front of Congress later in 1998 and fought off attempts to regulate the derivatives market, even after unregulated derivatives trading had caused the collapse of a big hedge fund that very summer. Greenspan simply stared in the face of Congress, alongside Bob Rubin, and said regulation of derivatives was a bad thing and would be dangerous.[43] What is more, Greenspan and Rubin then went on to actively support a bill[44] that would prohibit any regulation at all of the derivatives market.

After Brooksley Born left the Clinton administration in 1999, the President's working group on financial markets released a report that actually called for 'no regulations' of derivatives and swaps. This led to cooperation with Congress to introduce the Commodity Futures Modernization Act, a law that prohibited the CFTC or SEC from regulating the increasingly dangerous derivatives market. By allowing the trading in many types of mortgage-related swaps and other derivatives to go completely unregulated, this law would later lead to the kind of over-leveraging at a number of Wall Street securities firms that contributed to the failure of Lehman Brothers in 2008 and the near-collapse of big insurance groups like AIG.[45]

Greenspan, Rubin and Summers would leave the dangerous derivatives market totally unregulated. Michael Greenberger, a former colleague of Born's on the board of directors of the CFTC, summed up the situation left behind by Greenspan and Rubin in a PBS *Frontline* documentary about the Born incident called 'The Warning': 'So now this is an unregulated market,' says Greenberger.[46] 'No transparency, no capital reserve requirements, no prohibition on fraud, no prohibition on manipulation, no regulation of intermediaries. All the fundamental templates that we learned from the Great Depression are needed in order for markets to function smoothly are gone.'[47]

But The Three Marketeers did not stop there. They also performed legislative euthanasia on the single most important consumer protection law in American financial history. For years, Rubin and Summers had been developing plans to repeal the Glass–Steagall Act of 1933, the Depression-era law that had protected decades of American savers by keeping commercial banking separate from insurance and from investment banking and the securities industry.

It was thanks to Rubin and Summers, with the benevolent blessing of Alan Greenspan, that the Clinton administration teamed up with Republicans to repeal and replace Glass–Steagall. Truman notes that the law was being superseded already by the market reality and by merger fever on Wall Street. More and more banks were using loopholes in the law to get around the kinds of activity that Glass–Steagall was intended to stop.

With Bill Clinton still suffering the aftershocks of his impeachment in the Lewinsky scandal, Rubin and Greenspan took the lead, and pushed Congress to pass the Financial Services Modernization Act in November 1999.[48] Glass–Steagall was finally dead. Banks were free to buy risky trading operations, and still more of the groundwork was laid for what would a few years later turn out to be the biggest financial crisis since the 1930s. Truman notes that in some ways the new law merely formalised the reality in the marketplace, starting with the $70 billion merger that year of Citicorp, the biggest bank in the United States, and Travelers Group, which included retail brokerage (Smith Barney), investment banking (Salomon Brothers) and big insurance and consumer finance businesses. Citicorp announced the deal even before Glass–Steagall was repealed, and it was this merger that would effectively force Congress's hand.[49]

When the repeal was signed into law by President Bill Clinton,[50] Alan Greenspan stood just a few feet away, a proud smile on his face. He applauded as Clinton lifted his pen. The chairman of the Federal Reserve looked mightily pleased. After all, another piece of financial regulation had just been retired to the woodshed. Now Wall Street and the markets would be free to roam.

David Wessel, who knew Greenspan well in those days, says the Fed chairman 'was consistently dismissive' of the capacity of regulation to do any good. 'What Greenspan was really saying was that we're better off letting the wizards of Wall Street alone. They know what they're doing. They can self-regulate.'

Greenspan did not even believe that US regulators were sufficiently competent or up to the task of regulating. He had far more respect for the billionaires and bankers from Wall Street than for the government bureaucracy. 'His view', recalls Wessel,

> was that the kind of people we had as regulators were just incapable of fixing things, and that the bankers themselves had so much money on the table that they would police their own game. And that they would police it better than some $98,000 or $120,000-a-year government regulator and certainly better than some stupid rule that some idiot congressman could write. That is what he believed. What happened is that in the financial crisis of 2008 he was proved wrong, the table tipped over, and the rest of us got murdered.

The Molotov cocktail of unregulated markets exploded like a time bomb in September 2008, more than a decade after the first warnings from Brooksley Born and the Greenspan–Rubin campaign against regulation of derivatives trading. After Lehman Brothers was allowed to collapse, Wall Street and the world entered into the worst financial panic since the 1930s. It was bloody and it hit the

American economy like a tidal wave of destruction. The bundled subprime mortgages came home to roost. The derivatives market imploded. The very market at the heart of the financial crisis was the one that Alan Greenspan and Bob Rubin had worked so hard to keep free of regulations.

A year into the crisis, Born gave her own appraisal in *The Warning*. 'It was my worst nightmare coming true,' she recalled.

> Nobody really knew what was going on in the market. The toxic assets of many of our biggest banks are over-the-counter derivatives and they caused the economic downturn that made us lose our savings, lose our jobs, lose our homes. It was very frightening.[51]

In the wake of the 2008 crisis, Alan Greenspan would finally grudgingly admit that he had been wrong, and that his actions could have contributed to the crisis. He called it 'a flaw in my model, in my understanding of how the world works'.[52] But others are more direct. 'He certainly bears responsibility for the crisis,' says Ted Truman, 'but I think he has been cut down to size.'

As for Bob Rubin, he left the Clinton administration in the summer of 1999, handing off to Larry Summers the post of Treasury Secretary even as they battled to repeal Glass–Steagall that year.[53] Less than four months after resigning as Secretary of the Treasury, Rubin joined the board of Citibank, the bank that reaped the greatest benefits of the repeal of Glass–Steagall which Rubin had spearheaded as Treasury Secretary. At Citibank, Bob Rubin continued to believe in the supremacy of the markets and in the value of highly leveraged and high-risk investments.

As the bank's senior counsellor and a board member, he was involved in a board decision to ramp up risk-taking back in 2004 and 2005, a move that would eventually bring the bank to its knees during the crisis of 2008. Rubin would have a hard time later on trying to justify the fact that he had been paid $115 million between

1999 and 2009, at a time when under his leadership Citibank had lost $20 billion in one year alone and had been forced to accept a $50 billion government bailout to save the bank from collapse.[54] When Rubin finally left the bank in 2009, it was under a dark and pendulous cloud, but with a fair amount of cash in his pocket.[55]

Larry Summers, Rubin's hatchet man, never acknowledged the role he played in laying the groundwork for the financial crisis of 2008. Unlike Greenspan, he was not the sort of man to express any regret. Summers would later serve in the Obama administration, following a highly controversial stint as president of Harvard, having to leave after casting doubt on the ability of women to do well in science and mathematics.[56] He would later put himself forward for a seat on the Federal Reserve Board, but the Obama administration wasn't biting.[57] Finally, Summers would reinvent himself as a supporter of Hillary Clinton, trading his past deregulation mantra for a stern and politically correct belief in the need for far greater regulation of Wall Street.

'Larry was hoping for a job in the new Clinton administration, but that didn't work out too well,' recalls Wessel. 'Larry can be really cynical about things. He is quite capable of evacuating his previous position, taking a new one that's much more extreme on the left and never bothering to justify himself.'

In early 2017, as the Trump administration began taking shape, complete with its team of Goldman Sachs all-stars and its plans to roll back Dodd–Frank and other Wall Street regulation, Summers suddenly sounded like Bernie Sanders on steroids. He claimed that Donald Trump's policies were setting the stage for the next financial crisis.

'Deregulation in some areas like finance is hugely dangerous,'[58] said the man who had made deregulation his mantra and thereby contributed to laying the foundations for the 2008 financial crisis. Deregulation was dangerous, said the man who had helped Alan Greenspan and Bob Rubin to squash Brooksley Born nearly two decades earlier.

With the Trump administration planning to go even farther than the deregulation of the Clinton years, Summers will most likely end up being proved right. The unleashing of Wall Street's animal spirits, combined with huge corporate tax cuts, may well provide more economic growth for the United States in the short term, but many economists worry that it will all end badly again, eventually leading to another bubble on Wall Street. Tax cuts meanwhile will almost certainly add trillions of dollars to the national debt, raising it to levels that could become unsustainable in time.

Ted Truman believes that what the Trump administration has in mind could well lead to another financial crisis:

> I would say there is a counter-revolution that is now underway, with the dismantling of Dodd–Frank and the lifting of many restrictions on Wall Street over time likely. This will essentially reverse the pattern that has existed since the global financial crisis of 2008, and, depending on how far they go, on how far the pendulum swings, it will probably lay the foundation for another cycle of boom and bust.

The key question for Truman is not really whether there will be another cycle of boom and bust, but how long it will take. 'It could be a decade before the chickens really come home to roost this time,' he observes. He notes that the deregulation promised by the Trump administration marks a return to the Greenspan philosophy that the market will regulate itself, even though Alan Greenspan himself has admitted that he was wrong.

'People forget the lessons of the past,' notes Truman drily.

The lessons of the past are clear enough, but the Trump administration's embrace of tax cuts and deregulation means that Wall Street can party once again as if it were 1999. Donald Trump and his team from Goldman Sachs certainly will not fulfil their campaign promises to 'drain the swamp' of Wall Street lobbyists.[59] Team Goldman has been handed the keys to the government. The Trump administration's top economic team is 100 per cent Goldman Sachs. Some are even highly competent people. All are bitterly opposed to regulation, and all are sworn to undo the legacy of the Obama years. They are now actively engaged in dismantling the laws that were supposed to protect American savers from another financial crisis, with the enthusiastic cooperation of Republicans on Capitol Hill.

Under these circumstances, one does not need a crystal ball to see that after another prolonged period of deregulation, another financial bubble is virtually inevitable. It is only a question of time.

Those who do not learn from history are usually doomed to repeat it.

CHAPTER ELEVEN

TRUMP AND THE NEW WORLD DISORDER

To look into the eyes of Vladimir Putin is something of a rare privilege, especially when he welcomes you to his ornate suite of offices at the Kremlin. His gaze is impenetrable, aside from the mask of a diplomatic smile. Behind the mask are the cold blue eyes of a warrior, the dull stare of the master of martial arts. The President of Russia examines his visitor carefully, all the time affecting a poker face. He is wearing a sober dark blue suit with a white shirt and a blue tie. His black leather shoes are highly polished; they look new. He is impeccable, flawless, intense. His face seems tense and drawn and as he speaks, he fidgets frequently with his tie. Yet Putin emanates raw power as he sits there receiving a visitor, in front of a marble fireplace in the Chimney Room of the Kremlin.

Bush must have been endowed with supernatural powers to say he could look into Putin's eyes and read his soul. In the end, even he had to admit that he had misjudged the former KGB agent, to put it mildly. In fact, Putin seems a man of a thousand faces, the ultimate doyen of the intelligence community, perhaps the only head of state who is also operational in covert intelligence operations.

The most striking aspect of being in conversation with Vladimir Putin is the way he is capable, in a matter of minutes or even seconds, to change demeanour, to shift from being serious to playful, from formal to relaxed. I saw this happen in front of my own eyes when I went to see Putin at the Kremlin in the summer of 2015 in order to interview him for a biography I was writing about Silvio

Berlusconi, the former Italian Prime Minister who is a close friend of Putin's.[1] His mood changed very quickly indeed when he began speaking about his billionaire friend from Italy. His intense and menacing eyes were now positively twinkling with delight.

Putin's capacity for sudden mood shifts is very different from the way Donald Trump hops from subject to subject. With the tightly wound Putin, everything seems deliberate and carefully willed. The man never loses control. With Trump, everything is more impulsive. He genuinely seems unable or unwilling to stay on a single subject for more than a minute or two. Putin is always several steps ahead of his interlocutor, as though he were playing an imaginary game of three-dimensional chess. Trump is not a chess player. He is a crass and superficial real estate developer from New York who became a reality TV star along the way to the White House.

Putin and Trump could not be more different, yet both men share a fundamental character trait. Both men tend to filter the entire world through their ego. Both men are determined and driven narcissists. Putin is able to exert self-control and govern his narcissism. He can actually appear humble, even timid, in private, as though he were trying to downplay his own importance. Trump, as we all know by now, is not very good at hiding the high opinion he has of himself. He wears his ego on his sleeve and tweets or shouts praise for himself on a daily basis.

As ego-driven political leaders, both Putin and Trump like many of the same things. They enjoy having a court, an entourage, the trappings of power. They both love lavish pageantry, regardless of taste. They both have the greatest respect for other strongmen, for other forceful leaders, for nationalists and populists, for tough guys in general, whether they are dictators or democratically elected Western anti-establishment politicians. Strong leaders tend to admire other strong leaders. They feel they know how to deal with each other. They are comforted by the fact that they are alpha males, and they often behave as if they consider themselves invincible. In the case of the evolving relationship between Trump and Putin, however, the two men are anything but evenly matched. In terms of experience, cunning, sophistication, ruthlessness and self-control, Putin is miles ahead of Donald Trump, and thus far Putin's ability to play on Trump's ego has yielded solid results for the Kremlin. The Russian leader also has another advantage: while America was turned inward in 2016, distracted by the most chaotic presidential election campaign in modern history, Vladimir Putin went about redrawing the geopolitical map of half the planet, from Eastern Europe to the Middle East.

By the time Donald Trump took office, pledging to make America great again, Putin had already run circles around the Obama administration, carving out new spheres of influence and virtually pushing the United States out of the picture on critical world issues such as the bloody civil war in Syria. But Putin's finest and most diabolical achievement came during the 2016 election campaign. The Kremlin-ordered and -orchestrated hacking of Hillary Clinton's campaign and the Democratic National Committee[2] came straight out of the KGB playbook. The way Putin's men then exploited Julian Assange, another well-known narcissist, to release embarrassing emails via WikiLeaks, was exceedingly well planned and executed. The way that Trump then made endless and relentless use of the Kremlin-leaked hacked material on Hillary Clinton was solid proof of concept, and it must have been deeply satisfying for Putin. Trump's frequent and profuse expressions of friendship and admiration for the Russian leader throughout the presidential campaign, the transition period and the start of the Trump administration must have been reassuring.[3] Soon Putin could just sit back and revel in his good fortune. The plan seemed to be working.

If 2016 was the year that saw the most chaotic American presidential campaign in living memory, it also marked the most blatant use of the tools of cyber warfare by one sovereign nation against another. Vladimir Putin's army of hackers, carefully operating just outside the perimeter of Russian intelligence services, did a splendid job of causing mayhem, confusion, scandal and political crisis in America, nearly all of it to the benefit of Donald Trump.

Word of the Russian hacking of the Democratic National Committee first leaked out in June 2016, when the *Washington Post* reported that Russian spies had targeted the DNC's computer network and database. In Moscow, Kremlin spokesman Dmitry Peskov immediately denied any Russian involvement.[4]

Donald Trump, who by the middle of June had pretty much wrapped up the Republican nomination, ridiculed the allegations and claimed the Democrats had fabricated the entire story. Incredibly, he claimed that the Democrats had intentionally hacked themselves 'as a way to distract from the many issues facing their deeply flawed candidate and failed party leader. Too bad the DNC doesn't hack Hillary Clinton's 33,000 missing emails.'[5]

Trump's remark about Clinton's 33,000 emails was a reference to a separate scandal, and one that did not involve the Russians. It was the long-festering controversy over Hillary Clinton's personal server and a series of classified emails dating back to her time as Secretary of State in the Obama administration. The Republicans had placed Hillary under investigation for her unauthorised use of a private email server she had maintained while she had served in the Obama administration as Secretary of State. Some of the emails turned out to be classified documents and this was a technical violation of the rules on using only government email addresses for the transmission of state secrets. Now the Trump campaign was pushing the story of the Clinton emails relentlessly as their prime evidence of her being 'Crooked Hillary' and Trump was enjoying huge success with crowds during the campaign with his claims that the emails showed how Clinton had allowed access to the State Department in return for cash contributions to the Clinton Foundation by foreign governments, banks and companies.[6] The atmosphere was already phosphorescent in June 2016. Trump was leading campaign rallies across the country with the chant of 'Lock Her Up! Lock Her Up!', as was his soon-to-be National Security Adviser in the White House, former Defense Intelligence Agency chief General Michael Flynn.[7] Less than twelve months before he joined the Trump campaign,

Flynn had been a paid speaker in Moscow at an event sponsored by the Kremlin's main propaganda arm in Europe and the United States, the state-owned TV channel Russia Today.[8] Pictures of Flynn sitting happily at dinner next to Vladimir Putin would soon circulate, but Trump didn't seem to mind. His headaches with Flynn would come later, after he had brought him into the White House for what would turn out to be a short-lived stay.

As for the emails that Hillary Clinton sent and received during her time as Secretary of State on a private server, this was by now the subject of an increasingly controversial FBI investigation. Throughout the campaign, Trump kept up the pressure on Clinton, and he would go so far as to publicly invite Russian intelligence services to hack Hillary Clinton's mail.

'Russia, if you're listening, I hope you're able to find the 30,000 emails that are missing,' Mr Trump declared during a televised news conference during the summer of 2016.[9] It was a clear reference to Clinton's missing or deleted emails. Donald Trump, a presidential candidate, was actively encouraging a foreign government to conduct cyber espionage against his political opponent. It was utterly unprecedented – but then, with the dawning of the Era of Trump, so many things would soon become 'unprecedented' that the word would begin to lose its impact through overuse.

'I find those kinds of statements to be totally outrageous,' said Leon Panetta, a former CIA director and Clinton supporter, 'because you've got a presidential candidate who is, in fact, asking the Russians to engage in American politics. I just think that's beyond the pale.'[10]

Panetta's words ring true today, but there would be many more moments, and many more tweets, that went beyond the pale as the story of Russia's efforts to interfere in the American presidential campaign evolved during that fateful summer and autumn of 2016.

The Obama administration, meanwhile, had its hands full with Trump's repeated accusations that the Department of Justice was going easy on Hillary Clinton and that the FBI investigation of her email server was becoming a political whitewash. It was tricky stuff for Obama. No matter how much he may have despised Donald Trump, he did not want to be seen as providing political cover for the Democratic candidate by interfering in a Department of Justice matter. But as America prepared to go into convention season in the month of July, Trump was making highly effective use of Hillary Clinton's email scandal to counter claims that Russia had hacked the Democrats.[11]

Then, in the closing days of June 2016, Bill Clinton would lend Trump a hand, with one of the biggest mistakes of his long political career.

Loretta Lynch, Obama's Attorney General, was already under fire from Trump, with Trump claiming that the FBI's investigation of Clinton's emails would result in a cover-up with the Democratic administration deciding not to prosecute her. The FBI probe was winding down, and a final decision by the Justice Department on whether to prosecute Clinton was just days away.

'The investigation into the State Department email matter is going to be handled like any other matter,' said a defensive Lynch. 'We've got career agents and lawyers looking at that. They will follow the facts and follow the evidence wherever it leads and come to a conclusion.'[12]

Just a week after Lynch promised to be impartial in the delicate investigation of Hillary Clinton, on 27 June, she found herself in a most awkward meeting, with the husband of the presumptive Democratic nominee, former President Bill Clinton. The two met for about half an hour aboard a private jet on the tarmac at Sky Harbor International Airport in Phoenix, Arizona. It was not Lynch's idea. Bill Clinton, who was about to take off from the airport, had heard that the Attorney General was just landing. He waited for her to arrive and then strolled over to her plane, bounding up the steps and past the astonished Secret Service agents. Although Lynch would later claim the meeting had been 'primarily social', the damage had been done. News of the meeting set off a firestorm of criticism and accusations by Trump.[13]

Bill Clinton had just engineered a private meeting with the Attorney General of the United States, the top law enforcement official in the government, who ran the Justice Department, just days before the very same Attorney General was supposed to decide on whether or not to recommend criminal charges against Hillary Clinton. Whatever Bill Clinton's intentions might have been, it looked pretty bad. The Republicans immediately demanded that Lynch recuse herself from any decision.[14]

Trump himself had a field day with the news. He immediately went into attack mode and tweeted out his feelings: 'Only a fool would believe that the meeting between Bill Clinton and the U.S.A.G. was not arranged or that Crooked Hillary did not know,' he declared in a late-night outburst. He followed this up with a second tweet: 'Crooked Hillary Clinton knew that her husband wanted to meet with the U.S.A.G. to work out a deal. The system is totally rigged & corrupt!'[15]

The Attorney General would later admit that she 'regretted' the meeting.[16] But at the time, in early July 2016, she felt compelled to reassure the world that she would accept whatever 'determinations and findings' were arrived at by the FBI and by career prosecutors who had investigated Clinton's use of a private email server.[17]

Then, in the first of a series of controversial and extraordinarily dramatic appearances during the 2016 presidential campaign, the head of the FBI held a televised press conference on 5 July to announce that he would not be recommending that any charges be brought against Hillary Clinton.[18] James Comey laid out what at first appeared to be a case for the prosecution. Instead of using the usual FBI line that he could not comment on details of an ongoing investigation, Comey criticised Clinton for having been 'extremely careless' in her handling of classified information. Since other US government employees had been prosecuted for such carelessness in the past, the implication was that Hillary had broken the law but was not being prosecuted. The FBI chief, a Republican, seemed to be saying that any lesser figure could well have faced a criminal indictment and the risk of jail, but not Hillary Clinton. It was a bizarre performance in a bizarre year in American politics. If it was intended to shut down the Hillary Clinton email scandal, it failed, largely because Comey himself would return to the scene just eleven days before the 8 November election to announce that he had decided to reopen the investigation,[19] and then three days before the election to say it was closed again,[20] thus doing incalculable damage to Clinton's election prospects and giving a boost to Trump.

Trump was meanwhile benefiting from the WikiLeaks email releases, which caused more embarrassment and more damage for Hillary Clinton, courtesy of the Russian hackers. On the eve of the Democratic Party Convention in Philadelphia in late July, WikiLeaks released its first batch of nearly 20,000 Russian-hacked emails, revealing how the Democratic Party had favoured Hillary Clinton and worked behind the scenes at the Democratic National Committee to discredit and defeat Bernie Sanders during the primary season.[21] The fallout was immediate. Just one day before the convention began, the DNC chairwoman, Debbie Wasserman Schultz, was forced to resign.[22] Sanders supporters, hundreds of whom were delegates at the convention, were furious with Hillary Clinton.[23] Score One for Team Putin.

'The Russians are releasing these emails for the purpose of actually helping Donald Trump,' claimed Hillary Clinton's campaign manager, Robby Mook. 'I don't think it's coincidental that these emails were released on the eve our convention here.'[24]

Trump, meanwhile, went into overdrive in defence of Moscow. He fired off a Twitterstorm of attacks on the Democrats, and ridiculed the very idea that Russia might be behind the hacked emails. 'The new joke in town is that Russia leaked the disastrous DNC e-mails, which should never have been written (stupid), because Putin likes me,' tweeted Trump.[25]

It was a line that Trump would take on many occasions, both in public and in private, whenever the issue of Russian interference in the US election came up. Trump would continue to deny, ridicule and double down on any mention of the Putin-ordered hacking, even after it was documented and presented to him by the heads of the US intelligence community.[26]

In private, Trump spoke warmly of Putin, telling a visitor that summer that he was sure he could do business with the Russian leader, adding that the world's best prospect for defeating ISIS would be for Russia and the United States to join forces, and to achieve that would require having a good working relationship.

In public, Trump found himself increasingly on the defensive, especially for the effusive praise he was lavishing on the Russian dictator.

'If Putin wants to say nice things about me, what's wrong with that?' Trump asked one befuddled interviewer. 'If he says great things about me then I'm going to say great things about him,' he told another.[27]

But as evidence of Russian involvement in the hacking scandal grew, and the intelligence services confirmed that Russia was most definitely behind the hacking, Trump went to extraordinary lengths to deny that he had any ties to Putin whatsoever.

'I have no relationship with Vladimir Putin,' he told ABC News. 'He said very nice things about me, but I have no relationship with him. I've never met him.'[28]

In 2016, in the thick of the Russian hacking scandal, Trump declared over and over again that he had no relationship with Putin. Three years earlier, he had said exactly the opposite.

'I do have a relationship with Putin,' said a grinning Donald Trump in November 2013, just after returning from a Miss Universe pageant in Moscow.[29] During the trip he had hoped to have a meeting with Putin, who cancelled at the last minute but had sent Trump a personal note and gift.[30] 'I have spoken directly and indirectly with him,' Trump would later declare at a National Press Club luncheon in May 2014.[31] But Trump would reverse course during the final televised debate of the 2016 election campaign. 'I don't know Putin. I have no idea,' he now proclaimed. 'I never met

Putin. This is not my best friend. But if the US got along with Russia it wouldn't be so bad.'[32]

What was the truth? Amid the roar of the presidential election campaign, the contradictions in Trump's statements about his relationship with Putin fell by the wayside, one of many contradictory utterances by the reality TV star turned politician. In fact, as a businessman, Trump had cultivated Russia for many years, and had dealings with some of Putin's cronies. Among them is Aras Agalarov, a billionaire real estate mogul with ties to Putin who persuaded Trump to bring his Miss Universe pageant to Moscow.[33] He would later feature in the Russiagate scandal.

Trump has expressed his admiration for Putin for many years. His business dealings in Russia go back decades. In 2007, he praised Putin, saying, 'Whether you like him or don't like him, he is doing a great job.'[34] Before the Miss Universe pageant, he tweeted in pure Trump-style, wondering about Putin: 'Will he become my new best friend?'[35] He would later tell Larry King on *Russia Today* that 'I think he has really done a great job of outsmarting our country.'[36]

Trump's biggest nightmare was that Putin's interference in the US election would somehow delegitimise his victory. In early December 2016, his worst-case scenario seemed to materialise. The *Washington Post* revealed that the CIA had confirmed that the aim of the Russian hacking was to favour Trump against Clinton during the election campaign.[37] President Obama confirmed that the orders to act had come from the highest levels of the Kremlin. 'Not much happens in Russia without Vladimir Putin,' said a laconic Obama.[38]

Trump's reaction was to dismiss the CIA findings and attack the seventeen US intelligence agencies that had made the determination. Trump thus became the first president-elect in US history to get into an angry and very public shouting match with the US intelligence community over a matter of national security.

'These are the same people that said Saddam Hussein had weapons of mass destruction,' said a contemptuous Trump as he trashed the CIA's findings.[39]

By the end of December, with Trump still on the attack against the CIA and the White House, it seemed to many Americans that the campaign had never ended. The political atmosphere was incandescent. Trump was lashing out almost every day. America had never been more divided.

On 29 December, President Obama went on national television to announce that he was ordering the expulsion of thirty-five alleged Russian spies together with a raft of unprecedented sanctions against Russian intelligence officers and their proxies.[40] In normal times, no American President would take such a drastic foreign policy action with just weeks to go before Inauguration Day, but these were not normal times. Obama had directly accused Putin of masterminding the hacking and the WikiLeaks email dumps, both of which were aimed at helping Trump. It was a charge of direct interference in America's election campaign, and it had been proven. Now, with Trump trying to brush away the entire story, Obama was under pressure to act.

'Russia's cyber activities', said the White House, 'were intended to influence the election, erode faith in US democratic institutions, sow doubt about the integrity of our electoral process, and undermine confidence in the institutions of the US government.'[41]

If that had been Putin's plan, it seemed to be working, with a little help from Trump, who had claimed for many months now that the American electoral system was rigged.[42] Every time Putin was accused of a misdeed by the White House, Trump had come rushing to his defence. Now he downplayed the sanctions and said it was time to 'move on' from the Russian hacking story. He then praised Putin again, this time for not retaliating against the US sanctions.[43] On the same day that Obama was announcing sanctions, Trump's new National Security Adviser, General Michael Flynn, was on the phone with Russia's ambassador to Washington, not only planning ahead for Putin and Trump to speak right after the inauguration in January[44] but also, it would later be revealed, discussing the lifting of US sanctions against Russia.[45] Flynn was later forced to resign, after less than a month in office, when he was found to have lied about his talks with the Russians that day.[46] But the scandal that became known as Russiagate was destined to grow larger in the consciousness of most Americans, and to dominate the opening months of the Trump presidency.

Back in December 2016, America seemed to have two parallel governments, with Trump by now sounding off via tweet on a bewildering array of foreign policy issues even before taking office. He barged into the UN debate about Israeli settlements on the West Bank and seemed to throw into doubt the idea of a two-state solution for Israel and Palestine.[47] He baited China's leadership by speaking with the President of Taiwan and letting slip that he considered the long-standing US policy of recognising only 'One China' might be up for negotiation.[48] He bullied US car producers that dared to build a new factory in Mexico.[49] He went on Twitter benders, rampages, fits and outbursts, and the world looked on with amazement. But it was on Russia that Trump was the most vocal, and he kept lashing out in his attempts to play down the hacking story.

The situation became even more surreal in early January when Julian Assange went on Fox News and claimed, implausibly, that the WikiLeaks emails had not come from the Russian government.[50] Trump seized upon Assange's claim, treating him as a credible source and tweeting that Assange 'said Russians did not give him the info!'[51]

A few days later, after Trump finally sat down for a briefing on the hacking affair with the heads of the US intelligence community, he continued to pour ridicule on the facts.[52] He emerged from the meeting at Trump Tower calling the whole story 'a political witch-hunt' against him. While he acknowledged that Russia might have had a role in the hacking, he said China and other countries had done far worse.[53] He continued to dismiss the proof that had been presented to him of Russian interference, claiming in a statement and a tweet that 'there was absolutely no evidence that hacking affected the election results'.[54] Instead, he doubled down and attacked NBC for having done its job and reported on the intelligence findings, and he slammed the intelligence community for allegedly having leaked the information to NBC. Trump called for an investigation of the US television broadcaster, again avoiding the issue of Russia's interference in the election.[55]

The matter blew up again just a week before Trump's inauguration, when it emerged that during his meeting with the intelligence chiefs they had presented him not just with proof of Russia's interference in the election but with a separate dossier that contained unverified claims that the Russians had assembled compromising information on Trump. The dossier had been put together by a former British spy who had been assembling opposition research for some of Trump's Republican rivals during the primary season and then for the Clinton campaign. It was the stuff of John Le Carré. The intelligence chiefs said the material had been brought to Trump's attention because they believed they should make the President-elect aware that such allegations involving him were circulating among intelligence agencies.[56]

Donald Trump went ballistic. At a circus-like news conference held in Trump Tower on 11 January 2017,[57] his first since being elected, he put on the full Monty. Trump mixed his paid staffers together with the audience of journalists, and throughout the bizarre performance they applauded and cheered him as though it were a campaign rally.[58]

His daughter Ivanka and sons Eric and Don Junior stood stiffly to one side, alongside Mike Pence. They were supporting actors in the reality TV show that was unfolding in Trump Tower. The news conference had ostensibly been called to announce how Trump proposed to deal with the many conflicts of interest he would have as President. His approach was to come out bragging that he had just turned down a $2 billion deal that that had been offered to him by a business partner in Dubai. 'I didn't have to turn it down, because, as you know, I have a no-conflict situation because I'm President,' said Trump.[59]

The incoming President of the United States then promised to turn the running of the Trump Organization over to his sons, even though he would maintain ownership. He promised that he would never discuss his beloved Trump Organization with his sons, and said his daughter Ivanka would resign from all positions in the company. She was moving to Washington to occupy her own position in the White House, not far from her husband Jared Kushner, who would serve as a presidential adviser. Ivanka would also get her own West Wing office and a security clearance, but she got around the ethics rules by not taking a formal job or salary. More eyebrows were raised. Government ethics experts complained that this was nowhere near what was needed to avoid entangling conflicts of interests throughout the Trump administration, but the Queens brawler was having none of it. Like an outer-borough kid with a chip on his shoulder, Trump remained defiant, telling the news conference that if he really wanted to, there was nothing to stop him from managing the Trump Organization from the Oval Office.[60]

'I could actually run my business and run government at the same time. I don't like the way that looks, but I would be able to do that if I wanted to,' Trump declared to astonished onlookers. 'As President I could run the Trump Organization, a great, great company, and I could run the country,' he added for good measure. 'I'd do a very good job, but I don't want to do that.'[61]

To say that Trump's attitude to government ethics was cavalier would be an understatement. His remarks were unprecedented, but then America and the world were beginning to learn that with Donald Trump many things are unprecedented.

When Trump was asked about Russia's interference in the US election process and the alleged Russian dossier, he became apoplectic. He rambled, he insulted, he shouted. He called the allegations of compromising financial and personal information in the Russia dossier 'crap' and called the news website that had published the dossier, BuzzFeed, a 'failing pile of garbage'. He refused to take a question from a CNN reporter, saying, 'Not you. You're fake news.'[62] He mumbled from both sides of his mouth but managed to just about acknowledge that Russia had indeed been involved in the hacking. Extraordinarily, he promised that Putin would not engage in any hacking once he got to the White House. 'Russia will have much greater respect for our country when I'm leading than when other people have led it,' declared the new Commander-in-Chief. 'If Putin likes Donald Trump,' said Trump, 'then I consider that an asset, not a liability.'[63]

In his most extraordinary moment, and in a sign that Trump had every intention of continuing to use incendiary language even as President of the United States, Trump then laid into the US intelligence community again.

'I think it was disgraceful that the intelligence agencies allowed any information [out] that turned out to be so false and fake,' Trump told the news conference. 'That's something that Nazi Germany would have done and did.'[64]

Nazi Germany?

By now, Trump was taking America into uncharted waters. He was openly siding with the Kremlin on the Russian hacking scandal and comparing the US intelligence services to Nazi Germany. Outgoing CIA director John Brennan, who had only a few days left in office, decided that enough was enough. He called Trump's remarks 'repugnant' and challenged him to:

> tell the families of those 117 CIA officers who are forever memorialised on our wall of honor that their loved ones who gave their lives were akin to Nazis. Tell the CIA officers who are serving in harm's way right now and their families who are worried about them that they are akin to Nazi Germany.[65]

Trump didn't care. He was fighting to preserve the legitimacy of his election victory. His answer to Brennan was to suggest in a tweet that the CIA director himself had been 'the leaker of fake news'.[66] Trump belittled the intelligence community again when the Senate

Intelligence Committee decided to investigate the allegations of contacts between Moscow and the Trump entourage during the election campaign. He didn't mind when his own nominee for CIA director went to testify in Congress and acknowledged the Russian hacking.[67] He didn't mind when Rex Tillerson, his nominee as Secretary of State and Putin's former business partner, said all the right things at his Senate confirmation hearing.[68] Tillerson was careful to avoid pledging to maintain US sanctions against Russia; it was becoming clearer by the day that Trump wanted to use the sanctions as a bargaining chip in his dealings with Putin.

'They have sanctions on Russia – let's see if we can make some good deals with Russia,' he said in his first interview with the European press on the eve of his inauguration.[69] The remark offered insight into the way Trump perceives the world: as an endless series of deals to be made, a series of transactions. The same deal-making mentality was plain when he spoke of the Iran nuclear deal, which he had derided for more than a year. 'I don't want to say what I'm gonna do with the Iran deal. I just don't want to play the cards.'[70] Everything was up for grabs in Trump's worldview. The game of international politics was *The Art of the Deal*.[71]

But the rest of the interview, published just days before Trump took office on 20 January, produced an angry and astonished reaction across Europe. In the same interview, Donald Trump derided NATO as 'obsolete' and returned to his campaign theme of how NATO members were not contributing their fair share to the cost of the alliance. He went even further, questioning the very basis of the transatlantic alliance, which had kept the peace in the Western world for more than seventy years. Trump also called into question the European Union, praising Britain for having voted for Brexit and expressing the hope that other European countries would soon follow suit. He attacked German Chancellor Angela Merkel, calling her decision to open Germany's borders to Syrian war refugees a 'catastrophic' mistake.[72] He had said much the same thing on board his Boeing 757 on that sultry day in Texas in June of 2016.[73] But that had been Trump the presumptive Republican nominee. This time, the man speaking was about to move into the White House.

Angela Merkel reacted poorly,[74] as did the global financial and political elites who had meanwhile assembled in the Alpine ski resort of Davos for their annual meeting.[75] For the politically correct guardians of globalisation who assembled each year at the annual World Economic Forum in Davos, Donald Trump was anathema.

The corridors of Davos ran thick with talk of Trump. The new American President's shadow loomed over the Swiss ski resort in January 2017; his angry anti-establishment message was like a dark and pendulous great cloud. For the global elites gathered at Davos, Trump's election represented their worst nightmare. It was the quintessence of the anti-globalisation backlash, the symbol *par excellence* of the uprising of the masses against the elites, which had begun in 2016. The new leader of the free world was a winner-take-all protectionist who had made the hallmark of his election campaign a crusade against free trade and immigration. He was a cheerleader for Brexit who hoped that other countries would vote to leave the European Union. He was a xenophobe populist who blamed Merkel's open borders for half of Europe's woes and who warned that 'if refugees keep pouring into different parts of Europe I think it's gonna be very hard to keep it together'.[76] Even worse he was a denier of climate science, a man who called the entire science of climate change a hoax invented by China.[77]

For the Davos crowd of bankers, managers, political and media leaders, Trump symbolised the system gone wrong, upended, in tilt. With Brexit and Trump, the revolt of the peasants was now fully underway in America and across the European continent. His anti-immigrant platform, his bullying style, his narrow America First nationalism and his incendiary rhetoric, which had stoked the flames of hatred and racism during the election campaign, were among the reasons why the Davos elite was worried and fearful about the dawning of the Trump era. Although the Wall Street crowd and corporate America could see plenty of economic benefits in the short-term, many at Davos wondered what Trump would eventually mean to the liberal post-war order that has governed the world for the past seventy years. The arrival of Trump seemed to presage a period of darkness, or at least of uncertainty, and there could be no doubt that the globalists of Davos, who had made globalisation their religion for decades, were now in retreat. They were stopped dead in their tracks.

The problem, for the global elites at Davos, is that their vision of the world had been completely upended by the election of Donald Trump. All of their assumptions, all their ideas about Western society and the functioning of the global economy were suddenly being called into question. The norms and practices that had prevailed since the end of the Second World War across the industrialised West were now somehow being thrown into doubt, starting with the religion of globalisation, the belief that open trade and open borders bring progress and prosperity.

At Davos, Trump adviser Anthony Scaramucci, a controversial hedge fund manager, went around trying to reassure people and play down concerns, but executives worried that Scaramucci was just a decoy intended to mask Trump's plans for an aggressive and protectionist trade policy, which called for sacred cows and conventional norms to be thrown over in an isolationist foreign policy that favoured strongmen rather than America's traditional allies.[78] In this vision of the world order, it was fine for Trump to call into question the long-standing One China policy and even to openly proclaim that he considered it a bargaining chip for his trade talks with China. The old rules did not apply. With Trump, nothing would be predictable. His impulsive foreign policy would soon prove to be a mixture of aggressive isolationism and outbursts of angry bullying on the world stage.

It did not help matters when Scaramucci argued that European leaders needed to learn the lessons from Trump's electoral victory because it showed the growing popular distrust in global elites. He was right about that, even if he was representing a Trump administration that was itself stuffed with plutocrats and corporate executives. The reaction of the global elites was to make polite noises at Davos about the problem of widening income inequalities and the need for globalisation to become more inclusive.[79] These were, however, the same global elites who had preached globalisation for more than thirty years, and who still believed that its benefits outweighed its costs.

The real problem for the Davos elite is that they were actually more a part of the problem than the solution, and the Trump victory was only part of a much broader trend in Western democracies. Nearly everywhere in Europe, the post-war liberal order was under fire from demagogues and extremists, from anti-immigrant firebrand politicians and from nativists and nationalists. Trump was merely a manifestation of the tendency toward illiberal forms of democracy that was sweeping the Western world. The annual meeting of the global elites in Davos at the dawn of the Trump era came at a turning point in global politics, at a moment when populist strongmen with violent and inflammatory rhetoric were the emerging trend on the world stage, the new dominant figures in a more dangerous world. They were men like Trump and Putin, like Hungary's Viktor Orbán, Turkey's Recep Tayyip Erdoğan or Rodrigo Duterte in the Philippines. They were all part of the wave of populist and nationalist leaders who believed in a Darwinian form of survival on the world stage. Trump had campaigned against the job losses caused by free trade and globalisation, and he had managed to whip up enough anger and fear to count on the support of some of the many victims of globalisation in the United States.

It was against this backdrop that the President of China, a brutal dictator whose government has violated dozens of global trade commitments, was able to come to Davos in January 2016 and present himself as the benevolent defender of globalisation and free trade.[80] It was thanks to Donald Trump that the leader of China was able to take the stage at Davos and preach the gospel of togetherness. Trump's constant sabre rattling against Beijing had not been going down very well with the Chinese leadership. Nor had his disparagement of climate change as 'a Chinese hoax'. When Trump called into question the One China policy, Beijing had called Trump a 'rookie' and urged him to be careful.[81] They had criticised his Twitter outbursts, his constant threats and insults, but what bothered China the most was the risk that Trump could really upset the applecart and start a trade war from which no one would emerge as the winner.

When President Xi spoke at Davos, he presented China as a responsible member of the global community, a force for stability and peace, and above all a firm believer in economic globalisation, in free trade and in the battle against climate change. The gathered delegates of Davos broke into rapturous applause. Some acknowledged the irony of a Chinese leader who sounded like a Davos regular.[82] The President of China and head of the Chinese Communist Party was successfully presenting himself as a globalist and free trader while the billionaire real estate mogul who had just been elected President of the United States was an aggressive bully and protectionist. The world was being turned upside down. China was successfully moving into the vacuum that had been left by Trump's hostility to free trade deals like the TPP and NAFTA. China was now the most vocal champion of globalisation and free trade. China was calling for global implementation of the climate change accords that Trump had scorned. Trump was cooing his praise for Putin but he was insulting Angela Merkel, calling for more European countries to break up the European Union, and questioning NATO. And in a surreal twist, Vladimir Putin was emerging as Trump's most vocal defender.

With the arrival of Donald Trump at the White House, a number of certainties that had governed the post-war order would be called into question. This was a radical and populist revolution, a takeover of the White House, the Republican Party and Washington, and it was not in the Trump spirit to tread lightly. While the world tried to get used to the new Tweeter-in-Chief and persuade itself that in reality Trump would be a dealmaker, and he might be more pragmatic than his rhetoric implied, the truth was that he had rattled the world even before taking office. The new leader of the free world was proving a disruptive force on the world stage, and he didn't seem to mind. To the contrary, he seemed to revel in his newfound power as he tossed aside diplomatic convention and good manners. So what if the United States had guaranteed the stability of the world order for more than seven decades? Trump was quite willing to turn things upside down if there was a short-term gain to be had. He always came on strong, often in attack mode, gratuitously. Trump was prepared to bully and threaten, as long as it would help him to win, to close the deal, to make the transaction, to get his way. He was prepared to allow his adversaries to think that he was capable of flipping the table, of walking away, or of taking extreme and unexpected action. The Chinese began to perceive Trump's provocations as an opening bid, as a Trumpian method of negotiating a deal. Insult your opponent and then cut a deal and be friends afterwards. In the context of a reality TV show, where interpersonal melodrama and hysterics are encouraged, that would be reasonable enough. But in the delicate workings of international diplomacy, this was not what the world was used to. Yet with Donald Trump, everything was always on the table. Nothing was too crazy or extreme an option.

It would be highly comforting if it were to one day emerge that Trump actually had employed a systematic strategy, a method or style that was analogous to Richard Nixon's 'madman theory'.[83] Nixon believed in being unpredictable. He always wanted to keep his adversaries guessing. At one point during the Vietnam War, in order to spook the enemy, he deliberately raised US readiness to make it look like a nuclear strike was imminent.[84] The problem with Trump's evocation of the madman theory is that one can never be sure if he is being strategic or simply impulsive. A President who in the space of a few minutes can tweet an attack on Meryl Streep[85] and then heap praise on Vladimir Putin seems more unpredictable than strategic. It was going to take some time for the world to get used to the new American President, but the early view was that his foreign policy could best be understood as transactional in nature.

Over at the Council on Foreign Relations in New York, Gideon Rose, the editor of *Foreign Affairs* magazine, says the arrival of Trump means that the United States faces 'the period of greatest uncertainty in US foreign policy in my professional lifetime'. Rose adds that Trump has 'demonstrated no concern or respect for – or even appreciation of – the liberal international order that has been at the core of American Grand Strategy for the last fifty years'.[86]

On the eve of his inauguration, Trump joked with the entire assembled diplomatic corps in Washington. In front of ambassadors, he described his new Secretary of State Rex Tillerson with typical Trump swagger: 'He's led this charmed life,' he said with a smirk. 'He goes into a country, takes the oil, goes into another country. It's tough dealing with these politicians, right?'[87]

But with Donald Trump in the White House, the reality was slightly different from the rhetoric. By the start of 2017, it was becoming abundantly clear that the traditional world order, the liberal world order of open societies, open borders and free trade, was under siege. The President's top advisers included China hawks like trade adviser Peter Navarro and Breitbart veteran Steve Bannon. There was the unknown quantity of Trump's son-in-law Jared Kushner, perhaps the adviser closest to Trump. And then there was the short-lived tenure of General Michael Flynn, the controversial National Security Adviser, who had been fired by the Obama administration from his job as head of the Pentagon's intelligence agency because he had seemed flighty and unstable, endlessly pushing conspiracy theories and exaggerations which became known in the CIA as 'Flynn Facts'.[88] Flynn lasted less than twenty-three days at the White House before he was forced to resign at the start of the Russiagate scandal. His replacement, Lieutenant General Herbert McMaster, was said to be a more reasonable and stable National Security Adviser, and for a while the international community tried to reassure itself that strong figures like McMaster or Secretary of

Defense 'Mad Dog' Mattis and Secretary of State Rex Tillerson would stand up to Trump and moderate his more impulsive tendencies. That would prove to be wishful thinking. As for Tillerson's close friendship with Putin, dating back to their days as business partners in the Arctic Sea, that was presented as an asset rather than a liability by the Trump spin machine. And it was quite clear to most of the world that the dynamic between Donald Trump and Vladimir Putin would be central to the future of global stability.

From Putin's point of view, a disorientated American electorate and a polarised and highly partisan political divide was just what the doctor had ordered. A cooperative relationship with Donald Trump could solidify and even formalise Putin's revanchist ambitions and his dreams of trying to rebuild the Soviet Union or an even greater sphere of influence for Mother Russia. By the time Trump arrived in the White House, Putin was already the owner of Syria and in solid partnerships with both Turkey and Iran. He had annexed the Crimea in 2014, and had de facto control of Eastern Ukraine. But his military adventurism had cost him mightily in economic terms, and he needed an agreement with the Trump administration because he needed relief for his economy. Above all, he needed the US and European sanctions that had been imposed since the annexation of Crimea to be lifted, along with those imposed by Barack Obama as punishment for interference by Russian hackers. The sanctions were hurting some of Putin's closest cronies, and that could prove a problem over time. Putin meanwhile, must have been delighted to see the outbreak of anger and confusion inside NATO. When Donald Trump said that NATO was obsolete and needed a revamp, the Kremlin quickly issued its own statement, saying that Moscow agreed with Trump's initial assessment that yes, NATO was most definitely obsolete.[89]

This was the backdrop to the start of the Trump administration, a world where China was not interested in getting into a trade war but would take off the gloves if it felt provoked and where Putin and Trump seemed the world's newest Odd Couple. Putin wanted to rebuild Moscow's power and influence on the world stage. Trump wanted to make deals, and with Putin he wanted to see what he could get in exchange for lifting sanctions. Could he get Russia and the United States to join forces in the war against terrorism? Could he get a nuclear arms deal? Could he get a new trade deal, or more business for American firms? From Trump's point of view, the morality and principles that lay behind the sanctions didn't matter. The past did not matter; that was history. Now is now and it is all about the deal on the table.

'Trump sees the world as a zero-sum game in which one person's win comes at the expense of another person's loss and where co-operation is for suckers,' says Gideon Rose.

> It's a transactional view of the world in which you have no commitments beyond what you immediately agreed in return for other goods. It suggests that allies are only as useful as their last payment or service to you. It's essentially every country for itself. That's what Trump espoused during the campaign and that's in fact what he continues to espouse.

By giving recognition and enhanced standing to Vladimir Putin, Donald Trump may think he is making the deal of a lifetime. In many ways, it is not so hard to understand the dynamic of the relationship between Donald Trump and Vladimir Putin. Beyond their shared narcissism and fondness for grand gestures, both men want and need to make a deal. They both see a new phase of realpolitik as the best way forward. Putin is quite happy to be transactional with Trump, just as long as it advances his revanchist agenda. The problem is that future historians may well look back upon this moment, at the start of the Trump presidency, as the moment which codified Russia's rehabilitation on the world stage and marked the end of the post-Cold War phase in which the United States was the world's sole superpower. While effectively validating Russia again, Trump's policies are also likely to accelerate the emergence of China as a superpower of the twenty-first century, gaining influence and power throughout Asia and the world economy. The irony is that the more the Trump administration picks fights with Beijing, the more China's influence is likely to expand internationally.

The result of all this is that a tripolar world is now more and more likely to emerge over time, and a tripartite global power structure can be seen just over the horizon. In fact, it seems that the more that Trump pushes a narrow and strident nationalist approach to world affairs, the more Moscow and Beijing will succeed in carving out ever greater spheres of influence around the world. In the end, Trump's transactional approach to international relations, combined with his 'America First' agenda, could actually hasten the emergence of a new world order in which Washington is forced to share more power with Moscow and Beijing. Trump can deny it all and shout out that America is great again until he is blue in the face. He can say that he is the *Numero Uno*. But the cold winds of history are unforgiving. Not even Donald Trump can really stop the centrifugal dynamics of globalisation and the eventual emergence of a tripolar world. But he can be highly disruptive along the way.

CHAPTER TWELVE

THIS IS NOT AMERICA

Donald Trump began turning the world upside down within minutes of being sworn in as President. He came into office as he had campaigned: angry, self-aggrandising and vindictive. In his inaugural address,[1] pronounced on a grey and rainy Friday afternoon in Washington, Trump painted a dark portrait of America and then plunged straight into pure pitchfork populism. He broke with the tradition that had been observed by all incoming American Presidents in the past: there was no message of reconciliation here, no call for national unity or healing, no mention of hope. Instead, Trump went for the shock effect, using unusually harsh and aggressive language to attack the Washington establishment and then go into a protectionist and ultra-nationalist rant. This was not an inaugural address to the nation; it sounded more like a rancorous stump speech from the campaign trail. But there was a difference. The man who was speaking was now the President of the United States.

President Donald Trump seemed anything but presidential. He was still in campaign mode, still bombastic, still provocative, still prone to hyperbole and exaggeration, at times resorting to even violent and incendiary language.

Trump painted a grim portrait of America, a nation of 'mothers and children trapped in poverty in our inner cities, rusted-out factories scattered like tombstones across the landscape of our nation, an education system flush with cash but which leaves our young and beautiful students deprived of all knowledge'. He praised the police and lamented 'the crime and the gangs and the drugs that have stolen too many lives and robbed our country of so much unrealised potential'.

Then, with the kind of rhetoric one would more normally associate with a strongman or dictator than with a democratically elected President of the United States, Trump pronounced words of rage that will go down in history for their crude and authoritarian tone.

'This American carnage', declared a defiant and scowling President Donald Trump, 'stops right here, and stops right now!'

Never before in history had a President of the United States used such pungent language in an inaugural address. But Trump came out with both guns blazing.

The new President lamented the plight of the factory workers and the Americans who had been left behind by globalisation, swearing that 'the forgotten men and women of our country will be forgotten no longer'. There was more than a little irony in Trump's use of the term 'forgotten men'. It had been first coined back in 1932 by President Franklin Delano Roosevelt.[2] FDR had intended the forgotten man at the bottom of the economic pyramid and had launched a massive job creation programme of infrastructure projects, just as Trump intended to do. But FDR had created much of the social safety net and welfare functions of the federal government, the remains of which Trump was now preparing to dismantle.

Trump's 'forgotten men' reference was not the only time he seemed inspired by the 1930s. His 'America First' policy harked back to the late 1930s, when Charles Lindbergh led an isolationist and anti-Semitic movement that argued against US entry into World War II.[3] It was an eerie call to nationalism, and to an American ear it had the same boisterous ring that 'Deutschland Uber Alles' has to a German. Together with his pledge to make America great again, Trump had used 'America First' as his main campaign slogan, and now it would become his foreign policy doctrine. It would be his mantra, his reality and his general statement of principles.

'We, assembled here, today,' Trump proclaimed from the steps of the Capitol,

> are issuing a new decree to be heard in every city, in every foreign capital, and in every hall of power. From this day forward, a new vision will govern our land. From this day forward, it's going to be only America First, America First! Every decision on trade, on taxes, on immigration, on foreign affairs, will be made to benefit American workers and American families.

Just in case anyone had missed the point, Trump went into protectionist and xenophobe overdrive, declaring: 'We must protect our borders from the ravages of other countries making our products, stealing our companies, and destroying our jobs. Protection will lead to great prosperity and strength.'

With those words, it became clear there would be no pivot, from Candidate Trump to President Trump. He would not be acting presidential and his rhetoric sounded anything but presidential. His was a hostile and cruel view of a dog-eat-dog world where every nation is out for itself. For more than seventy years the world had grown accustomed to hearing American Presidents pledge America's commitment to democracy and human rights and other Western values, to a stable world order. Donald Trump instead put the world on notice that things were about to change. He articulated the crudest and most selfish narrow view of the world order, in which the United States would no longer subsidise 'the armies of other countries while allowing for the very sad depletion of our military'. He was essentially repudiating the long-standing bipartisan Washington consensus under which the United States would always shoulder its responsibilities as leader of the free world. Gone was any talk of promoting democracy. America, said Trump, would no longer 'seek to impose our way of life on anyone'. Instead, everything would be transactional, everything would depend on what kind of deal Washington could make on any given issue. America First seemed to mean America Alone; it was an aggressive, isolationist and transactional approach to the world.

As Trump's muscular rhetoric reverberated across the National

Mall, the television cameras showed a grimacing Hillary Clinton seated nearby on the inaugural platform. Michelle Obama could not hide her revulsion. She looked despairing at times. Barack Obama appeared tense, but he maintained his aplomb throughout, even muttering 'Good job!' to Trump at the end of the tirade. But the fiery rhetoric clearly appealed to Trump's base, and the guardian of the flame, the architect of the Trumpian worldview, Stephen Bannon, sat just a few feet away with a big grin on his face. Bannon, the alt-right guru of Breitbart News, was the master of fake news and the hero of the Ku Klux Klan and other white supremacists. He had been called 'the most dangerous operative in Washington' and he had fashioned some of the most controversial utterances of the Trump campaign, moments in which Trump's rhetoric seemed to incite racism and hatred. But now he was Trump's chief strategist in the White House, a populist hardliner who wanted to firebomb Washington, wage war on free trade and climate science, and form close relations with emerging far-right nationalist and populist movements across Europe.

Bannon proudly described Trump's inaugural address to the *Washington Post* as 'an unvarnished declaration of the basic principles' of Trump's brand of nationalism.[4] He even invited comparison between Trump's inaugural address and the speech that had been made a few days earlier in Davos by China's President Xi Jinping.

At Davos, the Chinese leader had spoken of the need for a more 'inclusive globalisation' and had strongly defended the principle of free trade and open markets. He had also defended the global treaty on climate change, which Obama had signed and Trump would eventually walk away from, making China the world's leading proponent of environmental protection.

'I think it'd be good if people compare Xi's speech at Davos and President Trump's speech in his inaugural,' Bannon declared. 'You'll see two different worldviews.'

If anyone had any doubts about what was happening, the climate change pages on the White House website disappeared within minutes of the Trump inauguration,[5] along with other vestiges of the Obama presidency, such as the webpage for the Office of National AIDS Policy. The site's pages dedicated to women and the LGBT community also disappeared,[6] as did the sections on civil rights[7] and, naturally enough, on affordable health care.[8]

Just a few hours later, as soon as he set foot in the Oval Office, Trump began to make good on his promise to abolish Obama's landmark healthcare law and remake the government in his own image. With the stroke of a pen, he signed an executive order that gave federal agencies the liberty to begin gutting parts of the Affordable Care Act.[9] It was a symbolic move, but it also gave the agencies wide discretion so that they could work with the Republican Congress during the exceedingly difficult phase of trying to repeal and replace Obamacare. Trump's second executive order put a freeze on the issuance of any new government regulations anywhere at all within the entire US government.[10] After signing these executive orders, Trump danced the night away with his wife at the inaugural ball, taking to the floor to the strains of Frank Sinatra's 'My Way', which seemed to just about say it all.[11] (Donald Trump was not the only billionaire former real estate mogul turned politician who had a taste for 'My Way'. Somewhere in a cavernous 72-room villa on the outskirts of Milan, a former Italian Prime Minister who could match Trump's narcissism pound for pound must have been watching Trump on TV and smiling a narcissistic smile as the old Sinatra song began to play.)

Outside on the streets of Washington, police had been battling angry protesters, arresting hundreds and using pepper spray and tear gas to beat back the crowds.[12] The next day, Saturday, saw the Women's March on Washington, with hundreds of thousands filling the streets of the nation's capital, the streets overflowing with a mass of humanity so thick that they had to cancel the idea of marching at all.[13]

Trump would not let the protesters spoil his jubilant mood. He sent his new spokesman, the hapless Sean Spicer, out to hold his first press conference in order to attack the 'dishonest media' and to claim, falsely, as it turned out, that they had under-reported the number of people who had attended the inaugural address on the Mall.[14] On his first full day in office he visited the CIA and spent half his time there talking in a rambling and incoherent fashion about himself and about what he now called his 'war' with the media.[15] Trump also tried to ignore the fact that on the day after he was sworn into office, millions of people had marched in dozens of cities across America and around the world in protest against his harsh and intolerant worldview. Trump actually entered the White House with the lowest approval rating in presidential history according to all surveys,[16] with CBS putting his support at just 32 per cent.[17] But he brushed the polls and the protests aside with a few more tweets and proceeded to launch his populist revolution.

In his first week in office, Trump made clear that he would govern as he had campaigned. He rescinded much of Obama's legacy by signing a raft of executive orders.[18] He withdrew the United States from the Trans-Pacific Partnership trade agreement[19] and announced that he would be renegotiating the NAFTA trade accord with Mexico and Canada,[20] making good on his threats to get tough on trade and adopt a protectionist approach to the world. He ordered the path to be cleared for environmentally sensitive energy projects like the Dakota and Keystone pipelines.[21] He froze all hiring in the federal government, but promised to build up the military.[22] He pressed ahead with his controversial plan to build a wall on the border with Mexico[23] and he tried twice to impose a ban on citizens of seven Muslim majority nations entering the United States.[24] He even said that Christians would be given priority among Syrians who apply for refugee status under a new system he called 'extreme vetting'.[25]

This was just for starters.

Trump's first two attempts at placing a travel ban on immigrants from seven Muslim majority nations were blocked by the courts, but he vowed to make good on his campaign pledge and railed at his detractors, including federal judges. He would take his battle to the Supreme Court, hoping his newest nominee to the Court, Neil Gorsuch, would vote to reinstate his travel ban.[26] Whenever Trump faced a setback, he found a scapegoat to tweet about, or he simply changed the subject. He seemed not to respect the institutions that made American democracy function, whether the courts or the free press; indeed, in many ways, Trump seemed to be actively working to undermine and delegitimise the institutions of American democracy.

Trump's greatest fear, as accusations of collusion between his campaign team and Russian agents continued to swirl about Washington, was that his election would somehow come to be seen as illegitimate, and that he was somehow not a legitimately elected President. Perhaps this is why he defended his newly named National Security Adviser, General Mike Flynn, long after he was told that Flynn had lied about his conversations with the Russian ambassador to the United States, Sergey I. Kislyak. The White House was fully warned by the Acting Attorney General, Sally Yates,[27] that Flynn had lied about his conversations, but Trump let nearly three weeks pass before taking action, and only acted then when it became clear Flynn had made a fool of Vice-President Mike Pence, assuring him that he and the Russian ambassador, who had met in December 2016, had never discussed the lifting of US sanctions on Russia.

Trump kept defending Flynn, even after the Justice Department informed him that Flynn was subject to blackmail from Russia. On 13 February he let Flynn resign,[28] but it would only emerge months later that Trump's own son-in-law and top adviser, Jared Kushner, had been present with Flynn during some of the most controversial meetings with the Russians, including one in December 2016 in which Kushner proposed to Ambassador Kislyak that they use Russian Embassy facilities to have a backchannel with Moscow that could not be spied upon by the US government – and this while another administration was still in office.[29]

The Russiagate scandal did not go away after Trump ditched Flynn and appointed yet another military man, in this case the kowtowing General H. R. McMaster, as the new National Security Adviser. Instead, based on what we now know, Trump asked FBI Director James Comey to pledge his loyalty and would even later ask Comey to drop the investigation into Flynn.[30] Critics in Congress, and across America, began to wonder if the President might not be guilty of obstruction of justice, especially after Trump unceremoniously fired Comey on 9 May, and then angrily attacked the appointing of Robert Mueller as a Special Prosecutor a few days later.[31] Kushner, according to all reports, was the only adviser who encouraged Trump to publicly attack the Special Prosecutor via tweet.[32] Many wondered what Kushner had to hide, and why he had been present at so many meetings with Russians, including a Russian bank chief who was a graduate of the FSB Academy, and an operative for Vladimir Putin.[33]

More and more, the Russiagate scandal began to resemble Watergate. Like Nixon, Trump had sacked the man who was investigating his White House. Nixon had fired Attorney General Elliot Richardson because he wouldn't fire Special Prosecutor Archibald Cox. Trump fired FBI Director James Comey after putting pressure on him to drop an investigation. In some ways, Trump's behaviour during the opening months of 2017 was even worse than that of Richard Nixon because it was more overt, more explicit. Nixon had been a pathological liar; so was Trump. But Nixon had never been as impulsive, as narcissistic, as crass as Trump.

After the departure of General Flynn from the White House, and with Congressional investigations underway into possible collusion during the 2016 campaign between Russian secret services and the Trump campaign, the new President decided to change the subject again. He woke up one Saturday morning at his Mar-a-Lago resort and accused his predecessor of criminal behaviour. Citing zero evidence, Trump accused Barack Obama of having personally ordered the wiretapping of his telephones at Trump Tower during the campaign.[34] He compared Obama to Richard Nixon during the Watergate scandal, and then he unleashed a burst of nasty tweets.

After it was explained to the White House that since the 1970s no US president has ever had the power to authorise a wiretap, Trump, as usual, doubled down with more accusations. It did not help when FBI director James Comey, just weeks before being sacked, went before the Senate Intelligence Committee and publicly denied Trump's outlandish claims.[35] The White House waffled, and Trump simmered, as was by now his custom.

The new President had suffered quite a credibility crisis early in his term: he had lost his National Security Adviser because of the growing Russiagate scandal; he had seen his two Muslim travel bans bogged down in court proceedings; he had failed in his first legislative attempt to repeal Obamacare and now he had been effectively called a liar by the head of the FBI, whom he had proceeded to sack. His son-in-law Jared Kushner was now a 'person of interest' to the Special Prosecutor, Robert Mueller, and the dark cloud of scandal that hung over the White House seemed unlikely to dissipate for a very long time.

Against this backdrop of scandal and controversy, it was not surprising that Trump was finding it difficult to get Congress to concentrate on his legislative agenda, whether his much-vaunted tax cuts or his efforts to slash welfare spending and repeal Obamacare.

The early healthcare reforms may have been bungled, but the hardest part would come next, as Trump's White House tried to work with a divided Republican Party on Capitol Hill on the legislation that was actually needed to press forward with its radical plans. Trump had appointed a number of deeply conservative Cabinet members and key advisers, and they were sworn to reduce regulation of Wall Street and the energy sector, to cut corporate taxes, to dismantle environmental regulations and to slash the federal budget. But the Republicans were divided between moderates who did not want to take many risks ahead of the 2018 mid-term elections and ultra-conservatives like the members of the Freedom Caucus, for whom ideological purity and fiscal discipline were the ultimate measures of success.

Nothing seemed off limits as Trump's team began to prepare for the deepest budget cuts in decades; their initial plan was to cut a whopping $800 billion of public spending on Medicaid, essentially health care for America's poor, over a decade.[36] The new head of Trump's Office of Management and Budget, a former Republican Congressman named Mick Mulvaney, was an ultra-conservative budget hawk who would happily embrace Trump's vision for welfare cuts.[37] In the Trump worldview of government, less is more. Public spending had to be slashed in order to pay for sharply lowered corporate taxes, new infrastructure projects and a rise in spending at the Pentagon. Trump's budget blueprint caused howls of protest from Democrats. In order to achieve such deep cuts, Trump's team was contemplating the complete elimination of a number of government programmes, including funding for initiatives aimed at protecting women from domestic violence, sexual assault and stalking.[38] No wonder hundreds of thousands of women had descended on Washington the day after Trump was sworn into office.

The Trump team also seemed keen to eliminate or sharply cut spending for the arts and humanities, potentially ending a decades-long pillar of American culture.[39] Also among the proposed cuts was the funding needed to implement the Paris Climate Change Agreement and an assortment of Department of Energy programmes designed to encourage the development of alternative and renewable energy.[40] Trump would later storm out of the Paris accords, announcing that the United States would immediately cease funding any climate change policies, isolating the United States from the rest of the world.[41]

Trump will face opposition to his harsh spending cuts, but sadly a number of them will go through, and the brunt of the axe is most likely to fall over time on low-income Americans, on the poor. The Trump administration's attempted cuts in entitlement programmes, in line with long-standing Republican proposals, target items such as spending on welfare and food stamps, on social assistance and education. Trump will likely give states greater leeway to administer or reallocate Medicaid spending on health care for the poor. In other words, America's remaining social safety net, already battered and slashed over the decades by Presidents Bill Clinton and George W. Bush, will soon be dismantled still further. The fundamental ideals of Lyndon Johnson's Great Society and War on Poverty may soon be extinguished for ever, and the most probable outcome, whatever the rhetoric, is that millions of poor, disabled and elderly Americans who rely on welfare or Medicaid could well see the floor drop away from beneath them.

The privatisation of Medicare may be a bridge too far even for Trump, but the partial privatisation of America's school system is not at all off limits. The new billionaire Secretary of Education, Betsy DeVos, has spent decades lobbying for cuts in the funding of public schools and for the redirection of a chunk of this money to issue vouchers for private schools.[42] Her vision, shared by Trump, would favour the rise of profit-making evangelical Christian and predominantly white private schools across America, while leaving inner-city minorities and the less mobile rural poor with even poorer schools. It is a cruel and racist version of America's future that DeVos espouses, and which Trump embraces. (It is not surprising that DeVos's brother is Republican donor Erik Prince, the man who founded Blackwater, the infamous private team of mercenaries and military subcontractors who were favoured in Iraq and Afghanistan by George W. Bush and Dick Cheney.)[43]

The greatest irony in all this is that among those who stand to suffer the most from Trump's budget cuts and economic policies are many of those millions of working-class Americans who voted for him. Trump will undoubtedly say that he is creating millions of jobs, and he will spend years patting himself on the back for every corporate announcement or positive economic indicator. But there is a different reality on the ground, out in the American heartland, a starkly different reality.

Nita Fischer,[44] now rehired by Walmart at $9 an hour at another store location in Lake Charles, Louisiana, is not likely to gain much from the Trump era, despite her high hopes for the man she voted for. She has a job but she still can't feed her infant son or afford medicines without food stamps and welfare. Thanks to the expected budget cuts, courtesy of the Trump administration, Nita Fischer may soon find that she has even less of a safety net. In fact, depending on the extent of the Trump spending cuts, she may risk not having a safety net at all any more.

For African-Americans, the Trump presidency did not get off to a very good start. Just days before the inauguration in January, a jury in the trial of Dylann Roof, the racist shooter who gunned down nine members of a Bible Study class at the AME Church in Charleston, South Carolina, finally convicted and sentenced him to death.[45] But the conviction was ignored in the media amid the hubbub and controversy that Trump was generating before and after taking office.

It was no coincidence that members of Black Lives Matter were among the hundreds of thousands who joined the Women's March in Washington on Donald Trump's first full day in the White House. Across American cities, black activists joined hands with the Women's March. They were angry, and frightened. In Donald Trump they saw a man who had fomented hatred and incited racism during the election campaign, a President who had appointed as his Attorney General Jeff Sessions, disparaged by his critics as 'a career racist' from Alabama. To make matters worse, the new team at the civil rights enforcement division of the Department of Justice included John Gore, a lawyer who had made a name for himself attacking civil rights while promoting Republican redistricting and voter suppression laws that targeted blacks and Hispanics.[46]

In Trump's view, there was nothing at all racist going on. After all, he had a token black man in his Cabinet, even if it was the eccentric Dr Ben Carson, a brain surgeon and former primary rival who had been given the improbable task of running the Department of Housing and Urban Development.[47] Carson was largely invisible but he spoke up gamely when Trump presented his welfare cuts to say that 'poverty is a state of mind'.[48] The truth was that Trump did not appear to be a racist, at least to those who know him, but he seemed happy to let Steve Bannon flirt freely with white supremacists if it helped shore up the base. The new President seemed to think that photo opportunities and publicity stunts with black TV stars could take the place of promoting diversity and racial harmony. He had posed happily in front of the cameras with an embarrassed-looking Kanye West.[49] He had recruited a black comedian and game show host, Steve Harvey, star of *Family Feud*, to supposedly help the good Dr Carson fix what was wrong with America's 'inner cities'.[50] He had hired Omarosa Manigault, a black woman he had fired three times during her appearances on *The Apprentice*, as a White House adviser.[51] This was perfectly normal behaviour for the star of a reality TV show. It was what one might expect from a President whose intellectual interests ranged from the Miss Universe beauty pageant to the latest adventures of Kim Kardashian. It did not, however, look very much like the actions of a President who wished to show leadership on the delicate matter of race relations. While Trump served up his old-fashioned concept of tokenism as a form of promoting race relations, his men were moving into position, with the Justice Department ready to go easy on civil rights enforcement and hard on voter suppression laws. Once again, the reality looked starkly different from the rhetoric. Hate crimes and racially inspired violence shot up dramatically in the opening months of the Trump administration. Many accused Trump of flirting with racism, with inciting racism with his anti-Muslim tweets and his incendiary rhetoric.

Back in Charleston, South Carolina, in the little two-storey building that houses the local branch of the NAACP, veteran civil rights campaigner Dot Scott had sighed the deepest of deep sighs when she asked whether Trump had triggered an increase in racial violence with his inflammatory rhetoric or was merely a manifestation of its enduring presence across the nation.[52] 'It would be far too easy to say that Trump is causing it all,' she had replied. 'Trump is just ripping the Band-Aid off racism in America, and he's not being very careful about it.'

Up in Newtown, Connecticut, the parents of the victims of the massacre at Sandy Hook Elementary School are not counting on Donald Trump.[53] Their efforts at gun violence prevention and gun control had flourished during the Obama years, but their hopes of somehow limiting the sale of the AR-15 assault rifle or any other dangerous firearms had been pretty much dashed by the election of Trump. Far from pressing for any meaningful gun control, the Trump administration was on course to pay back its partial electoral debts to the National Rifle Association, an early endorser and major financial backer of the Republican candidate. Not only were more stringent background checks for gun purchasers off the table in a Republican Congress; it now looked like controls could soon be relaxed on the carrying of concealed weapons across interstate lines. Trump could talk all he wanted about being the law and order President and about wanting to crack down on crime and violence. The reality was starkly different.

'Trump is a godsend for the gun lobby,' commented gun control advocate Tom Diaz shortly after the election. 'Now, with the Trump administration, we can be sure of one thing: that the industry will figure out how to sell more guns. That is the one certainty,' said Diaz.

In the north Florida coastal town of Ormond Beach, a waiter in a fast food restaurant named Gary Brock is also worried.[54] He had found a lifeline in the benefits of Obamacare, and as a minimum wage earner he had no other way to get affordable health care. 'I love my Obamacare,' he had said with a big smile. 'Obamacare saved my life.' Brock now wondered whether Trumpcare would offer him the same access to doctors or whether he would no longer be able to afford health care. His greatest reassurance, ironically enough, might ultimately come from the Republican Congress, which cannot easily afford to alienate the 20 million Americans who have signed on to Obamacare and who now fear losing their coverage. After all, they are potential voters.

For the billionaire denizens of Silicon Valley, who had previously worshipped at the altar of Hillary Clinton, life under Trump suddenly seemed fearful and challenging. They were aghast at his ban on refugees and immigrants from seven Muslim majority nations, they were disgusted by his withdrawal from the Paris climate accord, and they made their voices heard along with other corporate leaders from Ford and GE to Citicorp and even Goldman Sachs. But at the end of the day, the tech giants had important business interests to protect, and the Trump administration was still offering lower taxes and less regulation. They would ultimately try to get on with the Trump administration if it meant a tax amnesty that allowed them to repatriate hundreds of billions of dollars in offshore funds cheaply. Silicon Valley could bring its money back, Donald Trump could take credit, and he could claim that he was bringing more jobs back to America, even if that was unlikely to be true. The most likely reality is very different from Trump's fairy-tale vision.

Aside from token investments in a few show factories for the President to tweet about, Silicon Valley will likely continue to develop and roll out job-reducing automation and robotic technologies that pose a far greater threat to American jobs than the ravages of globalisation. Silicon Valley will bring its money back and the bulk of that money should fuel a fresh round of mergers and acquisitions, more tech company share buybacks and greater personal enrichment for the tech giants themselves. Silicon Valley will bring its money back to America and Wall Street will benefit.

The bankers on Wall Street, in turn, have been celebrating for months now. Their primary concern was whether they had already celebrated too soon, at a time when the exact nature of Trump's economic and trade policies was still taking shape. And the spectre of an extended Russiagate investigation would mean that Trump's tax cuts and other deregulation moves might be delayed to late 2017 or even until 2018. But Wall Street is surely right to bet on Trump in the long run, and on his economic team from Goldman Sachs. Even if Trump's protectionism creates more uncertainty, the bankers and hedge fund managers are still likely to be among the greatest beneficiaries of the Trump administration's tax cuts and planned deregulation of Wall Street. For Trump, there is little irony in the fact that thanks to his appointments, banking regulations will soon be dismantled by some of the very same hedge fund managers and bankers who helped to cause the financial crisis of 2008 in the first place. Donald Trump doesn't do irony. He does vitriol.

At the dawn of the Trump era, the main parlour game in Washington was to try to figure out if Trump would really do all of the implausible things he had said he would do, or whether he would moderate his more extreme positions. The hope at the time was expressed in the notion that Trump should be taken 'seriously but not literally'. Yet the way he came charging into the White House implied that he really did intend to put in place some of the most extreme ideas he had promised as a candidate. He really seemed willing to embrace extremist policies that questioned America's position in the world and the premises of its society at home. In his first few months at the White House, he presented himself as the most hotheaded and extremist President in living memory. This was a new kind of American leader, a new kind of populist President. He was prepared to throw red meat out to the base, with Steve Bannon always at his side to keep the populist messaging as virulent as possible.

Trump was happy to embrace the Second Amendment crowd and the pro-life Christian evangelicals, and he was happy to give the Republican hardline right a big win with the nomination of a new Supreme Court justice in the conservative mould of Justice Antonin Scalia. Trump's Supreme Court appointments would be among his most lasting legacies. With Supreme Court appointments, he could change the face of American society for a generation or more. To please the base, the nominee had to be pro-life, or at least sceptical about federal funding of contraceptives or a woman's right to choose. He had to be a justice who would reliably defend religious rights as well as the gun lobby, a *bona fide* ultra-conservative.

Trump found his man in Judge Neil Gorsuch, a Colorado Republican and favourite of the conservative legal establishment. Gorsuch was a former Justice Department official in the administration of George W. Bush and the son of a controversial former head of the Environmental Protection Agency during the Reagan administration who had been forced to resign over a toxic waste scandal.[55] Gorsuch was careful about hiding his views during confirmation hearings, but he was considered a reliable conservative, who could be expected to vote to limit gay rights, uphold restrictions on abortion and invalidate affirmative action programmes.

The naming of the gun-loving Judge Gorsuch to the Supreme Court brought immediate applause from the National Rifle Association.[56] Although he had not ruled on abortion rights, he was considered a reasonable choice by the pro-life community because he had written about the sanctity of life. Gorsuch was also known for backing religious rights and writing against euthanasia and assisted suicide.[57] His record over the years showed that he had repeatedly sided with big business over workers and had shown repeated hostility toward women's rights.

He was the perfect choice for Trump, especially since the new President was likely to have the opportunity to name another justice to the Supreme Court during his first term in office. Two of the nine judges are over the age of eighty, and if Trump is able to name a second, and even a third, justice to the court then he will be able to decisively shift it towards a deeply conservative vision of American society. Trump's appointments could well produce a Supreme Court that will be more amenable to calling into question not just abortion rights but also LGBT and women's rights, as well as voter rights and ultimately civil rights.

If Trump is able to nominate a second or third judge, he will make America a much darker society. The risks of America under Trump becoming a much less tolerant and open society are already clear to see, amid the rise in hate crimes and the increasing courage of white supremacists to come forward and praise Trump.

The Supreme Court appointments will leave their mark long after Trump has left the White House, and not in a good way. There will be resistance, especially in places like California and New York City, and in other progressive enclaves of enlightenment and tolerance across the nation, but much of America may well become a darker place, deeply divided, torn by racial conflict and income inequality, lacerated by hatred and fear.

While Trump sets about trying to remake American society, the greatest risk posed by his presidency undoubtedly lies in the international arena. It is here that Trump's unpredictable and impulsive style poses some very real challenges. He tends to attack first, but it is not always clear whether this is an opening gambit in a negotiation or whether Trump is simply allowing his ego to get the better of him. He hits back at criticism quickly and crudely, either in a spontaneous outburst or within the confines of 140 characters. The Trump style, distilled to its essence, is to shoot first and ask questions later. The style worked well enough during the 2016 election campaign, and it might make sense in the rough-and-tumble world of casino construction, but it is not the norm in international diplomacy. Trump doesn't care. He gave the most hostile and aggressive inaugural address in modern history. Then he began to make good on his threats.

In his first week in office, Trump managed to start a diplomatic crisis with Mexico. He first announced that he would soon hold talks on renegotiating NAFTA with President Enrique Peña Nieto of Mexico. Then he signed the order authorising construction of the wall, and he repeated his promise that Mexico would pay for it. The Mexican President found himself humiliated and announced that he had cancelled his meeting with Trump.[58] The two men finally had a phone call to try to patch things up.[59] But Trump had already shown his true colours.

British Prime Minister Theresa May was the first world leader to be received at the White House, and Trump put on his best behaviour in order to showcase the 'special relationship' between Washington and London, and happily accepted an invitation from Queen Elizabeth to visit Buckingham Palace during a state visit. Now that was the kind of gratification that the kid from Queens would have craved. But he could not resist using May's White House visit to praise the Brexit vote. 'Brexit is going to be fantastic,' he crowed, while an embarrassed British Prime Minister looked on.[60]

One day later, after May had left Washington, Trump signed the first Muslim ban, leaving the British premier and the rest of Europe in a state of shock.

Angela Merkel was still licking her wounds, having been attacked by Trump over her progressive immigration policies just days before he took office. With elections coming up later in September 2017, the last thing she needed was to be castigated by the new American President. But Trump had called her decision to allow a million Syrian war refugees and other immigrants entry to Germany 'catastrophic'. He was deliberately provoking the Chancellor of Germany and empowering her far-right opponents.

When Merkel made her first official visit to the White House, in March 2017, Trump refused to shake her hand and rambled on about how Germany owed billions of dollars in unpaid bills for the NATO alliance.[61] The day after Merkel left town, Trump tweeted a hostile claim for the money, only to be told by the German government that this was not the way NATO worked.[62]

Unsurprisingly, Europe's xenophobic populist parties were positively gleeful at the dawn of the Trump era in early 2017. Elections were scheduled to be held within the year in the Netherlands, France, Italy and Germany, and the far-right nationalists were rising in the polls everywhere. Europe, already suffering an existential crisis after Brexit and still unable to cope with the migrant crisis, now faced not only its own nationalists but a nationalist US president in Washington who scorned the euro, threatened NATO and favoured the disintegration of the EU. Trump's counterpart in the Netherlands, Geert Wilders, did not do as well as Steve Bannon might have hoped for, even after Bannon recommended a right-wing US think tank who made financial donations.[63] Likewise, Marine Le Pen lost in France and Merkel was likely to be re-elected in Germany.[64] But the rise of the populists and far-right nationalists did shift the boundaries of public discourse, and did focus more of European voters' attention on the issues of immigrants and terrorism, especially after the attacks outside the Houses of Parliament in London in March 2017 and the further attacks at the Ariana Grande concert in Manchester and at Borough Market. Trump would tweet about each of these atrocities, sometimes trying to take advantage of a British tragedy by taunting London's Mayor, Sadiq Khan, in a tweet.[65] It was the equivalent of Tony Blair tweeting an insult at Mayor Rudy Giuliani after 9/11, but Trump did not care. It was all more meat for his grinder, more blood for his dystopian worldview, more proof that his Muslim travel ban was the right thing to do. Trump's behaviour would cast a long shadow over Britain and over the rest of Europe. He seemed to favour Putin over Merkel. He liked strongmen, and strong leaders, like Erdoğan and Duterte of the Philippines.

In Moscow, Vladimir Putin was meanwhile biding his time. He would meet with Trump soon enough and the two men would try to make a deal. Putin could feel more than a little satisfied with his work over the previous year. He could happily deny that the Russian state had any responsibility for the hacking attacks and WikiLeaks campaign against Hillary Clinton. Putin attributed it to 'patriotic hackers' who were operating privately.[66] He even suggested that American hackers could have made it look like they were Russian as a form of dépistage.[67] A true double bluff from the master of deceit. Putin was a KGB agent with a diabolical sense of humour, and he must have enjoyed playing with the White House and the world.

The truth is that Donald Trump's arrival at the White House marked the beginning of a new world order, a new world disorder, a time of tumultuous change, and Russia (along with China) looked like it would be a chief beneficiary of that change. 'We do not seek to impose our way of life on anyone,' Trump had said from the steps of the Capitol. 'It is the right of all nations to put their own interests first,' he had decreed, before promising to 'reinforce old alliances and form new ones'.[68]

For Vladimir Putin, it must have been deeply satisfying to watch Donald Trump in action, blustering his way onto the world stage, reversing course and ditching the fundamentals of US foreign policy, even human rights. Putin enjoyed watching Trump who seemed to stagger around the world stage like an angry drunk, creating pockets of instability here or there, lecturing the Europeans, insulting his allies, placing in doubt the pillars of the post-war liberal world order. All of that worked quite well for Putin: it fed into his broader strategy of repositioning Russia as a Great Power once again, in an emerging tri-polar world where China and Russia would usurp US influence. If Trump was a bit jumpy, and alienated some world leader with an early morning tweet, Putin would know how to capitalise on the situation. He would know what to do.

The greatest challenge for Putin was Trump himself, and the risk of the spreading Russiagate scandal in Washington. The more it looked like Putin's intelligence services had colluded with hackers or WikiLeaks or the Trump campaign, the more difficult it became for President Trump to normalise relations with Moscow. But Trump would probably do what he wanted anyway, scandal or not.

Still, the world wondered. Could Trump's impulsive nature accidentally trigger a real international crisis? Surely, whispered the diplomats, Trump's more mercurial tendencies would be kept in check by his circle of hardnosed and pragmatic advisers, men and women who were prepared to stand up to him. The problem was that his circle of closest advisers contained the populist firebrand Steve Bannon, the chief apologist Kellyanne Conway and the inexperienced Jared Kushner, plus the dilettante daughter Ivanka Trump. Perhaps his closest adviser, the real Rasputin, was Kushner, the 35-year-old billionaire property magnate from New York who just happened to be Trump's son-in-law. Ivanka's husband, with no experience of international diplomacy, was also supposed to play the part of Middle East adviser.[69] His own ideology was pretty clear:

he was among those who had supported the building of new settlements by Israel on occupied Palestinian land. He was a big fan the uncompromising stance of Israeli premier Benjamin Netanyahu. But Kushner was a hawk when it came to Russiagate; after all, it was beginning to look as though he had something to hide.

The real moderates were housed *outside* the White House, even though they could be expected to have access to the new President. They were both men of stature and experience, veteran strategists and decision-makers. Secretary of Defense James 'Mad Dog' Mattis was supposed to be the grown-up on matters of national security and defence, and it seemed that he might exert a moderating influence on the Commander-in-Chief. Secretary of State Rex Tillerson may emerge as the other grown-up in the room, at least when it comes to being careful about taking risks in the international arena. The conventional wisdom was that 'Mad Dog' and Tillerson would hold Trump back from any really risky behaviour. The problem was that neither Mattis nor Tillerson had any control over Donald Trump's Twitter account. Both would prove ineffectual in countering Bannon's most extremist tendencies, and both would thus prove unable to perform the function of 'adults in the room' with a President who began to seem an ignorant and cantankerous man-baby to many Americans.

The world may eventually get used to Trump's Twitter outbursts, and prudent world leaders may learn to take Trump seriously but not literally. It may be that his tweets and provocations become so much the norm that the rest of the world just sighs and tries not to pay attention.

Still, in the delicate and nuanced arena of international affairs, words matter.

It matters to China if the President of the United States places the landmark One China policy in doubt, throwing it onto the negotiating table.

It matters to Mexico if the President of the United States treats the Mexicans with scorn and behaves like a bully.

It matters to Angela Merkel and to Europe if the President of the United States insults Germany and Europe with aggressive and hostile messages.

Yet in Trump's approach to the world, first you razz your adversary and then you make friends. First you directly threaten the interests of a foreign leader and then you have a meeting with them and try to cut a deal and come out saying your meeting was just 'amazing' or 'fantastic' or 'terrific'. It's all part of the negotiating process, it's all part of the show, and it's all part of keeping the populist base happy back in the American heartland.

As long as the foreign adversary accepts that it is OK to be criticised, humiliated or embarrassed by Trump before sitting down to the negotiating table to cut a deal, the Trump approach might even work. If a prickly foreign leader were to decide that it were time to stand up to Trump's provocations, then that could prove to be a bit of a problem. It has already been compounded by the way Donald Trump has abdicated so much of America's leadership role, especially with his withdrawal from the Paris climate accord.

As far back as in July 2016, amid the din of the Republican National Convention in Cleveland, Ohio, former presidential adviser David Gergen[70] sat down and tried to imagine the risks of a Trump presidency.

'I think the best thing we would have going for us if Donald Trump were elected President is the Constitution, because it does have checks and balances,' said Gergen, who served in the White House under Presidents Nixon, Ford, Reagan and Clinton. But Gergen noted that as Barack Obama had already demonstrated, 'the presidency does have informal powers that are not in the Constitution, and that is especially true overseas. So an unhinged Trump could be a problem.'

Gergen was not at all reassured by what he saw at the start of the Trump presidency.

'I think the Republic will survive,' he said, 'but I think that unless he gets serious and calms down, and gets both his temper and his impulses under control, and deals with his narcissism, you know, I think dangerous things could happen.'

Gergen hoped that Mattis and Tillerson would keep Trump's more reckless instincts in check, and he said he was glad to see the departure of Trump's first National Security Adviser, General Mike Flynn. He called Flynn 'a wild card at best, a conspiracy theorist, and a man with a lot of anger and desire for revenge'.

As for Trump himself, the former presidential adviser was even more concerned. He noted that there was already a move in the US Senate to introduce legislation that would forbid the President from launching a nuclear strike without first having Congress declare war. 'They're doing that', Gergen observed, 'to make sure that if he has an unstable or a wild moment that he is somehow constrained.'

'He is impulsive, he can lash out,' concluded Gergen, 'and I would be very concerned if a situation arose where he got into some *mano a mano* and felt he had to use force.'

In the world's fondest hopes, Donald Trump's bark will come to be seen as worse than his bite. The systemic shock of his early days will give way to realpolitik and the day-to-day business of nations. The truth is that Trump has not really changed his fundamental worldview since the campaign. In fact, he has been remarkably consistent, however harsh the message. He had already made many of the pronouncements that shocked Europe in early 2017 when we met aboard Trump Force One back in Houston during the summer of 2016. The big unanswered question now was just how far he could go with his populist revolution, how disruptive and destabilising a force his presidency could be in America and around the world. In domestic terms, if he were to accomplish even half of his agenda he would change the face of society for generations and call into question the very idea of America.

It is this that most worries those Americans who are opposed to Donald Trump. They worry that President Trump will take America to a darker place, a place that no longer reflects the most basic American values. The idea of America is a place of honour and dignity, a melting pot of fairness and freedom, a benevolent democracy that in the past has seemed unafraid to assume the mantle of leadership on the world stage. The idea of America is an idea about a liberal and tolerant society, a great and powerful nation that derives its strength through innovation and cultural diversity. It may have never really been that way, and perhaps the American dream is only half-true. But for a very long time America did signify hope for the rest of the world, hope and opportunity. Until now.

Trump has been elected President and he has the right to govern, but there are many Americans who fear for America's soul, and they have a duty to speak out. America will remain a divided nation for many years to come, and unfortunately most of the problems that plague the weakest members of society are likely to get even worse during the Trump years. In many ways, this great country has already lost its way. But the most probable result of an extended Trump presidency will be a nation that flourishes on Wall Street and yet becomes even more conflicted and unequal, more divided and racist, more cruel and desensitised as a society, as a culture. These are the risks; hopefully they are exaggerated and will never materialise. But the America now taking shape is not the America of my childhood dreams. It is not the America of Kennedy or of Reagan. This is not the America that we thought we knew so well. This America is an aberration. This is not America. This is some other place.

ENDNOTES

CHAPTER ONE

1 On 17 June 2016, I interviewed the Republican then-presumptive nominee Donald Trump for two articles published two days later in the British *Sunday Times* and the Italian *Corriere della Sera*.

Friedman, Alan. 'Putin, Kim, Cameron; I'll talk to them all'. *Sunday Times*, 19 June 2016. Available at: http://www.thetimes.co.uk/article/putin-kim-cameron-ill-talk-to-them-all-t98cks9f8

Friedman, Alan. 'Trump: "Pronto a invitare Putin e a trattare con Kim Jong-un"'. Corriere della Sera, 19 June 2016. Available at: http://www.corriere.it/esteri/16_giugno_19/trump-pronto-invitare-putin-b14d45f6-358e-11e6-8ef0-3c2327086418.shtml

2 Gass, Nick. 'Trump: I'll meet with Kim Jong Un in the US'. Politico, 15 June 2016. Available at: http://www.politico.com/story/2016/06/donald-trump-north-korea-nukes-224385

3 Trump, Donald and Schwartz, Tony. *Trump: The Art of the Deal*. Random House, 1987.

4 DeYoung, Karen and Miller, Greg. 'Key figures purged from Trump transition team'. *Washington Post*, 15 November 2016. Available at: https://www.washingtonpost.com/world/national-security/key-figures-purged-from-trump-transition-team/2016/11/15/ed4e2a36-ab6b-11e6-8b45-f8e493f06fcd_story.html

5 Friedman, Alan.

6 Samuelsohn, Darren. 'Trump's kids to run businesses via "blind trust", Trump attorney says'. *Politico*, 10 November 2016. http://www.politico.com/story/2016/11/trump-children-business-blind-trust-231179

7 Johnson, Jenna; Moravec, Eva Ruth and Sullivan, Sean. 'Trump accuses Obama of 'trying to make terrorism into guns,' days after mogul signaled openness to new restrictions'. *Washington Post*, 17 June 2016. Available at: https://www.washingtonpost.com/news/post-politics/wp/2016/06/17/trump-accuses-obama-of-trying-to-make-terrorism-into-guns-days-after-mogul-signaled-openness-to-new-restrictions/

8 Newell, Jim. 'Clinton Campaign Chairman Dismisses Rally for the Night'. Slate, 9 November 2016. Available at: http://www.slate.com/blogs/the_slatest/2016/11/09/john_podesta_says_clinton_campaign_is_calling_it_a_night.html

9 Kranish, Michael and O'Harrow Jr, Robert. 'Inside the government's racial bias case against Donald Trump's company, and how he fought it'. *Washington Post*, 23 January 2016. Available at: https://www.washingtonpost.com/politics/inside-the-governments-racial-bias-case-against-donald-trumps-company-and-how-he-fought-it/2016/01/23/fb90163e-bfbe-11e5-bcda-62a36b394160_story.html

10 O'Harrow Jr, Robert and Boburg, Shawn. 'The man who showed Donald Trump how

to exploit power and instill fear'. *Washington Post*, 16 June 2016. Available at: https://www.washingtonpost.com/investigations/former-mccarthy-aide-showed-trump-how-to-exploit-power-and-draw-attention/2016/06/16/e9f44f20-2bf3-11e6-9b37-42985f6a265c_story.html

Mahler, Jonathan and Flegenheimer, Matt. 'What Donald Trump Learned From Joseph McCarthy's Right-Hand Man'. *New York Times*, 20 June 2016. Available at: http://www.nytimes.com/2016/06/21/us/politics/donald-trump-roy-cohn.html

Kruse, Michael. 'He Brutalized For You'. Politico, 8 April 2016. Available at: http://www.politico.com/magazine/story/2016/04/donald-trump-roy-cohn-mentor-joseph-mccarthy-213799

11 Johnston, David Cay. 'Just What Were Donald Trump's Ties to the Mob?' Politico, 22 May 2016. Available at: http://www.politico.com/magazine/story/2016/05/donald-trump-2016-mob-organized-crime-213910

12 Glynn, Lenny. 'Trump's Taj – Open at Last, With a Scary Appetite'. *New York Times*, 8 April 1990. Available at: http://www.nytimes.com/1990/04/08/business/trump-s-taj-open-at-last-with-a-scary-appetite.html?pagewanted=all

13 Gara, Antoine. 'Billionaire Carl Icahn Closes The Trump Taj Mahal Casino After Union Standoff'. Forbes, 10 October 2016. Available at: http://www.forbes.com/sites/antoinegara/2016/10/10/billionaire-carl-icahn-closes-trump-taj-mahal-casino-after-union-standoff/#1a39475c21af

14 Peterson, Barbara. 'The Crash of Trump Air'. Daily Beast, 4 October 2015. Available at: http://www.thedailybeast.com/articles/2015/10/04/the-crash-of-trump-air.html

15 Eder, Steve and Parlapiano, Alicia. 'Donald Trump's Ventures Began With a Lot of Hype. Here's How They Turned Out'. New York Times, 6 October 2016. Available at: http://www.nytimes.com/2016/10/07/us/politics/donald-trump-business-deals.html?smid=tw-nytpolitics&smtyp=cur&_r=0

16 Mayer, Jane. 'Donald Trump's ghostwriter tells all'. *New Yorker*, 25 July 2016. Available at: http://www.newyorker.com/magazine/2016/07/25/donald-trumps-ghostwriter-tells-all

17 Eggen, Dan and Farnam, T. W. 'Trump's donation history shows Democratic favoritism'. *Washington Post*, 26 April 2011. Available at: https://www.washingtonpost.com/politics/trumps-donation-history-shows-democratic-favoritism/2011/04/25/AFDUddtE_story.html

18 Gass, Nick. 'Trump has spent years courting Hillary and other Dems'. Politico, 16 June 2016. Available at: http://www.politico.com/story/2015/06/donald-trump-donations-democrats-hillary-clinton-119071

19 'Company News; Trump's Plaza Hotel bankruptcy plan approved'. *New York Times*, 12 December 1992. Available at: http://www.nytimes.com/1992/12/12/business/company-news-trump-s-plaza-hotel-bankruptcy-plan-approved.html

20 'Chapter 11 For Taj Mahal'. *New York Times*, 18 July 1991. Available at: http://www.nytimes.com/1991/07/18/business/chapter-11-for-taj-mahal.html

21 Dowd, Maureen. 'When Hillary and Donald Were Friends'. *New York Times Magazine*, 2 November 2016. Available at: http://www.nytimes.com/2016/11/06/magazine/when-hillary-and-donald-were-friends.html

22 Farenthold, David A. 'Trump recorded having extremely lewd conversation about women in 2005'. *Washington Post*, 8 October 2016. Available at: https://www.washingtonpost.com/politics/trump-recorded-having-extremely-lewd-conversation-about-women-in-2005/2016/10/07/3b9ce776-8cb4-11e6-bf8a-3d26847eeed4_story.html?postshare=3561475870579757&tid=ss_tw

23 DelReal, Jose, A. 'Donald Trump announces presidential bid'. *Washington Post*, 16 June 2016. Available at: https://www.washingtonpost.com/news/post-politics/wp/2015/06/16/donald-trump-to-announce-his-presidential-plans-today/

24 Krieg, Gregory. 'It's official: Clinton swamps Trump in popular vote'. CNN, 22 December 2016. Available at: http://edition.cnn.com/2016/12/21/politics/donald-trump-hillary-clinton-popular-vote-final-count/

25 In 2015, 43 million Americans lived under the poverty line (13.5 per cent of the population), while 100 million Americans (31.7 per cent of the population) had family incomes below twice the poverty line. 'Income and Poverty in the United States: 2015'. United States Census Bureau. Available at: https://www.census.gov/content/dam/Census/library/publications/2016/demo/p60-256.pdf

CHAPTER TWO

1 Kennan, George F. ('X'), 'The Sources of Soviet Conduct'. *Foreign Affairs 25* (July 1947).

2 In 1952/53, the highest tax bracket was at 92 per cent. Tax Foundation, 'Federal Individual Income Tax Rates History (1913-2013)'. Available at: http://taxfoundation.org/sites/default/files/docs/fed_individual_rate_history_nominal.pdf

3 Source data is government spending as reported by the Office of Management and Budget or the United States Census Bureau, with the addition of interpolated data for the years not covered by the data sources.

4 Proctor, Bernadette D.; Semega, Jessica L. and Kollar, Melissa A. (2016). 'Income and Poverty in the United States: 2015'. United States Census Bureau. Available at: http://www.census.gov/library/publications/2016/demo/p60-256.html

5 According to the Congressional Research Service, the wars in Afghanistan and Iraq have cost US taxpayers $1.6 trillion. Belasco, Amy (2014). 'The Cost of Iraq, Afghanistan, and Other Global War on Terror Operations Since 9/11'. Congressional Research Service. Available at: https://www.fas.org/sgp/crs/natsec/RL33110.pdf

However, different studies calculated a much higher expense, taking into account various collateral costs. See among others: Bilmes, Linda J. (2013) 'The Financial Legacy of Iraq and Afghanistan: How Wartime Spending Decisions Will Constrain Future National Security Budgets'. Harvard Kennedy School. Available at: https://research.hks.harvard.edu/publications/workingpapers/citation.aspx?PubId=8956&type=WPN

6 From 165,000 Iraqi civilians to more than a million have died from the beginning of the conflict in 2003, depending on the source you consult. See: Crawford, Neta C. (2013). 'Civilian Death and Injury in the Iraq War, 2003–2013'. Costs of War. Boston University. Available at: http://watson.brown.edu/costsofwar/files/cow/imce/papers/2013/Civilian%20Death%20and%20Injury%20in%20the%20Iraq%20War%2C%202003-2013.pdf

'Iraq Body Count'. Available at: https://www.iraqbodycount.org

PSR, Physicians for Social Responsibility (2015). 'Body Count, Casualty Figures after 10 Years of the "War on Terror", Iraq, Afghanistan, Pakistan'. IPPNW Germany. Available at: http://www.psr.org/assets/pdfs/body-count.pdf

Roberts, Les et al., (2004). 'Mortality before and after the 2003 invasion of Iraq: cluster sample survey'. *The Lancet*. Roberts, Les et al., (2006). 'Mortality after the 2003 invasion of Iraq: a cross-sectional cluster sample survey', *The Lancet*.

Burnham, Gilbert, et al. (2006). 'The human cost of the war in Iraq: a mortality study, 2002–2006'. John Hopkins Bloomberg School of Public Health and Al Mustansiriya University School of Medicine. Available at: http://web.mit.edu/CIS/pdf/Human_Cost_of_War.pdf

With regard to the war in Afghanistan, which started in 2001, more than 31,000 civilians are estimated to have died violent deaths as a result of the war. See:

Crawford, Neta C. (2016). 'Update on the Human Costs of War for Afghanistan and Pakistan, 2001 to mid 2016'. Costs of War. Brown University. Available at: http://watson.brown.edu/costsofwar/files/cow/imce/papers/2016/War%20in%20Afghanistan%20and%20Pakistan%20UPDATE_FINAL_corrected%20date.pdf

7 See poverty rate from Census for years 2001 and 2008.

Proctor, Bernadette D. and Dalaker, Joseph (2002). 'Income and Poverty in the United States: 2001'. United States Census Bureau. Available at: https://www.census.gov/prod/2002pubs/p60-219.pdf

DeNavas-Walt, Carmen, Proctor, Bernadette D. and Smith, Jessica C. (2009). 'Income, Poverty, and Health Insurance Coverage in the United States: 2008'. United States Census Bureau. Available at: https://www.census.gov/prod/2009pubs/p60-236.pdf

8 Reilly, Katie. 'Read Hillary Clinton's "Basket of Deplorables" Remarks About Donald Trump Supporters', *Time*, 10 September 2016. Available at: http://time.com/4486502/hillary-clinton-basket-of-deplorables-transcript/

9 Among the 43 million Americans living below the poverty line in 2015, 19 million (6.1 per cent of the population) lived under half the poverty threshold. 'Income and Poverty in the United States: 2015'. United States Census Bureau.

10 The Fortune 2016 Global 500. Available at: http://beta.fortune.com/global500/

CHAPTER THREE

1 Nita Fischer, single mother, interviewed in Lake Charles, Louisiana, on 16 August 2016.

2 In Lake Charles, 23.6 per cent of the population is below the poverty level. Census Bureau, '2010–2014 American Community Survey 5-Year Estimates', data for 2014.

3 For 2015, the poverty threshold for one adult with a child was $16,337 per year. 'Income and Poverty in the United States: 2015'. United States Census Bureau.

4 The *Financial Times* reported this statement from Walmart on 1 July 2016 in an article that mentioned Nita Fischer's case. Whipp, Linda and Fleming, Sam. 'Push for higher wages squeezes US corporate profits'. *Financial Times*, 1 July 2016. Available at: https://www.ft.com/content/b9602ba0-3c91-11e6-8716-a4a71e8140b0

5 On 15 September 2016, I interviewed Dina Bakst, Elizabether Gedmark and Cara Suvall – respectively co-founder and co-president, staff attorney and director of the Southern office, attorney of the Southern office – from A Better Balance (phone interview).

6 Forbes (2016). 'America's Richest Families Net Worth'. Available at: http://www.forbes.com/families/list/#tab:overall

7 Randy Parraz, UFCW campaign director for Making Change at Walmart. Phone interview, 15 September 2016.

8 Fishman, Charles (2006) *The Wal-Mart Effect*. Penguin Press.

9 Parker-Pope, Tara. 'Injured Woman Wins Wal-Mart Saga', *New York Times*, 4 April 2008. Available at: http://well.blogs.nytimes.com/2008/04/04/injured-woman-wins-wal-mart-saga/

10 *Countdown with Keith Olbermann*, NBC News, 27 March 2008. Transcript available at: http://www.nbcnews.com/id/23848687/#.V-6Fq2MYH-Y

11 See, among others: Bivens, Josh; Gould, Elise; Mishel, Lawrence and Shierholz, Heidi (2014). 'Raising America's Pay. Why it's our central Economic Policy Challenge'. Economic Policy Institute. Available at: http://www.epi.org/publication/raising-americas-pay/

12 Public Affairs, UC Berkeley, 'Poverty-level wages cost US taxpayers $153 billion every year', *Berkeley News*, 13 April 2015. Available at: http://news.berkeley.edu/2015/04/13/poverty-level-wages-cost-u-s-taxpayers/

13 Jacobs, Ken; Perry, Ian and MacGillvary, Jenifer (2015). 'The High Public Cost of Low Wages'. UC Berkeley Center for Labor Research and Education. Available at: http://laborcenter.berkeley.edu/pdf/2015/the-high-public-cost-of-low-wages.pdf
14 Bernie Sanders speaking to supporters in Des Moines, Iowa, on 9 January 2016, during his presidential campaign. Video available at: https://www.youtube.com/watch?v=MbVHe9Tij_U
15 Bernie Sanders speaking to supporters in Keene, New Hampshire, on 2 February 2016, during his presidential campaign. Statement reported in Chipman, Kim, 'Bernie Sanders Calls Wal-Mart Walton Family Wealth Unacceptable', Bloomberg, 2 February 2016. Available at: http://www.bloomberg.com/politics/trackers/2016-02-02/bernie-sanders-calls-wal-mart-walton-family-wealth-unacceptable
16 Bernie Sanders speaking to supporters in Des Moines, Iowa, on 9 January 2016, during his presidential campaign. Video available at: https://www.youtube.com/watch?v=MbVHe9Tij_U
17 US Congress, Joint Economic Committee, 'Income Inequality in the United States', Washington, DC, January 2014. Video available at: https://www.youtube.com/watch?v=vFnT4AbJLrw
18 'Income and Poverty in the United States: 2015'. United States Census Bureau.
19 'Income and Poverty in the United States: 2015'. United States Census Bureau.
20 In the US, 14.5 million children (19.7 per cent of all US citizens under the age of eighteen) live under the poverty line. 'Income and Poverty in the United States: 2015'. United States Census Bureau.
21 Edin, Kathryn J. and Shaefer, Luke H. (2015). *\$2.00 a Day: Living on Almost Nothing in America*. Houghton Mifflin Harcourt.
22 See, among others, the percentage of unemployment in Leflore County, MS (10.9 per cent), Coahoma County, MS (10.3 per cent), Sunflower County, MS (10.8 per cent), Humphreys County, MS (12.9 per cent), Issaquena County, MS (16.9 per cent), Sharkey County, MS (9.9 per cent), Washington County, MS (10.5 per cent), Bolivar County, MS (7.9 per cent), Quitman County, MS (10.8 per cent). Bureau of Labor Statistics, US Department of Labor, 'Unemployment rates by county, not seasonally adjusted, Mississippi', 2015, annual. Data available at: http://data.bls.gov/map
23 See, among others, the percentage of people in poverty in Leflore County, MS (41.1 per cent), Coahoma County, MS (37.4 per cent), Sunflower County, MS (35.8 per cent), Humphreys County, MS (40.5 per cent), Issaquena County, MS (31.6 per cent), Sharkey County, MS (32.2 per cent), Washington County, MS (37.5 per cent), Bolivar County, MS (34.8 per cent), Quitman County, MS (38.6 per cent), Yazoo County. Census Bureau, '2010–2014 American Community Survey 5-Year Estimates', data for 2014.
24 In Mississippi, 1,788 African-American people are incarcerated out of every 100,000 people in the same ethnic group; the rate for white people is 600 out of every 100,000. Prison Policy initiative, 'Breaking Down Mass Incarceration in the 2010 Census: State-by-State Incarceration Rates by Race/Ethnicity'. Available at: http://www.prisonpolicy.org/reports/rates.html
25 See: Education Week, 'Quality Counts 2016'. Available at: http://www.edweek.org/ew/qc/2016/2016-state-report-cards-map.html?intc=EW-QC16-TOC

Social Science Research Council, 'The Measure of America 2013–2014'. Available at: http://www.measureofamerica.org/wp-content/uploads/2013/06/MOA-III.pdf

Guttmacher Institute (2014), 'US Teenage Pregnancies, Births and Abortions, 2010: National and State Trends by Age, Race and Ethnicity'. Available at: https://www.guttmacher.org/sites/default/files/report_pdf/ustptrends10.pdf
26 In 2015, the child poverty rate in Mississippi was 31.7 per cent. Schaefer, Andrew;

Carson, Jessica A. and Mattingly, Marybeth J. (2016). 'Overall Declines in Child Poverty Mask Relatively Stable Rates Across States'. Analysis based on American Community Survey, 1-Year Estimates, 2014 and 2015, US Census Bureau. University of New Hampshire, Carsey School of Public Policy. Available at: http://scholars.unh.edu/cgi/viewcontent.cgi?article=1281&context=carsey

27 Bill Luckett, Major of Clarksdale, Mississippi. Interviewed in Clarksdale on 12 August 2016.

28 Poverty rate in Clarksdale is 37.5 per cent versus a national rate of 13.5 per cent. '2010–2014 American Community Survey 5-Year Estimates'. United States Census Bureau; Income and Poverty in the United States: 2015. United States Census Bureau.

29 Desta Reff, Harvard Delta Fellow, interviewed in Clarksdale, Mississippi, on 12 August 2016.

30 Marian Wright Edelman to PBS journalist Kai Ryssdal, *PBS Newshour*, 'Poverty-stricken past and present in the Mississippi Delta', July 2016. Video available at: http://www.pbs.org/newshour/bb/poverty-stricken-past-present-mississippi-delta/

31 Peter Edelman to PBS journalist Kai Ryssdal, *PBS Newshour*, ibid.

32 Richard Grant, British writer, interviewed on 15 August 2016, in Jackson, Mississippi.

33 H. Luke Shaefer, Associate Professor of Social Work and Associate Professor of Public Policy, School of Social Work, University of Michigan, phone interview on 16 September 2016.

34 'Income and Poverty in the United States: 2015'. United States Census Bureau.

35 United States Department of Labor, Bureau of Labor Statistics, 'Unemployment rates by County, not seasonally adjusted, South Carolina', 2015, annual. Data available at: http://data.bls.gov/map

36 Census Bureau, '2010–2014 American Community Survey 5-Year Estimates', data for 2014.

37 Wilbur Cave, special projects director, Allendale County ALIVE, interviewed in Allendale, South Carolina, on 9 August 2016.

38 Calvin Wright, executive director of the Orangeburg-Calhoun-Allendale-Bamberg Community Action Agency, Inc. (OCAB), interviewed in Orangeburg, South Carolina, 10 August 2016.

39 'Income and Poverty in the United States: 2015'. United States Census Bureau.

40 In 2015, median income for all US households was $56,516, while the median income for black US households was $36,898. 'Income and Poverty in the United States: 2015'. United States Census Bureau.

41 The youth (sixteen to twenty-four years of age) unemployment rate in July 2016 was 11.5 per cent; for black youth, it was 20.6 per cent. United States Department of Labor, Bureau of Labor Statistics, 'Employment and Unemployment Among Youth Summary', August 2016. Available at: http://www.bls.gov/news.release/youth.nr0.htm

42 In 2015, 4.3 per cent of whites (not Hispanic) had income below half the poverty level (around 6,000 for an individual under the age of sixty-five years); among blacks the rate was 10.9 per cent. 'Income and Poverty in the United States: 2015'. United States Census Bureau.

CHAPTER FOUR

1 Rev. Eric Manning, pastor of Mother Emanuel AME Church, interviewed in Charleston, South Carolina, on 10 August 2016.

2 26 June 2015. 'On Remarks by the President in Eulogy for the Honorable Reverend Clementa Pinckney'. Available at: https://www.whitehouse.gov/the-press-office/2015/06/26/remarks-president-eulogy-honorable-reverend-clementa-pinckney

3 Jackson, Jesse. 'Charleston shooting: we need prayer, but also an end to this political genocide'. *The Guardian*, 20 June 2015. Available at: https://www.theguardian.com/commentisfree/2015/jun/20/jesse-jackson-south-caroline-shooting-racism-african-american
4 Ms Dot Scott and Rev. Joseph Darby, respectively president and vice-president of the Charleston branch of NAACP, interviewed in Charleston, South Carolina, on 11 August 2016.
5 Jones, Jeffrey M. 'Six in 10 Americans Say Racism Against Blacks Is Widespread'. Gallup.com, 17 August 2016. Available at: http://www.gallup.com/poll/194657/six-americans-say-racism-against-blacks-widespread.aspx
6 See the data collected for 2015 and 2016 by the *Washington Post* ('Fatal Force', available at: https://www.washingtonpost.com/graphics/national/police-shootings-2016/) and *The Guardian* ('The Counted', available at: https://www.theguardian.com/us-news/series/counted-us-police-killings).
7 Shoichet, Catherine E.; Berlinger, Joshua and Almasy, Steve. 'Alton Sterling shooting: Second video of deadly encounter emerges'. CNN, 7 July 2016. Available at: http://edition.cnn.com/2016/07/06/us/baton-rouge-shooting-alton-sterling/
8 'Philando Castile death: Aftermath of police shooting streamed live'. BBC News, 7 July 2016. Available at: http://www.bbc.com/news/world-us-canada-36732908
9 Statement by President Barack Obama at Warsaw Marriott, Warsaw, Poland, on 7 July 2016. Transcript available at: https://www.whitehouse.gov/the-press-office/2016/07/07/statement-president
10 Jody Owens, director and managing attorney of the Mississippi office of the Southern Poverty Center, interviewed in Jackson, Mississippi, on 15 August 2016.
11 Carson, Ann E. (2015) 'Prisoners in 2014'. US Department of Justice, Bureau of Justice Statistics. Available at: https://www.bjs.gov/content/pub/pdf/p14.pdf
12 Statement by President Barack Obama at Warsaw Marriott, Warsaw, Poland, on 7 July 2016.
13 The Kids Count Data Center measures the share of children under age eighteen who live in families with incomes below the federal poverty level, as defined by the US Office of Management and Budget, by race and ethnicity. In 2015, 36 per cent of black or African-American children lived in poverty; the rate is 12 per cent among white children. Kids Count Data Center (2015). 'Children in poverty by race and ethnicity'. Available at: http://datacenter.kidscount.org/data/tables/44-children-in-poverty-by-race-and-ethnicity#detailed/1/any/false/573/10,11,9,12,1,185,13/324,323
14 Stack, Liam. 'Video Released in Terence Crutcher's Killing by Tulsa Police'. *New York Times*, 19 September 2016. Available at: http://www.nytimes.com/2016/09/20/us/video-released-in-terence-crutchers-killing-by-tulsa-police.html?_r=0
15 Fausset, Richard and Alcindor, Yamiche. 'Video by Wife of Keith Scott Shows Her Pleas to Police'. *New York Times*, 23 September 2016. Available at: http://www.nytimes.com/2016/09/24/us/charlotte-keith-scott-shooting-video.html
16 'Audio: Calls from Zimmerman, neighbor capture last minutes of Martin's life'. *Washington Post*, 20 May 2012. Available at: http://www.washingtonpost.com/wp-srv/special/nation/last-minutes-trayvon-martin-911-calls/
17 Alvarez, Lizette and Buckley, Cara. 'Zimmerman Is Acquitted in Trayvon Martin Killing'. *New York Times*, 13 July 2016. Available at: http://www.nytimes.com/2013/07/14/us/george-zimmerman-verdict-trayvon-martin.html
18 Thompson, Krissah and Wilson, Scott. 'Obama on Trayvon Martin: "If I had a son, he'd look like Trayvon"'. *Washington Post*, 23 March 2012. Available at: https://www.washingtonpost.com/politics/obama-if-i-had-a-son-hed-look-like-trayvon/2012/03/23/gIQApKPpVS_story.html

19 Sybrina Fulton, Trayvon Martin's mother, interviewed in Miami Lakes, Florida, on 5 August 2016.
20 Drabold, Will. 'Meet the Mothers Of The Movement Speaking at the Democratic Convention'. *Time*, 26 July 2016. Available at: http://time.com/4423920/dnc-mothers-movement-speakers/
21 Mirkinson, Jack. 'Oprah: Trayvon Martin The "Same Thing" As Emmett Till'. Huffington Post, 8 May 2013. Available at: http://www.huffingtonpost.com/2013/08/05/oprah-trayvon-martin-emmett-till_n_3707096.html
22 Erica Gordon-Taylor speaks about the deaths of Emmet Till and Trayvon Martin on MSNBC, 23 August 2013. Video available at: http://www.nbcnews.com/video/thomas-roberts/52827832#52827832
23 'Pride Versus Humility: The Parable of the Pharisee and the Publican'. Sermon by Martin Luther King, Jr at Dexter Avenue Baptist Church, 25 September 1955. King, Martin Luther, Jr, Carson, Clayborne and Carson, Susan (2017). *The Papers of Martin Luther King, Jr., Volume VI: Advocate of the Social Gospel, September 1948 March 1963*. University of California Press.
24 'Black pastor leads "all lives matter" chant at GOP convention'. *Washington Post*, 21 July 2016. Available at: https://www.washingtonpost.com/video/politics/black-pastor-leads-all-lives-matter-chant-at-gop-convention/2016/07/21/561cede4-4fa1-11e6-bf27-405106836f96_video.html
25 Withers, Ali. 'Three Questions for Black Lives Matter's Alicia Garza'. Bloomberg, 4 August 2016. Available at: http://www.bloomberg.com/news/videos/2016-08-04/three-questions-for-black-lives-matter-s-alicia-garza
26 Donnella, Leah. 'Does It Matter When A White CEO Says "Black Lives Matter"?' NPR, 10 November 2016. Available at: http://www.npr.org/sections/codeswitch/2016/11/10/499633977/does-it-matter-when-a-white-ceo-says-black-lives-matter
27 The Fortune 2016 Global 500. Available at: http://beta.fortune.com/global500/list
28 Jackson, Jesse. 'Charleston shooting: we need prayer, but also an end to this political genocide', op. cit.
29 Berenson, Tessa. 'Donald Trump Just Picked Jeff Sessions for Attorney General. Here's What He Believes on 3 Key Issues'. *Time*, 18 November 2016. Available at: http://time.com/4576787/jeff-sessions-attorney-general-donald-trump/
30 The Editorial Board. 'Jeff Sessions as Attorney General: An Insult to Justice'. *New York Times*, 18 November 2016. Available at: http://www.nytimes.com/2016/11/19/opinion/jeff-sessions-as-attorney-general-an-insult-to-justice.html
31 Ferris, Sarah. 'Trump gets first Senate endorsement'. The Hill, 28 February 2016. Available at: http://thehill.com/blogs/ballot-box/presidential-races/271109-gop-senator-expected-to-endorse-trump
32 Apuzzo, Matt. 'Specter of Race Shadows Jeff Sessions, Potential Trump Nominee for Cabinet'. *New York Times*, 16 November 2016. Available at: http://www.nytimes.com/2016/11/17/us/politics/specter-of-race-shadows-jeff-sessions-potential-trump-nominee-for-cabinet.html
33 Apuzzo, Matt. 'Specter of Race Shadows Jeff Sessions, Potential Trump Nominee for Cabinet', op. cit.
34 Glover, Scott. 'Colleague, transcripts offer closer look at old allegations of racism against Sen. Jeff Sessions'. CNN, 18 November 2016. Available at: http://edition.cnn.com/2016/11/18/politics/jeff-sessions-racism-allegations/
35 Sullivan, Sean. 'Trump supporter Sen. Jeff Sessions reportedly said behavior Trump described in 2005 video is not sexual assault'. *Washington Post*, 10 October 2016. Available at: https://www.washingtonpost.com/news/post-politics/wp/2016/10/10/trump-supporter-sen-jeff-sessions-reportedly-said-behavior-trump-described-in-2005-video-is-not-sexual-assault/

CHAPTER FIVE

1 Statement by President Barack Obama on the school shooting in Newtown, Connecticut. James S. Brady Press Briefing Room, 14 December 2012. Transcript available at: https://www.whitehouse.gov/the-press-office/2012/12/14/statement-president-school-shooting-newtown-ct

2 David Stowe, vice-chair of the Newton Action Alliance, interviewed in Newtown, Connecticut, on 19 August 2016.

3 Remarks by President Barack Obama at Sandy Hook Interfaith Prayer Vigil, Newton High School, Newton, Connecticut, 16 December 2012. Transcript available at: https://www.whitehouse.gov/the-press-office/2012/12/16/remarks-president-sandy-hook-interfaith-prayer-vigil

4 Violent Crime Control and Law Enforcement Act of 1994, Public Safety and Recreational Firearms Use Protection Act. Text available at: https://www.congress.gov/bill/103rd-congress/house-bill/3355

5 Joshua Koskoff, attorney representing the Sandy Hook victims' families against Bushmaster, interviewed in Bridgeport, Connecticut, on 19 August 2016.

6 Murray, Shailagh and Horwitz, Sari. 'Rep. Gabrielle Giffords shot in Tucson rampage; federal judge killed'. *Washington Post*, 9 January 2011. Available at: http://www.washingtonpost.com/wp-dyn/content/article/2011/01/08/AR2011010802422.html

7 Large Capacity Ammunition Feeding Device Act. Text available at: https://www.congress.gov/112/bills/s32/BILLS-112s32is.pdf; Gun Show Background Check Act of 2011. Text available at: https://www.congress.gov/112/bills/s35/BILLS-112s35is.pdf; and Denying Firearms and Explosives to Dangerous Terrorists Act of 2011. Text available at: https://www.congress.gov/bill/112th-congress/senate-bill/34. The three bills were introduced in Senate by Senator Frank Lautenberg on 25 January 2011.

8 Clift, Eleanor. 'Congresswoman Carolyn McCarthy's Lonely Crusade for Smarter Gun Control'. Daily Beast, 21 July 2012. Available at: http://www.thedailybeast.com/articles/2012/07/20/congresswoman-carolyn-mccarthy-s-lonely-crusade-for-smarter-gun-control.html

9 Shrum, Robert. 'After Newtown, This Has to Be the Time for Gun Control'. Daily Beast, 14 December 2012. Available at: http://www.thedailybeast.com/articles/2012/12/14/after-newtown-this-has-to-be-the-time-for-gun-control.html

10 Lee, Carol E. 'Gun control group fails Obama'. Politico, 18 January 2010. Available at: http://www.politico.com/politico44/perm/0110/brady_campaign_f_4e52b8a5-4d03-44ce-9f5c-adbad49ed0bd.html

11 Manchin Amendment No. 715 to Safe Communities, Safe Schools Act of 2013. Text available at: https://www.congress.gov/amendment/113th-congress/senate-amendment/715

12 Blake, Aaron. 'Manchin-Toomey gun amendment fails'. *Washington Post*, 17 April 2013. Available at: https://www.washingtonpost.com/news/post-politics/wp/2013/04/17/manchin-toomey-gun-amendment-fails/

13 Statement by President Barack Obama at Rose Garden on 17 April 2013. Transcript available at: https://www.whitehouse.gov/the-press-office/2013/04/17/statement-president

14 Cillizza, Chris. 'How the NRA spent $32 million on politics in 2012'. *Washington Post*, 30 January 2016. Available at: https://www.washingtonpost.com/news/the-fix/wp/2013/01/30/how-the-nra-spent-32-million-in-2012/?utm_term=.1f0003eea798

15 Ingraham, Christopher. 'There are now more guns than people in the United States'. *Washington Post*, 5 October 2016. Available at: https://www.washingtonpost.com/news/wonk/wp/2015/10/05/guns-in-the-united-states-one-for-every-man-woman-and-child-and-then-some/?utm_term=.3fee836ffcd1

16 Pew Research Center, 'Opinions on Gun Policy and the 2016 Campaign' (August 2016). Available at: http://assets.pewresearch.org/wp-content/uploads/sites/5/2016/08/08-26-16-Gun-policy-release.pdf
17 In 2015, the database Mass Shooting Tracker registered 371 incidents where four or more people, including the assailant, were killed or injured in a single shooting spree. Data available at: https://massshootingtracker.org/data/2015
18 Grinshteyn, Erin and Hemenway, David. 'Violent Death Rates: The US Compared with Other High-income OECD Countries, 2010'. *American Journal of Medicine*, 2016. Available at: http://www.amjmed.com/article/S0002-9343(15)01030-X/fulltext
19 Lafrance, Adrienne. 'America's Top Killing Machine'. *The Atlantic*, 12 January 2015. Available at: http://www.theatlantic.com/technology/archive/2015/01/americas-top-killing-machine/384440/
20 Brady Handgun Violence Prevention Act, signed into law by President Bill Clinton on 30 November 1993. Text available at: https://www.congress.gov/103/bills/hr1025/BILLS-103hr1025enr.pdf
21 Tom Diaz, writer and advocate of gun control, phone interviews on 13 October and 25 November 2016.
22 Diaz, Tom. *Making a Killing: The Business of Guns in America*. New Press, 1999.
23 The White House, Press Office. FACT SHEET: New Executive Actions to Reduce Gun Violence and Make Our Communities Safer. 1 January 2016. Available at: https://www.whitehouse.gov/the-press-office/2016/01/04/fact-sheet-new-executive-actions-reduce-gun-violence-and-make-our
24 Wheaton, Sarah and Gass, Nick. 'Obama wipes away tears as he calls for new gun measures'. Politico, 5 January 2016. Available at: http://www.politico.com/story/2016/01/obama-gun-restrictions-217354
25 Steinhauer, Jennifer. 'Senate Rejects 4 Measures to Control Gun Sales'. *New York Times*, 20 June 2016. Available at: http://www.nytimes.com/2016/06/21/us/politics/gun-vote-senate.html?_r=0
26 Walsh, Deirdre and LoBianco, Tom. 'Nearly 15 hours later, Democratic senator ends filibuster over guns'. CNN, 16 June 2016. Available at: http://edition.cnn.com/2016/06/15/politics/gun-filibuster-senate-democrat/
27 Herszenhorn, David M. and Huetteman, Emmarie. 'House Democrats' Gun-Control Sit-In Turns Into Chaotic Showdown With Republicans'. *New York Times*, 22 June 2016. Available at: http://www.nytimes.com/2016/06/23/us/politics/house-democrats-stage-sit-in-to-push-for-action-on-gun-control.html
28 '"Assault Weapons" and "Large" Magazines'. NRA Institute for Legislative Action, 8 August 2016. Available at: https://www.nraila.org/issues/assault-weapons-large-magazines/#_edn1
29 Fernandez, Manny and Smith, Mitch. 'Gun Owners "Can Breathe Again": Trump's Win Emboldens Advocates'. *New York Times*, 22 November 2016. Available at: http://www.nytimes.com/2016/11/22/us/gun-supporters-trump.html
30 Berenson, Tessa. 'Hillary Clinton on Orlando Shooting: "Weapons of War Have No Place on Our Streets"'. *Time*, 13 June 2016. Available at: http://time.com/4366607/hillary-clinton-orlando-shooting-isis-guns/
31 Savransky, Rebecca. 'Clinton ad features daughter of Sandy Hook principal'. The Hill, 20 April 2016. Available at: http://thehill.com/blogs/ballot-box/presidential-races/276976-daughter-of-sandy-hook-principal-featured-in-new-clinton
32 Gearan, Anne. 'Hillary Clinton accuses gun lobby of intimidating Congress, harassing critics'. *Washington Post*, 21 April 2016. Available at: https://www.washingtonpost.com/news/post-politics/wp/2016/04/21/hillary-clinton-accuses-gun-lobby-of-intimidating-congress-harassing-critics/?utm_term=.0cccfbdefc90
33 Martin, Jonathan and Rappeport, Alan. 'Debbie Wasserman Schultz to Resign DNC Post'. *New York Times*, 24 July 2016. Available at: http://www.

nytimes.com/2016/07/25/us/politics/debbie-wasserman-schultz-dnc-wikileaks-emails.html
34 2016 Democratic Party Platform. 21 July 2016, as approved by the Democratic Platform Committee, 8–9 July 2016. Orlando, FL. Available at: https://www.demconvention.com/wp-content/uploads/2016/07/Democratic-Party-Platform-7.21.16-no-lines.pdf
35 Full transcript: Third 2016 presidential debate. Politico, 20 October 2016. Available at: http://www.politico.com/story/2016/10/full-transcript-third-2016-presidential-debate-230063
36 Spies, Mike and Balcerzak, Ashley. 'The NRA placed big bets on the 2016 election and won almost all of them'. The Trace, 9 November 2016. Available at: https://www.thetrace.org/2016/11/nra-big-bets-election-2016-results/

CHAPTER SIX

1 Mario Reyes, Webb County Sheriff's Office deputy, interviewed in Laredo, Texas, on 22 August 2016.
2 Nhan, Doris. 'Pew Report Reveals Demographics, Economics of US Hispanic Population'. *The Atlantic*, 21 September 2012. Available at: https://www.theatlantic.com/politics/archive/2012/09/pew-report-reveals-demographics-economics-of-us-hispanic-population/428856/
3 Vulliamy, Ed. *Amexica: War Along the Borderline*. Farrar, Straus and Giroux, 2010.
4 Ware, Michael. 'Los Zetas called Mexico's most dangerous drug cartel'. CNN, 6 August 2009. Available at: http://edition.cnn.com/2009/WORLD/americas/08/06/mexico.drug.cartels/index.html
5 Reed, Tristan. 'Mexico's Drug War: A New Way to Think About Mexican Organized Crime'. *Forbes*, 15 January 2015. Available at: http://www.forbes.com/sites/stratfor/2015/01/15/mexicos-drug-war-a-new-way-to-think-about-mexican-organized-crime/#51f6c7646ec5
6 'Polarization and Sustained Violence in Mexico's Cartel War'. Stratfor, 24 January 2012. Available at: https://www.stratfor.com/analysis/polarization-and-sustained-violence-mexicos-cartel-war
7 'Here's Donald Trump's Presidential Announcement Speech'. *Time*, 16 June 2015. Available at: http://time.com/3923128/donald-trump-announcement-speech/
8 Kendall, Brent. 'Trump Says Judge's Mexican Heritage Presents "Absolute Conflict"'. *Wall Street Journal*, 3 June 2016. Available at: http://www.wsj.com/articles/donald-trump-keeps-up-attacks-on-judge-gonzalo-curiel-1464911442
9 'Here's Donald Trump's Presidential Announcement Speech'. *Time*, op. cit.
10 Ye Hee Lee, Michelle. 'Trump's claim that 2 million or 3 million criminal aliens are "here illegally"'. *Washington Post*, 15 November 2016. Available at: https://www.washingtonpost.com/news/fact-checker/wp/2016/11/15/trumps-claim-that-two-million-or-three-million-criminal-aliens-are-here-illegally/?utm_term=.c3b40900c268
11 Bump, Philip. 'Here's what Donald Trump said in his big immigration speech, annotated'. *Washington Post*, 31 August 2016. Available at: https://www.washingtonpost.com/news/the-fix/wp/2016/08/31/heres-what-donald-trump-said-in-his-big-immigration-speech-annotated/?utm_term=.a32104a06ce5
12 Bump, Philip. 'Here's what Donald Trump said in his big immigration speech, annotated', op. cit.
13 Corasaniti, Nick. 'Donald Trump Visits Border in Laredo, "Despite the Great Danger"'. *New York Times*, 23 July 2015. Available at: http://www.nytimes.com/politics/first-draft/2015/07/23/donald-trumps-border-visit-stirs-passions-in-laredo/
14 Hector Garza, Border Patrol agent and president of Local 2455 in Laredo, interviewed in Laredo, Texas, on 22 August 2016.

15 Graff, Garret M. 'Donald Trump's Army on the Border'. Politico, 18 July 2016. Available at: http://www.politico.com/magazine/story/2016/07/2016-donald-trump-mexico-us-border-patrol-immigration-undocumented-illegal-customs-texas-rio-grande-214060
16 Corasaniti, Nick. 'Donald Trump Visits Border in Laredo, "Despite the Great Danger"', op. cit.
17 Urbino 'Benny' Martinez, Brooks County Sheriff, interviewed in Falfurrias, Texas on 23 August 2016.
18 The National Academies of Sciences, Engineering, and Medicine. *The Economic and Fiscal Consequences of Immigration*. The National Academies Press, 2016.
19 Brown, Anna and Stepler, Renee. 'Statistical Portrait of the Foreign-Born Population in the United States'. Pew Research, 19 April 2016. Available at: http://www.pewhispanic.org/2016/04/19/statistical-portrait-of-the-foreign-born-population-in-the-united-states-key-charts/
20 Zong, Jie and Batalova, Jeanne. 'Frequently Requested Statistics on Immigrants and Immigration in the United States'. Migration Policy Institute, 14 April 2016. Available at: http://www.migrationpolicy.org/article/frequently-requested-statistics-immigrants-and-immigration-united-states
21 'Modern Immigration Wave Brings 59 Million to US, Driving Population Growth and Change Through 2065'. Chapter 5: U.S. Foreign-Born Population Trends. Pew Research, 28 September 2015. Available at: http://www.pewhispanic.org/2015/09/28/chapter-5-u-s-foreign-born-population-trends/
22 Zong, Jie and Batalova, Jeanne. 'Mexican Immigrants in the United States'. Migration Policy Institute, 17 March 2016. Available at: http://www.migrationpolicy.org/article/mexican-immigrants-united-states
23 Rhodan, Maya. 'Donald Trump Raises Eyebrows With "Bad Hombres" Line'. *Time*, 19 October 2016. Available at: http://time.com/4537847/donald-trump-bad-hombres/
24 Gonzalez-Barrera, Ana. 'More Mexicans Leaving Than Coming to the US'. Pew Research Center, 19 November 2015. Available at: http://www.pewhispanic.org/2015/11/19/more-mexicans-leaving-than-coming-to-the-u-s/
25 Passel, Jeffrey S. and Cohn, D'Vera. 'Overall Number of US Unauthorized Immigrants Holds Steady Since 2009'. Pew Research Center, 20 September 2016. Available at: http://www.pewhispanic.org/2016/09/20/overall-number-of-u-s-unauthorized-immigrants-holds-steady-since-2009/
26 Cohen, Tom and Mears, Bill. 'Supreme Court mostly rejects Arizona immigration law; gov says "heart" remains'. CNN, 26 June 2012. Available at: http://edition.cnn.com/2012/06/25/politics/scotus-arizona-law/
27 Erlanger, Steven. 'Britain Votes to Leave EU; Cameron Plans to Step Down'. *New York Times*, 23 June 2016. Available at: http://www.nytimes.com/2016/06/25/world/europe/britain-brexit-european-union-referendum.html
28 The Editorial Board. 'France Elects Emmanuel Macron'. *New York Times*, 7 May 2017. Available at: https://www.nytimes.com/2017/05/07/opinion/france-elects-emmanuel-macron.html
29 Bergman, Matthew E. 'The Dutch pushed back against Geert Wilders's "Patriotic Spring". Here's what you need to know'. *Washington Post*. 16 March 2017. Available at: https://www.washingtonpost.com/news/monkey-cage/wp/2017/03/16/the-dutch-pushed-back-against-geert-wilderss-patriotic-spring-heres-what-you-need-to-know/?utm_term=.cfd779c142bc
30 Kirk, Ashley and Dunford, Daniel. 'EU referendum: How the results compare to the UK's educated, old and immigrant populations'. *Daily Telegraph*, 27 June 2016. Available at: http://www.telegraph.co.uk/news/2016/06/24/eu-referendum-how-the-results-compare-to-the-uks-educated-old-an/

31 Berenson, Tessa. 'Donald Trump Pushes for Muslim Ban After Orlando Shooting'. *Time*, 13 June 2016. Available at: http://time.com/4366912/donald-trump-orlando-shooting-muslim-ban/
32 Berenson, Tessa. 'Donald Trump Proposes "Extreme Vetting" for Immigrants'. *Time*, 15 August 2016. Available at: http://time.com/4452970/donald-trump-immigration-isis-terrorism/
33 Marr, Kendra. 'Donald Trump, birther?' Politico, 17 March 2011. Available at: http://www.politico.com/story/2011/03/donald-trump-birther-051473
34 Liptak, Adam and Shear, Michael D. 'Supreme Court Tie Blocks Obama Immigration Plan'. *New York Times*, 23 June 2016. Available at: http://www.nytimes.com/2016/06/24/us/supreme-court-immigration-obama-dapa.html
35 Weiner, Rachel. 'How immigration reform failed, over and over'. *Washington Post*, 30 January 2013. Available at: https://www.washingtonpost.com/news/the-fix/wp/2013/01/30/how-immigration-reform-failed-over-and-over/?utm_term=.bc71058a6b49
36 Cillizza, Chris. 'Why George W. Bush was right'. *Washington Post*, 31 January 2013. Available at: https://www.washingtonpost.com/news/the-fix/wp/2013/01/31/why-george-w-bush-was-right-on-immigration/?utm_term=.9b41243a8bae
37 The American Presidency Project. 'The President's News Conference With President Vicente Fox of Mexico in San Cristobal, Mexico'. 16 February 2001. Available at: http://www.presidency.ucsb.edu/ws/?pid=45868
38 The Immigration Reform and Control Act, enacted 6 November 1986, and signed into law by Ronald Reagan on 6 November 1986. Text available at: https://www.gpo.gov/fdsys/pkg/STATUTE-100/pdf/STATUTE-100-Pg3445.pdf
39 'A Reagan Legacy: Amnesty For Illegal Immigrants'. NPR, 4 July 2010. Available at: http://www.npr.org/templates/story/story.php?storyId=128303672
40 The Immigration Act of 1990, enacted 29 November 1990 and signed into law by George H. W. Bush on 29 November 1990. Text available at: https://www.gpo.gov/fdsys/pkg/STATUTE-104/pdf/STATUTE-104-Pg4978.pdf
41 Remarks by President George Bush and President Vicente Fox of Mexico at Arrival Ceremony. 5 September 2001. Transcription available at: https://georgewbush-whitehouse.archives.gov/news/releases/2001/09/20010905-2.html
42 Tom Jawetz, vice-president of immigration policy at the Center for American Progress, interviewed on 26 September 2016. Phone interview.
43 Budoff Brown, Carrie. 'Senate Gang of 8 immigration reform bill (full text)'. Politico, 17 April 2013. Available at: http://www.politico.com/story/2013/04/senate-gang-of-8-immigration-reform-bill-full-text-090192
44 Blake, Aaron. 'Manchin-Toomey gun amendment fails'. *Washington Post*, 17 April 2013. Available at: https://www.washingtonpost.com/news/post-politics/wp/2013/04/17/manchin-toomey-gun-amendment-fails/
45 Min Kim, Seung. 'Senate passes immigration bill'. Politico, 27 June 2013. Available at: http://www.politico.com/story/2013/06/immigration-bill-2013-senate-passes-093530
46 Min Kim, Seung. 'Senate passes immigration bill', op. cit.
47 The White House, Office of the Press Secretary. FACT SHEET: Immigration Accountability Executive Action. 20 November 2014. Available at: https://www.whitehouse.gov/the-press-office/2014/11/20/fact-sheet-immigration-accountability-executive-action
48 The White House, Office of the Press Secretary. Remarks by the President in Address to the Nation on Immigration. 20 November 2014. Available at: https://www.whitehouse.gov/the-press-office/2014/11/20/remarks-president-address-nation-immigration
49 Ford, Matt. 'A Ruling Against the Obama Administration on Immigration'. *The*

Atlantic. 10 November 2015. Available at: http://www.theatlantic.com/politics/archive/2015/11/fifth-circuit-obama-immigration/415077/
50 Liptak, Adam and Shear, Michael D. 'Supreme Court Tie Blocks Obama Immigration Plan', op. cit.
51 Chokshi, Niraj, Rogers, Katie and McPhate, Mike. 'A Brief Guide to Today's Supreme Court Decisions'. 23 June 2016. Available at: http://www.nytimes.com/2016/06/24/us/what-we-know-about-the-supreme-court-decisions.html
52 Piggot, Stephen. 'Jeff Sessions: Champion of Anti-Muslim and Anti-Immigrant Extremists'. Southern Poverty Law Center, 18 November 2016. Available at: https://www.splcenter.org/hatewatch/2016/11/18/jeff-sessions-champion-anti-muslim-and-anti-immigrant-extremists

CHAPTER SEVEN

1 Gary Brock, waiter, interviewed in Ormond Beach, Florida, on 8 August 2016.
2 The Patient Protection and Affordable Care Act, commonly known as 'Obamacare', was signed into law by President Obama on 23 March 2010. Text available at: https://www.gpo.gov/fdsys/pkg/PLAW-111publ148/pdf/PLAW-111publ148.pdf
3 In 2010, the percentage of people without health insurance was 16.3 per cent (49.9 million Americans). DeNavas-Walt, Carmen; Proctor, Bernadette D. and Smith, Jessica D. (2011) 'Income, Poverty, and Health Insurance Coverage in the United States: 2010'. United States Census Bureau. Available at: http://census.gov/content/dam/Census/library/publications/2011/demo/p60-239.pdf
4 In 2015, the percentage of people without health insurance was 9.1 per cent (29 million Americans). Barnett, Jessica C. and Vornovitsky, Marina S. (2016). 'Health Insurance Coverage in the United States: 2015'. Available at: http://census.gov/content/dam/Census/library/publications/2016/demo/p60-257.pdf
5 'Premium affordability, competition, and choice in the health insurance marketplace', 2014. US Department of Health & Human Services, office of the assistant secretary for planning and evaluation. Available at: https://aspe.hhs.gov/pdf-report/premium-affordability-competition-and-choice-health-insurance-marketplace-2014
6 West, Darrell M. and Bleiberg, Joshua. 'A look back at technical issues with Healthcare.gov'. Brookings Institution, 9 April 2015. Available at: https://www.brookings.edu/blog/techtank/2015/04/09/a-look-back-at-technical-issues-with-healthcare-gov/
7 Waters, Jennifer. 'Obamacare Aims to Close Medicare "Doughnut Hole"'. *Washington Post*, 6 October 2013. Available at: http://www.wsj.com/articles/SB10001424052702303722604579111170290397770
8 Pradhan, Rachana. 'Key Obamacare premiums to jump 25 per cent next year'. Politico, 24 October 2016. Available at: http://www.politico.com/story/2016/10/hhs-benchmark-obamacare-premiums-jump-25-percent-next-year-230263
9 Lim, Naomi. 'Bill Clinton calls Obamacare "the craziest thing in the world," later tries to walk it back'. CNN, 5 October 2016. Available at: http://edition.cnn.com/2016/10/04/politics/bill-clinton-obamacare-craziest-thing/
10 Jaffe, Alexandra. 'Bill Clinton Attempts to Clarify Scathing Obamacare Comments'. NBC News, 4 October 2016. Available at: http://www.nbcnews.com/politics/2016-election/bill-clinton-attempts-clarify-scathing-obamacare-comments-n659411
11 Lim, Naomi. 'Bill Clinton calls Obamacare "the craziest thing in the world," later tries to walk it back', op. cit.
12 Saenz, Arlette. 'White House Defends "Obamacare" After Bill Clinton Calls It "Craziest Thing"'. ABC News, 4 October 2016. Available at: http://abcnews.go.com/Politics/white-house-defends-obamacare-bill-clinton-calls-craziest/story?id=42564838
13 Ferris, Sarah. 'Bill Clinton slams ObamaCare: "It's the craziest thing in the

world"'. The Hill, 4 October 2016. Available at: http://thehill.com/policy/healthcare/299130-bill-clinton-slams-obamacare

14 McCaskill, Nolan D. 'Trump: Bill Clinton "went through hell last night"'. Politico, 4 October 2016. Available at: http://www.politico.com/story/2016/10/trump-clinton-hell-229118

15 Haberkorn, Jennifer. 'Supreme Court upholds individual mandate'. Politico, 28 June 2012. Available at: http://www.politico.com/story/2012/06/supreme-court-health-care-ruling-077935

16 Rosalind Hines, adviser for Health Insurance Application at Allendale County Alive, interviewed in Allendale, South Carolina, on 9 August 2016.

17 OECD, Health expenditure and financing (2015). Data available at: http://stats.oecd.org/Index.aspx?DataSetCode=SHA

18 Fuchs, Victor R. 'Why Do Other Rich Nations Spend So Much Less on Healthcare?' *The Atlantic*, 23 July 2014. Available at: http://www.theatlantic.com/business/archive/2014/07/why-do-other-rich-nations-spend-so-much-less-on-healthcare/374576/

19 Lee, MJ and Luhby, Tami. 'Trump issues executive order to start rolling back Obamacare'. CNN, 21 January 2017. Available at: http://edition.cnn.com/2017/01/20/politics/trump-signs-executive-order-on-obamacare/

20 Goldstein, Amy and Rucker, Philip. 'Trump names Rep. Tom Price as next HHS secretary'. *Washington Post*, 29 November 2016. Available at: https://www.washingtonpost.com/news/powerpost/wp/2016/11/28/trump-to-name-rep-tom-price-as-next-hhs-secretary/?utm_term=.cb3e7a931a62

21 Project Vote Smart. 'Tom Price's Political Summary on Issue: Guns'. Available at: https://votesmart.org/candidate/11853/tom-price?categoryId=37&type=V,S,R,E,F,P#.WGunu2NvjR0

22 Pear, Robert. 'Tom Price, Obamacare Critic, Is Trump's Choice for Health Secretary'. *New York Times*, 28 November 2016. Available at: http://www.nytimes.com/2016/11/28/us/politics/tom-price-secretary-health-and-human-services.html

23 Weisman, Jonathan. 'House Republican Budget Overhauls Medicare and Repeals the Health Law'. *New York Times*, 16 March 2015. Available at: http://www.nytimes.com/2015/03/17/us/politics/house-republican-budget-overhauls-medicare-and-repeals-the-health-law.html

24 Pear, Robert. 'Tom Price, Obamacare Critic, Is Trump's Choice for Health Secretary', op. cit.

25 Neel, Joe. 'Trump Chooses Rep. Tom Price, An Obamacare Foe, To Run HHS'. NPR, 28 November 2016. Available at: http://www.npr.org/sections/health-shots/2016/11/28/502566553/trump-chooses-rep-tom-price-an-obamacare-foe-to-run-hhs

26 Cancryn, Adam; Haberkorn, Jennifer and Pradhan, Rachana. 'Tom Price's radically conservative vision for American health care'. Politico, 29 November 2016. Available at: http://www.politico.com/story/2016/11/tom-price-radically-conservative-healthcare-vision-231965

27 Thomas, Katie. 'FDA Official Under Bush Is Trump's Choice to Lead Agency'. *New York Times*, 10 March 2017. Available at: https://www.nytimes.com/2017/03/10/health/fda-scott-gottlieb.html

28 Glenza, Jessica. 'Trump's pick for key health post known for punitive Medicaid plan'. *The Guardian*, 4 December 2016. Available at: https://www.theguardian.com/us-news/2016/dec/04/seema-verma-trump-centers-medicare-medicaid-cms

29 Cook, Tony. 'Seema Verma, powerful state health-care consultant, serves two bosses'. *Indianapolis Star*, 29 November 2016. Available at: http://www.indystar.com/story/news/politics/2014/08/25/powerful-state-healthcare-consultant-serves-two-bosses/14468683/

30 Pradhan, Rachana. 'Trump picks Seema Verma to head Centers for Medicare and Medicaid Services'. Politico, 29 November 2016. Available at: http://www.politico.com/blogs/donald-trump-administration/2016/11/seema-verma-to-head-centers-for-medicare-and-medicaid-services-231921
31 Medicaid and CHIP: October 2016 Monthly Applications, Eligibility Determinations and Enrollment Report, CMS. Available at: https://www.medicaid.gov/medicaid/program-information/medicaid-and-chip-enrollment-data/report-highlights/index.html
32 Liberto, Jennifer. 'Medicaid reduced by $1 trillion in GOP plan'. CNN, 5 April 2011. Available at: http://money.cnn.com/2011/04/05/news/economy/medicaid_cuts_budget_republicans/
33 Leventhal, Rajiv. 'Who is Seema Verma? Digging Deeper into Trump's Pick to Run CMS'. HealthCare Informatic, 5 December 2016. Available at: http://www.healthcare-informatics.com/article/who-seema-verma-digging-deeper-trump-s-pick-run-cms
34 H. Luke Shaefer, Associate Professor of Social Work and Associate Professor of Public Policy, School of Social Work, University of Michigan, phone interview on 16 September 2016.
35 Edin, Kathryn J. and Shaefer, Luke H. (2015). $2.00 a Day: Living on Almost Nothing in America. Houghton Mifflin Harcourt.
36 Personal Responsibility and Work Opportunity Act, signed into law by President Bill Clinton on 22 August 1996. Text available at: https://www.gpo.gov/fdsys/pkg/PLAW-104publ193/html/PLAW-104publ193.htm
37 Pear, Robert; Kaplan, Thomas and Haberman, Maggie. 'In Major Defeat for Trump, Push to Repeal Health Law Fails'. *New York Times*, 24 March 2017. Available at: https://www.nytimes.com/2017/03/24/us/politics/health-care-affordable-care-act.html
38 Pear, Robert and Kaplan, Thomas. 'House Passes Measure to Repeal and Replace the Affordable Care Act'. *New York Times*. 4 May 2017. Available at: https://www.nytimes.com/2017/05/04/us/politics/health-care-bill-vote.html
39 Pear, Robert. 'GOP Health Bill Would Leave 23 Million More Uninsured in a Decade, CBO Says'. *New York Times*, 24 May 2017. Available at: https://www.nytimes.com/2017/05/24/us/politics/cbo-congressional-budget-office-health-care.html
40 Weigel, David. '"Obamacare Lite," "RINOcare": Conservatives rebel against GOP's ACA bill'. *Washington Post*, 7 March 2017. Available at: https://www.washingtonpost.com/news/powerpost/wp/2017/03/07/obamacare-lite-rinocare-conservatives-rebel-against-gops-aca-bill/?utm_term=.3a1e2db91dfb
41 Pear, Robert. 'GOP Health Bill Would Leave 23 Million More Uninsured in a Decade, CBO Says', op. cit.
42 Wong, Scott; Hellmann, Jessie; Lillis, Mike and Marcos, Cristina. 'Trump delivers ultimatum to GOP on ObamaCare repeal'. The Hill 23 March 2017. Available at: http://thehill.com/homenews/house/325577-trump-delivers-ultimatum-to-gop-on-obamacare-repeal
43 Pear, Robert; Kaplan, Thomas and Haberman, Maggie. 'In Major Defeat for Trump, Push to Repeal Health Law Fails', op. cit.
44 Pear, Robert and Kaplan, Thomas. 'House Passes Measure to Repeal and Replace the Affordable Care Act', op. cit.

CHAPTER EIGHT

1 Busvine, Douglas and Soldatkin, Vladimir. 'Exxon, Rosneft unveil $500 billion offshore venture'. Reuters, 18 April 2012. Available at: http://www.reuters.com/article/us-exxon-rosneft-idUSBRE83H0UE20120418
2 Taylor, Adam. 'If ExxonMobil were a country, its economy would be bigger than Ireland's'. *Washington Post*, 13 December 2016. Available at: https://www.

washingtonpost.com/news/worldviews/wp/2016/12/12/if-exxonmobil-were-a-country-it-would-be-the-worlds-41st-largest-economy/?tid=sm_tw&utm_term=.e14b6734ba86

3 Coll, Steve. 'Rex Tillerson, from a corporate oil sovereign to the State Department'. *New Yorker*, 11 December 2016. Available at: http://www.newyorker.com/news/news-desk/rex-tillerson-from-a-corporate-oil-sovereign-to-the-state-department

4 Swartz, Mimi. 'An Extended Interview With Steve Coll'. *Texas Monthly*, May 2012. Available at: http://www.texasmonthly.com/articles/an-extended-interview-with-steve-coll/

5 Coll, Steve. *Private Empire: ExxonMobil and American Power*. Penguin Press, 2012.

6 Official Internet Resources of the President of Russia. 'Meeting with energy company heads'. 21 June 2013. Available at: http://en.kremlin.ru/events/president/news/18382

7 Franchetti, Mark. 'Jailed tycoon Mikhail Khodorkovsky "framed" by key Putin aide'. *Sunday Times*, 18 May 2008. Available at: http://www.thesundaytimes.co.uk/sto/news/world_news/article93267.ece

8 MacFarquhar, Neil and Kramer, Andrew E. 'How Rex Tillerson Changed His Tune on Russia and Came to Court Its Rulers'. *New York Times*, 20 December 2016. Available at: http://www.nytimes.com/2016/12/20/world/europe/russia-rex-tillerson-donald-trump-secretary-of-state.html

9 Skinner, Samuel K and Reilly, William K. (Prepared by the National Response Team). 'The EXXON VALDEZ Oil Spill, a report to the President'. May 1989. Available at: http://www.uscg.mil/history/webshipwrecks/ExxonValdezNRT1989Report.pdf

10 BBC Radio 4. 'Rex Tillerson "is one tough cookie"'. Podcast available at: http://www.bbc.co.uk/programmes/p04l2b1t

11 Forbes Global 2000 (2017). 'The World's Biggest Public Companies'. Available at: https://www.forbes.com/global2000/list/#tab:overall

12 Pfeifer, Sylvia. 'Exxon signs Kurd exploration contracts'. *Financial Times*, 10 November 2011. Available at: https://www.ft.com/content/4e44f860-0bda-11e1-9861-00144feabdc0

13 Kramer, Andrew E. and Krauss, Clifford. 'Rex Tillerson's Company, Exxon, Has Billions at Stake Over Sanctions on Russia'. *New York Times*, 12 December 2016. Available at: http://www.nytimes.com/2016/12/12/world/europe/rex-tillersons-company-exxon-has-billions-at-stake-over-russia-sanctions.html

14 Coll, Steve. *Private Empire: ExxonMobil and American Power*, op. cit.

15 'Priebus on Tillerson, Bolton and CIA report'. *Morning Joe*, MSNBC, 13 December 2016. Available at: http://www.msnbc.com/morning-joe/watch/priebus-on-tillerson-bolton-and-cia-report-831742532000

16 Sherman, Jake and Nussbaum, Matthew. 'Gates, Rice praise Tillerson for secretary of state'. Politico, 13 December 2016. Available at: http://www.politico.com/blogs/donald-trump-administration/2016/12/bob-gates-praises-tillerson-for-secretary-of-state-232555

17 Shelbourne, Mallory. 'Robert Gates strongly backs Trump pick for Secretary of State'. The Hill, 13 December 2016. Available at: http://thehill.com/homenews/administration/310116-gates-endorses-tillerson

18 Gates, Robert M. 'Sizing Up the Next Commander-in-Chief'. *Wall Street Journal*, 16 September 2016. Available at: http://www.wsj.com/articles/sizing-up-the-next-commander-in-chief-1474064606

19 Zimmerman, Neetzan. 'Condoleezza Rice calls for Trump to drop out: "Enough!"'. The Hill, 8 October 2016. Available at: http://thehill.com/blogs/blog-briefing-room/news/300038-condoleezza-rice-calls-for-trump-to-drop-out-enough

20 Conway, Madeline. 'James Baker: Tillerson will adopt "different outlook" on Putin'. Politico, 14 December 2016. Available at: http://www.politico.com/story/2016/12/james-baker-rex-tillerson-232624
21 Kranish, Michale; Gerean, Anne; Balz, Dan and Rucker, Philip. 'Trump wasn't happy with his State Department finalists. Then he heard a new name'. *Washington Post*, 13 December 2016. Available at: https://www.washingtonpost.com/politics/trump-wasnt-happy-with-his-state-department-finalists-then-he-heard-a-new-name/2016/12/13/0727658e-c161-11e6-8422-eac61c0ef74d_story.html
22 Graham, Todd. 'An "oops" that could mean "over" for Perry'. CNN, 11 November 2011. Available at: http://edition.cnn.com/2011/11/10/opinion/graham-debate-perry/
23 Davenport, Coral. 'Rick Perry, Ex-Governor of Texas, Is Trump's Pick as Energy Secretary'. *New York Times*, 13 December 2016. Available at: http://www.nytimes.com/2016/12/13/us/politics/rick-perry-energy-secretary-trump.html
24 Rauf, David Saleh. 'Rick Perry's corporate board positions prove lucrative'. *San Antonio Express-News*, 24 April 2016. Available at: http://www.expressnews.com/news/local/article/Rick-Perry-s-corporate-board-positions-prove-7307037.php
25 Vamburkar, Meenal. 'Energy Transfer Advances on Dakota Pipeline, Protests Grow'. Bloomberg, 11 October 2016. Available at: https://www.bloomberg.com/news/articles/2016-10-11/as-protests-rise-energy-transfer-moves-ahead-on-dakota-pipeline
26 Murphy, Ryan. 'On the Records: Perry's Financial Sector Donors'. *Texas Tribune*, 11 January 2012. Available at: https://www.texastribune.org/2012/01/11/records-perrys-big-financial-sector-donors/
27 Denning, Liam. 'Energy Transfer and the Art of Transference'. Bloomberg, 22 November 2016. Available at: https://www.bloomberg.com/gadfly/articles/2016-11-22/energy-transfer-partners-sunoco-logistics-deal-transferring-pain
28 Braun, Stephen. 'Perry brings oil industry ties to Energy Department'. PBS, 14 December 2016. Available at: http://www.pbs.org/newshour/rundown/perry-oil-industry-energy-department/
29 Hampton, Liz. 'Sunoco, behind protested Dakota pipeline, tops US crude spill charts'. Reuters, 23 September 2016. Available at: http://www.reuters.com/article/us-usa-pipeline-nativeamericans-safety-i-idUSKCN11T1UW
30 Vamburkar, Meenal. 'US Delays Dakota Pipeline as Trump Promises Quicker Review'. Bloomberg, 14 November 2016. Available at: https://www.bloomberg.com/news/articles/2016-11-14/obama-administration-extends-dakota-access-oil-pipeline-review
31 Davenport, Coral and Lipton, Eric. 'Trump Picks Scott Pruitt, Climate Change Denialist, to Lead EPA'. *New York Times*, 7 December 2016. Available at: https://www.nytimes.com/2016/12/07/us/politics/scott-pruitt-epa-trump.html?_r=0
32 Pruitt, Scott and Strange, Luther. 'The Climate-Change Gang'. *National Review*, 17 May 2016. Available at: http://www.nationalreview.com/article/435470/climate-change-attorneys-general
33 Cama, Thimothy. 'Oklahoma sues to stop Obama's climate rule'. The Hill, 1 July 2016. Available at: http://thehill.com/policy/energy-environment/246727-oklahoma-sues-to-stop-obamas-climate-rule
34 Milman, Oliver. 'Scott Pruitt's EPA: a dream for oil and gas firms is nightmare for environment'. *The Guardian*, 8 December 2016. Available at: https://www.theguardian.com/us-news/2016/dec/08/scott-pruitt-trump-administration-epa-oil-gas-environment
35 Balcerzak, Ashley. 'Rick Perry, with multiple ties to CEO of controversial pipeline project, tapped for Energy Dept'. Center for Responsive Politics, Open Secrets,

13 December 2016. Available at: https://www.opensecrets.org/news/2016/12/rick-perry-tapped-for-energy-dept/

36 Hampton, Liz and Volcovici, Valerie. 'Top executive behind Dakota Access has donated more than $100,000 to Trump'. Reuters, 25 October 2016. Available at: http://www.reuters.com/article/us-usa-election-trump-dakota-access-idUSKCN12Q2P2

37 Horn, Steve. 'This Trump Aide Stands To Profit From The Dakota Access Pipeline'. Huffington Post, 9 June 2016. Available at: http://www.huffingtonpost.com/entry/company-led-by-donald-trumps-energy-aide-says-its_us_57cf7dcee4b0eb9a57b69f06

38 Helderman, Rosalind S. and Harwell, Drew. 'Trump's stock holdings may give him a personal stake in rules on banks and oil firms'. *Washington Post*, 2 December 2016. Available at: https://www.washingtonpost.com/politics/trumps-complex-stock-portfolio-could-create-yet-more-conflicts/2016/12/01/25ec0e88-b663-11e6-959c-172c82123976_story.html?utm_term=.1597c2ffa6d0

39 Mufson, Steven. 'Trump dumped his stock in the Dakota Access pipeline owner over the summer'. *Washington Post*, 23 November 2016. Available at: https://www.washingtonpost.com/news/energy-environment/wp/2016/11/23/trump-dumped-his-stock-in-dakota-access-pipeline-owner-over-the-summer/?utm_term=.93ea0933e86b

40 Paletta, Damian; Lee, Carol E. and Browne, Andrew. 'Trump Spoke With Taiwan President in Break With Decades of US Policy'. *Wall Street Journal*, 2 December 2016. Available at: http://www.wsj.com/articles/donald-trump-spoke-with-taiwan-president-tsai-ing-wen-1480718423

41 Blake, Aaron. 'SNL makes fun of Trump's tweets, and Trump immediately tweets his disapproval. Sad!' *Washington Post*, 4 December 2016. Available at: https://www.washingtonpost.com/news/the-fix/wp/2016/12/04/snl-makes-fun-of-trumps-tweets-and-trump-immediately-tweets-his-disapproval-sad/?utm_term=.78951b757e3d

42 Nelso, Louis. 'Trump: Vanity Fair is "dead"'. Politico, 15 December 2016. Available at: http://www.politico.com/story/2016/12/trump-feud-vanity-fair-232675

43 'Sierra Club: Scott Pruitt is unfit to serve as Epa administrator'. Statement from Michael Brune, Sierra Club official website, 7 December 2016. Available at: http://content.sierraclub.org/press-releases/2016/12/sierra-club-scott-pruitt-unfit-serve-epa-administrator

44 Cama, Thimoty. 'Oil bubbles back to top with Trump'. The Hill, 14 December 2016. Available at: http://thehill.com/policy/energy-environment/310301-oil-bubbles-back-to-top-with-trump

45 Hurley, Lawrence. 'Supreme Court lets stand ruling throwing out "abortion pill" limits'. Reuters, 4 November 2013. Available at: http://www.reuters.com/article/us-usa-court-abortion-idUSBRE9A30JG20131104

46 Eger, Andrea. 'Oklahoma Attorney General Scott Pruitt defends Bible distribution in schools, says "religious freedoms are under attack"'. *Tulsa World*, 15 April 2015. Available at: http://www.tulsaworld.com/news/education/oklahoma-attorney-general-scott-pruitt-defends-bible-distribution-in-schools/article_592d20aa-2c46-51f6-a3fb-f11480542217.html

47 'E. Scott Pruitt's Political Summary'. Project Vote Smart. Available at: https://votesmart.org/candidate/23484/e-scott-pruitt#.WHkIhWNvjR0

48 Calkins Brubaker, Laurel. 'Oklahoma, Alabama Accuse NY of Stifling Climate Debate'. Bloomberg, 31 March 2016. Available at: https://www.bloomberg.com/news/articles/2016-03-30/oklahoma-alabama-support-exxon-mobil-in-ny-led-climate-probe

49 League of Conservation Voters. 'National Environmental Scorecard of Representative Ryan Zinke'. Available at: http://scorecard.lcv.org/moc/ryan-zinke

50 Kim Rin, Soo. 'Zinke's nomination could bring questions about super PAC ties'. Center for Responsive Politics, Open Secrets. 14 December 2016. Available at: https://www.opensecrets.org/news/2016/12/zinkes-nomination-bring-questions-super-pac-ties/
51 'Zinke weighs in on new BLM rule against oil and gas development on federal and tribal land'. Statement from Ryan Zinke, 15 November 2016. Available at: https://zinke.house.gov/media-center/press-releases/zinke-weighs-new-blm-rule-against-oil-and-gas-development-federal-and
52 'Zinke Makes History: Lifts the Ban on Crude Oil Exports'. Statement from Ryan Zinke, 18 December 2015. Available at: https://zinke.house.gov/media-center/press-releases/zinke-makes-history-lifts-ban-crude-oil-exports
53 Harder, Amy. 'Donald Trump Jr. Played a Key Role in Interior Pick'. *Wall Street Journal*, 15 December 2016. Available at: http://www.wsj.com/articles/donald-trump-jr-played-a-key-role-in-interior-pick-1481844976
54 Johnson, Charles S. 'Lewis, Zinke debate federal budget, health care, global warming'. *Billings Gazette*, 4 October 2014. Available at: http://billingsgazette.com/news/local/government-and-politics/lewis-zinke-debate-federal-budget-health-care-global-warming/article_d062bc3c-c8e9-5909-854f-5e78efc52868.html
55 Joseph, Cameron. 'House candidate calls Clinton "Antichrist"'. The Hill, 31 January 2014. Available at: http://thehill.com/blogs/ballot-box/197138-montana-gop-house-front-runner-calls-hillary-clinton-the-anti-christ
56 'Center for Biological Diversity Statement on Ryan Zinke as Trump's Choice for Interior Secretary'. Center for Biological Diversity, 13 December 2016. Available at: https://www.biologicaldiversity.org/news/press_releases/2016/ryan-zinke-12-13-2016.php
57 Shear, Michael D. 'Trump Picks Mick Mulvaney, South Carolina Congressman, as Budget Director'. *New York Times*, 16 December 2016. Available at: https://www.nytimes.com/2016/12/16/us/politics/mick-mulvaney-office-management-budget-trump.html
58 'Mick Mulvaney is a climate change denier'. Organizing for Action. Available at: https://www.barackobama.com/climate-change-deniers/mick-mulvaney-south-carolina/
59 'Mick Mulvaney's Voting Record on Energy'. Project Vote Smart. Available at: http://votesmart.org/candidate/key-votes/60348/mick-mulvaney/29/energy#.WHkojGNvit8
60 French, Lauren. '9 Republicans launch House Freedom Caucus'. Politico, 26 January 2016. Available at: http://www.politico.com/story/2015/01/house-freedom-caucus-conservative-legislation-114593
61 Weigel, David. 'House conservatives want Trump to undo regulations on climate, FDA, Uber'. *Washington Post*, 15 December 2016. Available at: https://www.washingtonpost.com/news/post-politics/wp/2016/12/15/house-conservatives-want-trump-to-undo-regulations-on-fda-climate-uber/?utm_term=.9a178dacba8f
62 Mufson, Steven and Eilperin, Juliet. 'Trump transition team for Energy Department seeks names of employees involved in climate meetings'. *Washington Post*, 9 December 2016. Available at: https://www.washingtonpost.com/news/energy-environment/wp/2016/12/09/trump-transition-team-for-energy-department-seeks-names-of-employees-involved-in-climate-meetings/?utm_term=.d7a57d3cc9ce
63 Boyer, Dave and Wolfgang, Ben. 'Energy Dept. rebuffs Trump's request for list of climate-change workers'. *Washington Times*, 13 December 2016. Available at: http://www.washingtontimes.com/news/2016/dec/13/energy-dept-rebuffs-donald-trumps-request-list-cli/
64 Schwartz, John; Steinhauer, Jennifer; Lipton, Eric and Nixon, Ron. 'Trump Meets With Al Gore on Climate Change While House G.O.P. Rebuffs Tariff Plan'. *New*

York Times, 5 December 2016. Available at: https://www.nytimes.com/2016/12/05/us/politics/donald-trump-transition.html?_r=0

65 Wright, David. 'Leonardo DiCaprio, Trump talk climate change'. CNN, 8 December 2016. Available at: http://edition.cnn.com/2016/12/08/politics/leonardo-dicaprio-trump-climate-change-meeting/

66 Karni, Annie. 'Ivanka Trump, climate czar?' Politico, 12 January 2016. Available at: http://www.politico.com/story/2016/11/ivanka-trump-climate-czar-232031

67 Sullivan, Sean and Costa, Robert. 'Donald Trump unveils child-care policy influenced by Ivanka Trump'. *Washington Post*, 13 September 2016. Available at: https://www.washingtonpost.com/news/post-politics/wp/2016/09/13/donald-trump-joined-by-ivanka-trump-to-outline-child-care-policy/?utm_term=.5f6d16820851

68 Shear, Michael D. 'Trump Will Withdraw U.S. From Paris Climate Agreement'. *New York Times*, 1 June 2017. Available at: https://www.nytimes.com/2017/06/01/climate/trump-paris-climate-agreement.html?hp&action=click&pgtype=Homepage&clickSource=story-heading&module=span-ab-top-region®ion=top-news&WT.nav=top-news

69 Smothers, Ronald. 'Democratic Donor Receives Two-Year Prison Sentence'. *New York Times*, 5 March 2005. Available at: http://www.nytimes.com/2005/03/05/nyregion/democratic-donor-receives-twoyear-prison-sentence.html

70 McMullen, Troy. 'Jared Kushner Is Keeping 90 Percent Of His Real Estate Holdings, Report says'. *Forbes*, 22 May 2017. Available at: https://www.forbes.com/sites/troymcmullen/2017/05/22/jared-kushner-is-keeping-90-percent-of-real-estate-holdings-report-says/#1b8b30b51b8b

71 Neidig, Harper. 'Critics bash Trump children's presence at tech meeting'. The Hill, 14 December 2016. Available at: http://thehill.com/homenews/administration/310498-critics-bash-trump-childrens-presence-at-tech-meeting

72 Calfas, Jennifer. 'Bill Gates compares Trump to JFK'. The Hill, 13 December 2016. Available at: http://thehill.com/homenews/administration/310151-bill-gates-to-meet-with-trump

73 Tabuchi, Hiroko and Fountain, Henry. 'Bill Gates Leads New Fund as Fears of U.S. Retreat on Climate Grow'. *New York Times*, 12 December 2016. Available at: https://www.nytimes.com/2016/12/12/business/energy-environment/bill-gates-breakthrough-energy-ventures.html

74 Clark, Pilita. 'US and China ratify Paris climate accord'. *Financial Times*, 3 September 2016. Available at: https://www.ft.com/content/e7a2c4ee-71b8-11e6-bf48-b372cdb1043a

75 Hirtenstein, Anna. 'Clean-Energy Jobs Surpass Oil Drilling for First Time in US'. Bloomberg, 25 May 2016. Available at: https://www.bloomberg.com/news/articles/2016-05-25/clean-energy-jobs-surpass-oil-drilling-for-first-time-in-u-s

CHAPTER NINE

1 Bradner, Eric; Chalian, David and Schleifer, Theodore. 'A gay Silicon Valley billionaire just made GOP history at the RNC'. CNN, 22 July 2016. Available at: http://edition.cnn.com/2016/07/21/politics/peter-thiel-gay-republican-national-convention/

2 Kosoff, Maya. 'Donald Trump berates media, cancels (and then uncancels) meeting with New York Times in failed "reset"'. *Vanity Fair*, 22 November 2016. Available at: http://www.vanityfair.com/news/2016/11/donald-trump-berates-tv-executives-cancels-meeting-with-new-york-times

3 'Donald Trump's New York Times Interview: Full Transcript'. *New York Times*, 23 November 2016. Available at: https://www.nytimes.com/2016/11/23/us/politics/trump-new-york-times-interview-transcript.html

4 Gibson, Ginger and Flitter, Emily. 'Trump revokes Washington Post's campaign

press credentials'. Reuters, 14 June 2016. Available at: http://www.reuters.com/article/us-usa-election-trump-media-idUSKCN0YZ2DA

5 The Washington Post Editorial Board. 'Is Mr. Trump a threat to democracy?' *Washington Post*, 27 February 2016. Available at: https://www.washingtonpost.com/opinions/is-mr-trump-a-threat-to-democracy/2016/02/26/d02ed222-dcd9-11e5-925f-1d10062cc82d_story.html?utm_term=.4c1a9e63f035

6 La Monica, Paul R. 'Jeff Bezos wants to send Donald Trump into space'. CNN, 7 December 2015. Available at: http://money.cnn.com/2015/12/07/investing/donald-trump-amazon-taxes/?iid=EL

7 Sutton, Kelsey. 'Jeff Bezos: Trump's treatment of the press "erodes our democracy around the edges"'. Politico, 20 October 2016. Available at: http://www.politico.com/blogs/on-media/2016/10/jeff-bezos-trumps-treatment-of-the-press-erodes-our-democracy-around-the-edges-230103

8 Weprin, Alex. 'Bezos pledges "open mind" to Trump administration'. Politico, 10 November 2016. Available at: http://www.politico.com/blogs/on-media/2016/11/bezos-pledges-open-mind-to-trump-administration-231178

9 Diamond, Jeremy. 'Trump calls for Apple boycott'. CNN, 20 February 2016. Available at: http://edition.cnn.com/2016/02/19/politics/donald-trump-apple-boycott/

10 Rogers, Katie. 'Kanye West Visits Donald Trump'. *New York Times*, 13 December 2016. Available at: https://www.nytimes.com/2016/12/13/us/politics/kanye-trump-tower-visit.html

11 Nelso, Louis. 'Trump: Vanity Fair is "dead"'. Politico, 15 December 2016. Available at: http://www.politico.com/story/2016/12/trump-feud-vanity-fair-232675

12 Swisher, Kara. 'As Trumplethinskin lets down his hair for tech, shame on Silicon Valley for climbing the Tower in silence'. Recode, 12 December 2016. Available at: http://www.recode.net/2016/12/12/13917982/trump-hair-tech-summit-shame-silicon-valley

13 'Transcript: Trump's Introductory Remarks With Tech Executives'. *Wall Street Journal*, 14 December 2016. Available at: http://www.wsj.com/articles/transcript-trumps-introductory-remarks-with-tech-executives-1481754651

14 'Transcript of Mitt Romney's Speech on Donald Trump'. *New York Times*, 3 March 2016. Available at: https://www.nytimes.com/2016/03/04/us/politics/mitt-romney-speech.html

15 Jackson, Henry C. and Isenstadt, Alex. 'Romney gushes over Trump after posh dinner'. Politico, 29 November 2016. Available at: http://www.politico.com/blogs/donald-trump-administration/2016/11/dinner-for-3-trump-romney-and-reince-231976

16 Mac, Ryan. 'Donald Trump To Tech Leaders: I'm On Your Side'. *Forbes*, 14 December 2016. Available at: http://www.forbes.com/sites/mattdrange/2016/12/14/donald-trump-to-techs-leaders-im-on-your-side/#7810b83e40ce

17 Kara Swisher, journalist and co-founder of Recode, interviewed on 23 December 2016. Phone interview.

18 Panzarino, Matthew. 'Tim Cook explains to Apple employees why he met with President-elect Trump'. Techcrunch, 19 December 2016. Available at: https://techcrunch.com/2016/12/19/tim-cook-explains-to-apple-employees-why-he-met-with-president-elect-trump/

19 Browning, Linnley. 'Trump's Offshore Tax-Cut Pitch Falls Flat in Silicon Valley'. Bloomberg, 24 August 2016. Available at: https://www.bloomberg.com/news/articles/2016-08-24/trump-s-offshore-tax-cut-pitch-falls-flat-in-silicon-valley

20 Fleming, Sam and Jopson, Barney. 'US companies braced for tax shake-up as Apple feud escalates'. *Financial Times*, 25 August 2016. Available at: https://www.ft.com/content/e2ed8c00-6a0f-11e6-a0b1-d87a9fea034f

21 Rubin, Richard. 'US Companies Are Stashing $2.1 Trillion Overseas to Avoid

Taxes'. Bloomberg, 4 March 2015. Available at: https://www.bloomberg.com/news/articles/2015-03-04/u-s-companies-are-stashing-2-1-trillion-overseas-to-avoid-taxes

22 'Moody's: US corporate cash pile, led by tech sector, to grow to $1.77 trillion by end of 2016'. Moody's, 3 November 2016. Available at: https://www.moodys.com/research/Moodys-US-corporate-cash-pile-led-by-tech-sector-to--PR_357576

23 Chasmar, Jessica. 'Bill Gates compares Donald Trump to JFK on innovation'. *Washington Times*, 13 December 2016. Available at: http://www.washingtontimes.com/news/2016/dec/13/bill-gates-compares-donald-trump-to-jfk-on-innovat/

24 'The full transcript from the Trump transition team's Tuesday call to reporters'. *Washington Post*, 13 December 2016. Available at: https://www.washingtonpost.com/news/post-politics/wp/2016/12/13/the-full-transcript-from-the-trump-transition-teams-tuesday-call-to-reporters-3/?utm_term=.7ced7ee86b53

25 Justin Smith, chief executive of Bloomberg Media, interviewed on 22 December 2016. Phone interview.

26 Frey, Carl Benedikt and Osborne, Michael A. (2013) 'The future of employment: How susceptible are jobs to computerisation?' Oxford Martin School, University of Oxford. Available at: http://www.oxfordmartin.ox.ac.uk/downloads/academic/The_Future_of_Employment.pdf

27 Central Intelligence Agency. The World Factbook (United States, 2016 est.). Available at: https://www.cia.gov/library/publications/the-world-factbook/geos/us.html

28 Swisher, Kara. 'Who said what inside the Trump tech meeting: Immigration, paid maternity leave and becoming the "software president"'. Recode, 15 December 2016. Available at: https://www.recode.net/2016/12/15/13976806/immigration-maternity-leave-grid-software-president-trump-tech-meeting

CHAPTER TEN

1 Merle, Renae. 'From Goldman Sachs to "Suicide Squad": Meet Steven Mnuchin, Donald Trump's pick for Treasury secretary'. *Washington Post*, 29 November 2016. Available at: https://www.washingtonpost.com/news/wonk/wp/2016/11/29/from-goldman-sachs-to-suicide-squad-meet-steven-mnuchin-donald-trumps-pick-for-treasury-secretary/?utm_term=.24e3345ccc6b

2 Green, Joshua. 'This Man Is the Most Dangerous Political Operative in America'. Bloomberg, 8 October 2015. Available at: https://www.bloomberg.com/politics/graphics/2015-steve-bannon/

3 Paletta, Damian and Timiraos Nick. 'Trump Names Goldman President Gary Cohn Director of National Economic Council'. *Wall Street Journal*, 12 December 2016. Available at: http://www.wsj.com/articles/trump-names-goldman-president-gary-cohn-as-director-of-national-economic-council-1481573082

4 Picker, Leslie. 'Donald Trump Nominates Wall Street Lawyer to Head SEC'. *New York Times*, 4 January 2016. Available at: https://www.nytimes.com/2017/01/04/business/dealbook/donald-trump-sec-jay-clayton.html

5 White, Ben and Karni, Annie. 'Goldman Sachs partner to join Trump administration'. Politico, 11 January 2017. Available at: http://www.politico.com/story/2017/01/dina-powell-goldman-sachs-joins-trump-233476

6 Diamond, Jeremy. 'Donald Trump: Banks have "total control" over Ted Cruz'. CNN, 19 February 2016. Available at: http://edition.cnn.com/2016/02/19/politics/donald-trump-ted-cruz-goldman-sachs/

7 Schleifer, Theodore. 'Donald Trump makes wild threat to "spill the beans" on Ted Cruz's wife'. CNN, 24 March 2016. Available at: http://edition.cnn.com/2016/03/22/politics/ted-cruz-melania-trump-twitter-donald-trump-heidi/

8 Confessore, Nicholas and Horowitz, Jason. 'Hillary Clinton's Paid Speeches to Wall

Street Animate Her Opponents'. *New York Times*, 21 January 2017. Available at: https://www.nytimes.com/2016/01/22/us/politics/in-race-defined-by-income-gap-hillary-clintons-wall-street-ties-incite-rivals.html

9 Diamond, Jeremy. 'Donald Trump: Banks have "total control" over Ted Cruz', op. cit.

10 Wootson Jr, Cleve R. 'Sen. Al Franken claims that Donald Trump's new ad on the economy is anti-Semitic'. *Washington Post*, 6 November 2016. Available at: https://www.washingtonpost.com/news/the-fix/wp/2016/11/06/sen-al-franken-claims-that-donald-trumps-new-ad-on-the-economy-is-anti-semitic/?utm_term=.483a4aba43a3

11 McCormick, John. '"Tax Wall Street," Trump Pledges After Worst Market Week Since 2011'. Bloomberg, 9 January 2016. Available at: https://www.bloomberg.com/politics/articles/2016-01-09/-tax-wall-street-trump-pledges-after-stock-market-selloff

12 Shen, Lucinda. 'Here's What Goldman Sachs CEO Lloyd Blankfein Told Employees About Trump's Win'. *Fortune*, 11 November 2016. Available at: http://fortune.com/2016/11/11/donald-trump-goldman-sachs/

13 Greenfeld, Karl Taro. 'From IndyMac to OneWest: Steven Mnuchin's Big Score'. Bloomberg, 22 March 2012. Available at: https://www.bloomberg.com/news/articles/2012-03-22/from-indymac-to-onewest-steven-mnuchins-big-score

Vardi, Nathan. 'John Paulson and George Soros Score Big Selling OneWest Bank For $3.4 Billion'. *Forbes*, 22 July 2014. Available at: http://www.forbes.com/sites/nathanvardi/2014/07/22/john-paulson-and-george-soros-score-big-selling-onewest-bank-for-3-4-billion/#51ddb59a5ab0

DexHeimer, Elizabeth. 'Mnuchin to Get $4.5 Million Pay as Vice Chairman of CIT'. Bloomberg, 26 July 2014. Available at: https://www.bloomberg.com/news/articles/2014-07-25/mnuchin-to-get-4-5-million-pay-as-vice-chairman-of-cit

14 Woellert, Lorraine. 'Trump Treasury pick made millions after his bank foreclosed on homeowners'. Politico, 12 January 2016. http://www.politico.com/story/2016/12/trump-treasury-foreclosed-homes-mnuchin-232038

15 Dayen, David. 'Treasury Nominee Steve Mnuchin's Bank Accused of "Widespread Misconduct" in Leaked Memo'. The Intercept, 3 January 2017. Available at: https://theintercept.com/2017/01/03/treasury-nominee-steve-mnuchins-bank-accused-of-widespread-misconduct-in-leaked-memo/

16 Dayen, David. 'Treasury nominee Steve Mnuchin's bank accused of "widespread misconduct" in leaked memo', op. cit.

17 McLannahan, Ben and Fleming, Sam. 'Steve Mnuchin faces tough road to Treasury post'. *Financial Times*, 8 January 2017. Available at: https://www.ft.com/content/cc5036c0-d466-11e6-9341-7393bb2e1b51

18 'Led by Merkley, Warren and Sanders, Senate Democrats Roll Out New Website Inviting Personal Stories from Americans Hurt by Foreclosure King Steve Mnuchin'. Senator Elizabeth Warren official website, 16 December 2016. Available at: https://www.warren.senate.gov/?p=press_release&id=1330

19 Mui, Ylan Q. and Costa, Robert. 'Trump expected to tap billionaire investor Wilbur Ross for commerce secretary'. *Washington Post*, 24 November 2016. Available at: https://www.washingtonpost.com/news/powerpost/wp/2016/11/24/trump-expected-to-tap-billionaire-investor-wilbur-ross-for-commerce-secretary/?utm_term=.63e3440399f7

Withorn-Peterson, Chase. 'What You Need To Know About Commerce Secretary Pick Wilbur Ross, Trump's Billionaire Pal'. *Forbes*, 29 November 2016. Available at: http://www.forbes.com/sites/chasewithorn/2016/11/29/what-you-need-to-know-about-likely-commerce-secretary-wilbur-ross-trumps-billionaire-pal/#3de0b2368d60

20 Kosman, Josh. 'Icahn, Ross saved Trump brand from Taj Mahal casino mess'. *New York Post*, 25 November 2016. Available at: http://nypost.com/2016/11/25/icahn-ross-saved-trump-brand-from-taj-mahal-casino-mess/
21 Benoit, David. 'Trump Names Carl Icahn as Adviser on Regulatory Overhaul'. *Wall Street Journal*, 21 December 2016. Available at: http://www.wsj.com/articles/trump-to-name-icahn-as-adviser-on-regulatory-overhaul-1482354552
22 Lynch, Sarah N. 'Trump's SEC pick Clayton points to capital formation, not enforcement'. Reuters, 5 January 2017. Available at: http://www.reuters.com/article/us-usa-trump-sec-idUSKBN14N1Y9
23 Shen Lucinda. 'Here's How Closely Donald Trump's Pick for SEC Chair Is Tied to Goldman Sachs'. Fortune, 6 January 2017. Available at: http://fortune.com/2017/01/05/donald-trump-sec-jo-white-jay-clayton/
24 Herbst-Basiliss, Svea and Holland, Steve. 'Wall Street lawyer Jay Clayton emerges as Trump's top SEC choice'. Reuters, 3 January 2017. Available at: http://www.reuters.com/article/usa-trump-sec-idUSL1N1EU00A
25 Michaels, Dave and Hoffman, Liz. 'SEC Pick Jay Clayton Is a 180 From Chairman Mary Jo White'. *Wall Street Journal*, 4 January 2017. Available at: http://www.wsj.com/articles/president-elect-trump-to-nominate-jay-clayton-securities-and-exchange-commission-chairman-1483545999
26 Rep. Adam Schiff on his Twitter profile, 5 January 2017. Available at: https://twitter.com/RepAdamSchiff/status/817105044143304712
27 Lynch, Sarah N. 'Trump's SEC pick Clayton points to capital formation, not enforcement', op. cit.
28 Bain, Ben. 'Trump to Pick Deals Lawyer Clayton to Lead Wall Street Cop'. *Washington Post* with Bloomberg, 6 January 2017. Available at: http://washpost.bloomberg.com/Story?docId=1376-OJ8CJ66JIJUO01-2KHJKG5GK554C2HG1L124FCU3M
29 Verdi, Nathan. 'Carl Icahn's Investment Fund Plunged By 20% In 2016'. Forbes, 12 January 2017. Available at: http://www.forbes.com/sites/nathanvardi/2017/01/12/carl-icahns-investment-fund-plunged-by-20-in-2016/#d8cfac416372
30 Picket, Leslie. 'Donald Trump Nominates Wall Street Lawyer to Head SEC'. *New York Times*, 4 January 2016. Available at: https://www.nytimes.com/2017/01/04/business/dealbook/donald-trump-sec-jay-clayton.html
31 Wieczner, Jen. 'Donald Trump Bump Investors Have This Unlikely Stock to Thank For Dow Record'. Fortune, 12 December 2016. Available at: http://fortune.com/2016/12/09/trump-stock-market-dow-close-goldman-sachs/
32 Limitone, Julia. 'Mnuchin and Ross's Top Priorities for Trump's First 90 Days'. FOXBusiness, 30 November 2016. Available at: http://www.foxbusiness.com/politics/2016/11/30/mnuchin-and-rosss-top-priorities-for-trumps-first-90-days.html
33 Schlesinger, Jacob M. 'Trump Treasury Choice Steven Mnuchin Vows to "Strip Back" Dodd-Frank'. *Wall Street Journal*, 30 November 2016. Available at: http://www.wsj.com/articles/trump-treasury-choice-steven-mnuchin-vows-to-strip-back-dodd-frank-1480513188
34 Cohan, William D. 'Rethinking Robert Rubin'. Bloomberg, 30 September 2012. Available at: https://www.bloomberg.com/news/articles/2012-09-30/rethinking-robert-rubin
35 *Time* magazine's cover. 'Rubin, Greenspan & Summers'. *Time*, 15 February 1999. Available at: http://content.time.com/time/covers/0,16641,19990215,00.html
36 Ramo, Joshua Cooper. 'The Three Marketeers'. *Time*, 15 February 1999. Available at: http://content.time.com/time/world/article/0,8599,2054093,00.html
37 Edwin 'Ted' Truman, economist, Senior Fellow with the Peterson Institute for International Economics, interviewed in Washington, DC, on 9 November 2016. Phone interview on 13 January 2017.

38 Schroeder, Michael. 'CFTC Chief Refuses to Take Back Seat in Derivatives Debate'. *Wall Street Journal*, 3 November 1998. Available at: http://www.wsj.com/articles/SB909726692140470500
39 'CFTC issues concept release concerning over-the-counter derivatives market'. US Commodity Futures Trading Commission, 7 May 1998. Available at: http://www.cftc.gov/opa/press98/opa4142-98.htm
Concept release available at: http://www.cftc.gov/opa/press98/opamntn.htm
40 Testimony of Chairman Alan Greenspan. 'The regulation of OTC derivatives'. Before the Committee on Banking and Financial Services, US House of Representatives. The Federal Reserve Board, 24 July 1998. Available at: https://www.federalreserve.gov/boarddocs/testimony/1998/19980724.htm
41 David Wessel, writer and journalist, interviewed in Washington, DC, on 9 November 2016.
42 Hirsh, Michael. *Capital Offense: How Washington's Wise Men Turned America's Future Over to Wall Street*. John Wiley & Sons, 2010.
43 Testimony of chairman Alan Greenspan. 'The regulation of OTC derivatives'. Before the Committee on Banking and Financial Services, US House of Representatives. The Federal Reserve Board, 24 July 1998.
44 105th Congress, Public Law 277, October. 21, 1998. Text available at: https://www.gpo.gov/fdsys/pkg/PLAW-105publ277/pdf/PLAW-105publ277.pdf
45 Blumenthal, Paul. 'How Congress Rushed a Bill that Helped Bring the Economy to Its Knees'. Huffington Post, 25 May 2011. Available at: http://www.huffingtonpost.com/paul-blumenthal/how-congress-rushed-a-bil_b_181926.html
46 'The Warning', *Frontline*, PBS. Available at: http://www.pbs.org/wgbh/pages/frontline/warning/
47 'Interview: Michael Greenberger'. 14 July 2009. Transcript available at: http://www.pbs.org/wgbh/pages/frontline/warning/interviews/greenberger.html
48 The Gramm–Leach–Bliley Act (GLBA), also known as the Financial Services Modernization Act of 1999, enacted 12 November 1999. 106th Congress, Public Law 102. Text available at: https://www.congress.gov/106/plaws/publ102/PLAW-106publ102.pdf
49 Martin, Mitchell and International Herald Tribune. 'Citicorp and Travelers Plan to Merge in Record $70 Billion Deal: A New No. 1: Financial Giants Unite'. *New York Times*, 7 April 1998. Available at: http://www.nytimes.com/1998/04/07/news/citicorp-and-travelers-plan-to-merge-in-record-70-billion-deal-a-new-no.html
50 'Statement of President Bill Clinton on Signing the Gramm-Leach-Bliley Act'. 12 November 1999. Transcript available at: http://www.presidency.ucsb.edu/ws/?pid=56922
51 'Interview: Brooksley Born'. 28 August 2009. Transcript available at: http://www.pbs.org/wgbh/pages/frontline/warning/interviews/born.html
52 'Greenspan Admits "Flaw" to Congress, Predicts More Economic Problems'. *PBS Newshour*, 23 October 2008. Available at: http://www.pbs.org/newshour/bb/business-july-dec08-crisishearing_10-23/
53 'Treasury Secretary Rubin resigns'. CNN, 12 May 1999. Available at: http://edition.cnn.com/ALLPOLITICS/stories/1999/05/12/rubin/
54 Brown, Ken and Enrich, David. 'Rubin, Under Fire, Defends His Role at Citi'. *Wall Street Journal*, 29 November 2008. Available at: http://www.wsj.com/articles/SB122791795940965645
55 Stempel, Jonathan and Wilchins, Dan. 'Robert Rubin quits Citigroup amid criticism'. Reuters, 9 January 2009. Available at: http://www.reuters.com/article/us-citigroup-rubin-idUSN0930738020090109
56 Finder, Alan; Healy, Patrick D. and Zernike, Kate. 'President of Harvard Resigns,

Ending Stormy 5-Year Tenure'. *New York Times*, 22 February 2006. Available at: http://www.nytimes.com/2006/02/22/education/22harvard.html

57 Goldfarb, Zachary A. and Mui, Ylan Q. 'Larry Summers withdraws name from Fed consideration'. *Washington Post*, 15 September 2013. Available at: https://www.washingtonpost.com/business/economy/larry-summers-withdraws-name-from-fed-consideration/2013/09/15/7565c888-1e44-11e3-94a2-6c66b668ea55_story.html?utm_term=.109116cc3aa2

58 Condon, Christopher. 'Summers Warns of Financial-Crisis Risk From Trump Economic Plans'. Bloomberg, 8 January 2017. Available at: https://www.bloomberg.com/news/articles/2017-01-08/summers-warns-of-financial-crisis-risk-from-trump-economic-plans

59 Hagen, Lisa. 'Trump proposes new lobbying ban: "Time to drain the swamp" in DC'. The Hill, 17 October 2016. Available at: http://thehill.com/blogs/ballot-box/presidential-races/301464-trump-proposes-new-lobbying-ban-time-to-drain-the-swamp

CHAPTER ELEVEN

1 I interviewed the Russian President Vladimir Putin in Moscow on 27 July 2015.

2 Entous, Adam; Nakashima, Ellen and Miller, Greg. 'Secret CIA assessment says Russia was trying to help Trump win White House'. *Washington Post*, 9 December 2016. Available at: https://www.washingtonpost.com/world/national-security/obama-orders-review-of-russian-hacking-during-presidential-campaign/2016/12/09/31d6b300-be2a-11e6-94ac-3d324840106c_story.html?utm_term=.f75520d01c26

Calabresi, Massimo and Rebala, Pratheek. 'Here's The Evidence Russia Hacked The Democratic National Committee'. *Time*, 13 December 2016. Available at: http://time.com/4600177/election-hack-russia-hillary-clinton-donald-trump/

3 See among others: Diamond, Jeremy. 'Timeline: Donald Trump's praise for Vladimir Putin'. CNN, 29 July 2017. Available at: http://edition.cnn.com/2016/07/28/politics/donald-trump-vladimir-putin-quotes/

Demirjian, Karoun 'Trump praises Putin's response to sanctions, calls Russian leader "very smart!"'. *Washington Post*, 30 December 2016. Available at: https://www.washingtonpost.com/news/powerpost/wp/2016/12/30/trump-praises-putins-response-to-sanctions-calls-russian-leader-very-smart/?utm_term=.8b385c4f0946

4 Nakashima, Ellen. 'Russian government hackers penetrated DNC, stole opposition research on Trump'. *Washington Post*, 14 June 2016. Available at: https://www.washingtonpost.com/world/national-security/russian-government-hackers-penetrated-dnc-stole-opposition-research-on-trump/2016/06/14/cf006cb4-316e-11e6-8ff7-7b6c1998b7a0_story.html?utm_term=.19acc0610378

5 Bradner, Eric. 'Trump: DNC hacked itself'. CNN, 16 June 2016. Available at: http://edition.cnn.com/2016/06/15/politics/dnc-hack-donald-trump/

6 Bolton, Alexander. 'Trump, GOP see gold in Clinton Foundation attacks'. The Hill, 24 August 2016. Available at: http://thehill.com/homenews/campaign/292410-trump-gop-see-gold-in-clinton-foundation-attacks

7 'Michael Flynn leads chants of "lock her up" at Republican Convention'. *Washington Post*, 11 August 2016. Available at: https://www.washingtonpost.com/video/national/michael-flynn-leads-chants-of-lock-her-up-at-republican-convention/2016/08/11/788253f8-6016-11e6-84c1-6d27287896b5_video.html

8 'RT to mark its 10 year anniversary with international conference on media and politics'. Russia Today, press release, 1 December 2015. Available at: https://www.rt.com/about-us/press-releases/conference-rt-10-years/

Rosenberg, Matthew; Mazzetti, Mark and Goldman, Adam. 'Trump's National

Security Pick Sees Ally in Fight Against Islamists: Russia'. *New York Times*, 10 January 2017. Available at: https://www.nytimes.com/2017/01/10/us/politics/trumps-national-security-pick-sees-ally-in-fight-against-islamists-russia.html

9 Parker, Ashley and Sanger, David E. 'Donald Trump Calls on Russia to Find Hillary Clinton's Missing Emails'. *New York Times*, 27 July 2016. Available at: https://www.nytimes.com/2016/07/28/us/politics/donald-trump-russia-clinton-emails.html

10 Krever, Mick. 'Former CIA chief: Trump "beyond the pale," not qualified to be president'. CNN, 28 July 2016. Available at: http://edition.cnn.com/2016/07/27/world/leon-panetta-amanpour-trump-russia-hillary-clinton/

11 See between others: Byrnes, Jesse. 'Trump: Clinton "guilty as hell"'. The Hill, 12 April 2016. Available at: http://thehill.com/blogs/ballot-box/presidential-races/275968-trump-clinton-guilty-as-hell

12 LoBianco, Tom. 'Lynch: Clinton email probe handled the same as any other'. CNN, 19 June 2016. Available at: http://edition.cnn.com/2016/06/19/politics/loretta-lynch-hillary-clinton-email/

13 Landler, Mark. 'Meeting Between Bill Clinton and Loretta Lynch Provokes Political Furor'. *New York Magazine*, 30 June 2016. Available at: https://www.nytimes.com/2016/07/01/us/politics/meeting-between-bill-clinton-and-loretta-lynch-provokes-political-furor.html

14 Hattem, Julian. 'Lynch pressured to recuse herself after Clinton tarmac meeting'. The Hill, 1 July 2016. Available at: http://thehill.com/policy/national-security/286202-lynch-pressured-to-recuse-herself-after-clinton-tarmac-meeting

15 Reston, Maeve and Collinson, Stephen. 'Clintons return to political storm'. CNN, 3 July 2016. Available at: http://edition.cnn.com/2016/07/02/politics/hillary-clinton-fbi-interview-bill-clinton/

16 Morin, Rebecca. 'Lynch says she "regrets" June conversation with Bill Clinton'. 18 December 2016. Available at: http://www.politico.com/story/2016/12/lynch-says-she-regrets-sit-down-conversation-with-bill-clinton-232788

17 Landler, Mark; Apuzzo, Matt and Chozick, Amy. 'Loretta Lynch to Accept FBI Recommendations in Clinton Email Inquiry'. *New York Times*, 1 July 2016. Available at: https://www.nytimes.com/2016/07/02/us/politics/loretta-lynch-hillary-clinton-email-server.html

18 Landler, Mark and Lichtblau, Eric. 'FBI Director James Comey Recommends No Charges for Hillary Clinton on Email'. *New York Times*, 5 July 2016. Available at: https://www.nytimes.com/2016/07/06/us/politics/hillary-clinton-fbi-email-comey.html

19 'Letter to Congress from FBI Director on Clinton Email Case'. *New York Times*, 28 October 2016. Available at: https://www.nytimes.com/interactive/2016/10/28/us/politics/fbi-letter.html?_r=0

20 Apuzzo, Matt; Schmidt, Michael S. and Goldman, Adam. 'Emails Warrant No New Action Against Hillary Clinton, FBI Director Says'. *New York Times*. 6 November 2016. Available at: https://www.nytimes.com/2016/11/07/us/politics/hilary-clinton-male-voters-donald-trump.html

21 Hamburger, Tom and Tumulty, Karen. 'WikiLeaks releases thousands of documents about Clinton and internal deliberations'. *Washington Post*, 22 July 2016. Available at: https://www.washingtonpost.com/news/post-politics/wp/2016/07/22/on-eve-of-democratic-convention-wikileaks-releases-thousands-of-documents-about-clinton-the-campaign-and-internal-deliberations/?utm_term=.4427051ce2ba

22 Martin, Jonathan and Rappeport, Alan. 'Debbie Wasserman Schultz to Resign DNC Post'. *Washington Post*, 24 July 2016. Available at: https://www.nytimes.com/2016/07/25/us/politics/debbie-wasserman-schultz-dnc-wikileaks-emails.html

23 Trip, Gabriel. 'Bernie Sanders Backers March Against Hillary Clinton in

Philadelphia'. *New York Times*, 24 July 2016. Available at: https://www.nytimes.com/2016/07/25/us/politics/protests-convention-bernie-sanders-philadelphia.html

24 Herb, Jeremy. 'Mook suggests Russians leaked DNC emails to help Trump'. Politico, 24 July 2016. Available at: http://www.politico.com/story/2016/07/robby-mook-russians-emails-trump-226084

25 Gass, Nick. 'Trump blasts "joke" that Russia leaked DNC emails to help him'. Politico, 25 July 2016. Available at: http://www.politico.com/story/2016/07/dnc-leak-russia-trump-226108

26 Miller, Zeke J. 'Donald Trump Meets With Intelligence Leaders But Still Doesn't Publicly Blame Russia for Hacks'. *Time*, 6 January 2017. Available at: http://time.com/4626515/donald-trump-intelligence-meeting-russia-hacks/

27 Cillizza, Chris. 'Donald Trump's answer on Russia and Vladimir Putin at the NBC forum was totally bananas'. *Washington Post*, 8 September 2016. Available at: https://www.washingtonpost.com/news/the-fix/wp/2016/09/08/donald-trumps-answer-on-russia-and-vladimir-putin-at-the-commander-in-chief-forum-was-bananas/?utm_term=.85d145101052

28 Cillizza, Chris. 'Donald Trump's ABC interview may be his best/worst yet'. *Washington Post*, 1 August 2016. Available at: https://www.washingtonpost.com/news/the-fix/wp/2016/08/01/donald-trumps-abc-interview-may-be-his-bestworst-yet/?utm_term=.bff62f7b3546

29 'Donald Trump discusses Putin relationship in 2013'. MSNBC Live with Thomas Roberts, 28 July 2016. Available at: http://www.msnbc.com/thomas-roberts/watch/trump-discusses-putin-in-2013-734124099973

30 Donald Trump declared on 6 March 2014, at the Conservative Political Action Conference in National Harbor, Maryland: 'You know, I was in Moscow a couple of months ago. I own the Miss Universe Pageant and they treated me so great. Putin even sent me a present, a beautiful present.'

Schwab, Nikki. 'Donald Trump Peppers CPAC Speeches With Humblebrags'. US News & World Report, 6 March 2014. Available at: http://www.usnews.com/news/blogs/washington-whispers/2014/03/06/donald-trump-peppers-cpac-speeches-with-humblebrags

Video available at: http://www.politico.com/video/2014/03/donald-trump-speech-at-cpac-2014-003845

31 Donald Trump declared on 27 May 2014, at the the National Press Club in Washington DC: 'Russia does not respect our country any longer. They see we've been greatly weakened, both militarily and otherwise, and he certainly does not respect President Obama. So what I would do – as an example, I own Miss Universe, I was in Russia, I was in Moscow recently and I spoke, indirectly and directly, with President Putin, who could not have been nicer, and we had a tremendous success. The show was live from Moscow, and we had tremendous success there and it was amazing, but to do well, you have to get the other side to respect you, and he does not respect our president, which is very sad.' Video available at: http://www.press.org/events/npc-luncheon-donald-trump-chairman-and-president-trump-organization

32 Blake, Aaron. 'The final Trump-Clinton debate transcript, annotated'. 19 October 2016. Available at: https://www.washingtonpost.com/news/the-fix/wp/2016/10/19/the-final-trump-clinton-debate-transcript-annotated/?utm_term=.e43eb614d0c9

33 Crowley, Michael. 'When Donald Trump brought Miss Universe to Moscow'. Politico, 15 May 2016. Available at: http://www.politico.com/story/2016/05/donald-trump-russia-moscow-miss-universe-223173

34 During an interview with CNN host Larry King, on 15 October 2007, Trump said: 'Look at Putin – what he's doing with Russia – I mean, you know, what's going on over there. I mean this guy has done – whether you like him or don't like him – he's

doing a great job in rebuilding the image of Russia and also rebuilding Russia period.' Transcript available at: http://edition.cnn.com/TRANSCRIPTS/0710/15/lkl.01.html

35 Crowley, Michael. 'When Donald Trump brought Miss Universe to Moscow', op. cit.

36 Trump's words referred to Putin successful efforts to dissuade the US from striking Syria by arranging with the US for the removal of Syria's chemical weapons.

'Politicking with Larry King'. Russia Today, 4 October 2013. Available at: https://www.rt.com/shows/politicking-larry-king/donald-trump-larry-king-557/

37 Entous, Adam; Nakashima, Ellen and Miller, Greg. 'Secret CIA assessment says Russia was trying to help Trump win White House', op. cit.

38 'Transcript: Obama's end-of-year news conference on Syria, Russian hacking and more'. *Washington Post*, 16 December 2016. Available at: https://www.washingtonpost.com/news/post-politics/wp/2016/12/16/transcript-obamas-end-of-year-news-conference-on-syria-russian-hacking-and-more/?utm_term=.865ef5309417

39 Toosi, Nahal. 'Trump team rejects intel agencies' claims of Russian meddling'. 12 September 2016. Available at: http://www.politico.com/story/2016/12/trump-team-russia-cia-intel-election-232460

40 Sanger, David E. 'Obama Strikes Back at Russia for Election Hacking'. *New York Times*, 29 December 2016. Available at: https://www.nytimes.com/2016/12/29/us/politics/russia-election-hacking-sanctions.html

41 The White House, Office of the Press Secretary. 'Fact Sheet: Actions in Response to Russian Malicious Cyber Activity and Harassment'. 29 December 2016. Available at: https://www.whitehouse.gov/the-press-office/2016/12/29/fact-sheet-actions-response-russian-malicious-cyber-activity-and

42 Samuelsohn, Darren. 'A guide to Donald Trump's "rigged" election'. Politico, 25 October 2016. Available at: http://www.politico.com/story/2016/10/donald-trump-rigged-election-guide-230302

43 Wagner, John and Demirjian, Karoun. 'After Obama sanctions Russia, Trump says it's time "to move on to bigger and better things"'. *Washington Post*, 29 December 2016. Available at: https://www.washingtonpost.com/news/post-politics/wp/2016/12/29/after-obama-sanctions-russia-trump-says-its-time-to-move-on-to-bigger-and-better-things/?utm_term=.6e8b2181fd4c

44 Landay, Jonathan and Mohammed, Arshad. 'Trump adviser had five calls with Russian envoy on day of sanctions: sources'. Reuters, 13 January 2017. Available at: http://www.reuters.com/article/us-usa-trump-russia-idUSKBN14X1YX

45 Miller, Greg; Entous, Adam and Nakashima, Ellen. 'National security adviser Flynn discussed sanctions with Russian ambassador, despite denials, officials say'. *Washington Post*. 9 February 2017. Available at: https://www.washingtonpost.com/world/national-security/national-security-adviser-flynn-discussed-sanctions-with-russian-ambassador-despite-denials-officials-say/2017/02/09/f85b29d6-ee11-11e6-b4ff-ac2cf509efe5_story.html?tid=a_inl&utm_term=.b03ba2f159ca

46 Miller, Greg and Rucker, Philip. 'Michael Flynn resigns as national security adviser'. *New York Times*, 14 February 2017. Available at: https://www.washingtonpost.com/world/national-security/michael-flynn-resigns-as-national-security-adviser/2017/02/13/0007c0a8-f26e-11e6-8d72-263470bf0401_story.html?utm_term=.7f047635dd4f

47 DeYoung, Karen. 'Trump, Obama on possible collision course over Israeli settlement vote'. *Washington Post*, 22 December 2016. Available at: https://www.washingtonpost.com/world/national-security/trump-obama-on-possible-collision-course-over-israeli-settlement-vote/2016/12/22/3b0e3f1c-c846-11e6-8bee-54e800ef2a63_story.html?utm_term=.7e1eb06363fc

48 Nicholas, Peter; Beckett, Paul and Seib, Gerald F. 'Trump Open to Shift on Russia Sanctions, "One China" Policy'. *Wall Street Journal*, 13 January 2017. Available at: http://www.wsj.com/articles/donald-trump-sets-a-bar-for-russia-and-china-1484360380
49 Rogers, Christina; Mauldin, William and Colias, Mike. 'Trump Puts Auto Makers, Trade Policy in Spotlight'. *Wall Street Journal*, 3 January 2017. Available at: http://www.wsj.com/articles/trump-targets-gm-on-chevy-cruzes-imported-from-mexico-1483448986
50 'Assange: Russian government not the source of WikiLeaks emails'. FoxNews, 3 January 2017. Video available at: http://www.foxnews.com/politics/2017/01/03/assange-russian-government-not-source-wikileaks-emails.html
51 Nelson, Louis. 'Trump sides with Assange on Russia hacking'. Politico, 4 January 2017. Available at: http://www.politico.com/story/2017/01/trump-julian-assange-russia-hacking-233169
52 Miller, Zeke J. 'Donald Trump Meets With Intelligence Leaders But Still Doesn't Publicly Blame Russia for Hacks'. *Time*, 6 January 2017. Available at: http://time.com/4626515/donald-trump-intelligence-meeting-russia-hacks/
53 Shear, Michael D. and Sanger, David E. 'Putin Led a Complex Cyberattack Scheme to Aid Trump, Report Finds'. *New York Times*, 6 January 2017. Available at: https://www.nytimes.com/2017/01/06/us/politics/donald-trump-wall-hack-russia.html
54 Blake, Aaron. 'Trump's bogus claim that intelligence report says Russia didn't impact the 2016 election outcome'. *Washington Post*, 7 January 2017. Available at: https://www.washingtonpost.com/news/the-fix/wp/2017/01/07/trumps-bogus-claim-that-intelligence-says-russia-didnt-impact-the-2016-election-outcome/?utm_term=.3ab0d165346c
55 Smilowitz, Elliot and Kamisar, Ben. 'Trump calls for investigation into intel leaks to NBC'. The Hill, 6 January 2017. Available at: http://thehill.com/policy/national-security/313021-trump-calls-for-investigation-into-intel-leaks-to-nbc
56 Shane, Scott; Confessore, Nicholas and Rosenberg, Matthew. 'How a Sensational, Unverified Dossier Became a Crisis for Donald Trump'. *New York Times*, 11 January 2017. Available at: https://www.nytimes.com/2017/01/11/us/politics/donald-trump-russia-intelligence.html
57 'Donald Trump's News Conference: Full Transcript and Video'. *New York Times*, 11 January 2017. Available at: https://www.nytimes.com/2017/01/11/us/politics/trump-press-conference-transcript.html?_r=0
58 Karni, Annie. 'Trump pits his staff against the media'. Politico, 11 January 2017. Available at: http://www.politico.com/story/2017/01/trump-press-conference-paid-staffers-media-233496
59 'Donald Trump's News Conference: Full Transcript and Video'. *New York Times*, 11 January 2017.
60 Craig, Susanne and Lipton, Eric. 'Trump's Plans on Businesses May Fall Short'. *New York Times*, 11 January 2017. Available at: https://www.nytimes.com/2017/01/11/us/politics/trump-organization-business-conflicts.html
61 'Donald Trump's News Conference: Full Transcript and Video'. *New York Times*, 11 January 2017. Available at: https://www.nytimes.com/2017/01/11/us/politics/trump-press-conference-transcript.html?_r=0
62 Sutton, Kelsey. 'Trump calls CNN "fake news," as channel defends its reporting on intelligence briefing'. Politico, 11 January 2017. Available at: http://www.politico.com/blogs/on-media/2017/01/trump-refusing-to-answer-question-from-cnn-reporter-you-are-fake-news-233485
63 Hirschfeld Davis, Julie and Haberman, Maggie. 'Donald Trump Concedes Russia's Interference in Election'. *New York Times*, 11 January 2017. Available at: https://

www.nytimes.com/2017/01/11/us/politics/trumps-press-conference-highlights-russia.html

64 Begley, Sarah. 'Donald Trump Suggests Intelligence Agencies Released Russia Allegations'. *Time*, 11 January 2017. Available at: http://time.com/4631494/donald-trump-russia-allegations-intelligence-agencies/

65 Mettler, Katie. 'CIA director says Trump crossed "the line" by comparing CIA officers to Nazis'. *Washington Post*, 17 January 2017. Available at: https://www.washingtonpost.com/news/morning-mix/wp/2017/01/17/cia-director-says-trump-crossed-the-line-by-comparing-cia-officers-to-nazis/?utm_term=.29b20a727fb6

66 Master, Cyra. 'Trump on outgoing CIA director: "Was this the leaker of Fake News?"' The Hill, 15 January 2017. Available at: http://thehill.com/homenews/administration/314436-trump-on-outgoing-cia-director-was-this-the-leaker-of-fake-news

67 Killough, Ashley. 'Trump's CIA pick: Russian hacking "aggressive action" by senior leaders'. CNN, 12 January 2017. Available at: http://edition.cnn.com/2017/01/12/politics/mike-pompeo-cia-director-hearing-donald-trump/

68 O'Keefe, Ed and Gearan, Anne. 'Tillerson calls US intelligence findings on Russian interference in election "troubling"'. *Washington Post*, 11 January 2017. Available at: https://www.washingtonpost.com/world/national-security/tillerson-set-for-confirmation-hearings-that-are-likely-to-discuss-his-links-with-autocratic-leaders/2017/01/10/090604b0-d76d-11e6-b8b2-cb5164beba6b_story.html?utm_term=.1dfcfc343306

69 Biskup, Daniel. 'Donald Trump: "Brexit will be a great thing… you were so smart"'. *The Times*, 16 January 2017. Available at: http://www.thetimes.co.uk/article/brexit-will-be-a-great-thing-you-were-so-smart-to-get-out-09gp9z357

70 Biskup, Daniel. 'Donald Trump: "Brexit will be a great thing… you were so smart"', op. cit.

71 Trump, Donald and Schwartz, Tony. *Trump: The Art of the Deal*. Random House, 1987.

72 Biskup, Daniel. 'Donald Trump: "Brexit will be a great thing… you were so smart"', op. cit.

73 See note 1, Chapter 1.

74 King, Esther. 'Angela Merkel: We'll respond to Trump's criticism when he takes office'. Politico, 16 January 2017. Available at: http://www.politico.eu/article/angela-merkel-well-respond-to-trumps-criticism-when-he-takes-office/

75 Giles, Chris. 'Why Davos 2017 matters: 10 things to watch for'. *Financial Times*, 16 January 2017. Available at: https://www.ft.com/content/576fb394-dbcd-11e6-86ac-f253db7791c6

76 Biskup, Daniel. 'Donald Trump: "Brexit will be a great thing… you were so smart"', op. cit.

77 Wong, Edward. 'Trump Has Called Climate Change a Chinese Hoax. Beijing Says It Is Anything But'. *New York Times*, 18 November 2016. Available at: https://www.nytimes.com/2016/11/19/world/asia/china-trump-climate-change.html

78 Tett, Gillian. 'Donald Trump is committed to globalisation, Davos told'. *Financial Times*, 17 January 2017. Available at: https://www.ft.com/content/0a15c89c-dcb6-11e6-9d7c-be108f1c1dce

79 Cohen, David. 'Global report sees rise in inequality in US'. Politico, 15 January 2017. Available at: http://www.politico.com/story/2017/01/inequality-economy-united-states-233642

80 'President Xi's speech to Davos in full'. World Economic Forum, 17 January 2017. Available at: https://www.weforum.org/agenda/2017/01/full-text-of-xi-jinping-keynote-at-the-world-economic-forum

81 John, Tara. 'China's State Media Tells Donald Trump to "Stop Acting Like

a Diplomatic Rookie"'. *Time*, 6 December 2016. Available at: http://time.com/4591829/china-donald-trump-diplomatic-rookie/

82 'The new Davos man. Xi Jinping portrays China as a rock of stability'. *The Economist*, 17 January 2017. Available at: http://www.economist.com/news/china/21715035-does-he-really-want-be-global-leader-xi-jinping-portrays-china-rock-stability

83 Swaim, Barton. 'How might Nixon's "madman theory" apply to Trump?' *Washington Post*, 15 December 2016. Available at: https://www.washingtonpost.com/blogs/post-partisan/wp/2016/12/15/how-might-nixons-madman-theory-apply-to-trump/?utm_term=.3c3aea8961a2

84 Sagan, Scott D. and Suri, Jeremi. 'The Madman Nuclear Alert. Secrecy, Signaling, and Safety in October 1969'. *International Security*, Vol. 27, No. 4 (Spring 2003). Stanford University. Available at: https://fsi.stanford.edu/sites/default/files/sagan_is_spr03.pdf

85 Balluck, Kyle. 'Trump fires back at "overrated" Meryl Streep'. The Hill, 9 January 2017. Available at: http://thehill.com/blogs/in-the-know/in-the-know/313267-trump-fires-back-at-overrated-meryl-streep

86 Gideon Rose, editor of *Foreign Affairs* magazine, interviewed on 19 December 2016. Phone interview.

87 Haberman, Maggie. 'President-Elect Trump, Back in Washington, Resembles Candidate Trump'. *New York Times*, 17 January 2017. Available at: https://www.nytimes.com/2017/01/17/us/politics/president-elect-trump-back-in-washington-resembles-candidate-trump.html

88 Priest, Dana and Miller, Greg. 'He was one of the most respected intel officers of his generation. Now he's leading "Lock her up" chants'. *Washington Post*, 15 August 2016. Available at: https://www.washingtonpost.com/world/national-security/nearly-the-entire-national-security-establishment-has-rejected-trumpexcept-for-this-man/2016/08/15/d5072d96-5e4b-11e6-8e45-477372e89d78_story.html?utm_term=.ac1334f90672

89 'Kremlin agrees with Trump that NATO is "vestige of past"'. TASS, 16 January 2017. Available at: http://tass.com/politics/925204

CHAPTER TWELVE

1 'Donald Trump's Full Inauguration Speech'. *Time*, 20 January 2017. Available at: http://time.com/4640707/donald-trump-inauguration-speech-transcript/

2 Roosevelt, Franklin D. 'Radio Address From Albany, New York: The "Forgotten Man" Speech'. 7 April 1932. The American Presidency Project, University of California, Santa Barbara. Available at: http://www.presidency.ucsb.edu/ws/?pid=88408

3 Calamur, Krishnadev. 'A Short History of "America First"'. *The Atlantic*, 21 January 2017. Available at: https://www.theatlantic.com/politics/archive/2017/01/trump-america-first/514037/

4 Costa, Robert. 'Bannon calls Trump's speech "Jacksonian"'. *Washington Post*, 20 January 2017. Available at: https://www.washingtonpost.com/local/2017/live-updates/politics/live-coverage-of-trumps-inauguration/bannon-calls-trumps-speech-jacksonian/?utm_term=.2439fdc63df7

5 Greenwood, Max. 'White House climate change webpage disappears after Trump's inauguration'. The Hill, 20 January 2017. Available at: http://thehill.com/homenews/administration/315284-white-house-climate-change-webpage-disappears-after-trumps

6 Wheeler, Lydia. 'LGBT rights page gone from White House website'. The Hill, 20 January 2017. Available at: http://thehill.com/policy/technology/315379-lgbt-rights-page-gone-from-white-house-website

7 Ross, Janell. 'Civil rights page also deleted from White House website'. *Washington Post*, 20 January 2017. Available at: https://www.washingtonpost.com/local/2017/live-updates/politics/live-coverage-of-trumps-inauguration/civil-rights-page-also-deleted-from-white-house-website/?utm_term=.e75cf70582ce
8 Parker, Ashley. 'On a largely ceremonial day, Trump revamps the White House website and takes a few executive actions'. *Washington Post*, 20 January 2017. Available at: https://www.washingtonpost.com/news/post-politics/wp/2017/01/20/moments-after-taking-the-oath-president-trump-transforms-white-house-website/?utm_term=.66f1c7c07a03
9 Parker, Ashley and Goldstein, Amy. 'Trump signs executive order that could effectively gut Affordable Care Act's individual mandate'. *Washington Post*, 20 January 2017. Available at: https://www.washingtonpost.com/politics/trump-signs-executive-order-that-could-lift-affordable-care-acts-individual-mandate/2017/01/20/8c99e35e-df70-11e6-b2cf-b67fe3285cbc_story.html?utm_term=.56c2872e98dc
10 Kopan, Tal. 'Trump puts freeze on new regulations'. CNN, 21 January 2017. Available at: http://edition.cnn.com/2017/01/20/politics/reince-priebus-regulations-memo/
11 Rogers, Katie. 'Inaugural Balls: The Trumps' First Dance'. *New York Times*, 20 January 2017. Available at: https://www.nytimes.com/2017/01/20/us/politics/inaugural-balls.html
12 Woodrow Cox, John; Jamison, Peter; Davis, Aaron C. and Bahrampour, Tara. 'Inauguration Day 2017: Pomp and chaos collide as Trump becomes president'. *Washington Post*, 20 January 2017. Available at: https://www.washingtonpost.com/news/local/wp/2017/01/20/inauguration-day-2017-washington-prepares-for-celebration-protests-and-donald-trump/?utm_term=.5757b568230c
13 Stein, Perry; Hendrix, Steve and Hauslohner, Abigail. 'Women's marches: More than one million protesters vow to resist President Trump'. *Washington Post*, 22 January 2017. Available at: https://www.washingtonpost.com/local/womens-march-on-washington-a-sea-of-pink-hatted-protesters-vow-to-resist-donald-trump/2017/01/21/ae4def62-dfdf-11e6-acdf-14da832ae861_story.html?utm_term=.5719764b20b3
14 Hirschfeld Davis, Julie and Rosenberg, Matthew. 'With False Claims, Trump Attacks Media on Turnout and Intelligence Rift'. *New York Times*, 21 January 2017. Available at: https://www.nytimes.com/2017/01/21/us/politics/trump-white-house-briefing-inauguration-crowd-size.html
15 Rucker, Philip; Wagner, John and Miller, Greg. 'Trump wages war against the media as demonstrators protest his presidency'. *Washington Post*, 21 January 2017. Available at: https://www.washingtonpost.com/politics/trump-wages-war-against-the-media-as-demonstrators-protest-his-presidency/2017/01/21/705be9a2-e00c-11e6-ad42-f3375f271c9c_story.html?utm_term=.c9296cdb8d6c
16 Baker, Peter. 'Trump Entering White House Unbent and Unpopular'. 17 January 2017. Available at: https://www.nytimes.com/2017/01/17/us/politics/donald-trump-obama-approval-rating.html
17 Dutton, Sarah; De Pinto, Jennifer; Backus, Fred; Khanna, Kabir and Salvanto, Anthony. 'More Americans disapprove than approve Trump's handling of transition'. CBS News, 18 January 2017. Available at: http://www.cbsnews.com/news/more-americans-disapprove-than-approve-trumps-handling-of-transition/
18 Goldmacher, Shane. 'Trump starts Day Three with a trio of executive orders'. Politico, 23 January 2017. Available at: http://www.politico.com/story/2017/01/trump-executive-orders-agenda-234040
19 Baker, Peter. 'Trump Abandons Trans-Pacific Partnership, Obama's Signature Trade Deal'. *New York Times*, 23 January 2017. Available at: https://www.nytimes.com/2017/01/23/us/politics/tpp-trump-trade-nafta.html?_r=0

20 Bradner, Eric. 'Trump to begin renegotiating NAFTA with leaders of Mexico, Canada'. CNN, 23 January 2017. Available at: http://edition.cnn.com/2017/01/22/politics/trump-renegotiate-nafta/

21 Baker, Peter and Davenport, Coral. 'Trump Revives Keystone Pipeline Rejected by Obama'. *New York Times*, 24 January 2017. Available at: https://www.nytimes.com/2017/01/24/us/politics/keystone-dakota-pipeline-trump.html

22 Shear, Michael D. 'Trump Orders Broad Hiring Freeze for Federal Government'. *New York Times*, 23 January 2017. Available at: https://www.nytimes.com/2017/01/23/us/politics/federal-hiring-freeze.html

23 Nakamura, David. 'Trump signs directive to start border wall with Mexico, ramp up immigration enforcement'. *Washington Post*, 26 January 2017. Available at: https://www.washingtonpost.com/politics/trump-pledges-to-start-work-on-border-wall-within-months/2017/01/25/dddae6ee-e31e-11e6-ba11-63c4b4fb5a63_story.html?utm_term=.f4a7731cf315

24 Burns, Alexandre. '2 Federal Judges Rule Against Trump's Latest Travel Ban'. *New York Times*, 15 March 2017. Available at: https://www.nytimes.com/2017/03/15/us/politics/trump-travel-ban.html

25 The Editorial Board. 'The Extreme Foolishness in Extreme Vetting Proposals'. *New York Times*, 10 April 2017. Available at: https://www.nytimes.com/2017/04/10/opinion/the-extreme-foolishness-in-extreme-vetting-proposals.html?_r=0

26 Liptak, Adam. 'Trump Administration Asks Supreme Court to Revive Travel Ban'. *New York Times*, 2 June 2017. Available at: https://www.nytimes.com/2017/06/02/us/politics/trump-travel-ban-supreme-court.html

27 Entous, Adam; Nakashima, Ellen and Rucker. 'Justice Department warned White House that Flynn could be vulnerable to Russian blackmail, officials say'. *New York Times*, 13 February 2017. Available at: https://www.washingtonpost.com/world/national-security/justice-department-warned-white-house-that-flynn-could-be-vulnerable-to-russian-blackmail-officials-say/2017/02/13/fc5dab88-f228-11e6-8d72-263470bf0401_story.html?utm_term=.6ab79f22427a

28 Miller, Greg and Rucker, Philip. 'Michael Flynn resigns as national security adviser'. *New York Times*, 14 February 2017. Available at: https://www.washingtonpost.com/world/national-security/michael-flynn-resigns-as-national-security-adviser/2017/02/13/0007c0a8-f26e-11e6-8d72-263470bf0401_story.html?utm_term=.7f047635dd4f

29 Nakashima, Ellen; Entous, Adam and Miller, Greg. 'Russian ambassador told Moscow that Kushner wanted secret communications channel with Kremlin'. *Washington Post*, 26 May 2017. Available at: https://www.washingtonpost.com/world/national-security/russian-ambassador-told-moscow-that-kushner-wanted-secret-communications-channel-with-kremlin/2017/05/26/520a14b4-422d-11e7-9869-bac8b446820a_story.html?utm_term=.2c219e85d606

30 Schmidt, Michael S. 'In a Private Dinner, Trump Demanded Loyalty. Comey Demurred'. *New York Times*, 11 May 2017. Available at: https://www.nytimes.com/2017/05/11/us/politics/trump-comey-firing.html

Schmidt, Michael S. 'Comey Memo Says Trump Asked Him to End Flynn Investigation'. *New York Times*, 16 May 2017. Available at: https://www.nytimes.com/2017/05/16/us/politics/james-comey-trump-flynn-russia-investigation.html

31 Shear, Michael D. and Apuzzo, Matt. 'FBI Director James Comey Is Fired by Trump'. *New York Times*, 9 May 2017. Available at: https://www.nytimes.com/2017/05/09/us/politics/james-comey-fired-fbi.html

Tapper, Jake; Collinson, Stephen and Merica, Dan. 'Trump says special counsel appointment "hurts our country"'. CNN, 19 May 2017. Available at: http://edition.cnn.com/2017/05/18/politics/donald-trump-robert-mueller-appointment/index.html

32 Savransky, Rebecca. 'Report: Kushner urged aggressive Trump response to special counsel'. The Hill. 18 May 2017. Available at: http://thehill.com/homenews/administration/334056-report-kushner-urged-trump-to-attack-after-special-counsel
33 Filipov, David; Brittain, Amy; Helderman, Rosalind, S. and Hamburger, Tom. 'Explanations for Kushner's meeting with head of Kremlin-linked bank don't match up'. *Washington Post*, 1 June 2017. Available at: https://www.washingtonpost.com/politics/explanations-for-kushners-meeting-with-head-of-kremlin-linked-bank-dont-match-up/2017/06/01/dd1bdbb0-460a-11e7-bcde-624ad94170ab_story.html?utm_term=.968d178a3776
34 Shear, Michael D. and Schmidt, Michael S. 'Trump, Offering No Evidence, Says Obama Tapped His Phones'. *New York Times*, 4 March 2017. Available at: https://www.nytimes.com/2017/03/04/us/politics/trump-obama-tap-phones.html
35 Rosenberg, Matthew; Huetteman, Emmarie and Schmidt, Michael S. 'Comey Confirms FBI Inquiry on Russia; Sees No Evidence of Wiretapping'. *New York Times*, 20 March 2017. Available at: https://www.nytimes.com/2017/03/20/us/politics/intelligence-committee-russia-donald-trump.html
36 Hirschfeld Davis, Julie. 'Trump's Budget Cuts Deeply Into Medicaid and Anti-Poverty Efforts'. *New York Times*, 22 May 2017. Available at: https://www.nytimes.com/2017/05/22/us/politics/trump-budget-cuts.html
37 Steinhauer, Jennifer and Shear, Michael D. 'In Mick Mulvaney, Trump Finds Anti-Establishment Leader for Budget Office'. *New York Times*, 17 December 2016. Available at: https://www.nytimes.com/2016/12/17/us/politics/trump-mick-mulvaney-budget-office.html
38 Landsbaum, Claire. 'There's New Reason to Be Worried That Trump Will Slash Funding to Violence Against Women Programs'. *New York Magazine*, 19 January 2017. Available at: http://nymag.com/thecut/2017/01/trumps-team-could-cut-violence-against-women-programs.html
39 Bump, Philip. 'Trump reportedly wants to cut cultural programs that make up 0.02 percent of federal spending'. *Washington Post*, 19 January 2017. Available at: https://www.washingtonpost.com/news/the-fix/wp/2017/01/19/trump-reportedly-wants-to-cut-cultural-programs-that-make-up-0-02-percent-of-federal-spending/?utm_term=.5538bccfbf92
40 Bolton, Alexander. 'Trump team prepares dramatic cuts'. The Hill, 19 January 2017. Available at: http://thehill.com/policy/finance/314991-trump-team-prepares-dramatic-cuts
41 Shear, Michael D. 'Trump Will Withdraw US From Paris Climate Agreement'. *New York Times*, 1 June 2017. Available at: https://www.nytimes.com/2017/06/01/climate/trump-paris-climate-agreement.html?hp&action=click&pgtype=Homepage&clickSource=story-heading&module=span-ab-top-region®ion=top-news&WT.nav=top-news
42 Zernike, Kate. 'Betsy DeVos, Trump's Education Pick, Has Steered Money From Public Schools'. *New York Times*, 23 November 2016. Available at: https://www.nytimes.com/2016/11/23/us/politics/betsy-devos-trumps-education-pick-has-steered-money-from-public-schools.html
43 Pérez-Peña, Richard. 'Betsy DeVos is Publicly Polite, but a Political Fighter'. *New York Times*, 23 February 2017. Available at: https://www.nytimes.com/2017/02/23/us/politics/education-secretary-betsy-devos-donald-trump.html
44 See Chapter 3.
45 Blinder, Alan and Sack, Kevin. 'Dylann Roof Is Sentenced to Death in Charleston Church Massacre'. *New York Times*, 10 January 2017. Available at: https://www.nytimes.com/2017/01/10/us/dylann-roof-trial-charleston.html
46 Savage, Charlie and Lichtblau, Eric. 'Civil Rights Group Rebukes Trump Justice

Dept. Over Case Delays'. *New York Times*, 24 January 2017. Available at: https://www.nytimes.com/2017/01/24/us/politics/civil-rights-trump-administration-sessions.html

47 Gabriel, Trip. 'Trump Chooses Ben Carson to Lead HUD'. *New York Times*, 5 December 2016. Available at: https://www.nytimes.com/2016/12/05/us/politics/ben-carson-housing-urban-development-trump.html

48 DelReal, Jose A. 'Ben Carson calls poverty "a state of mind" during interview'. *New York Times*, 24 May 2017. Available at: https://www.washingtonpost.com/news/post-politics/wp/2017/05/24/ben-carson-calls-poverty-a-state-of-mind-during-interview/?utm_term=.47e39af54efc

49 Rogers, Katie. 'Kanye West Visits Donald Trump', *New York Times*, 13 December 2016. Available at: https://www.nytimes.com/2016/12/13/us/politics/kanye-trump-tower-visit.html

50 Deb, Sopan. 'Steve Harvey Talks Housing With President-Elect Trump'. *New York Times*, 13 January 2017. Available at: https://www.nytimes.com/2017/01/13/arts/steve-harvey-donald-trump.html

51 Malveaux, Suzanne and Diaz, Daniella. 'Omarosa to join Trump team, focus on public engagement'. CNN, 5 January 2017. Available at: http://edition.cnn.com/2017/01/04/politics/omarosa-manigault-donald-trump-white-house-outreach/

52 See Chapter 4.

53 See Chapter 5.

54 See Chapter 7.

55 Dennis, Brady and Mooney, Chris. 'Neil Gorsuch's mother once ran the EPA. It didn't go well'. *Washington Post*, 1 February 2017. Available at: https://www.washingtonpost.com/news/energy-environment/wp/2017/02/01/neil-gorsuchs-mother-once-ran-the-epa-it-was-a-disaster/?utm_term=.62d1a678c26e

56 'NRA Applauds Neil Gorsuch's Nomination to the US Supreme Court'. NRA-Institute for Legislative Action, 31 January 2017. Available at: https://www.nraila.org/articles/20170131/nra-applauds-neil-gorsuchs-nomination-to-the-us-supreme-court

57 Haberkorn, Jennifer. 'Gorsuch pick affirms Trump vow to pick "pro-life" justice'. Politico. 31 January 2017. Available at: http://www.politico.com/story/2017/01/gorsuch-pick-affirms-trump-vow-to-pick-pro-life-justice-234465

58 Diaz, Daniella. 'Mexican president cancels meeting with Trump'. CNN, 27 January 2017. Available at: http://edition.cnn.com/2017/01/25/politics/mexico-president-donald-trump-enrique-pena-nieto-border-wall/

59 Acosta, Jim and Merica, Dan. 'Trump, Mexican President talk on phone after canceled meeting'. CNN, 28 January 2017. Available at: http://edition.cnn.com/2017/01/27/politics/trump-mexican-president-talk-on-phone-after-canceled-meeting/

60 'Trump: Brexit Will Be a Fantastic Thing for UK'. Bloomberg, 27 January 2017. Available at: https://www.bloomberg.com/politics/videos/2017-01-27/trump-brexit-will-be-a-fantastic-thing-for-u-k

61 Landler, Mark. 'Merkel Meets Trump, the Defender Versus the Disrupter'. *New York Times*, 17 March 2017. Available at: https://www.nytimes.com/2017/03/17/world/europe/angela-merkel-donald-trump.html?hp&action=click&pgtype=Homepage&clickSource=story-heading&module=first-column-region®ion=top-news&WT.nav=top-news&_r=0

62 Rinke, Andreas; Martin, Michelle and Neely, Jason. 'Germany rejects Trump's claim it owes NATO and US "vast sums" for defense'. Reuters, 19 March 2017. Available at: http://www.reuters.com/article/us-usa-trump-germany-defence-idUSKBN16Q0D8

63 Rubin, Alissa J. 'Geert Wilders Falls Short in Election, as Wary Dutch Scatter Their Votes'. *New York Times*, 15 March 2017. Available at: https://www.nytimes.com/2017/03/15/world/europe/geert-wilders-netherlands-far-right-vote.html

O'Harrow, Robert Jr and Boburg, Shawn. 'How a "shadow" universe of charities joined with political warriors to fuel Trump's rise'. *Washington Post*, 3 June 2017. Available at: https://www.washingtonpost.com/investigations/how-a-shadow-universe-of-charities-joined-with-political-warriors-to-fuel-trumps-rise/2017/06/03/ff5626ac-3a77-11e7-a058-ddbb23c75d82_story.html?utm_term=.a1b9ab8a25e8

64 Stanley-Becker, Isaac. 'Marine Le Pen falls short in far-right bid for the presidency of France'. *Washington Post*, 7 May 2017. Available at: https://www.washingtonpost.com/world/europe/marine-le-pen-congratulates-emmanuel-macron-on-his-victory-in-french-presidential-race/2017/05/07/afe9064e-3021-11e7-a335-fa0ae1940305_story.html?utm_term=.1b57bb9f90b4

Stelzenmüller, Constanze. 'In Germany, more momentum for Merkel'. *Washington Post*, 15 May 2017. Available at: https://www.washingtonpost.com/news/global-opinions/wp/2017/05/15/in-germany-more-momentum-for-merkel/?utm_term=.633a64e3cc16

65 Wootson, Cleve R. 'A brief history of Donald Trump's feud with Sadiq Khan, London's first Muslim mayor'. *Washington Post*, 6 June 2017. Available at: https://www.washingtonpost.com/news/worldviews/wp/2017/06/06/a-brief-history-of-donald-trumps-feud-with-sadiq-khan-londons-first-muslim-mayor/?utm_term=.a2df2db0ae37

66 McKirdy, Euan and Ilyushina, Mary. 'Putin: "Patriotic" Russian hackers may have targeted US election'. CNN, 2 June 2017. Available at: http://edition.cnn.com/2017/06/01/politics/russia-putin-hackers-election/index.html

67 Siemaszko, Corky. 'Vladimir Putin Tells Megyn Kelly: US Hackers Could Have Framed Russia'. NBC News, 2 June 2017. Available at: http://www.nbcnews.com/news/world/vladimir-putin-tells-megyn-kelly-u-s-hackers-could-have-n767641

68 'Donald Trump's Full Inauguration Speech'. *Time*, 20 January 2017.

69 Johnson, Alan. 'What will Jared Kushner and Donald Trump's Middle East look like?' CNN, 18 January 2017. Available at: http://edition.cnn.com/2017/01/18/opinions/jared-kushner-donald-trump-middle-east-opinion-johnson/

70 David Gergen, political commentator and former presidential adviser, interviewed in Cleveland on 20 July 2016 and phone interview on 27 January 2017.

BIBLIOGRAPHY

J. BAUDRILLARD, *America*, Verso Books, 2010 (trad. it. *America*, se, Milano 2009).

J. C. COBB, *The Most Southern Place on Earth: The Mississippi Delta and the Roots of Regional Identity*, Oxford University Press, 1992.

S. COLL, *Private Empire: ExxonMobil and American Power*, Penguin Press, 2012.

A. DE TOCQUEVILLE, *Democracy in America and Two Essays on America*, Penguin, 2003 (trad. it. *La democrazia in America*, utet, Torino 2013).

T. DIAZ, *Making A Killing: The Business of Guns in America*, The New Press, 1999.

ID., *The Last Gun: How Changes in the Gun Industry are Killing Americans And What It Will Take To Stop It*, The New Press, 2013.

K. J. EDIN, H. L. SHAEFER, *$2.00 A Day: Living on Almost Nothing in America*, Mariner Books, 2015.

C. FISHMAN, *The Wal-Mart Effect: How an Out-of-Town Superstore Became a Superpower*, Penguin Books, 2006 (trad. it. *Walmart Story*, egea, Milano 2014).

T. F. GEITHNER, *Stress Test: Reflections on Financial Crises*, Crown Publishers, 2014.

R. GRANT, *Dispatches from Pluto: Lost and Found in the Mississippi Delta*, Simon & Schuster, 2015.

M. HIRSH, *Capital Offense: How Washington's Wise Men Turned America's Future Over to Wall Street*, John Wiley & Sons, 2010.

R. HOFSTADTER, *The Paranoid Style in American Politics*, Vintage Books, 1952.

ID., *Anti-intellectualism in American Life*, Vintage Books, 1962 (trad. it. *Società e intellettuali in America*, Einaudi, Torino 1968).

M. KRANISH, M. FISHER, *Trump revealed: An American Journey of Ambition, Ego, Money and Power*, Simon & Schuster, 2016.

P. KRUGMAN, *The Conscience of a Liberal*, W. W. Norton & Co Inc., 2009 (trad. it. *La coscienza di un liberal*, Laterza, Roma-Bari 2009).

J. R. MACARTHUR, *The Outrageous Barriers to Democracy in America*, Melville House, 2008.

S. MALLABY, *The Man Who Knew The Life and Times of Alan Greenspan*, Bloomsbury, 2016.

H. MILLER, *The Air-Conditioned Nightmare*, New Directions, 1945 (trad. it. *Incubo ad aria condizionata*, Feltrinelli, Milano 2013).

C. MURRAY, *Coming Apart: The State of White America, 1960-2010*, Crown Forum, 2012.

T. PIKETTY, *Capital in the Twenty-First Century*, Belknap Press, 2014 (trad. it. *Il capitale nel xxi secolo*, Bompiani, Milano 2016).

R. REICH, *Aftershock: The Next Economy and America's Future*, Knops, 2010 (trad. it. *Aftershock: il futuro dell'economia dopo la crisi*, Fazi, Roma 2012).

P. THEROUX, *Deep South*, Penguin Books, 2005.

H. S. THOMPSON, *Fear and Loathing in Las Vegas: A Savage Journey to the Heart of the American Dream*, Tandem Library, 1998 (trad. it. *Paura e disgusto a Las Vegas: una selvaggia cavalcata nel cuore del sogno americano*, Bompiani, Milano 2016).

D. TRUMP, T. SCHWARTZ, *Trump: The Art of the Deal*, Random House, 1987 (trad. it. *Trump: l'arte di fare affari*, Sperling & Kupfer, Milano 1989).

E. VULLIAMY, *Amexica: War Along the Borderline*, Farrar, Straus and Giroux, 2010.

S. WALTON, J. HUEY, *Sam Walton: Made in America*, Bantam Books, 1992.

D. WESSEL, *In Fed We Trust: Ben Bernanke's War on the Great Panic*, Crown Business, 2009.

T. WOLFE, *You Can't Go Home Again*, Scribner, 2011 (trad. it. *Non puoi tornare a casa*, Mondadori, Milano 1962).

T. WOLFE, F. W. JOHNSON, *The New Journalism*, Picador, 1975.

D. YERGIN, *Shattered Peace: The Origins of the Cold War and the National Security State*, Penguin Books, 1977.